THE FEDERAL COURTS

Richard A. Posner

THE FEDERAL COURTS

Crisis and Reform

HARVARD UNIVERSITY PRESS
Cambridge, Massachusetts, and London, England   1985

LIBRARY OF CONGRESS CATALOGING IN PUBLICATION DATA

Posner, Richard A.
  The federal courts.

  Includes index.
  1. Courts—United States.   2. Judicial process—
United States.   3. Judges—United States.   4. Court
congestion and delay—United States.   I. Title.
KF8700.P67   1985   347.73′2   84-19126
ISBN 0-674-29625-7   347.3071

For Charlene

Preface

ARTICLE III of the Constitution ordained the creation of a Supreme Court, authorized Congress to create other, inferior federal courts, and empowered federal courts to exercise jurisdiction over specified types of cases thought to be of national concern—mainly cases between citizens of different states, admiralty cases, and cases arising under federal law. These are the constitutive provisions of Article III, and out of them has grown the complex, extensive, powerful, controversial, overworked judicial system that is the subject of this book. My intent is to describe, and as best I can to explain, the system; to examine the proposals for improving it; to make my own suggestions for improvement; and, not least, to register my concern that the system is on the verge of being radically changed for the worse under pressure of the rapid and unremitting growth in caseload that is traced in Chapter 3.

The scope of the book is broad, the treatment suggestive rather than exhaustive, the conclusions tentative rather than definitive. Such novelty as the book possesses comes from its eclectic approach: I use economic and political theory, statistics, and history, as well as the traditional methods of legal analysis, and also draw on my own experience as a federal court of appeals judge. In its descriptive aspect the book is in the tradition of Frankfurter and Landis's *The Business of the Supreme Court* (1928) and also has affinities with the political science literature on judicial administration, a literature illustrated by such works as Marvin Schick's *Learned Hand's Court* (1970) and J. Woodford Howard's *Courts of Appeals in the Federal Judicial System* (1981). Analytically it draws heavily both on the economic approach to law and on what for want of a better name might be called the Harvard Law School approach to federal jurisdiction—an approach shaped by notable graduates of the Harvard Law School in its happier days, including Oliver Wendell Holmes, Louis Brandeis, Learned Hand, Felix Frankfurter, Henry Hart, Alexander Bickel, and Henry Friendly. Illustrative works in this tradition on which I have drawn in this book are Hart and Sacks, *The Legal Process* (tent. ed. 1958), and Friendly, *Federal Jurisdiction: A General View* (1974). In its personal aspect, as the confessions of a sitting judge, this book has elements in common with a genre that stretches from Cardozo's *The Nature of the Judicial Process* (1921) to Coffin's *The Ways of a Judge* (1980). But the personal element must not be overemphasized; after three years as a judge I am not ready to write my memoirs. This is not primarily an insider's book, but grows out of my long-standing academic interest in judicial administration.

The book has four parts. Part I is introductory; it presents some theoretical observations about the judicial process that are employed in later chapters and a number of background facts concerning the history, structure, and personnel of the federal court system. Specialists in federal jurisdiction will no doubt find some of the material in Part I overly familiar; but the book is not intended for them alone, although I hope they will read it. The problems of the federal courts cannot be solved only by lawyers and judges, and this book is intended in part to stimulate the interest of economists, historians, public administrators, and others who may have significant contributions to make to improving the federal courts.

Part II takes up the most urgent problem of the federal courts today—their enormous caseload, the product of two decades of extremely rapid docket growth. It discusses the extent, causes, and consequences of this growth and considers a number of the proposals for dealing with it—proposals I call "palliatives," as distinct from the more fundamental reorientation considered in Part III. There I sketch what I conceive to be the ideal role of the federal courts in our federal system of government today—a more limited role than they are now playing. This leads to a discussion of the Fourteenth Amendment, a major instrument by which the federal courts have overflowed their proper banks, and then on to the great question of judicial self-restraint—a commodity in insufficient supply in the federal courts today—and the enduring question of judicial craft.

The measures proposed in Chapters 5 through 8 (the last chapter of Part II, and the whole of Part III) would, if adopted, go some way toward solving the caseload problem. The federal court system would be somewhat smaller and less busy; perhaps it would be somewhat less important. But it would still be quite large, quite busy, and quite important; and therefore it is worth considering how it can perform better the essential, the irreducible, functions of a federal court system. This question is examined in Part IV. From an appellate perspective—the dominant perspective throughout this book—the basic functions that the federal court system performs, and will continue to perform after every feasible reform designed to cope with the caseload crisis has been adopted, are the interpretation of constitutional and statutory provisions and the elaboration of federal common law doctrines. The argument put forth in Part IV is that the federal courts could do a better job in these areas than they are doing today. The last chapter provides a brief summary of the book and discusses the unfulfilled role of legal education and scholarship in improving the federal courts.

The basic statistics used in this book (particularly in Chapters 2 through 4) are complete through the middle of 1983 in the case of statistics on caseloads in the federal courts, and through the end of 1983 in the case of number and salaries of federal judges. But the world will not stand still for writers, and there have been some significant developments since my research was completed. In particular, in June 1984 Congress created 85 new federal judgeships—61 in the district courts and 24 in the courts of appeals. The result is to raise from 132 to 156 the number of judgeships in the regional federal courts of appeals (excluding the Court of Appeals for the Federal Circuit, a specialized court discussed in Chapter 2). The largest circuit, the Ninth Circuit, now has 28 judgeships, rather than 23 as before. These changes are likely to exacerbate the problems discussed in the book that have been created by having a large number of federal trial and particularly appellate judges. The same act of Congress has slightly improved the retirement provisions for federal judges, by allowing judges who are between 65 and 70 years of age to retire if the sum of age plus years of service is 80 or more. Thus a judge who is 67 and has been a federal judge for 13 years can retire; previously he could not have retired until he had 15 years of service, since only judges 70 or older could retire with fewer than 15 years of service.

Two other developments in the summer of 1984 deserve note. First, the Comprehensive Crime Control Act of 1984 (Pub. L. 98–473) includes a provision that will allow both the prosecutor and the defendant in a federal criminal case to appeal a sentence that falls outside sentencing guidelines to be set by an as-yet-to-be appointed Sentencing Commission. It remains to be seen how much this provision will add to the federal appellate caseload, but the addition could in the long run be substantial. Second, federal judges received a modest pay increase, retroactive to January 1, 1981, which brings the salary of a Supreme Court justice up to $100,600, that of a circuit judge up to $80,400, and that of a district judge up to $76,000.

Statistics are now available for the federal district courts and courts of appeals for the 1984 reporting year, which ended on June 30, 1984, and for the Supreme Court's 1983 term, which ended at about the same time. The number of civil and criminal cases filed in the district courts was 298,330, an increase of 7.7 percent over the previous year (see Table 3.2). This is, of course, a very large increase for one year. The number of cases filed in the courts of appeals was 31,490, an increase of 6.5 percent—also very large. The opinion workload of the courts of appeals increased as well: the number of signed, published opinions per court of appeals judgeship rose from 42 in the previous year to 49. Case filings in the Supreme Court, however, rose only from 4,201 to 4,222, and majority opinions from 162 to 163. (The source of all these statistics, except number of Supreme Court opinions which is from the November 1984 *Harvard Law Review,* is the Administrative Office of the United States Courts.)

I should also like to acknowledge belatedly a very interesting paper by Professor Bernard Meltzer, "Inflation and the NLRB," *Regulation,* Sept.-Oct. 1980, at p. 43, which argues that the expansion in number of cases before the National Labor Relations Board (and hence, on petition for judicial review, in the federal courts of appeals), discussed in Chapter 3 of this book, may be due in part to inflation. In 1959 the Board limited its jurisdiction by indicating minimum dollar volumes of business below which it would not assert jurisdiction over firms in various industries. These minimums, not having been adjusted for inflation, have become progressively less restricting over the years.

These changes in data and analysis do not make this book less timely; the increase in the number of judges and number of cases makes it more so. But they should be kept in mind in reading the chapters to which they pertain.

Some readers may think the heavy emphasis throughout the book on the federal courts of appeals, at the expense of both the federal district courts (the federal trial courts) and the Supreme Court, excessive. As a court of appeals judge I must plead guilty to parochialism in this regard. But in mitigation I point out that the enormous literature on the Supreme Court invites a treatment in which the lower federal courts receive more than usual emphasis, that 99 percent of all federal appeals are finally decided by the courts of appeals, and that the caseload crisis is more serious in the courts of appeals than in the district courts, or for that matter than in the Supreme Court.

*   *   *

Sections of Chapters 4 and 5 are adapted, though with many changes of both substance and style, from my article "Will the Federal Courts of Appeals Survive until 1984? An Essay on Delegation and Specialization of the Judicial Function," 56 *So. Cal. L. Rev.* 761 (1983), copyright 1983 by the University of Southern California. The first section of Chapter 6 is a thoroughly revised and greatly expanded version of my article "Toward an Economic Theory of Federal Jurisdiction," 6 *Harv. J. Law & Pub. Policy* 42 (1982), copyright 1982 by the Harvard Society for Law and Public Policy, Inc. Chapter 7 is based on "The Meaning of Judicial Self-Restraint," 59 *Ind. L.J.* 1 (1983), copyright 1984 by the Trustees of Indiana University. Chapter 9 is an amalgam, but again with many additions and changes, of two articles, "Economics, Politics, and the Reading of Statutes and Constitutions," 49 *U. Chi. L. Rev.* 263 (1982), copyright 1982 by The University of Chicago, and "Statutory Construction—In the Classroom and in the Courtroom," 50 *U. Chi. L. Rev.* 800 (1983), copyright 1983 by The University of Chicago. Chapter 11 borrows some passages from Part I of the last-cited article and from "The Present Situation in Legal Scholarship," 90 *Yale L.J.* 1113 (1981), copyright 1981 by The Yale Law Journal Co., Inc. The rest of the book is completely new.

I am grateful to Barbara Donagan and David Vandermeulen for their excellent research assistance; to Vandermeulen, Andrew Miller, and Michael Williams for checking the citations; to the Law and Economics Program of the University of Chicago Law School for defraying the costs of research assistance and citation checking; and to the following friends and colleagues who read and commented on all or part of the manuscript: Michael Aronson, Walter Blum, Stephen Breyer, Frank Easterbrook, Philip Elman, Jesse Eschbach, Henry Friendly, Jerry Goldman, William Landes, John Langbein, Edward Levi, William McLauchlan, Geoffrey Miller, Andrew Rosenfield, A. W. B. Simpson, and George Stigler. Professor Goldman has my very special thanks for having read and made a great number of helpful suggestions on two entire drafts of the manuscript; Professor Easterbrook's extensive comments also require special acknowledgment. James McCafferty, the Chief of the Statistical Analysis and Reports Division of the Administrative Office of the United States Courts, and his staff provided valuable statistical information and assistance. Finally, my wife, Charlene, made a number of helpful contributions as critic and researcher, and to her the book is gratefully dedicated.

Contents

Figures

Tables

I

THE INSTITUTION

1

The Judicial Process

SOME ELEMENTARY facts about courts in general will help to set the stage for this study of the federal court system. A court is a public body for resolving disputes in accordance with law. In every case the court must determine what the facts are and what their legal significance is. If the court determines their legal significance by applying an existing rule of law unchanged, it is engaged in pure dispute resolution. But if to resolve the dispute the court must create a new rule or modify an old one, that is law creation. Judges defending themselves from accusations of judicial activism sometimes say they do not make law, they only apply it. It is true that in our system judges are not supposed to and generally do not make new law with the same freedom that legislatures can and do; they are, in Oliver Wendell Holmes's phrase, "confined from molar to molecular motions."[1] The qualification is important, but the fact remains that judges make, and do not just find and apply, law.

Two different kinds of law creation should be distinguished, however. The first is the derivation of a new rule, by deduction, from unquestioned premises. This we may call the "formalistic" kind. The second kind of law creation, the "political" as we may call it (not using the word in any partisan or pejorative sense), involves the court's deriving a new rule from (or with the aid of) political, ethical, economic, or sociological ideas that do not command universal assent in the society. Most law creation involves at least a tincture of the political in the broad sense in which I am using the word; but the more political law creation a court engages in, the more like a legislature it becomes.

Dispute resolution and law creation (of either kind) are separable, and many judges are just dispute resolvers. This is true of the lay

1. Southern Pacific Co. v. Jensen, 244 U.S. 205, 221 (1917) (dissenting opinion).

judges whom we call jurors and the private judges whom we call arbitrators, but it is also true of many publicly employed professional judges—indeed, it is true of most such judges most of the time. There is a rule of thumb for determining whether a particular judicial decision involves only dispute resolution: whether or not the decision is published. An unpublished decision is unlikely to create a new rule or modify an old one. A rule of law is a public statement of the form, if X fact then Y legal consequence. A decision unaccompanied by any published statement of facts and reasons discloses just the consequence. Without some explanation of what the facts were that led to the consequence it will usually be impossible to infer what rule the court was applying, let alone that it was a new rule or a modification of an old one.

Although many courts engage only in dispute resolution, none engages only in law creation. This follows from the definition of a court as an agency engaged in applying law to resolve disputes. Pure law creation—the creation of law apart from any concrete dispute—is the domain of constitutional conventions, legislatures, and administrative agencies authorized to make rules in legislative fashion. Courts can create law only as an incident to resolving disputes. Thus a "court" that did nothing but issue advisory opinions—opinions on disputes that had not yet arisen—would not be a real court; it would be a counselor.

Why do courts have the incidental function of creating law? There are three reasons. The first is that they have it by default. Until well into the nineteenth century, English and American legislatures concerned themselves mainly with revenue measures and local administration rather than with enacting general rules of conduct.[2] With some notable exceptions[3] they left the regulation of safety and health, trade and commerce, employment, inheritance, internal security—almost the whole range of social interactions—to be regulated by judge-made law, "common law" in the nontechnical sense in which I shall use the term throughout this book. Generations of English judges beginning in the Middle Ages had by the end of the eighteenth century, as a by-product of thousands of decisions, created a body of rules of great complexity,

2. See, for example, the tables of statutes prefixed to volumes 20 and 23 of Danby Pickering, *The Statutes at Large* [of Great Britain] (1765, 1766). On the history of English law see, for example, Theodore F. T. Plucknett, *A Concise History of the Common Law* (5th ed. 1956); on the history of appellate judging in England and the continent, see John P. Dawson, *The Oracles of the Law* (1968); and on the reception of the common law in America, see, for example, Lawrence W. Friedman, *A History of American Law* 96–99 (1973); Spencer L. Kimball, *Historical Introduction to the Legal System* 263–309 (1966).

3. See, for example, William Hunt, *The Puritan Moment: The Coming of Revolution in an English County* 69–70 (1983).

owing little to legislation; and these rules were taken over almost intact by the courts of our new nation. Such important fields of law as criminal law, torts (for example, negligence, defamation, assault), property, contracts, admiralty, and procedure are, at least in their origins, common law fields.

The second reason for judicial law creation, which explains its persistence into the modern age of statutes, is the judges' access to a body of information that legislators do not possess: the information generated by the parties to concrete disputes. The legislature passes a rule, thinking it knows what the effects will be, but it cannot have a precise understanding of them in advance of the actual application of the rule. The judge has the advantage of seeing the rule in operation, and he can deal with problems of application that the legislature did not foresee. So, assuming that the rule as enacted by the legislature has enough play in the joints to give the judge discretion in interpretation, he can refine the rule to make it a more apt instrument of the legislature's purposes.

The third reason for judicial law creation comes from the differences between the composition of legislatures (and, even more clearly, of constitutional conventions) and of courts. As large, representative bodies elected at frequent intervals in partisan elections, legislatures are handicapped in dealing effectively with technical questions, quite apart from the inherent limitations of foresight. The process of gaining agreement in a diverse, factious assembly results in compromises that are unclear and sometimes incoherent, while the built-in impediments to getting legislation passed—impediments designed to reduce the legislators' power, to weed out proposed legislation that lacks real support, and to increase the stability of legislation once enacted—make it difficult for the legislature to withdraw or revise misconceived or poorly drafted legislation. In contrast, judges operate in a less political and (until recently) less hectic atmosphere which allows them to apply a measure of relatively disinterested repair to the sometimes badly damaged products of the legislative process. Whether they should undertake this function, however, raises questions that I postpone to Chapter 8.

I have thus far treated the law-creation function of courts as problematic (as indeed it must be in a system of representative government) and the dispute-resolution function as self-evident. But it is self-evident only if one ignores the fact that dispute resolution has another goal besides assuring the efficacy of the legal rule by preventing people from denying that the rule is addressed to their conduct. Part of our biological inheritance is the sense of indignation, and its complement the desire for retribution (by violent means if necessary), that is aroused when someone invades an interest that we value highly—be it bodily security, or self-esteem, or family affection, or material possessions.[4] The emotions and institutions that cluster around the idea of retribution—vengeance, retaliation, the feud, the duel—constitute the system for maintaining public order in a prepolitical society.[5] The courts provide a substitute for the costly self-help methods that people would otherwise resort to.[6] In this perspective it is less important that the court decide a case correctly than that its decision be accepted as authoritative—though there is no doubt a positive correlation between the correctness and the authority of a court's decisions. The archaic, ritualistic, apparently nonutilitarian features of the judicial process—the robe, signifying impersonality; the raised bench, symbolizing authority; the special vocabulary, more distant from ordinary speech than is strictly necessary; the oath; the theatrical format of the Anglo-American trial, with its surprises and confrontations and general adversary zest—all seem related to the function of judicial dispute resolution as a substitute for retribution. This explains the odd fact noted by many judges that a plaintiff who loses his lawsuit may nevertheless feel happier for having sued and lost than if he had not sued at all. He has had his day in court, has probably in the course of the trial scored some points against the defendant and at least has forced the defendant to defend himself, and in turn has been led to diffuse the blame for what he may still believe to have been an outrageous invasion of his interests among the defendant, the lawyers, the judges, and some mysterious external entity called the law.

The law's delay, a subject of much adverse comment since Shakespeare and no doubt long before,[7] assumes in this perspective a less purely negative light. The passion for revenge fades with time. The law channels the passion into the litigation process, where it is allowed to run its course harmlessly (though not costlessly); and by the time the process is completed, even if the plaintiff has lost the case, his indignation has cooled. (Of course, if delay is too great, victims of aggression may seek retribution outside the legal system.) This brings me to the first of several critical observations in this book about the judicial process as practiced in the United States Supreme Court today, and this a

4. See *The Dominance Relations: An Ethological View of Human Conflict and Social Interaction* 279–280 (Donald R. Omark, F. F. Strayer, and Daniel G. Freedman eds. 1980), and the references cited there.

5. See Richard A. Posner, *The Economics of Justice*, chap. 8 (1981), for development of this point and supporting references.

6. For an excellent recent case study, see Jenny Wormald, "Bloodfeud, Kindred and Government in Early Modern Scotland," 87 *Past & Present* 54 (1980).

7. See *Hamlet*, act 3, sc. 1, l. 73.

slightly esoteric one: the Court's insistence on clearing its docket each year before it rises for its summer recess prevents it, if not completely,[8] from exploiting delay as a method of calming passions. The Supreme Court deals with some of the most passionate disputes in American society, and part of its function should be to cool these disputes. Sometimes it could do this simply by carrying a case on its docket, as most other courts do routinely, over the summer. Of course, the Court's practice is effective in forcing slowpokes to hurry up, but at a high price, and in the face of more flexible alternatives; for example, the Chief Justice might simply refuse to assign additional opinions to a slow justice. At the very least, the normal deadline should be lifted for cases argued at the end of the term.

A third judicial function in addition to dispute resolution and law creation should be mentioned: keeping the other branches of government within the bounds set by the Constitution. (No one has discovered how to keep the judges within proper bounds, a problem I return to in Chapter 7.) This function is largely an American innovation, and it is particularly important for the federal courts (above all the Supreme Court) because they have responsibilities under the Constitution for checking all branches of state government as well as the legislative and executive branches of the federal government. In one sense this is just a special case of dispute resolution and law creation. But when the dispute is between a private person and the state or federal government, and the law to be applied is a constitutional norm that the judge is asked not merely to apply but to elaborate, he is playing so distinctive a role in maintaining the structure of government that separate consideration of that role is warranted.

THE DEMAND FOR AND SUPPLY OF JUDICIAL SERVICES

I have sketched the judicial function, but I have not said how it is brought into play or how it is exercised. It will be convenient in discussing these topics to think of judicial services, such as a trial or an appeal,

---

8. Under the Court's rules, a case, to be carried over, must be reargued. Although this has proved an effective deterrent to carrying over cases, a few exceptionally sensitive cases have been carried over in this manner. And the principle of discretionary jurisdiction enables the Court to delay action on sensitive matters, as it did in the 1950s with regard to the constitutionality of state statutes forbidding miscegenation. See Naim v. Naim, 350 U.S. 985 (1956) (per curiam); Alexander M. Bickel, *The Least Dangerous Branch* 174 (1962). See generally Lawrence Baum, "Policy Goals in Judicial Gatekeeping: A Proximity Model of Discretionary Jurisdiction," 22 *Am. J. Pol. Sci.* 13 (1977); Gregory A. Caldeira, "The United States Supreme Court and Criminal Cases, 1935–1976: Alternative Models of Agenda Building," 11 *Brit. J. Pol. Sci.* 449 (1981); Doris Marie Provine, *Case Selection in the United States Supreme Court* (1980).

as a "product" that the parties (in the first instance, the plaintiff) "buy" when they decide to bring a suit or to continue with a suit that they have already brought, and that the court therefore "sells" to them. The amount of judicial services supplied can therefore be thought of as the intersection of the demand for and the supply of those services, and we can explore the forces that will cause that intersection to shift over time, as has been happening in recent years in both the federal and the state courts.[9]

The aggregate demand for judicial services is the sum of the demands of all potential plaintiffs, and thus depends on how many potential plaintiffs there are. This in turn depends on how broadly legal rights are defined and how extensive is the activity to which the rights pertain. For example, if people who injure others in accidents are strictly liable (that is, regardless of whether they are careless or not) to their victims for damages, the demand for judicial services will rise with the number of accidents, and at any level of accidents will be greater than if only negligent injurers are liable. Demand also depends critically on the value of asserting legal rights. Although I have suggested that some litigants derive satisfaction from the judicial process even when they lose, everyone prefers winning to losing and winning big to winning small; so I shall be on safe ground in asserting that the demand for judicial services by a potential plaintiff, that is, an individual having a possible legal claim, is positively related to the probablity that he will win if the case goes to judgment, and to the amount of money or other gain that he can anticipate from victory. I am speaking of net gains, of course; the plaintiff, unless he wants to hurt the defendant as well as help himself—as he may, if I am right about the importance of retribution in the legal process—is interested in the judgment he can expect to obtain minus the costs of obtaining it. Those costs include not only the costs of the judicial services themselves but also the costs of the lawyer he must hire and any incidental expenses he must incur (for expert witnesses and the like) to prosecute the suit successfully.

9. The economic model of litigation is sketched in Richard A. Posner, *Economic Analysis of Law* pt. VI (2d ed. 1977), especially chap. 21. The seminal article is William M. Landes, "An Economic Analysis of the Courts," 14 *J. Law & Econ.* 61 (1971). For notable recent contributions to the literature see Steven Shavell, "Suit, Settlement and Trial: A Theoretical Analysis under Alternative Methods for the Allocation of Legal Costs," 11 *J. Legal Stud.* 55 (1982); George L. Priest and Benjamin Klein, "The Selection of Disputes for Litigation," 13 *J. Legal Stud.* 1 (1984). And for empirical evidence that supports the model see Patricia Munch Danzon and Lee A. Lillard, "Settlement Out of Court: The Disposition of Medical Malpractice Claims," 12 *J. Legal Stud.* 345 (1983); David M. Trubek et al., "The Costs of Ordinary Litigation," 31 *U.C.L.A. L. Rev.* 72 (1983).

Another type of cost is also relevant to assessing demand: the cost of substitute products or services to which a buyer might turn. The cheaper, or otherwise more attractive, that substitutes for the courts are, the smaller will be the demand for judicial services. An important substitute, though one largely limited to cases in which the parties have a relationship preexisting their dispute, is private arbitration. But the most important substitute is the out-of-court settlement. (Whether it occurs before a lawsuit is filed, or before it ends, is of no moment here.) As long as it is cheaper to settle a case than to litigate it, in the sense that the legal fees and other expenses that the parties must bear will be lower if the case is settled (as they surely will be if the case is settled before the judicial proceeding is far advanced), settlement should be an attractive substitute for litigation to both parties. The main (but not the only) thing likely to derail the settlement process is if both parties are optimistic about the outcome of the litigation. To take a very simple example, assume that the plaintiff will win $1,000 if the case is tried to judgment, his probability of winning is 60 percent, and the expenses of the suit will be $200 to him and the same to the defendant (under the usual American rule, each party must bear his own expenses regardless of the outcome of the suit). If both parties agree that the plaintiff has a 60 percent chance of winning, the case will almost certainly be settled. The plaintiff has an expected gain from litigation of $400 ($1,000 × 0.6 − $200), and the defendant an expected loss from litigation of $800 ($1,000 × 0.6 + $200, since he must pay the expenses of suit on top of whatever judgment the plaintiff obtains). So at any settlement price between $400 and $800, both parties will be better off than litigating. (I assume that the cost of settlement is zero, but the analysis will be unaffected qualitatively as long as that cost is less than $200 for each party.) Of course, each party might be so stubborn in trying to engross the greater part of the potential gains from settlement that negotiations would break down; but such breakdowns are rare. Suppose, however, that the defendant in my example thinks the plaintiff has only a 10 percent chance of winning. Then the maximum settlement price he will offer is $300 ($1,000 × 0.1 + $200), and the plaintiff will refuse to settle.

Now in most classes of litigation, as this analysis suggests, the vast majority of cases will in fact be settled either before there is any formal lawsuit or early in the judicial process.[10] Small changes in the settlement rate therefore can have dramatic effects on the demand for judi-

10. Most federal suits are settled. See, for example, Joel B. Grossman et al., "Measuring the Pace of Civil Litigation in Federal and State Trial Courts," 65 *Judicature* 86, 106 (1981) (table 6), and the data in Chapter 4 of this book on dispositions without court action.

cial services. This in turn makes uncertainty a key determinant of the amount of litigation, for uncertainty about outcome is a necessary condition for *both* parties to expect to do well at trial. It also suggests a mechanism by which the settlement rate is automatically maintained, by a process analogous to Adam Smith's "invisible hand," at a high—but not too high—level. If the settlement rate is extremely high, implying that there are few cases being tried to judgment, potential parties will lack up-to-date information about how the judicial process works in their type of case. This will make it difficult for them to converge in their estimates of the probable outcome if the case is tried, will make it more likely for the settlement process to break down, and will therefore increase the likelihood that the case will be tried. If the case is tried, the trial will yield information about the judicial process that will make it easier for future disputants to settle their disputes. Hence swings in the settlement rate should be self-correcting, and I am led to predict that settlement rates will change only slowly over long periods of time. (Unfortunately, I have found no data with which to test this hypothesis.)

I want to turn now to the supply of judicial services. It is an oddity of modern American judicial systems, at least if one takes an economic view of things, that they do not charge—except trivial filing fees—for their services. Yet these services are not cheap; the budget of the federal courts alone, a small part of the nation's judiciary, is approaching $1 billion a year, almost all paid for by the taxpayers rather than the litigants. An argument can be made for shifting at least part of that cost to the groups that either use disproportionately or benefit disproportionately from the services provided by the judicial system. There is also an argument, however, against trying to support the courts entirely out of fees charged to the individual litigants. The fact that a lawsuit provides information that enables other disputants to settle their disputes without litigation means that the parties to the suit are conferring benefits on other people, and they ought to be able to shift some of the costs of the litigation to those beneficiaries; otherwise there might actually be more litigation in the long run. If this seems counterintuitive, consider how a test case can sometimes head off future litigation. I do not suggest that our present "free" system is ideal from this standpoint (and I shall propose some changes in Chapter 5), but it is important to understand why courts probably should not try to operate entirely on a user-fee basis—all notions of "fairness" aside.

But since they do not charge fees to users, the courts are deprived of the method which the private market uses, and which a court system financed entirely out of user fees could use, to match supply to demand. If the demand for judicial services increases, the courts do not respond by raising their fees, which would serve both to limit demand and to provide funds to defray the costs of increased supply (more judges, for example). A judicial system's short-run response to higher demand is delay. Delay not only postpones but reduces demand; it diminishes the expected benefit of litigating to the plaintiff by reducing the present value of any judgment he receives (unless, as is rare, prejudgment interest is awarded at market rates), and thus makes substitutes such as settlement and (assuming it is faster) arbitration more attractive. The usual long-run response to higher demand for judicial services is to add judges and supporting personnel. This process can, as we shall see, impose very substantial social costs, but in the absence of user fees those costs do not serve to check demand. It is like building an expensive highway to relieve congestion but charging users nothing: there is no incentive for the users to seek substitutes that may be cheaper for society as a whole, so congestion soon reasserts itself.

I want now to consider the supply of judicial services more concretely by looking first at the organization and then at the personnel of court systems. For courts engaged only in dispute resolution, structure is not a problem because there is no great need to coordinate the work of the judges making up the system. Thus the American Arbitration Association, a large private court, has a very loose structure with virtually no hierarchy.[11] In contrast, court systems engaged in law creation, such as the federal court system and the court systems of the various states, are hierarchical. Generally there are three tiers: a lowest tier of trial judges each sitting by himself (though panels of trial judges are not unknown); a middle tier of appellate judges sitting in panels of three; and a supreme court composed usually of seven or nine judges, sitting en banc (that is, as a single panel) instead of in separate panels, and exercising a discretionary rather than, as in the intermediate appellate court, an obligatory jurisdiction. The English judicial system is similar. This structure is so persistent over time and so uniform across jurisdictions that it must have some definite advantages.

11. On private arbitration generally see, for example, Steven Lazarus et al., *Resolving Business Disputes: The Potential of Commercial Arbitration* (1965); Herbert M. Kritzer and Jill K. Anderson, "The Arbitration Alternative: A Comparative Analysis of Case Processing Time, Disposition Mode, and Cost in the American Arbitration Association and the Courts," 8 *Justice System J.* 6 (1983); William M. Landes and Richard A. Posner, "Adjudication as a Private Good," 8 *J. Legal Stud.* 235, 245–53 (1979). Arbitration appears to be growing in popularity as a dispute-settlement mechanism, but there are few statistics. We do know, however, that between 1971 and 1977 the number of arbitrations conducted under the aegis of the American Arbitration Association increased from 22,459 to 47,066 (1977–1978 AAA Ann. Rep. 13).

The advantages, indeed, are not hard to see. The basic job of the trial judge is the management of the trial, an executive function best performed by one person. Since the law-creation function of the individual trial judge is relatively small and the losing litigant has a right of appeal, there is no reason to worry greatly about uniformity of results at the trial, and hence no good reason to have trial judges sit in panels, which would be costly both directly and in reducing the efficiency of trial management. But law creation, to be effective, must be consistent; it will not do to subject people to inconsistent rules. Thus every jurisdiction must have a single tribunal that has the final say on what the rules of decision are. There must be, in other words, a supreme court; and since it will be powerful because of its monopoly of law creation, there must be more than one judge in order to reduce the power of any individual, ameliorate the consequences of low-quality appointments, obtain the benefits of collective deliberation, and in all these ways enhance the legitimacy and hence the authority of the court's decisions. In general, the more powerful the court is, the larger will be the number of judges on a panel (within rather tight limits, however). This is a risk-averse strategy: there will be leveling down as well as up (dilution of the best as well as the worst).

Having a panel of judges rather than a single judge at the appellate level involves less redundancy than one might think. Law creation requires the writing of judicial opinions for publication—and opinion writing is an appellate judge's most time-consuming task—but only one judge on the panel will be assigned to write the panel opinion. If one judge hears 180 cases a year he will be responsible for 180 opinions (of course, he will not have to worry about having to write any dissenting or concurring opinions!); if he sits in a panel of three he will be responsible for only 60; and if he sits in a panel of nine he will be responsible for only 20. Incidentally, this implies that the federal court system should be organized in such a way that the Supreme Court hears more appeals than any court of appeals panel (provided the Court's cases are not substantially more time-consuming), since the Supreme Court with its nine members sits en banc while each of the courts of appeals, whatever its size, sits in panels of three. But in fact each of those panels hears more appeals than the Supreme Court, a point to which I shall return in Chapter 5.

The only reason to have an intermediate appellate court—something all the states, and the federal system, did without for many years[12]—is

12. The federal courts of appeals were not created till 1891, although some intermediate appellate review of federal district court decisions was provided by the federal circuit courts before then. On the growth of state intermediate courts see Robert A. Kagan,

to relieve the pressure on the supreme court. But once there is an intermediate court, then quite apart from workload it makes sense for the supreme court to exercise a discretionary rather than mandatory jurisdiction. Unless the intermediate appellate court decides an appeal in a fashion contrary to another intermediate court in the same jurisdiction, or contrary to the rule laid down in an earlier supreme court decision, there will usually be no need for further appellate review—if, as I have argued, the principal reason for appellate review is to ensure the production of a consistent set of legal rules. But it is not the only reason. One certainly would like to have, to the extent possible, correct as well as consistent rules. But if several intermediate appellate panels agree on the answer to a legal question and none disagrees, the answer probably is right; and if they disagree, this is, as we have just seen, an independent reason for further appellate review. Sometimes a question is so important that the community cannot wait for several intermediate appellate panels to chew it over successively; sometimes the question is such that it cannot arise before more than one panel; and sometimes even though all the intermediate panels agree on one answer, the supreme court, with its broader perspective and (perhaps) more carefully selected membership, may rightly reject the answer given by the intermediate courts.

There would be some appellate review of trial courts even if courts in our system had no law-creation function: the traditional American hostility to concentrated governmental power has made it inevitable that single trial judges would not be allowed to exercise an unchecked discretion, though in fact appellate review of fact-finding and trial management by the trial judge is quite limited.[13] But if all that appellate courts did was to correct trial errors, there would be less concern with creating an appellate structure that promoted consistency among appellate decisions in the same jurisdiction, for there would not be a potential problem of subjecting the people in the jurisdiction to inconsistent legal obligations.

The three-tier judicial structure that I have outlined creates the familiar judicial pyramid, illustrated by the federal court system with its 500-odd district judges, 100-odd circuit judges (intermediate appellate

Bliss Cartwright, Lawrence W. Friedman, and Stanton Wheeler, "The Evolution of State Supreme Courts," 76 *Mich. L. Rev.* 961 (1978). And see generally John A. Stookey, "Creating an Intermediate Court of Appeals," in *The Analysis of Judicial Reform* 153 (Philip L. Dubois ed. 1982).

13. Arbitration usually does not have an appellate stage. But arbitration is (normally) optional; courts are governmental, and hence coercive, institutions, so there is less tolerance of their mistakes.

judges), and 9 Supreme Court justices. A significant limitation of the pyramidal structure should be noted: it cannot be expanded symmetrically to accommodate growth in the demand for judicial services. The base of trial judges can be enlarged without too much difficulty, but the intermediate tier and especially the apex are difficult to enlarge, at least beyond the point we have already reached in the federal court system. The Supreme Court would not be more productive if it had 11 members rather than 9 because more negotiations among the members would be necessary to construct a majority in each case, and this additional burden would offset the reduced burden of opinion writing for each judge. The number of links required to connect all the members of a set grows exponentially with the size of the set, in accordance with the formula $n(n-1)/2$.[14] Thus, 36 links are necessary to connect all the members of a set of 9, and 55 for a set of 11—half again as many. But the reduction in the number of opinion assignments per capita would be less than one-fifth (it would be 2/11). And if instead of increasing the membership of the Supreme Court you were to split the Court in two, you would have to create a Super Supreme Court above the halves to ensure consistency of legal rules. The need for consistency imposes similar if less stringent limitations on the expansion of the intermediate appellate courts (in the federal system the courts of appeals): either each court of appeals must be allowed to become unwieldy in size (several now have more than 9 active judges, and one has 23), or the number of courts of appeals has to be increased—which means more intercircuit conflicts and therefore more work for the Supreme Court. Specialized courts provide a way around the pyramidal structure of appellate review, but they have problems of their own, as we shall see in Chapter 5.

I have equated the trial judges with dispute resolution and the appellate judges, intermediate or final, with law creation, but of course these equations are too rigid. A trial judge must create law when precedents provide no sure guidance, and appellate courts engage in dispute resolution when they review findings of fact, though they do this under a deferential standard that weights the trial judge's factual determinations heavily. But the correlation of the appellate process with law creation is a strong one; some evidence for this is the fact that the American Arbitration Association, and most other private courts, do

14. Each member must establish a link with every other one (that is, with $n - 1$, the one being himself). For n members, the number of these links is $n(n - 1)$. Division by 2 is necessary to eliminate the duplicate link between each pair that is implied by multiplying n by $n - 1$. (Since A will have a link with everyone else in the set, including B, and B with everyone else including A, one of the $A - B$ links is redundant.)

not provide appellate review. The increasing ratio of law creation to dispute resolution as one moves up the judicial hierarchy is also shown by the increasing ratio of published to unpublished decisions (and very few arbitration decisions are published); as mentioned earlier, publication is essential to law creation but incidental to dispute resolution. In the federal system, for example, a very small fraction of district court opinions are published, about half of the court of appeals opinions are published, and all of the Supreme Court's opinions are published.

SELECTING AND MOTIVATING JUDGES

Turning from court organization to personnel, one encounters fascinating problems of selection and motivation that deserve separate consideration. An ordinary firm has a pretty good idea of the "value added" of an individual executive, and armed with that knowledge can decide whether to fire him or to pay him a bonus. Both the carrot and the stick are in play, and together they give the executive a strong incentive to do his best work. But it is hard to determine a judge's value added. The ordinary firm has profits (or losses), and if it can figure out how much better off or worse off it would be without a particular executive, it knows exactly what he is worth. But in part because of the decision not to finance the courts out of user fees, society has little if any idea what the social value of any of its public court systems is, and thus the effort to set a value on the individual judge's output fails at the threshold. Yet this would not be a catastrophic failure, provided judges could be ranked against one another; then the situation would be no worse, if no better, than that of any other government agency whose output—like the output of most government agencies—is not sold in the market. It might be possible to rank judges, at least below the level of the Supreme Court: one could look at the number of cases that a trial or appellate judge decided each year and adjust the number downward for delay and for the number of times he was reversed and upward for the number of times he was affirmed and the number of times he was cited approvingly by other judges. These would admittedly be crude measures of quality, but perhaps they could be refined in various ways. The Continental judicial systems (such as those of France and Germany), which are career judiciaries, promote judges up through the ranks using evaluation methods not unlike those of other large organizations, public and private.[15]

15. See, for example, Bradley C. Canon, "British, French and American Systems of Justice Compared," 61 *Current History* 97, 101–102 (1971); Henry W. Ehrmann, *Comparative Legal Cultures* 76–78 (1976); Daniel J. Meador, "German Appellate Judges: Career

What is lacking in the American scene is the will rather than the way. In any system where workers' pay, tenure, and rank depend on the decisions of their superiors, power is concentrated at the level where those decisions are made.[16] And no matter how objective the criteria employed at that level are, there is bound to be concern, in a culture like ours where distrust of officialdom is deeply ingrained, that the bosses will abuse their power. One cannot imagine the American public's accepting a system where the Chief Justice of the United States determined the selection, pay, tenure, and rank of the other federal judges. The Constitution set the tone for the federal judiciary by requiring presidential appointment and senatorial confirmation of federal judges[17] and by guaranteeing the judges against removal except by the laborious process of impeachment by the House of Representatives and conviction by the Senate on the ground of misbehavior, and against any reduction in pay; and although none of the states has gone as far to assure the independence of judges, all have gone some distance in that direction. Judicial independence is normally thought of as independence from political control of the judicial process, but it would be more accurate to describe it as independence from control by superior officials, whether or not political, to the end of diffusing judicial power.

It is a myth that independence guarantees a nonpolitical judiciary. Its tendency, rather, is to make the court system an autonomous center of political power. Independence means that once the judge is appointed he cannot be compelled or even induced to do the bidding of the appointing authority. Federal judges are almost completely impervious to the usual methods of controlling agents and employees—the threat to fire or cut wages if performance is poor and the prospect of a raise or a bonus for excellent performance.[18] Apart from the prospect of professional commendation for doing a good job (an uncertain prospect, be-

---

Patterns and American-English Comparisons," 67 *Judicature,* June-July 1983, at 16, 22, 26; Martin Shapiro, *Courts: A Comparative and Political Analysis* 151 (1981). Cf. John Paul Ryan, "Evaluating Judicial Performance: Problems of Measurement and Politics," in *The Analysis of Judicial Reform,* supra note 12, at 121, and references cited; Joel Davidow, "Beyond Merit Selection: Judicial Careers through Merit Promotion," 12 *Tex. Tech. L. Rev.* 851 (1981). An interesting paper by Joachim Herrmann, "The Independence of the Judge in the Federal Republic of Germany," in *Contemporary Problems in Criminal Justice: Essays in Honor of Professor Shigemitsu Dando* 61 (1983), expresses concern about the effect of evaluations of judicial performance on judicial independence.

16. As noted by Shapiro in reference to the Continental systems, supra note 15, at 152.

17. Article II, § 2, requires confirmation of Supreme Court justices and other officers of the United States, which has been assumed to include judges of the lower federal courts.

18. The Judicial Council of each circuit has some—though very rarely used—powers to censure judges in the circuit, withdraw cases from them, and force them to retire for disability. See 28 U.S.C. § 372.

cause legal scholarship and opinion are themselves political to a significant extent), only a small carrot is in play. That is the limited prospect for district judges of advancement to the court of appeals, which pays a slightly higher salary and involves somewhat less taxing work and greater prestige (at least within the judiciary itself), and the extremely limited prospect for court of appeals judges of advancement to the Supreme Court. Otherwise the judge is, at least if he wants to be, principal rather than agent. And although the appointing authority may try to select as judges those whose views it knows, finds compatible with its own, and believes to be permanent rather than transitory, these are difficult criteria to apply in practice. This may be one reason why ideological appointments to the federal courts are infrequent below the level of the Supreme Court.

Independence is a necessary rather than a sufficient condition for exercising political power. The appointees might not have a taste for or skill at wielding such power; but independence makes it likely (though less likely than in an elective judiciary) that many judges will have such a taste. It makes a judgeship a plum, and thus an apt instrument of political patronage. And the people whom politicians reward with patronage appointments are generally people who have rendered political services. Not all such people are politicians and not all federal judicial appointments are patronage appointments; but in a system in which judges are appointed by politicians, it would be unrealistic to expect all or most judges to be apolitical technicians.

If one thinks of the most influential judges in the history of this country—judges such as John Marshall, Roger Taney, Oliver Wendell Holmes, Louis Brandeis, Benjamin Cardozo, William Howard Taft, Charles Evans Hughes, Felix Frankfurter, Robert Jackson, Harlan Fiske Stone, Hugo Black, Earl Warren, William Brennan, William Rehnquist, Learned Hand, Roger Traynor, Jerome Frank, Henry Friendly—and asks how many of them would have been on the supreme court or intermediate appellate court of a judicial system organized as a career bureaucracy, as the Continental judiciaries are, or on the English Court of Appeal or House of Lords, which today recruit exclusively from the ranks of the senior barristers and of lower-court judges previously recruited from those ranks, the answer is very few, perhaps none. Only Cardozo was an American equivalent of a Queen's Counsel (that is, a senior full-time trial lawyer); and none of our great judges, I imagine, would have found a career in a European-style career judiciary very congenial. The American judicial system, perhaps especially at the federal level where judicial independence is most fully secured, allows and indeed encourages the appointment as judges of people who have experience and aptitude that transcend technical legal analysis and trial skills, and that equip them to engage in the political law creation that has always been a conspicuous feature of American judiciaries. Nor is this pattern contrary to the spirit of the Constitution: the federal judiciary was modeled on the English judiciary, and eighteenth-century English judges were powerful public officials.[19] True, Article III gave the federal courts only a limited jurisdiction. And true, the growth of legislative activity by Parliament in the nineteenth and twentieth centuries, and doubtless other factors, have virtually extinguished the policymaking role of the English judge; today, in contrast to his American counterparts, he really is a technician. England is now part way to the Continental system of a career judiciary, where a person is recruited into the judiciary from law school and spends his career as a judge, rising through the ranks untroubled by fear of lateral entry. In England judges are appointed to the trial bench after careers as barristers, but they are promoted as in the Continental systems. More important, the appointments are meritocratic rather than political (as they were when the courts were politically powerful); and having been appointed for their excellence as technicians, the judges behave like technicians.[20]

The American system, unchanged since the Revolution, is now almost at the opposite extreme from the English. Our federal and state judiciaries are not narrowly meritocratic; our judges are not merely technicians of the law. (These two negatives are related.) Just why these things should be so is not entirely clear, but one reason must be the fact that American law is inherently more political than English—and not merely more political because it is administered by judges who are more political. The Constitution has given the federal courts broad authority with (in many places) imprecise direction, and the authority granted is thus inherently political. In contrast, there are no justiciable constitutional rights in England. And the United States Congress, though it has become a powerful legislative body in this century, has never become a disciplined legislative body like the British Parliament,

19. See Louis L. Jaffe, *English and American Judges as Lawmakers* 60 (1969).

20. There is a rich literature on the history and present organization and character of the English judiciary. See, for example, Brian Abel-Smith and Robert Stevens, *In Search of Justice: Society and the Legal System* (1968); R. M. Jackson, *The Machinery of Justice in England* (7th ed. 1977); Gareth Jones, "Should Judges Be Politicians? The English Experience," 57 *Ind. L.J.* 211 (1982); Robert Megarry, "Barristers and Judges in England Today," 51 *Fordham L. Rev.* 387 (1982); Shimon Shetreet, *Judges on Trial: A Study of the Appointment and Accountability of the English Judiciary* (1976). Jaffe's *English and American Judges,* supra note 19, is a particularly good introduction to the contemporary differences between English and American judges, while Delmar Karlen, "Civil Appeals: English and American Approaches Compared," 21 *William & Mary L. Rev.* 121 (1979), is a highly readable account of English appellate justice.

and has become even less disciplined with the decline in the power of committee chairmen. Parliament is effectively unicameral and is most of the time firmly controlled by the executive (that is, the Cabinet). Our federal legislative power is divided up among the two houses of Congress and the Presidency, and often one of the three is controlled by a different political party from the other two; but even when all three are in theory controlled by the same party, the reality is different because the parties are weak and decentralized—increasingly so. The result of all this is that federal statutes often emerge from the legislative process radically incomplete, and the courts are left to complete them by a process that is only formally interpretive. In addition, the interactions between legislation and the Constitution and between federal law and the law of 50 quasi-sovereign states have made many fields of American law immensely complex, with a multitude of ill-fitting seams that require continuous, and highly creative, judicial patchwork to avoid chaos. And when judges have to bring in political concepts to resolve questions for which the technical legal materials of decision provide no answers, they often must choose among competing concepts because none commands a consensus in our contentious society. When judges make such choices, they are exercising political power.

The institution of judicial independence, which in England guarantees the complete insulation of judges from politics, in America fosters the exercise of political power by individual judges. It does this both by protecting the judges from retribution by the overtly political branches and by influencing the selection process in favor of politically well connected lawyers, many of whom have tastes and skills for functioning as political judges. Thus, even though the federal courts are the most protected of all courts from political interference, they wield greater political power than any other courts in the world. Judicial independence has not taken our judges out of politics; in our political culture, it has put the judges securely in politics.

Since the term politics has a pejorative ring in a discussion of law, I hasten to add that the exercise of political power by the federal courts is not usurpative, although particular exercises may be; it is implicit in the constitutional scheme. When the framers of the Constitution rejected the colonial model of judges subservient to the Crown[21] in favor of judicial independence on the model of the eighteenth-century English judiciary,[22] which had played (or at least was thought to have played) a big role in securing the rights of Englishmen against the Crown, they

21. See Gordon S. Wood, *The Creation of the American Republic 1776–1787*, at 160 (1969).
22. See, for example, 25 *Papers of Alexander Hamilton* 574–575 (Harold C. Syrett ed. 1977).

were creating, deliberately it would seem, a separate and powerful branch of government. The main difference between the original and the copy was that the framers thought the danger of tyranny would come not from the executive, as in England, but from the legislature—that is, from Congress. Although the Constitution does not say in so many words that federal courts can invalidate statutes that violate the Constitution, the provision in Article VI that "This Constitution . . . shall be the supreme law of the land" and the provision in Article III extending the judicial power of the United States "to all cases . . . arising under this Constitution," together with the many affirmations of the judicial power to review the constitutionality of legislation in the debates preceding the adoption and ratification of the Constitution,[23] make clear beyond reasonable doubt that constitutional questions were indeed intended to be justiciable. Thus, the framers envisaged a judiciary of unprecedented power.

This is not to say, of course, that federal or other American judges were ever supposed to be or are in fact completely free-wheeling political actors. In vesting the legislative power of the United States in Congress in Article I and the judicial power in the courts in Article III, the framers of the Constitution obviously intended these to be different powers, the difference being captured in the Holmes quotation at the beginning of this chapter. A legislature is quintessentially political; the appropriate scope of a court as a political body was obviously supposed to be less. The Constitution also established a number of important checks on the exercise of political power by judges that help to differentiate their role from that of legislators. The first consists of the limitations on the nature of the federal judicial power itself. By confining federal judges to the decision of cases, Article III limited the occasions for judicial intervention in the life of the nation.[24] Not only must the judge wait for a case to come up to him before he can lay down a rule, but with cases coming up to him in random order he will find it difficult to establish an agenda for political action. He must take the cases as they come; his role is inherently one of reacting rather than initiating. The framers did not anticipate, however, the discretionary jurisdiction of the Supreme Court, which in the present period of enormous caseloads enables the Court, by picking and choosing among the thousands of applications for review, to establish an agenda for action

23. The classic statement is in Hamilton's *Federalist* No. 78, but there are many other similar statements in the constitutional debates; for a very serviceable collection of the references in the debates to the federal judiciary see George J. Schulz, Creation of the Federal Judiciary: A Review of the Debates in the Federal and State Constitutional Conventions; and Other Papers, S. Doc. No. 91, 75th Cong., 1st Sess. (1937; GPO 1938).

24. As astutely observed by de Tocqueville. See 1 *Democracy in America* 100 (Reeve trans., rev. ed., 1899).

(or would enable it to do so, if the justices pulled together more).

Another check on the power of judges comes from the powers that the other branches retain over the judiciary, albeit not over the individual judge. Congress can refuse to raise judges' salaries in times of inflation, can curtail their perquisites, can be stingy in appropriating money for essential support services, can impose onerous duties on the judges with one hand and curtail their jurisdiction with the other, can overrule nonconstitutional decisions, can initiate constitutional amendments, can add new judges and new courts, and in these and other ways can show effective displeasure with the judges. A neglected point, moreover, is that the fewer judges there are, the more each judge's conduct contributes to the likelihood of legislative retribution, and the bigger price therefore the individual judge pays for setting his political will against that of the other branches of government. It was expected, and apparently intended for the foregoing reason,[25] that the federal judiciary would be small (it still is, relative to the state judiciaries). This point has a corollary: while an increase in the number of judges in one obvious sense dilutes the power of the individual judge, in another sense it increases it (more precisely, makes it cheaper to exercise) by reducing the price the individual must pay for being irresponsible. This, as we shall see, is one of the costs of increasing the number of judges in a judicial system in order to meet increases in the demand for judicial services.

There is another subtle check on judicial usurpation. The institution of judicial independence, by stripping away the usual incentives that motivate people to bend their efforts in one direction or another, brings to the fore another incentive: that of maintaining status. The prestige of being a federal judge is an emolument of the position that helps explain the willingness of so many lawyers to accept a large cut in pay to become a judge.[26] Now it is easier to maintain one's judicial prestige by keeping a low judicial profile than by striving to take power away from a competing branch of government. Admittedly, although an aggressive judicial posture invites criticism and antagonism in some quarters, it

25. Charles Warren, "New Light on the History of the Federal Judiciary Act of 1789," 37 *Harv. L. Rev.* 49, 76 (1923), quotes one of the draftsmen of that Act as observing that "numbers [of judges] rather lessened responsibility."

26. For evidence of this willingness, see Chapter 2. Federal judges traditionally score high on prestige rankings—well above lawyers and county and local judges, the only types of state judge for whom prestige rankings are reported. See Donald J. Treiman, *Occupational Prestige in Comparative Perspective* 319 (1977); Paul Mathew Siegel, "Prestige in the American Occupational Structure" 70–71 (Ph.D. diss., University of Chicago Dept. of Sociology, March 1971); National Opinion Research Center, "Jobs and Occupations: A Popular Evaluation," in *Class, Status and Power: A Reader in Social Stratification* 412 (Reinhard Bendix and Seymour Martin Lipset eds. 1953).

invites praise in others, and if successful can enhance one's judicial prestige. But it is a somewhat risky game, and relatively few judges have had the stomach for it. This is one reason why only a minority of federal judges have been judicial activists, even though federal judges are insulated from direct retribution for wielding their power boldly. The effectiveness of professional critics in constraining judicial behavior is enhanced by the tradition (now on the wane in the federal courts of appeals) that the judge must explain his decision in a published opinion, which if it falls below professional expectations of principled judicial decision making may become a focus of searing criticism. So federal judges are not all-powerful; but it would be naive to suppose that they do not have and exercise power.

2

The Federal Court System

THIS CHAPTER traces changes in the organization, personnel, and jurisdiction of the federal courts since their establishment in 1789. Consideration of caseload, including the caseload explosion that has occurred in the last quarter-century, is postponed to the next chapter, and many historical details, ably treated in other studies of the federal courts,[1] are omitted altogether.

ORGANIZATION

Article III of the Constitution and the first Judiciary Act[2] between them created three different types of federal courts—district courts, circuit courts, and the Supreme Court—though manned by only two types of judges—district judges and Supreme Court justices. The district courts were trial courts and were manned by district judges, sitting alone. The Supreme Court was mainly (today it is almost exclusively) an appellate court, composed of justices sitting en banc rather than in separate panels. The circuit courts were manned by one district judge and two Supreme Court justices—a panel of three. Although the circuit courts had some appellate responsibilities in relation to the district courts, they were mainly trial courts themselves. Appeals could come to the Supreme Court not only from the district and circuit courts, but from

1. The classic study remains Felix Frankfurter and James M. Landis, *The Business of the Supreme Court: A Study of the Federal Judicial System* (1927); despite the title, it is a comprehensive history of federal jurisdiction. Two extremely serviceable and up-to-date summaries of the evolution of the federal court system, by a law professor and a political scientist, respectively, are Charles Alan Wright, *The Law of Federal Courts,* chap. 1 (4th ed. 1983), and John R. Schmidhauser, *Judges and Justices: The Federal Appellate Judiciary* (1979).
2. Act of September 24, 1789, chap. 20, 1 Stat. 73.

state supreme courts if a question of federal law was involved. Appeal in all cases was a matter of right rather than at the discretion of the appellate court. Apart from Supreme Court review of state court decisions, then, the federal court system as first created would have been a two-tier system had it not been for the circuit courts.

The circuit courts were a problem from the start, primarily because of the hardships to the Supreme Court justices of having to "ride circuit" at a time when transportation was very slow and uncomfortable. Improvements in transportation were outdistanced by increases in the size of the country and, more important, by increases in the Supreme Court's own workload which could not be matched by increasing the number of Supreme Court justices proportionally and which therefore increased the opportunity costs of circuit riding. Various stopgaps were attempted until 1891, when Congress in the Evarts Act[3] created the courts of appeals (initially and confusingly—because there were still circuit courts—called "circuit courts of appeals").[4] By the logic of judicial administration developed in Chapter 1, the creation of the courts of appeals should have been accompanied by the abolition of the circuit courts and the conversion of the Supreme Court's obligatory review jurisdiction to a discretionary one; instead, the circuit courts lingered on until 1911, and the conversion of the Supreme Court's review jurisdiction, which began as one would expect in 1891 and assumed its modern form of a predominantly discretionary jurisdiction in 1925,[5] remains incomplete to this day. In addition, the idea of trial panels did not die with the circuit courts; it survived in the three-judge district court (generally composed of two district judges and one circuit judge) with right of direct appeal to the Supreme Court. Formerly common, three-judge district courts are now largely limited to reapportionment cases.

The basic organizing principle of the federal court system has always

3. Act of March 3, 1891, chap. 517, 26 Stat. 826.

4. The members of the federal courts of appeals are still called "circuit judges," a title that in the federal system goes back to a time before there were courts of appeals, when as one of the stopgap measures to relieve the burdens of circuit riding on the Supreme Court justices, Congress created a circuit judge in each circuit to help man the circuit courts.

It should be noted that the Court of Appeals for the District of Columbia Circuit, established in 1893, was not really created *ex nihilo* like the other federal courts of appeals. It was the successor to the Supreme Court of the District of Columbia, which had long exercised appellate jurisdiction over the trial courts of the district. Though federal, these courts exercised a largely local jurisdiction similar to that exercised in states by state trial courts. See U.S. Court of Appeals for the D.C. Circuit, *History of the United States Court of Appeals for the District of Columbia Circuit in the Country's Bicentennial Year* 1–5 (1977).

5. See Act of February 13, 1925, chap. 229, 43 Stat. 936.

been regional, and increases in caseload have been accommodated partly by increasing the number of geographic units into which the system is divided. Originally each state was a single federal district; now many states are divided into several districts—as many as four— and there are 91 districts in all. Originally there were 3 circuits; when the circuit courts of appeals were created in 1891 there were 9; there are now 13, though one of these (the "Federal Circuit") is not regional. There is nothing inevitable about organizing courts along regional lines, and the cost of transportation, which was once a big factor in regionalization, is now a small one. The alternative to regionalization is specialization: a federal court could have jurisdiction over all cases of a particular type in the nation rather than jurisdiction over all cases, of whatever type, in a region.

The earliest specialized federal court was the Court of Claims, established before the Civil War to hear money claims against the federal government. Four major specialized courts were created in this century. The first was the Court of Customs Appeals, which as the name implies had jurisdiction over appeals in cases arising under the customs laws (laws imposing import duties). The second was the Commerce Court, which was given jurisdiction to review orders of the Interstate Commerce Commission other than orders for the payment of money. This court was a complete failure and was abolished three years after it was created.[6] The Court of Patent Appeals was created next, to decide appeals from determinations of patent validity by the Commissioner of Patents. It was later merged with the Court of Customs Appeals to form the Court of Customs and Patent Appeals, and finally in 1982 was merged with the appellate division of the Court of Claims to form the United States Court of Appeals for the Federal Circuit. As well as succeeding to the jurisdiction of these former courts, the new court was given exclusive jurisdiction of appeals from decisions of the district courts dealing with patent validity and infringement, and of certain other matters. The creation of the Federal Circuit has given renewed impetus to perennial calls for greater specialization in the federal court system, an issue I take up in Chapter 5. There is also a temporary court—the Emergency Court of Appeals—which is staffed by regular circuit judges, serving on the court on a part-time basis, to decide appeals in certain energy-regulation cases.

My omission of the Tax Court may have distressed those of my readers who are cognoscenti of federal jurisdiction. I have left it out because it is not a court established under Article III of the Constitution. Article

6. See Frankfurter and Landis, supra note 1, at 153–174.

III defines not only the judicial power of the United States but who may exercise it: judges who have lifetime tenure and are guaranteed against any reduction in salary. Although it may seem the height of technicality to make the definition of a federal court turn on whether it is created pursuant to Article III or Article I, under which the Tax Court was created, the concept of federal judicial power must be bounded somewhere to keep this book to a manageable length, and the line between Article III and other federal judicial tribunals provides a convenient, if rather arbitrary, boundary. The truth is that there are thousands of non–Article III federal judges—the administrative law judges and other adjudicative officers of federal administrative agencies, bankruptcy judges, military judges, and federal magistrates, as well as the judges of Article I courts explicitly so called, such as the Tax Court. Indeed, one of the most important developments in the history of the federal courts has been the progressive shift of the judicial function from Article III judges to Article I judges, particularly in the administrative agencies. (The only retrograde movement has been the diminution in the number of territorial courts—non-Article III courts—as the territories achieved statehood.) But rather than treating this as a shift within the federal court system, as well I might, I have decided to treat it as a shift from the federal court system to an alternative court system.

The shift has altered the responsibilities of the federal courts. Federal district courts now function as review courts for many federal administrative decisions; and not only do the courts of appeals exercise a second tier of judicial review of administrative action by reviewing the district courts' administrative-review decisions, but many administrative decisions are reviewable directly in the courts of appeals, without initial review in the district courts. (As we shall see in Chapter 8, the division of initial review jurisdiction between district courts and courts of appeals follows no rational pattern.) Thus, the federal judicial pyramid is asymmetrical: just as the Supreme Court reviews decisions of state supreme courts as well as of federal courts of appeals, so the courts of appeals review decisions of federal administrative agencies (and Article I courts such as the Tax Court) as well as of federal district courts. Bankruptcy judges and federal magistrates, finally, occupy a kind of dual role: as independent adjudicators whose decisions are reviewed by the district courts (and often directly by the courts of appeals), and as adjuncts to the district courts in the broad sense in which special masters, and less clearly law clerks, staff attorneys, and externs, are all judicial adjuncts.

In one sense the organization of the federal courts is rigidly hierarchical, in that each court can nullify any decision appealed to it from a court in a lower tier. In another sense it is extremely loose-knit. Judges have no authority to appoint or remove other Article III judges or to reassign them to another district or circuit, although Article II of the Constitution implies that judges could be empowered to appoint Article III judges, and although, as mentioned in the first chapter, the Judicial Councils have some de facto power over judicial tenures. The most important exception to the principle that judges do not control the tenures of other judges is that once a judge takes senior status, usually at age 65 or 70, his continued service is essentially at the pleasure of the judges in active service on his court.

As shown in Table 2.1, Article III judges are a diminishing proportion of the total employees of the federal court system. This trend began well before 1960 and seems to have accelerated decisively sometime between 1970 and 1975. Neither increases in the number of judges

Table 2.1. Personnel and budget of the federal courts, 1925–1983

				Budget[b]	
				Current	1967
	Total	Number of Article III	Percentage of Article III	dollars	dollars
Year	employees	judges[a]	judges	(millions)	(millions)
1925	1,284	179	13.9	14	27
1930	1,517	200	13.2	15	30
1935	1,620	189	11.7	15	36
1940	2,171	256	11.8	11	26
1945	2,253	261	11.6	14	26
1950	2,836	289	10.2	24	33
1955	3,259	321	9.8	32	40
1960	3,200	322	10.1	50	56
1965	4,478	394	8.8	76	80
1970	5,346	507	9.5	126	108
1975	7,619	506	6.6	313	194
1980	10,075	657	6.5	606	245
1982	10,587	657	6.2	749	256
1983	11,046	657	5.9	823	275
1984	11,755	657	5.9	925	305

Source: Appendices to Budgets of the United States for the years listed.

a. From Appendix B at the end of the book; senior judges are excluded.

b. Appropriations. Before 1940 there was no separate budget for the judiciary, and figures for earlier years include some nonjudicial expenditures of the Department of Justice.

nor increases in their salaries can explain the very rapid real increases in the federal judicial budget recently; only the addition of non–Article III personnel can. Judges' salaries and fringe benefits were 20 percent of the federal judicial budget in 1960 but only 9 percent in 1980.[7] Since 1960 the total number of judges has doubled, but the total number of judicial employees has almost quadrupled. And several "off budget" items should be noted. Many federal judges (excluding Supreme Court justices) employ externs, who are law students working part-time for course credit given by their schools. This practice was unknown 25 years ago. Some district judges appoint private practitioners (unpaid) to represent indigent civil litigants, such as state and federal prisoners with civil rights complaints; these lawyers function partly as judicial adjuncts, helping the judge to winnow out the frivolous cases. This also was unknown 25 years ago. Finally, though I know of no statistics on the question, my impression is that the use of special masters has grown; these are private practitioners, appointed by the judge but paid for by the parties, who assist the judge in ruling on discovery motions and in calculating damages, and sometimes in deciding liability issues. Thus the growth in the budget and employment of the federal courts understates the expansion of the federal court system.

Despite the constitutionally ordained independence of Article III judges, and the fact that Congress has fixed the pay, perquisites, and even precedence of the judges in minute detail, a considerable scope for administration remains; and in any case statutes regulating the federal courts are, in part at least, the result of proposals made by the federal judiciary. The administrative hierarchy of the federal courts consists principally of the Chief Justice, the Judicial Conference of the United States (consisting of the Chief Justice, the chief judges of the courts of appeals, and some district judges), the chief judges of the circuits and districts, the circuit Judicial Councils (composed of the circuit judges and some district judges), the Administrative Office of the United States Courts, and the professional administrators of the courts of appeals (circuit executives). The fact that the Chief Justice of the United States, a nonelected official with life tenure, is not only the chief judge of the Supreme Court but the administrative head of the entire federal court system at once guarantees the substantial independence of the federal judiciary from the other branches of federal government and imparts to the position of Chief Justice a faintly monarchical air.

7. Wolf Heydebrand and Carroll Seron, "The Double Bind of the Capitalist Judicial System," 9 *Int'l J. of Sociology of Law* 407, 418 (1981) (table 2). (Readers should not be alarmed by the title of this mainly descriptive article!) My estimates, based on the U.S. Budget, are 21 percent and 10 percent, respectively.

THE JUDGES

The key personnel of the federal court system are (still) the judges, and the key facts about them are their independence from the usual methods for motivating workers and the method of their selection. In regard to selection I will expand briefly on what I said in Chapter 1.[8] I noted that the appointive power is divided between the President and the Senate. By a process not clear to me, the balance has worked itself out approximately as follows: district judges are in fact appointed by the senior senator from the judge's state who is of the President's party, if there is such a senator; if both senators are from the opposing party, the state chairman of the President's party has the appointive power (though often he is really just a clearing house for proposals, and the Attorney General or the White House or powerful local politicians have the real power). Although each circuit (except the District of Columbia and Federal Circuits) includes several states, circuit judgeships are informally allocated among the states of the circuit usually in rough proportion to the number of court of appeals cases that arise in the state. The power to appoint circuit judges is shared by the senior senator of the President's party in the state to which the judgeship in question has been allocated (or the state chairman, if both senators are of the opposing party) and the President, each normally being entitled to veto the choice of the other. The exact balance of power between them depends on specific, often local, political factors (the senator's standing with the White House, the President's standing with the electorate and with other senators, and so forth). The President has largely a free hand with Supreme Court appointments, particularly if the Senate is controlled by his party. The same thing is true of those federal courts (mainly the new Federal Circuit, and the district courts and court of appeals for the District of Columbia Circuit) that are not located in a state.

Appointments at all levels of the federal judiciary can be divided

8. What follows draws in part on personal experience, but mainly on a substantial scholarly and journalistic literature whose highlights include the following: Henry J. Abraham, *Justices and Presidents: A Political History of Appointments to the Supreme Court* (1974); Harold W. Chase, *Federal Judges: The Appointing Process* (1972); Jerome Corsi, *Judicial Politics: An Introduction* (1984); Sheldon Goldman and Thomas P. Jahnige, *The Federal Courts as a Political System* 49–76 (1971); Joel B. Grossman, *The ABA and the Politics of Judicial Selection* (1965); J. Woodford Howard, *Courts of Appeals in the Federal Judicial System*, chap. 4 (1981); William D. Mitchell, "Appointment of Federal Judges," 17 *A.B.A.J.* 569 (1931); Schmidhauser, supra note 1, chaps 2–3; Rayman L. Solomon, "The Politics of Appointment and the Federal Courts' Role in Regulating America: U.S. Courts of Appeals Judgeships from T.R. to F.D.R." (Sept. 1, 1983, forthcoming in *Am. Bar Foundation Research J.*); Nina Totenberg, "Will Judges Be Chosen Rationally?" 60 *Judicature* (Aug.–Sept. 1976) at 93.

(with some unavoidable crudeness) into three types: merit appointments, patronage appointments, and ideological appointments. (I mean these terms to be descriptive, not evaluative.) Merit appointments, in the sense of appointments motivated solely by the appointee's suitability for the position, are rare, especially for a first appointment, but merit promotion of district judges to the courts of appeals is common. Patronage appointments—rewarding good friends and faithful supporters of the senator or the President, or currying favor with a powerful interest group—are the most common type of federal judicial appointment below the Supreme Court level. Ideological appointments—usually initiated by the President rather than by a senator, and based not on the political loyalty or deserts of the judicial appointee but on his views on matters likely to come before the court—are rare at the district court level, somewhat more common at the court of appeals level, and very common at the Supreme Court level, the difference in incidence corresponding to the different importance of the three levels in the creation of law. Most appointments partake of all three elements—merit, patronage, and ideology—in the sense that a candidate who is seriously deficient with respect to any one of them is unlikely to be appointed. The screening function performed by the American Bar Association's Standing Committee on the Judiciary, although in my opinion unduly biased in favor of candidates having extensive experience as trial lawyers, assures that most candidates will have a minimum competence.[9] But in virtually every Administration a few federal judges are nominated and confirmed who are rated as unqualified by the ABA committee. And an ideologically desirable or meritocratic candidate who has offended powerful politicans in the President's party is unlikely to be appointed, and similarly with a patronage candidate who is ideologically unacceptable.

In an article published in 1966, Professor Surrency summarized the system of selection as he saw it: "The appointment of [federal district] judges has long been considered a matter of political patronage . . . Rarely has any President appointed anyone to the bench from other than his own party . . . While during the Nineteenth Century the only

9. Members of the Standing Committee, some of them anyway, know perfectly well that extensive trial experience is not a prerequisite for distinguished service at any level of the federal judiciary, but will defend the committee's emphasis on such experience on the following *realpolitik* ground. Confining judicial selection to full-time trial lawyers (the tendency, though not the invariable outcome, of the committee's approach) will tend to screen out lawyers who spend a lot of their time politicking rather than practicing, and will thus raise the average quality of the federal bench. A Senator will be able to tell a loyal supporter, "I would like to appoint you, but the ABA would not approve you because you're not an experienced trial lawyer."

qualification was loyalty to the party in power, beginning with Theodore Roosevelt the general trend has been to give some consideration to the candidates' qualifications. Increasingly the American Bar Association is consulted."[10] Today, of course, it is consulted in all cases. With regard to circuit judges, Professor Howard has written more recently: "Judgeships normally are rewards for political service."[11]

Although there may be an element of overstatement in these evaluations, politics does play a large role in federal judicial selection. Yet this, of course, does not exclude the possibility that more judges than just those appointed on a strictly meritocratic basis will have extraordinary merit. If Learned Hand and Henry Friendly illustrate meritocratic appointments of judges who turned out indeed to have extraordinary merit, Holmes and Brandeis illustrate judges of extraordinary merit who were appointed primarily on grounds other than strict merit—ideology in Holmes's case (I am thinking of Holmes's appointment to the U.S. Supreme Court rather than to the Supreme Judicial Court of Massachusetts, the latter having been a merit appointment for Holmes), ideology and patronage in Brandeis's. There are many fine federal judges who were appointed not because—at least not mainly because—they were fine candidates but because they were good friends of the senator of the right party at the right time in the right state.

If exceptional merit were the sole criterion of appointment, rather than a serendipitous outcome of appointments more often than not based mainly on other factors, the federal bench would be of higher quality than it is. But it is unrealistic to think that political (patronage and ideological) factors can be eliminated from the appointing process. As noted in Chapter 1, the conditions guaranteeing independence of the federal judiciary make political appointments irresistible to the appointing authorities. The life tenure of federal judges not only makes the job something of a plum and so encourages patronage appointments; it also enables a politician to project his ideas beyond his own term of office by appointing a like-minded person to a lifetime job, and thus encourages ideological appointments as well. The only way to get politics out of the selection process would be either to greatly reduce the political independence of federal judges, which would however reduce the attractiveness of the job to many of the people most highly qualified for it, or (as in England and the Continent) to reduce the po-

10. Erwin C. Surrency, "Federal District Court Judges and the History of Their Courts," 40 F.R.D. 139, 150 (1966). See also Evan A. Evans, "Political Influences in the Selection of Federal Judges," 1948 Wis. L. Rev. 330; J. Earl Major, "Federal Judges as Political Patronage," 38 Chi. Bar Record 7 (1956).

11. Howard, supra note 8, at 90.

Table 2.2. Federal judicial salaries, 1800–1983, in current and constant (1983) dollars

Year	Supreme Court[a]		Court of Appeals		District Court	
	Current dollars	1983 dollars	Current dollars	1983 dollars	Current dollars	1983 dollars
1800	3,500	20,828	—	—	800–1,800[b]	4,761–10,712
1820	4,500	32,518	—	—	1,000–3,000[b]	7,226–21,679
1860	6,000	67,444	—	—	2,000–5,000[b, c]	21,679–54,196[c]
1900	10,000	121,400	6,000	72,840	5,000	60,700
1913[d]	14,500	148,173	7,000	71,532	6,000	61,313
1940	20,000	144,524	12,500	90,327	10,000	72,262
1960	35,000	119,758	25,500	87,252	22,500	76,987
1983	96,700	96,700	77,300	77,300	73,100	73,100

a. Associate justices. Between 1789 and 1968 the Chief Justice was paid an extra $500 a year; since then the differential has widened and is now $3,700.

b. Depending on judicial workload of district. See Schmidhauser, *Judges and Justices: The Federal Appellate Judiciary* 142–143 (1979).

c. 1855.

d. This year is included because it is the first year of regularly collected consumer price index figures. Earlier figures are rough estimates. See note following Table B.1 in Appendix B at end of book.

litical power of the federal courts. That would reduce both the incentive of the appointing authorities to make ideological appointments and the interest of politically minded lawyers in seeking appointment—points to which I shall return in Chapter 8.

A discussion of the quality of the federal bench would not be complete without an examination of the trend in salaries of federal judges[12] and the increase in the number of judges and supporting personnel. Table 2.2 presents an overview of the salary picture (for complete figures and source of deflator see Table B.1 in Appendix B at the end of the book).

One can see from this table that Supreme Court justices' salaries in real (that is, net of inflation) terms are substantially lower today than they were in 1900, and about a third lower than they were in 1940. There is abundant if anecdotal evidence that their salaries were considered very low throughout the nineteenth century,[13] in which event they

12. On the general subject of compensating senior federal officers, see *The Rewards of Public Service: Compensating Top Federal Officials* (Robert W. Hartman and Arnold R. Weber eds. 1980).

13. See Schmidhauser, supra note 1, at 141–145. Compare the scattered evidence of nineteenth-century lawyers' incomes collected in James Willard Hurst, *The Growth of American Law: The Law Makers* 311–312 (1950).

must be low today as well. The salaries of circuit judges have barely kept pace with inflation in this century (district judges have done a little better), a period when incomes in most other occupational groups were growing markedly. But this does not mean that the judges are "falling behind" in a meaningful sense. The real incomes of the elite members of most occupations, including law, probably have not grown in this period, though evidence is sparse. Between 1901 and 1915, Louis Brandeis, reputed to be one of the highest-paid lawyers in America, averaged $73,000 a year in income from the private practice of law (about $800,000 in today's dollars—an extremely high income for a lawyer).[14] What has happened in this century is not so much a deterioration in the average federal judicial salary as a compression of the salary distribution, as a result of which the Supreme Court justices have done the worst and the district judges the best. A tendency toward greater equality of incomes within each profession seems to be a general feature of twentieth-century society. In 1882 the annual salary of a newly hired associate at a prominent Boston law firm was $800,[15] 8 percent of a U.S. Supreme Court justice's salary and maybe 2 percent of a top practitioner's income. Today that associate's salary would be at least a third as large as the justice's salary, but also about 10 percent of a top partner's income. So it is not clear that the federal judges alone have lost ground in this century; other senior members of the legal profession have too. But of course this does not show that the judges' salaries were or are adequate.

The first concerted expression of dissatisfaction with federal judicial salaries in this century is found in hearings on a 1926 bill to raise them.[16] Because federal judicial salaries are not adjusted frequently, they fluctuate significantly in real (that is, inflation- and deflation-adjusted) terms; and 1926 was one of the trough years, the culmination of a period when federal judicial salaries had markedly deteriorated in real terms because of inflation. District and circuit judges were being paid $7,500 and $8,500, respectively, and associate justices of the Supreme Court $14,500; the equivalent salaries in 1983 dollars would be

14. Alpheus Thomas Mason, *Brandeis: A Free Man's Life* 691 (1956). Note the unintended touch of irony in Mason's subtitle.

15. Robert A. Silverman, *Law and Urban Growth: Civil Litigation in the Boston Trial Courts, 1880–1900*, at 35 (1981). And in 1900 the average annual earnings of a public school teacher were $328, those of a manufacturing worker $435, and those of a federal employee $1,033 (U.S. Dept. of Commerce, Bureau of the Census, *Historical Statistics of the United States* 91 [1960] [table D 603–617])—roughly 3, 4, and 10 percent, respectively, of a Supreme Court justice's income. Today the percentages would be much higher. On the general trend toward compression of professionals' salaries see George J. Stigler, *Trends in Employment in the Service Industries* 128–129 (1956).

16. Salaries of Judges, Joint Hearing before Judic. Comm., 69th Cong., 1st Sess., ser. 3 (1926).

$43,357, $49,138, and $83,824, respectively. (The bill, which passed, raised the salaries, effective the same year, to $10,000, $12,500, and $20,000.) The 1926 hearings have a distinctly contemporary ring, allowing for changing fashions in rhetoric. Here is a typical statement, by Charles Evans Hughes, at the time a former U.S. Supreme Court justice:

> Consider the situation in the city of New York. The Federal district judge dealing with intricate patent cases, complicated corporation cases, the most difficult and responsible receivership cases, a vast number of criminal cases, involving the integrity of the administration of the criminal law, receives $7,500 a year—and he can not get an apartment of five rooms in even a moderately desirable neighborhood for less than $3,000 a year.
>
> How do you expect him to live? What right have you to suppose that a man worthy of a seat on that bench, when he can go out any day and pick up five or six times the amount of his salary, will stay there?[17]

Anticipating the reply—"Are not our courts well manned?"—Hughes pointed out that there had been recent resignations from the federal bench in New York, and, more important, that the low salaries were restricting the field of selection.[18] But at the time he was writing, the average salary of the circuit and district judges was $8,000; today it is $75,000, roughly 50 percent higher in real terms.

The alarm was next sounded in 1954, another trough year, when district and circuit judge salaries were $15,000 and $17,500, respectively, and the salary of Supreme Court justices $25,000.[19] In 1983 dollars these figures are $56,553, $65,978, and $94,255, which (except for the last) are significantly below today's salaries. At the time, the average lawyer's salary was about $10,000, but it was pointed out that successful trial lawyers could expect to earn $35,000 to $50,000, with many earning more.[20] In 1955 federal judicial salaries were raised substantially, to the levels shown for 1960 in Table 2.2. And during the 1960s, a period of big increases in government salaries generally, there were two substantial raises, which by 1969 had brought district judges' salaries to $40,000, circuit judges' to $42,500, and Supreme Court justices' to $60,000.

Although federal judicial salaries in 1969 may be assumed to have

17. *Id.* at 25.
18. *Id.* at 15–17.
19. Judicial and Congressional Salaries: Reports of the Task Forces of the Commission on Judicial and Congressional Salaries, S. Doc. No. 97, 83d Cong., 2d Sess. (1954).
20. *Id.* at 61.

been adequate, they were hardly princely. Yet they represent the peak in real terms; in 1983 dollars they were worth $110,565, $117,475, and $165,847, respectively. Since then there has been a marked deterioration, as is plain from Table 2.2. Although the cost of living has almost tripled since 1969, the salaries of federal judges have not even doubled. The failure of judicial salaries to keep pace with inflation is particularly marked in the case of Supreme Court justices. It is true that the immense power and prestige of the Supreme Court, coupled with the very few vacancies to be filled, make recruitment of highly qualified lawyers easy even at present salaries. And since many Supreme Court justices are appointed from other courts, the salary of a justice represents a raise for these appointees, however paltry that salary might seem to a successful practitioner. Yet it seems odd, considering the trifling amounts involved, that society should risk narrowing the field of selection for such an important post even slightly, by fixing the salary at a level so far below the opportunity costs of so many highly qualified candidates.

There is, of course, no iron law that ordains that all salaries shall keep pace with inflation. As a matter of fact, rapid inflations such as this country experienced in the 1970s are frequently symptomatic of a decline in living standards, implying that most salaries (especially after-tax salaries, in a country like ours that has a progressive income tax) will not keep pace with inflation. Most lawyers' salaries evidently did not keep pace; according to the only lawyer-income series that spans the relevant years (the National Survey of Professional, Administrative, Technical, and Clerical Pay conducted annually by the Department of Labor's Bureau of Labor Statistics), the average lawyer's income rose from $19,000 in 1969 to $40,000 in 1982 (current, not constant, dollars). But though less than the rate of inflation, this was a bigger increase than federal judges enjoyed. And the incomes of the elite of the legal profession apparently have kept up with inflation, though systematic data are lacking: many partners at major law firms earn $100,000 a year by the time they are 40 years old and $250,000 by the time they are 50.[21] These salaries compare favorably in real terms with partners' salaries in the 1960s.

The infrequency with which federal judicial salaries are raised has interacted with the increasing instability of prices (due mainly to inflation, although there was a severe deflation in the 1930s) to produce the

21. According to a survey, in 1981 beginning associates at large New York law firms earned an average of $43,500 a year, and associates in their seventh year $71,800— almost as much as a federal judge is paid today (Catalyst Legal Services, Inc., *1981– 1983 Survey* 71 [1982]). For Atlanta, the corresponding figures were $30,000 and $60,200 (*id.* at 2).

sharp sawtooth pattern of Figure 2.1, where federal judicial salaries since 1820 are plotted in 1983 dollars.[22] Between 1915 and 1920 a Supreme Court justice's real salary fell by about 50 percent. It doubled in the next eight years and then began a protracted decline which ended, in 1954, almost 40 percent lower than it had been twenty years earlier. It then rose irregularly by about 80 percent in the period ending in 1969, and has since plunged about 40 percent. The fluctuations in the real salaries of the other federal judges have been similar. These patterns are not sensible from the standpoint of recruiting and retaining able judges.

Salary figures, even when adjusted for inflation, do not tell the complete story of the trend in real federal judicial salaries. Another factor is the tremendous increase in the caseload of the federal courts that has occurred at every level. This increase has been met in part by increasing the number of judges at all levels except the Supreme Court. But not only has the increase in judges been proportionately less than the increase in caseload, so that the caseload per judge has risen during this period; an increase in the number of judges could reduce the prestige of the individual judge, and prestige is an important form of nonpecuniary compensation for federal judges. It is unlikely, however, that any substantial reduction in prestige has yet occurred.[23] Although the number of federal judges has grown significantly in recent years, as shown in Figure 2.2, the absolute number is still small and has actually declined as a fraction of the total number of lawyers. Since 1969 the number of circuit judges has risen by less than 50 percent and the number of district judges by little more than 20 percent (the two groups together increasing from about 500 to about 650, not counting senior judges); in the same period the number of lawyers doubled.

But the increase in caseload per judge has been substantial and has been accompanied by a reduction in the opportunities for federal judges to supplement their judicial salaries. This reduction is a consequence both of the greater workload, which has reduced the time available for extracurricular activities, and of new ethical standards (some embodied in federal statutes) which have limited both the activities that federal judges may engage in off the bench (for example, they may no longer serve as corporate directors) and in some cases even the

22. Although the courts of appeals were not created until 1891, the first circuit judge was appointed in 1869, and circuit judges' salaries are shown from that date in Figure 2.1. District judges' salaries are shown from 1891, when they were made uniform for the first time. Supreme Court salaries are for associate justices. See Appendix B for the table (B.1) from which Figure 2.1 was made.

23. The studies of prestige rankings cited in Chapter 1 do not help with this question; the data appear to be mostly from before 1965.

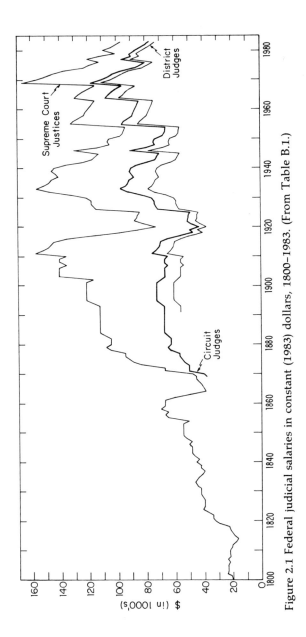

Figure 2.1 Federal judicial salaries in constant (1983) dollars, 1800–1983. (From Table B.1.)

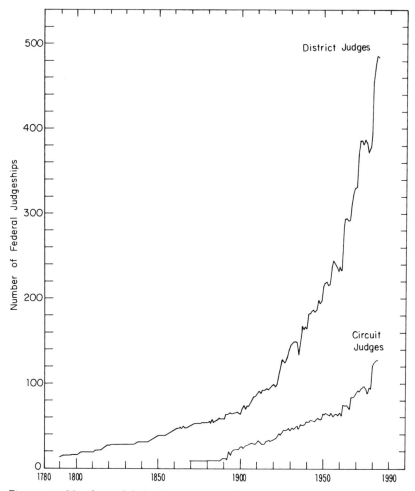

Figure 2.2 Number of federal circuit and district judges, 1789–1983. (From Table B.3.)

amount of income they may obtain from a permitted activity (for example, they may accept no honorarium of more than $2,000).[24] Another recent disamenity is the requirement that federal judges annually file elaborate financial statements which are open to public inspection. The growing budgets of the federal court system, shown in Table 2.1, have

24. For a partial set of restrictions see Code of Judicial Conduct for United States Judges; 2 U.S.C. § 441; 18 U.S.C. §§ 458, 1910; 20 U.S.C. §§ 454, 455; Ethics in Government Act of 1978, P.L. 95–521, Tit. III, §§ 301–309, as amended.

gone not to improve the remuneration of federal judges in real terms but to support more judges and in particular more supporting personnel, whose number relative to the number of judges has grown substantially. The federal courts increasingly resemble executive branch and independent agencies, where a few poorly paid senior officials preside over a bureaucracy. The convergence is not complete, but the specter of bureaucracy increasingly haunts the federal judiciary. And unlike other senior government officials, federal judges are not expected to "cash in" on their government service by returning to the private sector after a few years in office—in fact most do not.

Against all this two points can be argued. The first is that low turnover is a sign of job satisfaction, and federal judicial turnover is low; resignations by federal judges are infrequent. In the 1950s, for example, a "trough" period for federal judicial salaries (see Figure 2.1), only 7 judges—an average of less than one a year out of a corps of almost 300—resigned.[25] True, this figure rose to 8 in the 1960s, to 24 in the 1970s (a very large increase even if one corrects for the larger size of the federal judiciary), and to 12 in the first four years of the 1980s (that is, a rate of 30 per decade—higher than the 1970s); but the turnover is still very low compared to other professions. This low turnover rate is misleading, however. The average age of appointment of federal district judges is 50, and that of circuit judges 53.[26] Anyone who accepts such an appointment does so with knowledge of current and likely future salary conditions; and even though over a period of a decade or more unexpected inflation may upset financial expectations, few people have a taste for switching careers after age 60, especially since the financial attractiveness of a federal judgeship increases as retirement age approaches.

The problem with inadequate salaries is not that they can be expected to trigger an avalanche of resignations but rather, as Charles Evans Hughes pointed out more than fifty years ago, that they limit the field of selection. Against this the second point may be argued, however: there is no scarcity of candidates for federal judgeships even at present salary levels. This is true, and would be so even at substantially lower salaries, simply because there are no demanding entrance requirements. A fair number of lawyers would be rated as qualified by the American Bar Association's Standing Committee on the Judiciary in every district and circuit in the country, but most of them would add

25. Administrative Office of the U.S. Courts, Salary Increases for Justices and Judges of the United States Courts 15 (unpublished memo submitted to the Federal Commission on Executive, Legislative and Judicial Salaries, 1980).

26. Id. at 47 (table 14).

little luster to the bench. Moreover, there is an important difference between qualified candidates and candidates who are actually eligible. Eligibility is determined not only by merit but by political factors (patronage and ideology) that greatly narrow the field from which the appointment will actually be made. There may be a dozen people who are well qualified by intellect, character, and temperament to fill a particular vacancy on the federal bench, yet of those all but two or three may be disqualified because they have the wrong ideology or political connections or live in the wrong state or district. Any further narrowing of the field because of inadequate salary could have a substantial adverse impact on the quality of appointments.

All this is not meant to suggest that it is necessary to pay dollar for dollar what a lawyer earns in private practice to induce him to accept a federal judgeship, unless like many lawyers he feels that a judicial career would not suit his personality. Apart from the intrinsic interest, challenge, and satisfactions of a federal judgeship, the opportunity it offers for constructive public service, and the prestige of such a judgeship both within and outside the legal profession, certain disamenities of private practice—in particular the need to beat the bushes for clients and the lawyer's subservient role as his client's agent—are absent from the judge's life. And the terms of retirement are highly attractive for judges, at least for an older appointee: retirement at full pay is permitted at age 65 with fifteen years of service, and at 70 with ten years; the judge makes no contribution toward retirement, can work as a judge as much or as little as he wants after retirement ("senior status"), and participates in any pay raise granted active judges after his retirement. The only drawback is the absence of surviving spouse's benefits, apart from those provided by a not very munificent contributory plan that federal judges can join.

Retirement provisions obviously are a very important part of the total compensation of a position whose occupants are middle-aged when appointed; so if these provisions had improved substantially in recent years, this might offset the failure to raise salaries. But, surprisingly, as early as 1869 federal judges were allowed to retire at full pay at age 70 with 10 years of service on the federal bench.[27] In 1919 "senior status" was created, allowing the retired judge to continue serving on a part-time basis.[28] In 1948 retired judges were allowed to participate in any pay raises after the date of their retirement, and in 1954 judges with

27. Act of April 10, 1869, chap. 22, 16 Stat. 44.
28. Act of February 25, 1919, chap. 29, § 6, 40 Stat. 1156.

fifteen years of service were allowed to retire at age 65.[29] So there has been significant, but not dramatic, improvement in the retirement provisions for federal judges over the last century, but no improvement in the last thirty years.

Two other aspects of remuneration should be mentioned. The first is the geographic uniformity of federal judicial salaries. These salaries, though low on average, may be adequate in the lower-cost areas of the nation. Second, federal judges are allowed to supplement their incomes by part-time teaching, writing, and lecturing (and many do). Of course this income is not free; it entails additional work at a time when the judicial workload is heavier than ever, and there is always the danger that it will distract some judges from their judicial responsibilities.

With all these points granted, since few lawyers not fortunate enough to be independently wealthy will accept a drastic reduction in their standard of living in order to accept a federal judgeship, the present salary levels do limit the field of selection. There is no point telling a person that he ought to be content with an income of $75,000—an income far above the national average. If he makes and spends $250,000 a year, he will perceive a reduction in his income to $75,000 as entailing a drastic and probably unacceptable drop in his standard of living. It is not that one cannot live comfortably on $75,000 a year, or that a person earning more cannot "afford" a reduction in income to that level; most Americans live quite happily on far less. But just as a person living happily on $75,000 a year will still eagerly accept a raise to $250,000, so a person living on $250,000 will be highly reluctant to take a cut in his income to $75,000, even if he has no fixed commitments that would drive him into bankruptcy. This is human nature, and there is no use railing at it.

The Administrative Office study cited earlier reported that in 1980 the average income of lawyers appointed to the federal bench from private practice was (before their appointment) $131,000,[30] more than twice what federal lower court judges' salaries were then. Even allowing for geographical differences in lawyers' incomes, $131,000 was far below the average income of the most successful trial lawyers in 1980. This suggests, and other studies confirm, that, at least in big cities, federal judges generally are not being appointed from the very top rank of the practicing bar, but from just below the top.[31] The pay cut required

29. Act of June 25, 1948, chap. 646, 62 Stat. 903; Act of February 10, 1954, chap. 6, § 4, 68 Stat. 12. The current retirement provisions are in 28 U.S.C. § 371.

30. Administrative Office, supra note 25, at 17.

31. See Howard, supra note 8, at 94.

of the top rank is just too great. Of course, the second rank contains many lawyers capable of serving with great distinction as federal judges; Learned Hand and Oliver Wendell Holmes are examples of distinguished judicial appointments from this category (neither had been an outstanding success at the bar). But so, of course, does the first rank—Cardozo, Brandeis, and Friendly being examples. It is also true that more consideration could and should be given to appointing distinguished government lawyers and distinguished academics—two relatively impecunious groups, by the standards of the legal profession—to federal judgeships, whether or not they have extensive (or any) trial experience. But the political character of the appointive process limits the practical possibilities.

It would be a big mistake to write off the most successful law-firm practitioners as candidates for federal judgeships. The average quality of the federal bench must suffer; and society cannot afford that. I mentioned earlier that most appointments to the federal bench are not based on merit alone. This would not be at all troubling if the job of a federal judge did not require much ability or if it were unimportant to society whether the job was done badly or well. But being a judge of a major court in America is an extremely difficult job, requiring if it is to be performed well a combination of intellectual skills and character attributes that is rare. Few judges in our history are thought to have performed with great distinction, and even they are criticized a good deal. Since the federal courts are a powerful institution of government whose decisions in the aggregate have a significant effect on the welfare of the American people, it is important to society as a whole, and not just to law professors and others who value legal analytical skills for their own sake, that the courts be manned by very good judges. There are no grounds for complacency about the federal judiciary or for indifference to the problems of recruiting the best people into it.

The social costs of substantially increasing the salaries of federal judges would be very small; there are fewer than 700 such judges, and if the salary of each were increased by $50,000 a year, the total annual cost to the taxpayers of America would be only $35 million, a few hundredths of 1 percent of the federal budget. But the political costs would be very great, not only because the federal judiciary is quite unpopular in some quarters today but also because the public has difficulty understanding why this relatively obscure (as federal judges other than the Supreme Court justices are) corps of government officials should be paid so much more than the average American worker.

Modest improvement in the compensation of federal judges might be possible, however, by abandoning the geographic uniformity of federal judicial salaries. They were not always uniform; the first Judiciary Act created (as shown in Table 2.2) substantial differentials in the salaries of federal district judges (though motivated by differences in workload rather than regional differences in the cost of living), depending on where they sat, and these differentials persisted until late in the nineteenth century. The restoration of these differentials, which could be easily achieved at both the district court and the court of appeals levels (at the latter by basing the cost-of-living differential on the cost of living in the district where the circuit judge actually resides), would be a step forward in rationalizing judicial compensation. There is a substantial difference in the cost of living between urban areas such as New York, San Francisco, and other major cities, on the one hand, and largely rural districts in the South and the Midwest, on the other. The cost of living is almost 60 percent higher in Honolulu than it is in the average nonmetropolitan area in the South; this is the largest difference, but the cost of living in Boston is 30 percent higher than in Atlanta—still a dramatic difference.[32] I do not, of course, suggest lowering any federal judge's salary—that would violate Article III—to finance an increase for judges who live in areas where the cost of living is above the national average. I merely suggest that the next time Congress decides to raise the salaries of federal judges, it vary the raises according to the differences in the cost of living among the various districts and circuits.

My other observation has to do with the difference in salary between district and circuit judges. This difference, though no longer great, has two potential effects that are undesirable. First, it may induce some district judges to accept appointment to the court of appeals who would be happier and more productive as district judges but who have a natural human reluctance to turn down a raise.[33] Second, it contributes to a symbology in which the appellate judge is "higher" in the judicial pecking order than the district judge—which reinforces the tendency of district judges to accept appointment to the court of appeals regardless of aptitude. The truth is that the jobs of trial judges and of appellate judges are not differentiable on grounds of social importance, inherent difficulty, or scarcity of the requisite combinations of skills (which are different). An appellate court is more powerful than a trial court in the same system, but in recognition of this the appellate judge's power is

32. U.S. Department of Labor, Bureau of Labor Statistics, "Autumn 1981 Urban Family Budgets and Comparative Indexes for Selected Urban Areas," table 6 (News Release, April 16, 1982) (family on "higher budget").

33. Even with the salary differentials, district judges occasionally, though rarely, turn down appointment to the court of appeals.

diluted by making appellate decision making collective rather than individual.

An analogy is provided by the difference between a line and a staff job in the military. General Eisenhower, when he was northern European theater commander in World War II, was subordinate to General Marshall, the army chief of staff, yet did not have a less demanding, less responsible, or less prestigious position than Marshall. We should foster a similar attitude with respect to trial judges and (excepting the Supreme Court) appellate judges in the federal system. The appellate judge's job is slower-paced, more impersonal, more cerebral. Hair-trigger judgmental reflexes, a commanding presence, and trial experience are not essential to the effective performance of his job. But they are significant (I do not say indispensable) factors in the district judge's effective performance of his job—along with the sheer emotional stamina that is necessary to cope with today's enormous caseloads: in the busier districts, district judges may spend as many as 150 days a year on trial. As an appellate judge who has, however, conducted a half dozen civil trials in the past two years in federal district courts,[34] I can testify from personal experience to the heavy emotional as well as intellectual demands that conducting a trial makes and to the great difference in the "feel" of district court and court of appeals work.

There is also an important difference in the audiences for the two types of work. Since relatively little of a trial judge's work product takes the form of published opinions designed to shape the law of the future, the primary audience for the trial judge is found in the courtroom itself—the parties and their counsel, jurors, witnesses, and court watchers. The appearance of fairness, the maintenance of authority, keeping things moving along—these become ends in themselves for the trial judge, and quite properly so. It is different at the appellate level: the primary audience for the appellate judge consists not of the parties and their counsel but of other judges and other lawyers—the people who read appellate opinions—to whom the important thing is the quality of the opinion (consisting of the decision and the supporting reasoning) rather than the judge's courtroom management and deportment.

Lest I be misunderstood, especially as a judge who was appointed to the court of appeals without having been a district judge, I emphasize that I am not proposing that the practice of appointing district judges to the courts of appeals cease. Not only is the experience of having been a

34. The chief judges of the courts of appeals are empowered to designate court of appeals judges to sit in the district courts of the circuit. I have conducted no criminal trials, which usually are even more taxing on the judge than civil trials.

trial judge a most valuable one for an appellate judge,[35] and not only do many district judges demonstrate their fitness for appellate appointments (Learned Hand being a conspicuous, but not a rare, example), but also, as I mentioned earlier, merit often plays a larger role in appointing district judges than nonjudges to the courts of appeals. I am merely suggesting that we eliminate a pay differential which, together with a symbolic differential that it reinforces, may lead occasionally to suboptimal appointments to the courts of appeals.[36] I do not think we need fear thereby undermining the indispensable element of hierarchy in the judicial system; such deference as district judges feel toward circuit judges is not a function of what is now little more than a nominal salary difference. And I do not think that the prestige of circuit judges depends on their being paid a few thousand dollars more than district judges.

This discussion of federal judicial salaries has been so protracted that readers may suspect that I have a personal interest in it—which of course I have. But my main purpose has not been to complain; it has been to show how persistent and intractable the problem of federal judicial salaries is. If these salaries remain, as I believe they probably will, inadequate in the sense in which I have suggested they are inadequate, this will make all the more troublesome the problem of a rapidly growing caseload which puts the federal judicial system to an unhappy choice between placing more work on the backs of its underpaid judges and adding to the ranks of those judges—and thus, by diluting the individual judge's influence and status, making them even more underpaid, when "pay" is understood as it should be to include nonpecuniary compensation.

As a mild antidote to the parochialism that afflicts some federal judges and many scholars and practitioners as well, it may be well to remind the reader at this point that the federal courts are only a small, though a disproportionately powerful, component of the American judicial system. There are about 27,000 state (including local) and federal judges in the United States (excluding administrative law judges and other executive and administrative officers who perform judicial functions),[37] of whom fewer than 3 percent are Article III federal judges. The biggest states have bigger judicial systems than the federal. In

35. So much so that I would be inclined to think it a good idea to make it possible for every newly appointed circuit judge who had not served as a district judge (or the equivalent in a state court system) to spend his first six months sitting in the district court rather than the court of appeals.

36. I shall return to the differences between the federal trial and appellate benches in Chapter 8.

37. "Lawscope," 69 *A.B.A.J.* 890 (1983).

1979, when federal expenditures on judicial services were only $370 million, local expenditures on such services were $1.2 billion and state expenditures $1.8 billion.[38] Comparison in anything other than the grossest terms is difficult, however, because of the different functions performed by the state and federal systems; many of the 27,000 state and local judges are justices of the peace and traffic or family-court judges. But there is a rough correspondence in function and position in the judicial hierarchy between state trial courts of general jurisdiction (that is, courts whose jurisdiction depends on there being a minimum amount in controversy, but there is no maximum) and federal district courts; between state supreme and intermediate appellate courts and federal courts of appeals; and between state supreme courts and the U.S. Supreme Court. The comparison is fuzziest in the middle, where federal courts of appeals resemble state intermediate appellate courts in their position relative to district courts but resemble state supreme courts in the number of judges and in their position relative to the U.S. Supreme Court. The total number of judges in state supreme courts, intermediate appellate courts, and major trial courts is 7,930—more than ten times the number of Article III federal judges.[39]

Whatever the difficulty of drawing exact parallels, there is no doubt that the average conditions of employment in the state judicial systems are inferior to those in the federal system. (Some indirect but powerful evidence is that, while it is not uncommon for state judges to accept appointments as federal judges, the reverse has been extremely rare in modern times.) Table 2.3 compares the average salaries of state supreme court justices and federal circuit judges. The figure for the state judges is an unweighted average; the salaries in the highest and lowest states are also given. The salary comparison tells only part of the story. In most states all or most state judges are elected rather than appointed, though the electoral process is often less contentious than for other public officials. For example, in some states, for some judicial offices, an incumbent who seeks reelection cannot be opposed by another candidate and is reelected automatically if he receives a certain percentage (such as 60 percent, in Illinois) of the votes cast. Nevertheless, any electoral process will discourage a very large number of well qualified persons from seeking judicial office. This is not only because many people find campaigning distasteful or are not very good at it (or both), but also because electoral selection diminishes judicial independence, which is

38. U.S. Department of Commerce, Bureau of the Census, *Statistical Abstract of the United States 1982–1983*, at 183.
39. Computed from Council of State Governments, *Book of the States 1982–1983*, at 254–255 (1982).

Table 2.3.   Salaries of state supreme court justices and federal circuit judges compared (in dollars)

Year	State highest	State lowest	State average	Federal	Ratio of state average to federal
1919	13,700	3,000	6,167	8,500	0.73
1937	22,000	4,800	8,878	12,500	0.71
1945	23,000	5,000	9,300	12,500	0.74
1955	35,500	8,500	14,911	25,500	0.58
1965	39,500	14,000	22,270	33,000	0.67
1975	60,575	26,000	37,299	44,600	0.84
1980	72,855	36,637	49,690	57,500	0.86
1982	76,498	40,392	54,003	74,300	0.73

Sources: 1919: ABA Reports, 1924, 1937; 1980: National Center for State Courts, Survey of Judicial Salaries (July 1980); other years: Council of State Governments, Book of the States, various years.

an important nonpecuniary return to being a judge. It does this both directly in systems where the judge must stand for reelection, and indirectly: the expense of campaigning creates all sorts of subtle and not so subtle conflicts of interest, since the trial bar is usually a major source of campaign contributions to judicial candidates.

The differences between the employment conditions of federal and state judges go right back to 1789, when Article III and the first Judiciary Act established the federal judiciary on a higher plane in terms of conditions of employment than most state judges of the time enjoyed;[40] and these differences grew larger in the early nineteenth century as state after state went to an electoral system for judges.[41] Some reasons for the disparities, historically and at present, in the employment conditions of state and federal judges will be explored in Chapter 6.

JURISDICTION

Having said something about the federal courts and their personnel, I want now to describe briefly the evolution and contemporary extent of the federal courts' jurisdiction. Article III set the limits of the judicial power of the United States but left to Congress the task of defining the

40. See Evan Haynes, The Selection and Tenure of Judges (1944), for the history of judicial appointment and tenure provisions in each state, and Council of State Governments, Book of the States 1982–1983, for the current provisions.
41. See William E. Nelson, The Roots of American Bureaucracy, 1830–1900, at 39–40 (1982).

actual jurisdiction of the federal courts within those limits. The first Judiciary Act, having created lower federal courts, did not grant them an extensive jurisdiction. The district courts were given jurisdiction mainly in admiralty and criminal cases and the circuit courts mainly in diversity cases, but neither type of court was given general jurisdiction over cases arising under federal law ("federal-question" cases as they have come to be called); that was not to come till 1875. The Supreme Court was given appellate jurisdiction over the decisions of the district and circuit courts, with the exception—a surprising one in view of later developments—of criminal judgments, and also appellate jurisdiction over state court decisions interpreting federal law. The fact that the district and circuit courts were not given a general federal-question jurisdiction assured that state courts would frequently be called upon to interpret and apply federal law. The first Judiciary Act also established the practice, which persists to this day in diversity of citizenship cases, of fixing a minimum amount in controversy for a plaintiff wanting to litigate in federal court ($500, raised in steps to $10,000 in 1958).[42]

Some features of the pattern of jurisdiction created by the first Judiciary Act are easier to explain than others. The conferral of admiralty jurisdiction and of jurisdiction over disputes between citizens and foreigners (a part of the diversity jurisdiction, broadly defined) seems designed to promote the foreign commerce of the United States by assuring foreigners of access to national, and presumptively therefore more uniform and expert and less xenophobic and parochial, courts.[43] The rest of the diversity jurisdiction may seem explicable in similar terms, although doubts about this will be explored in later chapters.

The fact that the lower federal courts were not given jurisdiction over federal-question cases suggests, somewhat surprisingly from a modern perspective, that the framers of the first Judiciary Act were not much concerned that state courts might be prejudiced against persons asserting federal claims. Perhaps the new American government was thought too weak to invite the antagonism of state courts, or perhaps there were just so few federal rights that their beneficiaries were not numerous enough to have the political muscle to get their own tribunals, as it were, for the vindication of such rights.

Why, then, it was thought necessary to have federal crimes tried in federal courts may seem a puzzle. The traditional refusal of the courts of one sovereign to enforce the penal laws of another provides a suffi-

42. Technically, amount in controversy must *exceed* $10,000. To simplify exposition, I shall pretend that the amount must be *at least* $10,000.

43. As emphasized in 25 *Papers of Alexander Hamilton* 477–479 (Harold C. Syrett ed. 1977). See also 1 Julius Goebel, *The Oliver Wendell Holmes Devise History of the Supreme Court of the United States: Antedecents and Beginnings to 1801*, at xvii (1971).

cient doctrinal reason; a functional explanation, though one having little application to conditions in 1789, will be proposed in Chapter 6. The
withholding of appellate jurisdiction over federal criminal cases, much
as it cuts against the modern grain, can be explained in various ways.
Since (with a few exceptions) it would violate double jeopardy to allow
a prosecutor to appeal an acquittal, allowing the defendant to appeal his
conviction would have created a bias in favor of erroneous acquittals.
And since the defendant had all the benefits of the criminal procedure
provisions of the Bill of Rights, the chance of convicting an innocent
man must have seemed slight. The modern view of criminal appeals is,
of course, different.

Conspicuous in the first Judiciary Act is an evident parsimoniousness
in the creation of federal jurisdiction. The jurisdiction conferred was
about the minimum one can imgine that would have allowed the federal judiciary to play the role envisioned for it in the Constitution; and
the amount-in-controversy requirement assured that the federal courts
would not have to resolve petty disputes even within the limited area of
their jurisdiction. No doubt this parsimony was for the most part simply a reflection of the temper of the times, which believed in limited
government and above all in limited national government. The creation
of lower federal courts was a controversial issue, which is why Article
III merely authorized Congress to create them. But there may also have
been a sense—there are hints of it in the *Federalist* No. 78 (Hamilton)—
that the proper performance of the constitutional role of the federal judiciary required that it be kept small. As I have indicated, the more
judges there are in a court system the less responsibly they can be expected to exercise their power, since political retribution for judicial
excesses short of impeachable offenses must, by virtue of Article III's
provisions relating to tenure and pay, be visited on the entire judiciary
(or at least entire courts) and not just on the errant judge.

Several judicial developments before the Civil War completed the
pattern of federal jurisdiction sketched in the first Judiciary Act. The
first was the assumption by the Supreme Court of the power to declare
state and federal legislation and executive acts unconstitutional (a
power implicit, as we have seen, but not explicit, in the Constitution),[44]
coupled with the assertion—which the assumption of the power of constitutional review itself exemplified—of the principle of flexible (dis-
paragingly, "loose") interpretation of the Constitution.[45] The idea of a
justiciable constitution, flexibly interpreted, marked a breathtaking ex-

44. See Marbury v. Madison, 1 U.S. (1 Cranch) 137 (1803); M'Culloch v. Maryland, 17
U.S. (4 Wheat.) 316 (1819).

45. Epitomized in Chief Jusice Marshall's statement in *M'Culloch*: "it must never be
forgotten that it is a *constitution* we are expounding." 17 U.S. at 407.

pansion in judicial power over English and colonial antecedents, and an expansion that by its nature was bound to grow; for with every passing year the Constitution receded further into history, making it more difficult to reconstruct the intended meaning of the constitutional text and progressively freeing the judges to imbue it with their own values. Holding this power in check, though, was the insistence by Chief Justice Marshall and his brethren on taking seriously the Constitution's limitation of federal judicial power to the decision of actual cases or controversies, and thus on refusing to issue advisory opinions[46] or to resolve even the most momentous constitutional issues other than as required to decide a lawsuit properly before the court. The framers of the Constitution had considered and rejected a proposal to create a Council of Revision to pass on not only the constitutionality but the wisdom of federal laws before they were enacted.[47] The Supreme Court in the John Marshall era complied with the framers' desire both to confine the federal courts to the mode of proceeding that had become customary in the English courts of the eighteenth century and to require the federal courts to make a distinction between the constitutionality and the wisdom of the actions of the other branches of government.

In *Swift v. Tyson*[48] the Supreme Court expanded federal judicial power in diversity cases by holding that the law applicable in a diversity case dealing with rights under a bill of exchange was general common law to be formulated by the federal courts rather than the common law of the state where the bill had been issued or of some other state concerned in the transaction. One view of *Swift v. Tyson* is that the Court misread the Rules of Decision Act (a part of the first Judiciary Act), which provided that federal courts should use as their rules of decision the laws of the states, unless otherwise directed by Congress or the Constitution.[49] *Swift* confined "laws" to statutes, and the argument is that it did so contrary to the intentions of the framers. The original draft of the Rules of Decision Act included decisional law, and it appears—though not very clearly—that the explicit reference to it was deleted in order to simplify rather than to change the meaning of the act.[50] This view has been challenged, most recently by Professor Havenkamp, who suggests that the Court in *Swift* may simply have

---

46. See Wright, supra note 1, at 57–58.

47. See 1 *Records of the Federal Convention* 73, 77, 78 (Max Farrand rev. ed. 1937); Gordon S. Wood, *The Creation of the American Republic 1776–1787*, at 552 (1969).

48. 41 U.S. (16 Pet.) 1 (1842).

49. Section 34 of the Act of September 24, 1789, chap. 20, 1 Stat. 92; now 28 U.S.C. § 1652.

50. See Charles Warren, "New Light on the History of the Federal Judiciary Act of 1789," 37 *Harv. L. Rev.* 49 (1923).

been trying to select the rule of decision which, under conflict-of-laws principles, the states themselves would have followed had the case been decided in state court.[51] However that may be, for almost a century following *Swift* the federal courts developed general common law principles to govern virtually all nonlocal ("local" meaning primarily real property) diversity cases in the absence of applicable state statutes. We need not try to determine whether this development was motivated by a desire to protect interstate businesses from populist legal doctrines made by elected state judges, to foster enterprise by bringing about greater uniformity of legal obligation for those businesses, or to set an example that might encourage greater uniformity of American common law—or just by a confusion over whether common law decisions are mere instantiations of a body of natural law equally accessible to federal and to state judges, or emanations of the sovereign will of the state.

The Civil War led to profound changes in the jurisdiction of the federal courts by fundamentally changing the relationship between the federal government and the states. Before the Civil War virtually the only activity of the lower federal courts in relation to the states was to adjudicate diversity cases, and the only activity of the Supreme Court in relation to the states was to invalidate state laws that were in conflict with federal laws or that impaired the obligations of contracts. The Fourteenth Amendment, adopted in 1868, forbade the states (among other things) to deprive persons of life, liberty, or property without due process of law, or to deny persons the equal protection of the laws. Congress passed a series of civil rights acts creating criminal and tort remedies for violations of the Fourteenth Amendment. A notable example of the tort remedies was the Ku Klux Klan Act of 1871, section 1 of which, recodified as 42 U.S.C. § 1983, is of immense importance to the work of the federal courts today. Also of great importance today is the Habeas Corpus Act of 1867 (now 28 U.S.C. §§ 2241 *et seq.*), which extended federal habeas corpus to persons in state custody. Another illustration of the changing relationship between the federal government and the states is the conferral of general federal-question jurisdiction on the federal courts in 1875.[52]

The full implications of the Fourteenth Amendment for the jurisdiction of the federal courts were not to be felt for another century, and indeed the amendment had little impact of any sort until the 1890s. But beginning then the federal courts became extremely active in limiting the power of the states to regulate commercial conduct, finding in the

51. Howard Havenkamp, "Federalism Revised" (review of Tony Freyer, *Harmony and Dissonance: The Swift and Erie Cases in American Federalism*), 34 *Hastings L.J.* 201 (1982).

52. Act of March 3, 1875, chap. 137, 18 Stat. 470.

due process clause a constitutional commitment to liberty of contract or laissez-faire. This era, typified by the famous decision in *Lochner v. New York*[53] invalidating a state maximum-hours law, ended abruptly in the late 1930s with a change in the Supreme Court's membership. But this did not end the federal courts' activities in enforcing the Fourteenth Amendment. Rather, there was a change from protecting economic liberty to protecting other concepts of liberty—what we now call civil liberties and civil rights. From the equal protection clause came the idea of equal rights for blacks, and later (and in somewhat diluted form) for women and girls (and then for men and boys), for aliens, children born out of wedlock, and other groups. From the Bill of Rights, loosely read—and much of it rather arbitrarily read into the due process clause of the Fourteenth Amendment—came the ideas that the states could not interfere with freedom of speech or religion, must accord criminal defendants elaborate procedural rights, must provide humane prison conditions, must allow abortions, and so forth. From the concept of due process itself came the idea that the state has to grant a hearing to anyone whose entitlement it wants to take away—for example, to a tenured public school teacher whom it wants to fire.

The list of rights protected in the name of the Fourteenth Amendment has grown steadily over the last 50 years, to the point where that amendment is today the direct or indirect source of much of the business of the federal courts. The two most important procedural vehicles for enforcing Fourteenth Amendment rights in federal courts have already been mentioned: section 1 of the Ku Klux Klan Act of 1871, which created damage remedies for violations of federal rights by state officers, and the Habeas Corpus Act of 1867, which has been interpreted to allow prisoners to challenge the constitutionality of their state convictions by civil proceedings in federal court.

It is plain enough why Congress wanted persons claiming that their rights under the Fourteenth Amendment had been violated to be able to sue in federal courts: the state was often the de facto defendant, and its courts were unlikely to be sympathetic to the plaintiff. (Whether this is a fair assumption today is a question examined in Chapter 6.) It is only a little less obvious why Congress decided for the first time in 1875 that anyone with a financially significant federal cause of action should be allowed to sue in federal court. The Civil War had both revealed and exacerbated deep sectional tensions, and it could no longer be assumed that state courts would be sympathetic to assertions of federal right whoever the defendant was. But why, if the federal claimant preferred

53. 198 U.S. 45 (1905).

to sue in state court, the defendant should have been allowed to remove the case into federal court for trial there is unclear from this perspective. Nevertheless, the right of removal, which defendants had had in diversity cases since the first Judiciary Act (though removal was not mentioned in Article III and had been unknown to the common law), and which made perfectly good sense in a diversity case in which the plaintiff was a resident and the defendant a nonresident of the state in which the suit was brought, was carried over to the federal-question jurisdiction. The Civil War also ushered in the era, in which we still find ourselves, of active federal government. As Congress passed more and more laws, displacing more and more state law, it could no longer be assumed that state courts in any part of the country would always be sympathetic to assertions of federal rights. On both grounds—sectional tension and growth of federal power—it was no longer feasible to place exclusive jurisdiction for enforcement of federal rights in state courts.

Once the general federal-question jurisdiction was in place, the expansion of federal regulation guaranteed a steady increase in the business of the federal courts. When the courts themselves seemed unlikely to be sympathetic to a particular type of regulation, or for any other reason unlikely to be suitable instruments for regulation, Congress would create an administrative agency, but the federal courts would retain a review jurisdiction. It seems, however, though adequate data are lacking, that only since the late 1930s has the docket of the federal courts assumed anything like its characteristic modern shape (see Tables 3.1 and 3.2). Of the opinions of the Seventh Circuit between 1892 and 1911, for example, 56 percent were diversity cases, 22 percent patent cases, 7 percent bankruptcy cases, 4 percent criminal cases, and 1 percent review of administrative action.[54] In the period 1932–1941, diversity cases accounted for only 19 percent of the opinions and patent cases 10 percent, while criminal cases had risen to 9 percent, tax and administrative agency cases accounted for 32 percent, and bankruptcies (not surprisingly in the depression era) for 18 percent.[55] These patterns are broadly consistent with those for a similar study of several other federal courts of appeals,[56] and the pattern in the later period resembles, if only generally, the present distribution of cases.

Three more developments should be mentioned to complete this

54. Solomon, supra note 8, at 23.

55. Id.

56. See Lawrence Baum, Sheldon Goldman, and Austin Sarat, "The Evolution of Litigation in the Federal Courts of Appeals, 1895–1975," 16 Law & Soc'y Rev. 291 (1981–1982).

thumbnail sketch of federal jurisdiction. First, by the end of the nineteenth century federal criminal convictions had been made appealable by the defendant, and such appeals now supply a significant part of the caseload of the courts of appeals and the Supreme Court. Second, the *Erie* decision in 1938, overruling *Swift v. Tyson,* held that federal courts in diversity actions must follow state decisional as well as statutory law.[57] In principle this was a very substantial blow struck for federalism in its modern sense of state autonomy. But its practical significance has been somewhat less. Civil appeals are relatively infrequent unless there is some uncertainty about the applicable law; mere uncertainty over the facts is not a promising basis for appeal because appellate review of the factual determinations made at trial is quite limited. So a sizable fraction of diversity appeals involve cases in which state decisional law is unclear, and in those cases the federal court of appeals is perforce creating law. Of course, the state courts may pay no attention to what a federal court of appeals has done in their name, but that was true before *Erie.* The big difference is that should a state court disapprove of a federal diversity decision, the federal courts would have to stop following that decision in subsequent cases. This could make a significant difference for the caseload of the federal courts because the common law rules created by federal courts tended to be more favorable to defendants than the counterpart rules in the states, and they thereby gave nonresident defendants an incentive to remove diversity cases to federal court that was independent of any procedural or institutional differences between the two court systems. This incentive was removed, at least in areas where the law was well settled, by the *Erie* decision.

The third development also occurred in 1938: the Supreme Court promulgated rules of civil procedure for federal courts, pursuant to the Rules Enabling Act.[58] Until then federal courts followed the rules of procedure of the state in which the federal court was located, except in equity and admiralty cases, where federal rules had been promulgated earlier. There was a tension between the promulgation of the federal rules of civil procedure and *Erie.* This was due partly to the fact that the difference between substance and procedure—the former governed in diversity cases by state decisional as well as statutory law, the latter governed in diversity as in all other federal cases by the federal rules—is difficult to determine in many cases; and partly to the fact that the Federal Rules of Civil Procedure, by suddenly making federal procedure sharply different from state procedure, created a host of new incentives

---

57. Erie R.R. v. Tompkins, 304 U.S. 64 (1938).
58. Act of June 19, 1934, chap. 651, 48 Stat. 1064; now 28 U.S.C. § 2072.

to bring a diversity case in federal rather than state court or to remove it to federal court. No longer would considerations of local bias, and differences in judges and juries, alone enter into the decision whether to sue in federal court; now advantages and disadvantages stemming from differences in the rules of procedure had to be considered. So the adoption of the federal rules may have created an incentive to litigate diversity cases in the federal courts that offset the contrary incentive created by *Erie*; unfortunately, there are no statistics on the number of diversity cases in the 1930s. The federal rules also brought into existence a class of lawyers specializing in federal practice, facilitated the nationwide practice of federal law, and drove a wedge between state and federal courts. The wedge is diminishing, however, because state procedural codes are increasingly patterned on the federal rules. Although the federal rules are much criticized for having increased the length and cost of litigation, and could also be criticized for being unduly pro-plaintiff, judged by the tests of survival and imitation they have been a smashing success.

II

THE CRISIS

3

Extent and Causes of the

Caseload Explosion

IN THE LAST chapter, the growth of the federal courts' caseload was reflected only indirectly—in the creation of new federal courts, the increase in the number of federal judges and supporting personnel, the growth of the federal judicial budget, and other institutional responses to the growing demand for federal judicial services. This chapter focuses on the caseload itself, and particularly on the explosion in federal judicial business that has taken place since about 1960.

EXTENT

The enormous increase in the population of the United States, and in the power and reach of the federal government after the Civil War, made it inevitable that the caseload of the federal courts would expand from its humble beginnings. Nevertheless, until roughly 1960, which as the last year of the Eisenhower Administration has seemed to many observers a watershed in the modern social and political history of the nation, the rate of growth had been modest and easily accommodated by the creation in 1891 of a three-tier system. Between 1904, the first year for which statistics on the number of cases filed in the federal district courts are available, and 1960, the number of such cases rose from 33,376 to 89,112—an annual compound rate of increase of only 1.8 percent.[1] Although there are no statistics for total number of federal

1. Apparently the figures include cases filed in the circuit courts, abolished in 1911. See *1874 Attorney General Ann. Rep.* 5–6, 22–31.

Unless otherwise indicated, all caseload statistics in this book for the federal district

ᴄᴀ𝗌ᴇs filed prior to 1904, we do know (from the reports of the Attorney General, first issued in 1874) that the number of private civil cases filed in the federal courts was actually lower in 1904 than it had been in 1873.[2]

The caseload rose steeply during the 1920s and 1930s, when Prohibition led to a very substantial rise in the number of both criminal and U.S. civil (mainly forfeiture and penalty) case filings.[3] But the end of Prohibition led to an equally precipitous drop. In 1934, after the surge of Prohibition cases had abated, 70,111 civil and criminal cases were filed in the federal district courts; and between that year and 1960 the number of criminal cases actually fell, from 34,152 to 29,828. All of the

---

courts and courts of appeal are taken from or calculated from annual reports of the Attorney General of the U.S. (before 1940) and annual reports (normally published together with the annual proceedings of the Judicial Conference) of the Administrative Office (AO) of the U.S. Courts (1940 to the present). Specific sources are not separately indicated where they are easily found in the relevant report. Bankruptcy proceedings are omitted. On the range of available federal judicial statistics see James A. McCafferty, "Federal Judicial Statistics" (AO, August 1983, unpublished); on the methodology of collection and reporting see the Administrative Office's *Guide to Judiciary Policies and Procedures*, vols. XI and XI-A (Statistical Analysis Manual); and for detailed analysis of the statistics up to 1932 see American Law Institute, *A Study of the Business of the Federal Courts* (2 vols., 1934). Statistics for the Supreme Court are, unless otherwise indicated, taken from Gerhard Casper and Richard A. Posner, *The Workload of the Supreme Court* (1976), as updated to the present using the same sources and methods as in the original study.

Federal judicial statistics are referred to in a number of studies, some cited in this book; but the number of studies to which statistics are central is rather small. Some examples (in addition to the ALI and Casper and Posner studies) are Lawrence Baum, Sheldon Goldman, and Austin Sarat, "The Evolution of Litigation in the Federal Courts of Appeals, 1895–1975," 16 *Law & Soc'y Rev.* 291 (1981–1982); Gregory A. Caldeira, "A Tale of Two Reforms: On the Work of the U.S. Supreme Court," in *The Analysis of Judicial Reform* 137 (Philip E. Dubois ed. 1982); David S. Clark, "Adjudication to Administration: A Statistical Analysis of Federal District Courts in the Twentieth Century," 55 *So. Cal. L. Rev* 65 (1981); Joel B. Grossman and Austin Sarat, "Litigation in the Federal Courts: A Comparative Perspective," 9 *Law & Soc'y Rev.* 321 (1975); Arthur D. Hellman, "Error Correction, Lawmaking, and the Supreme Court's Exercise of Discretionary Review," 44 *U. Pitt. L. Rev.* 795 (1983); William P. McLauchlan, *Federal Court Caseloads* (1984). McLauchlan's study, a recent and rich compendium of descriptive statistics on the federal court system, emphasizing differences among circuits, deserves special note. Statistical studies of particular areas of federal jurisdiction include Karen M. Allen, Nathan A. Schachtman, and David R. Wilson, "Federal Habeas Corpus and Its Reform: An Empirical Analysis," 13 *Rutgers L.J.* 675 (1982); Paul D. Carrington, "United States Appeals in Civil Cases: A Field and Statistical Study," 11 *Houston L.J.* 1101 (1974); Hessel E. Yntema, "The Jurisdiction of the Federal Courts in Controversies between Citizens of Different States—III," 19 *A.B.A.J.* 265 (1933). A number of other studies are referenced in *Forecasting the Impact of Legislation on Courts* 101–105 (Keith O. Boyum and Sam Krislov eds. 1980).

2. See 1 American Law Institute, supra note 1, at 107 (detailed table 1).

3. See *id.* at 32–36; 2 *id.* at 37. The result was the huge bulge in filings per district judge shown in Figure 4.2 in the next chapter.

growth in the period therefore was in civil cases, which rose from 35,959 to 59,284—a compound annual rate of increase of 1.9 percent. For the whole docket (criminal as well as civil), the compound annual rate of increase between 1934 and 1960 was only 0.9 percent.

In 1891, the first year of the federal courts of appeals (or circuit courts of appeals, as they were called then), a total of 841 cases were filed in

Table 3.1. Case filings in lower federal courts, 1960

Type of case	District courts (%)		Courts of appeals (%)[a]	
Criminal	28,137	(35.5)	623	(22.2)
Civil	51,063	(64.5)	2,188	(77.8)
U.S. Civil	20,840	(26.3)	788	(28.0)
Condemnation	1,009	(1.3)	30	(1.1)
FLSA	1,206	(1.5)	22	(1.0)
Contract	8,295	(10.5)	34	(1.2)
Tax	1,545	(2.0)	155	(5.5)
Civil rights[b]	26	(0.0)	N.A.	
Postconviction	1,305	(1.6)	179	(6.4)
FTCA	1,253	(1.6)	50	(1.8)
Forfeiture and penalty	2,371	(3.0)	12	(0.4)
Social security laws[b]	537	(0.1)	N.A.	
Private	30,233	(38.2)	1,400	(49.8)
Diversity	17,048	(21.5)	740	(26.3)
Admirality	3,968	(5.0)	128	(4.6)
Antitrust	222	(0.3)	47	(1.7)
Civil rights	280	(0.4)	44	(1.6)
Intellectual property	1,451	(1.8)	155	(5.5)
FELA	1,096	(1.4)	30	(1.1)
Postconviction	872	(1.1)	111	(3.9)
Jones Act	2,646	(3.3)	38	(1.4)
LMRA	322	(0.4)	64	(2.3)
RLA	68	(0.1)	13	(0.5)
Administrative appeals	—		737	
Other[c]	—		217	
Total	79,200		3,765[d]	

a. Percentages just of cases appealed from district courts (N = 2,811).
b. Not reported in 1960; the figure is for 1961.
c. Like administrative appeals, these are not appeals from the district court; most are bankruptcy cases.
d. 2,811 from district courts.

those courts. This number rose to 3,406 in 1934, representing a compound annual rate of increase of 4.8 percent. Between 1934 and 1960, however, the rate of growth slowed very markedly, to 0.5 percent; only 3,889 cases were filed in 1960.

In the Supreme Court, comparisons with the early years of the century are difficult because of the marked contraction of the Court's obligatory jurisdiction by the Judiciary Act of 1925. But between 1934 and 1960 the number of applications for Supreme Court review doubled, from 937 to 1,940. This represents a compound annual rate of growth of 2.8 percent. But the number of cases decided on the merits by the Supreme Court with full opinion, as distinct from the number of applications for review processed, fell from 156 in 1934 to 110 in 1960.

The increase in applications for Supreme Court review would have been the only ominous note to a student of federal judicial caseloads in 1960—ominous because of the great difficulty of expanding the Supreme Court's capacity to dispose of judicial business. Since the number of appeals to the courts of appeals was growing much less rapidly than the number of district court filings, the *rate* of appeal to the courts of appeals must have been in decline in 1960, implying that future increases in the district courts' workload could be met by adding trial judges without the necessity of adding significant numbers of new appellate judges as well. As suggested in Chapter 1, a judicial system can adapt to caseload growth more easily by adding trial judges than by adding appellate judges.

Table 3.1 presents a snapshot of the caseloads of the district courts and the courts of appeals in 1960, the eve of explosion.[4] The discrep-

4. For the nonlawyer, some of the subject-matter categories may require elucidation. "FLSA" stands for Fair Labor Standards Act, which is the federal minimum wage and also maximum hours law. "Postconviction" refers to suits (nominally civil) by which persons who have been convicted of a crime and have exhausted their appellate remedies may later attempt to set aside their convictions, generally on constitutional grounds. The postconviction cases under "U.S. Civil" are cases brought by federal prisoners; those under "Private" (meaning the United States is not a party to the suit) are cases brought by state prisoners, including civil rights cases attacking prison conditions rather than the legality of the prisoner's conviction. "FTCA" is the Federal Tort Claims Act, which allows the government to be sued for certain torts committed by federal employees. "Intellectual property" refers to cases under the patent, copyright, and trademark laws. "FELA" refers to the Federal Employers Liability Act, which governs the tort liability of railroads to their workers. The Jones Act is a similar statute for maritime employees. "LMRA" is the Labor Management Relations Act (Taft-Hartley), section 301 of which confers on the federal courts jurisdiction to enforce collective bargaining contracts. "RLA" is the Railway Labor Act, which establishes a scheme of compulsory arbitration for railroad workers' disputes with their employers and empowers the federal district courts to enforce the arbitration awards.

A deficiency of the Administrative Office's subject-matter classification should be

ancy between the total number of district court cases in the table and the number just given in the text (and the much smaller discrepancy for the courts of appeals) reflects the omission from the table of some 10,000 cases arising under the "local" jurisdiction of the federal courts. This refers to their jurisdiction over matters ordinarily within the jurisdiction of state courts—such as divorce, probate, most tort, property, and contract disputes, and most crimes—in parts of the country that are not states, which by 1960 meant principally the District of Columbia. In 1970 a separate system of local courts was created for the District, and the local jurisdiction of the federal district courts in the District was abolished.[5] Since this was a one-time change with no significance for the future, it would give a misleading impression of the caseload growth since 1967 to reflect the change in the table.

Table 3.1 shows that the jurisdiction of the district courts in 1960 was a little more than one-third criminal. If to direct appeals from federal criminal convictions one adds postconviction proceedings by federal prisoners attacking their federal convictions, and by state prisoners attacking their state convictions on federal constitutional grounds, the figure is still well under 40 percent. The civil docket of the federal courts in 1960 was dominated by diversity cases, which were more than 20 percent of the district courts' entire caseload. The picture was similar in the courts of appeals. Exclusive of administrative appeals, which were about 20 percent of the courts of appeals' docket, criminal cases including postconviction proceedings were about a third of the rest of the docket. But a much larger proportion of these cases were postconviction proceedings than direct appeals, for a very low appeal rate for federal convictions was balanced by a high appeal rate for postconviction proceedings. A quarter of the courts of appeals' docket (excluding administrative appeals) consisted of diversity cases.

Table 3.2 presents the comparable figures for case filings in 1983.[6] The changes are dramatic: the number of cases filed in the district courts more than tripled, roughly from 80,000 to 280,000—a 250 per-

---

noted: every case is placed in just one category even if it presents claims in two (for example, a federal securities claim with a pendent state-law tort claim), as many cases do. The lawyer filing the case indicates which claim he thinks most important, and that is how the case is classified.

5. See District of Columbia Court Reform and Criminal Procedure Act of 1970, 84 Stat. 473.

6. The statistics reported by the Administrative Office for the district courts and the courts of appeals are for a July 1 to June 30 fiscal year (not really "fiscal"—the federal fiscal year is now October 1 to September 30—but I shall retain the term to describe the judicial reporting year). Statistics for the Supreme Court are by annual term of court, which begins on the first Monday in October.

Table 3.2. Case filings in lower federal courts, 1983

Type of case	District courts (%)		Courts of appeals (%)[a]	
Criminal	35,872	(12.9)	4,790	(19.2)
Civil	241,159	(87.1)	20,199	(80.8)
U.S. Civil	95,803	(34.6)	5,820	(23.3)
Condemnation	917	(0.3)	55	(0.2)
FLSA	821	(0.3)	47	(0.2)
Contract	47,052	(17.0)	232	(0.9)
Tax	4,117	(1.5)	468	(1.9)
Civil rights	1,937	(0.7)	709	(2.8)
Postconviction	4,354	(1.6)	1,258	(5.0)
FTCA	2,887	(1.0)	496	(2.0)
Forfeiture and penalty	3,463	(1.3)	128	(0.4)
Social security laws	20,309	(7.3)	992	(3.4)
Private	145,356	(54.8)	14,379	(57.5)
Diversity	57,421	(20.1)	3,610	(14.4)
Admiralty	5,628	(2.0)	229	(1.0)
Antitrust	1,192	(0.4)	345	(1.4)
Civil rights	17,798	(6.4)	3,043	(12.2)
Intellectual property	5,413	(2.0)	334	(1.3)
FELA	2,102	(0.8)	77	(0.3)
Postconviction	26,411	(9.5)	4,069	(16.3)
Jones Act	4,053	(1.5)	282	(1.1)
LMRA	4,017	(1.5)	423	(1.7)
RLA	182	(0.1)	43	(0.2)
Administrative appeals	—		3,069	
Other[b]	—		1,522	
Total	277,031		29,580[c]	

a. See Table 3.1.
b. See Table 3.1
c. 24,989 from district courts.

cent increase, compared with less than 30 percent in the preceding quarter-century. The compound annual rate of increase was 5.6 percent—six times the annual rate in the preceding period. Contrary to popular impression, the growth has been larger on the civil than on the criminal side of the calendar, even when "criminal" is defined to include postconviction proceedings and prisoner civil rights proceedings (both classes of cases are nominally civil). The number of federal criminal prosecutions was only 27 percent greater in 1983 than it had been in 1960, and even when one adds to that the much larger number of federal (4,354) and especially state (26,411) prisoner postconviction and prisoner civil rights proceedings, the increase in criminal cases, from 30,314 in 1960 to 66,637 in 1983 (120 percent) is much less than the increase in "pure" civil cases, from 48,886 to 210,503 (more than 330 percent).

The increase in district court cases, dramatic as it has been, is dwarfed by the increase in court of appeals cases—from 3,765 in 1960 (excluding, as with the district courts, cases arising under local jurisdiction) to 29,580 in 1983. This is an increase of 686 percent (789 percent if only appeals from district courts are included), compared to 250 percent for the district courts. The composition of cases has also changed more in the courts of appeals than in the district courts. Criminal cases, including postconviction and prisoner civil rights cases, now account for 40 percent of the courts of appeals' docket (excluding administrative appeals), which means they have grown faster in these courts than in the district courts. As a matter of fact they have grown more than tenfold—from 913 in 1960 to 10,117 in 1983. Diversity cases have shrunk to 14 percent of the docket, little more than the number of civil rights cases—a category so small in 1960 that the number of civil rights appeals was not separately recorded. The compound annual rate of increase for the whole court of appeals docket since 1960 has been 9.4 percent, compared to only one-half of 1 percent in the preceding 26 years.

It is, of course, potentially misleading to generalize from a comparison of only two widely separated years. In particular, any generalization is extremely sensitive to the choice of the first year. If I had started not with 1960 but with 1934, the annual rates of growth that I have computed would be much lower. But in fact 1960 does identify, though only approximately, a turning point for the federal court system. Figure 3.1 is a graph of caseload growth in the district courts and the courts of appeals since 1904 (the earliest year for which complete statistics of case filings in the district courts are available). Although the change in the rate of caseload growth cannot be pinpointed to 1960, it is apparent that the period 1958–1962, of which 1960 is the midpoint, represents a sharp turning point. For a long time before these transition years caseload growth had been moderate in the district courts and virtually nil in the courts of appeals; since then it has been consistently very great in both.

Figure 3.2 provides a more precise picture of the turning points. The same numbers are plotted as in Figure 3.1, but on semi-logarithmic

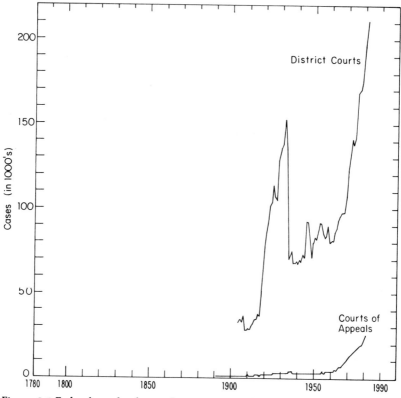

Figure 3.1 Federal caseload growth, 1891–1983. (From Table B.2.)

paper, in which vertical intervals measure proportionate rather than absolute growth. Figure 3.2 shows a sharp increase in the rate of docket growth for the district courts beginning in 1961 and the courts of appeals beginning in 1959—an increase that has been sustained for more than 20 years.

Of course, figures on case filings cannot tell the whole story about caseload. A case is not a standard measurement like a quart or a constant (that is, inflation-free) dollar. If an increase in case filings were associated with a decrease in the difficulty of the average case, the figures on caseload growth would exaggerate the actual increase in the workload of the courts. For the district courts, a slightly better measure of caseload change may be the number of cases that go to trial as distinct from the number disposed of before trial. This is not a good measure, however, since one response of district judges to workload pressures might be to make it more difficult for litigants to get a trial—since a trial

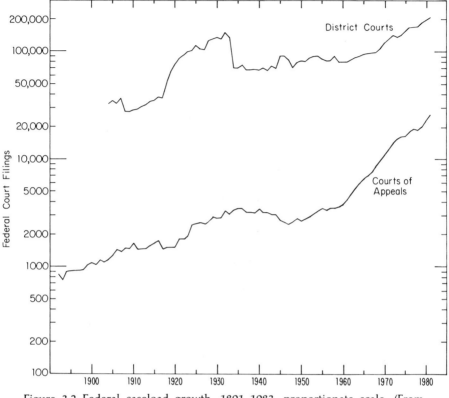

Figure 3.2 Federal caseload growth, 1891–1983, proportionate scale. (From Table B.2.)

takes more time than disposing of a case before trial—by granting motions to dismiss and motions for summary judgment more freely and by putting more pressure on the parties to settle their case before it gets to trial. But for what it is worth, Table 3.3 compares the number of trials completed in 1960 and 1983, and shows a smaller increase than in the number of case filings—110 percent rather than 250 percent.[7] Now if there is more pressure to dispose of cases one way or another before trial, the cases that run the gauntlet successfully and are tried are likely to be bigger cases than if trials are more freely allowed. This hypothesis is supported by the more than 40 percent increase in the average length

7. The percentage of federal district court cases reaching trial declined from 11.4 percent in 1962 to 5.4 percent in 1983. (These figures are for civil cases only.)

of a trial over the period, from 2.2 to 3.1 days, shown in Table 3.3. Putting these figures together with the figures on number of trials, one can see that the number of trial days in the federal district courts has roughly tripled in the last 23 years.

A comparable effort to get a better measure of workload, as distinct from raw caseload, is made for the courts of appeals in Table 3.4 by distinguishing between all terminations, on the one hand, and terminations either after oral argument or after the case is submitted to a panel of judges without oral argument, on the other. Terminations after argument or submission exclude cases that are settled, or otherwise fall by the wayside, between the filing of the appeal and its dismissal or other disposition. The increase in terminations after argument or submission is less dramatic than that for the caseload as a whole, but it is still almost 400 percent.

Table 3.4 makes another adjustment. A case in which the district court (or the administrative agency, in the case of an administrative appeal) is reversed is likely to be more difficult than one in which the district court or the agency is affirmed. The fraction of completely insubstantial appeals, requiring minimal judge time, is bound to be larger in the affirmed than in the reversed category; and the appellate court can rely more heavily on the trial court's analysis. Hence a change in the fraction of appeals decided in favor of the appellant is some index of the changing difficulty of the appellate caseload. The figures in Table 3.4, which show a dramatic fall in the reversal rate between 1960 and 1983, from 24.5 percent to 15.9 percent, imply that the average case

Table 3.3. Number and length of trials, 1960 and 1983

	1960	1983
Trials completed		
Criminal	3,515	6,656
Civil	6,488	14,391
Total	10,003	21,047
Average length (days)[a]	2.2	3.1

a. Computed by taking the midpoint of brackets used by the Administrative Office to report differences in lengths of trials. (For example, if the Administrative Office reports the number of trials lasting between 4 and 6 days, I assume, for purposes of computing an average length for all trials, that all trials in the 4–6 day bracket lasted 5 days.) This may lead to some overestimation, since there are probably more trials at the lower end of each bracket than at the higher end. For trials lasting 20 days or more, the AO reports the length of each trial. There were 45 such trials in 1960, lasting an average of 29 days each, and 160 in 1983, lasting an average of 37 days each.

Table 3.4. Terminations in courts of appeals, 1960 and 1983 (percentage reversing district court)

Type of termination	1960		1983	
All terminations	3,713		28,660	
Terminations after				
hearing or submission	2,681	(24.5)	13,217	(15.9)
Criminal	441	(17.7)	2,859	(9.4)
U.S. civil	534	(24.9)	2,472	(20.0)
Private civil	1,198	(26.5)	6,223	(17.8)
Administrative appeals	361	(25.2)	1,292	(11.1)
Original proceedings	56	—	96	—

Note: The disposition affirmance in part, reversal in part is treated as affirmance in these statistics. Bankruptcy proceedings are omitted from the breakdown.

on the appellate docket is becoming easier. But even if one assumed, contrary to the truth, that no affirmance, even a partial affirmance (see note to Table 3.4), required any judge time at all—so that only complete reversals measured the actual workload of the courts of appeals—and if one therefore multiplied terminations after argument or submission by the percentage of cases in which the lower court or the agency was reversed, the workload increase would still be more than 200 percent. The real increase in workload has obviously been greater.

Another way of looking at workload changes in the courts of appeals is to focus on the signed, published, majority opinion (hereafter referred to as "signed opinion" for brevity). This is the method used for disposing of the more difficult appeals (whether affirming or reversing); the published per curiam opinion (an opinion not signed by an individual judge) and the unpublished (almost always per curiam) opinion are normally reserved for the less difficult cases.[8] Although the number of signed court of appeals opinions in 1960 is not a recorded figure, it has been estimated to be 1,972.[9] In 1983 the number (by then recorded) was 5,572,[10] an increase of 183 percent. This, of course, is a much smaller increase than that for all contested terminations—terminations after

8. These different modes of appellate decision are discussed more fully in the next chapter.

9. See William M. Landes and Richard A. Posner, "Legal Precedent: A Theoretical and Empirical Analysis," 19 *J. Law & Econ.* 249, 300, 303 (1976).

10. Calculated from *Federal Court Management Statistics 1983*, at 13 (Adm. Off. of U.S. Cts. 1983).

hearing or submission (Table 3.4)—implying that a smaller percentage of such terminations was by signed opinion in 1983 than in 1960. The percentage was indeed smaller: 42 percent versus 74 percent. The reason for this could be that the cases were becoming easier to decide, but it could also be that the judges simply did not have time to write more signed opinions than they did write, as is suggested by the fact that in

Table 3.5. Percentage distribution of signed court of appeals opinions, 1960 and 1983, compared to distribution of terminations in contested cases (in parentheses)

Type of case	1960		1983	
Criminal	11	(17, 16)	20	(22)
Civil	67	(58, 65)	64	(66)
U.S. Civil	23	(21, 20)	23	(19)
Condemnation	1	(1)	1	(0)
FLSA	3	(1)	0	(0)
Contract	3	(1)	1	(1)
Tax	5	(4)	0	(1)
Civil rights	0	(N.A.)	4	(2)
Postconviction	6	(5)	6	(4)
FTCA	1	(1)	1	(1)
Forfeiture and penalty	1	(N.A.)	0	(0)
Social security laws	0	(0)	4	(4)
Other	3	(3)	6	(6)
Private civil	44	(37, 45)	41	(47)
Diversity	22	(20)	8	(12)
Admiralty	5	(3)	3	(1)
Antitrust	2	(1)	2	(1)
Civil rights	0	(1)	5	(11)
Intellectual property	7	(4)	4	(1)
FELA	0	(1)	0	(0)
Postconviction	3	(3)	7	(12)
Jones Act	0	(1)	1	(1)
LMRA	0	(2)	3	(2)
RLA	1	(0)	0	(0)
Other	4	(1)	8	(6)
Administrative appeals	19	(20, 13)	14	(10)
Other	3	(6, 5)	3	(3)
Total	100	(101, 99)	100	(101)

1960 the average number of signed opinions per court of appeals judge is estimated to have been only 31, while in 1983 it was close to 42.[11]

Changes in the character of court of appeals opinions may tell us even more about the change in workload. But unfortunately there are no published statistics on those opinions (as distinct from filings and terminations) except number and circuit; and the sheer volume makes reading all the opinions issued in two years out of the question. I therefore drew samples of the 1960 and 1983 opinions, 100 for each year. Opinions are published in the *Federal Reporter* in roughly chronological order. I chose for each year the volume in which the first opinion was dated January (that is, the beginning of the second half of the fiscal year) and then counted off the first 100 cases in that or (if necessary) the succeeding volume, subject to the constraint that each circuit be represented in each sample in the same proportion that it bore to all signed opinions for the fiscal year.[12] For 1960 the sample contains opinions published in January through March in volumes 274 and 275 of the *Federal Reporter, Second Series* (F.2d), and for 1983 opinions published in January and February in volume 689 of F.2d.

The results are presented in Tables 3.5 and 3.6. Table 3.5 compares the breakdown by subject matter of the signed opinions in the two periods, as well as comparing the breakdown of signed opinions with that of all terminations in contested cases.[13] With respect to the latter comparison, the table shows that certain very challenging fields of law, such as admiralty, antitrust, and intellectual property, are consistently overrepresented among the cases disposed of by signed opinion, while cer-

11. The 1960 figure was obtained by dividing the estimate in Landes and Posner, supra note 9, at 303 (table B2), of the number of signed opinions in 1960 (1,972) by the number of active circuit judges that year (66). Landes and Posner provide alternative estimates of the number of signed opinions, but for the reasons explained on page 300 of the article, the one I have used here seems the most accurate. The 1983 figure, which is from the source in note 10 supra, is also an estimate. The figure actually measures the number of signed opinions per judgeship, not per judge. This understates the number of opinions per judge to the extent that there are vacancies, and overstates it to the extent that visiting judges (mainly senior and circuit judges) nowadays write many of the opinions. These distortions are to some extent offsetting, but I suspect that on balance the average number of signed opinions per active circuit judge is somewhat overstated. (This is a less serious problem for 1960, when visiting judges were used less.)

The reasons for the declining percentage of appeals decided by signed opinion are explored further in the last section of Chapter 4.

12. For 1960 I used the distribution among circuits in contested terminations; no distribution of published opinions is available for that year.

13. This figure is unavailable for the fine subject-matter classifications for 1960, so for these I used the breakdown in case filings from Table 3.2. The first figure in parentheses in the 1960 column for major classifications is the breakdown in case filings, the second the breakdown in terminations in contested cases.

Table 3.6. Comparisons between 1960 and 1983 signed opinions

	1960	1983
Percent affirming (in whole or in part)	69[a]	58
Percent remanding	77[b]	69[c]
Percent appealed from final judgment	94[d]	88
Percent appealed from judgment after trial	62[e]	51[d]
Percent in which opinion was unanimous	85	81
Percent first appeal in case	94	94
Average length of opinion	3.82 pages	5.36 pages
	2,863 words	4,020 words
Average no. of footnotes	3.8	7.0
Average no. of citations	12.4	24.7
Average no. of issue categories	1.1	1.4

a. Number (N) of cases on which percentage or average is calculated is 100 unless otherwise indicated. For this figure N was 99.
  b. N = 35.
  c. N = 45.
  d. N = 97.
  e. N = 98.

tain other fields, notably criminal appeals in 1960 and private civil rights cases and state postconviction cases in 1983, are underrepresented, probably because these latter areas all contain a high proportion of appellants not represented by counsel.[14] Otherwise the subject-matter breakdowns of signed opinions and of contested terminations are similar for each year, meaning that the shift in the composition of signed opinions mirrors that in the composition of the filings. Thus, 20 percent of the signed opinions in 1960 were in criminal cases (broadly defined to include postconviction proceedings), while the proportion in 1983 was 33 percent. Signed opinions in civil rights and social security cases went from zero in 1960 to 13 percent of the 1983 opinions, while the percentage of diversity opinions fell from 22 percent to 12 percent.

Table 3.6 looks at other aspects of the opinion sample. The first is the percentage of opinions that affirm the district court or administrative agency. This percentage was significantly higher in 1960, suggesting that the cases decided by signed opinion that year probably were easier than their counterparts in 1983. Further support for this hypothesis is given by the finding in the table that a higher (though not much higher) percentage of decisions were unanimous in 1960 than in 1983. A find-

14. 1960 predated the Criminal Justice Act, which funds indigent criminal defendants (including appellants) and is discussed in the next section of this chapter.

ing that cuts the other way is that a higher percentage of the 1960 opinions decided appeals from judgments after a trial, so that the court of appeals had a longer record to wade through. (A related finding is that more of the appeals in 1983 were interlocutory, that is, not from final judgments.) The lower percentage of tried cases in 1983 no doubt reflects the increasing use of summary judgment and judgment on the pleadings by district judges to cope with their own workloads—further evidence that these workloads (and not merely number of cases) really have increased substantially.

Although I did not try to count the number of issues discussed in each opinion in the sample, I did classify each opinion in an issue category. These categories will be discussed in detail in Chapter 10, where, using the same opinion sample, I attempt to convey a more precise sense of the change in the character of courts of appeals' work between 1960 and 1983; for now the thing to note is the greater number of multiple classifications for the cases in the 1983 group, suggesting that these are more complex cases on average. Table 4.6 in the next chapter provides some additional evidence. However, the great increases in the length of opinions and in the number of footnotes and citations are more ambiguous indicators of greater complexity; they also will be discussed in the next chapter.[15] Here it remains only to note that the courts of appeals, perhaps sensitive to the heavy workload of the district courts, seem less prone today to remand for further proceedings in the district court than they were in 1960. (Remands to administrative agencies were not counted in calculating this percentage, nor were affirmances in full, where by definition there is no remand.)

Although the evidence is far from definitive, Tables 3.5 and 3.6 do suggest that the caseload increase experienced by the courts of appeals over the past 23 years is not a statistical mirage but represents a real and very great increase in workload—all of which would be obvious enough were it not for the fact that, as we shall see, there is a school of thought that disparages the increase. But I want first to discuss very briefly the situation in the specialized courts and in the Supreme Court.

In 1960 the principal specialized Article III courts, both appellate, were the Court of Customs and Patent Appeals and (the appellate division of) the Court of Claims, and together they delivered 337 opinions in that year (I do not have data on the number of filings). By 1983 these tribunals had been merged to form the Court of Appeals for the Federal

15. Incidentally, some confirmation that the sample is a representative one is supplied by the fact that the average number of citations per case in 1960, 12.4, is very close to the average found in another study—12.1—based on a sample of 223 court of appeals opinions published in 1960. See Landes and Posner, supra note 9, at 252–253, 257.

Circuit; but since the court was not formed until well into the 1983 fiscal year, only nine months of results are available. In those nine months 694 cases were filed in the court, which is the equivalent of an annual rate of 925. Some appeals that formerly went to the regional courts of appeals now go to the Federal Circuit, but I follow convention in treating it separately. Thus, the data in Table 3.2 do not include cases filed in the Federal Circuit but do include cases filed in the District of Columbia Circuit court of appeals, even though that court, like the Federal Circuit, is more specialized than the remaining courts of appeals.

Although the plausible assumption that the maximum feasible number of Supreme Court justices is nine and that the Court must decide every case en banc limits the number of cases that the Court can accept for decision on the merits, the number so decided has increased substantially since 1960—from 110 to 162 (1982 term). The number of cases in which review was asked for, a number over which the Court has no direct control, rose from 1,940 in 1960 to 4,201 in 1982, which represents a compound annual rate of increase of 3.6 percent, compared to a 2.8 percent increase from the previous quarter-century. Still, not only is the rate of increase of case filings in the Supreme Court lower than in the district courts or the courts of appeals; the only increase beyond the Court's control is in the number of cases to be screened, and it is possible for the Court to delegate much of the screening function to subordinate personnel (namely law clerks), though not without some danger to quality. But the relatively modest rate at which the Court's applications docket is increasing is of small comfort at best; it may simply reflect the decreasing probability of the application's being granted and hence the lessened value of applying. If the number of federal court of appeals and state court decisions reviewable by the Supreme Court becomes so great that there is only an infinitesimal probability of the Court's granting an application for review in a given case, naturally applicants will be discouraged. This would be an example of limiting demand by a form of queuing; it would not be a healthy sign.

Table 3.7 presents a comparison of the Supreme Court's decisions on the merits (that is, decisions in the cases that it accepted for review) in the 1960 and 1982 terms. The small number of fine subject-matter categories reflects the wide scatter of the Court's decisions across such categories, and highlights the very low probability of Supreme Court review in many important areas of federal law. The table shows, however, that in both terms the Supreme Court was primarily a court for reviewing federal court (almost entirely court of appeals) decisions; its original (trial) jurisdiction is small, and only about 20 percent of its docket (less in 1960) comes from cases decided in state courts. As one

Table 3.7. Supreme Court decisions on the merits, 1960 and 1982 terms

Type of case	1960 (%)		1983 (%)	
Original jurisdiction	1	(1.0)	4	(2.5)
From federal courts	87	(82.9)	129	(79.6)
Criminal	16	(15.2)	7	(4.3)
Civil	71	(67.6)	122	(75.3)
U.S. civil	51	(48.6)	66	(40.7)
Tax	14	(13.3)	6	(3.7)
Civil rights	3	(2.9)	5	(3.1)
Postconviction	3	(2.9)	11	(6.8)
Administrative review	18	(17.1)	19	(11.7)
Private	19	(18.1)	56	(34.6)
Civil rights	N.A.		9	(5.6)
Labor	7	(6.7)	5	(3.1)
From state courts	17	(16.2)	29	(17.9)
Criminal	7	(6.7)	15	(9.3)
Civil	10	(9.5)	14	(8.6)
Total	105		162	

Source: *Harv. L. Rev.*, November 1961, November 1983 (table III).

might expect, civil rights and postconviction cases were a bigger fraction of the docket in 1982 than in 1960, although the fact that the *Harvard Law Review* (which compiled the data on which Table 3.7 is based) does not report state prisoner cases separately understates the increase. The most startling changes shown in the table are the big drop in the fraction of tax cases (13.3 percent to 3.7 percent) and the big increase in the fraction of private cases (which includes cases between an individual or firm and a state or its officers) from the lower federal courts. This increase reflects the increase in the number of statutes that create federal rights and in the growth of state-prisoner postconviction litigation, which is buried in the broad category. The table also illustrates the dramatic increase in the number of cases that the Supreme Court is deciding on the merits, though as I have said that number is within the Court's own control. It should also be noted that the Court is increasingly a constitutional court; according to the *Harvard Law Review*'s data, in only 24.8 percent of the Court's decisions in 1960 was the principal issue a constitutional one, while for 1982 the figure is 41.4 percent.

Although raw caseload figures may exaggerate the significance of the caseload explosion since 1960, and although as a former professor I understand the joys of contradicting received wisdom, I find unpersuasive Professor Marc Galanter's recent suggestion that the "litigation explosion" is merely "an item of elite folklore."[16] He writes: "Portentous pronouncements were made by established dignitaries and published in what appear to be learned journals. Could one imagine public health specialists or poultry breeders conjuring up epidemics and cures with such cavalier disregard of the incompleteness of the data and the untested nature of the theory?"[17] Professor Galanter points to interesting though very spotty data suggesting that the per capita rate of litigation may have been higher in colonial and nineteenth-century America than it is today.[18] Although he concedes that there has been a "dramatic rise in federal court filings in recent decades," including a "striking growth of appeals,"[19] Galanter points out that the federal court system is only a small part of the nation's judiciary, and anyway that most cases are settled before trial. He cites Professor David Clark's exemplary statistical study of the federal district courts, which shows that delay in civil cases has actually declined since 1900 and terminations per judge have declined since the Prohibition caseload surge.[20] He infers, as does Clark, that the federal district courts have (in Clark's words) "exhibited tremendous resilience in coping with widely varying workloads."[21]

But all this does not show that the growth of the federal caseload since 1960 is not something to be concerned about. The situation is quite different from what it was in the last period of rapid and steep federal caseload growth, the 1920s and early 1930s. The cause then was clear: Prohibition. The cure was clear: repeal Prohibition. The current pattern of rapid and steep caseload growth is not the result of a single factor; and its causation is not only complex, but unclear. The fact that the growth has been greatest at the appellate level (in contrast to the Prohibition era, when, as is apparent from Figures 3.1 and 3.2, the court of appeals docket was little affected by the surge in district court cases) is particularly ominous because the appellate level is the big potential bottleneck in a judicial system. And at current appellate caseload levels

16. Marc Galanter, "Reading the Landscape of Disputes: What We Know and Don't Know (and Think We Know) about Our Allegedly Contentious and Litigious Society," 31 *U.C.L.A. L. Rev.* 4, 64 (1983).

17. *Id.* at 71.

18. *Id.* at 38–41. See also Lawrence M. Friedman, "Courts over Time: A Survey of Theories and Research," in *Empirical Theories About Courts* 9, 20–25 (Keith O. Boyum and Lynn Mather eds. 1983).

19. Galanter, supra note 16, at 37–38.

20. See Clark, supra note 1, at 80, 83. I shall consider the question of delay in the federal courts in the next chapter.

21. *Id.* at 152.

it will be extremely difficult to expand the capacity of the federal judicial system to meet any new increments of demand.

Granted, there would be no crisis if the judges had been so underemployed in 1960 that the increase in work merely took up the embarrassing slack in their workload. But, in fact, even in the 1950s the judges were complaining about being overworked. In 1958, for example, Chief Justice Warren deplored "the choking congestion in the Federal Courts today."[22] This was an overstatement; and the literature of judicial administration contains many other instances of crying wolf. But while federal judges undoubtedly led a more leisurely life in 1960 than they do now, I can find no evidence that they were underworked; nor do conversations with judges who were sitting then suggest that they were. Very little of the increase in workload since then could have been absorbed simply by bringing an underemployed judiciary up to full steam.

CAUSES

A nation of 230 million cannot get by with as few federal judges as when the population was 3 million. But there is no reason to think that the kind of population and economic growth that we have had since 1960 makes it inevitable that the caseload of the federal courts would rise, let alone rise at the extraordinary rate it has. Population and economic activity both grew more rapidly in the preceding quarter-century,[23] yet there was little growth in the caseload of the federal courts then.

Rather than viewing caseload as a function of broad social aggregates such as population and GNP, I prefer using the economic model sketched in the first chapter, which conceives of federal judicial services as a product whose output, like that of other products, is governed by the laws of demand and supply. My present concern is with demand. Demand for a product will grow either if the price of the product to the consumer falls (movement down a demand curve) or if the value of the product to the consumer rises (demand curve shifting outward). Both phenomena have been at work in the federal courts in the last quarter-century. The fall in the (indirect) price of federal judicial services is dramatically illustrated by the effect of inflation on the minimum amount

22. Earl Warren, "Delay and Congestion in the Federal Courts," 42 *J. Am. Judic. Soc'y* 6–7 (1958).

23. The resident population of the United States increased by 29 percent between 1960 and 1982, but by 39 percent between 1938 and 1960 (computed from U.S. Department of Commerce, Bureau of the Census, *Statistical Abstract of the United States 1982–1983*, at 6). The GNP, in 1967 dollars (that is, correcting for inflation), grew by 86 percent between 1960 and 1980—but by 140 percent between 1940 and 1960 (computed from *id.* at 418).

Table 3.8. Diversity filings, 1956–1963

	Diversity cases filed	
Year	District court	Court of appeals
1956	20,524	742
1957	23,223	750
1958	25,709	788
1959	17,342	756
1960	17,028	740
1961	17,402	N.A.
1962	18,359	N.A.
1963	18,990	N.A.

in controversy required to litigate a case in federal court under the diversity jurisdiction. The amount was raised in 1958 from $3,000 to $10,-000, and the next year diversity filings in the district courts fell by 32.6 percent. The pattern of diversity filings in the years preceding and following the change in the minimum amount in controversy, shown in Table 3.8, and the absence of any alternative explanation, suggest that the drop in filings was indeed caused by the change in the minimum amount. Unfortunately, it is not possible to determine the effect of the change on the number of appeals in diversity cases. The Administrative Office stopped reporting this figure for several years after 1960, and that year was too early for the change to have had much effect at the court of appeals level; relatively few cases filed in district courts in 1959 would have been decided and appealed as early as 1960. In any event, Table 3.8 shows no effect in the courts of appeals; indeed, there was a bigger drop in diversity appeals from 1958 to 1959 than from 1959 to 1960.

The $10,000 minimum-amount-in-controversy requirement in diversity cases has not been changed since 1958. But the inflation since then has reduced the purchasing power of the dollar by more than two-thirds.[24] The Consumer Price Index (1967 = 100) was 86.6 in 1958;

24. As a matter of fact, the amount has been changed only three times since 1789. The first time was in 1877, when it was raised from $500 to $2,000, and the second in 1911, when it was raised to $3,000. Unfortunately, the number of diversity cases filed was not reported in those periods, so it is not possible to estimate the response of litigants to the changes. But for what it is worth, I note that the number of private civil cases filed—of which diversity cases were an unknown, but probably large, fraction (see Chapter 2, notes 56–58)—fell slightly in both 1877 (from 11,366 in 1876 to 10,258) and 1911 (from 10,618 in 1910 to 10,191). See 2 American Law Institute, supra note 1, at 107 (detailed table I).

it was 303.5 in December 1983. Thus, many diversity claimants who would have been priced out of the federal judicial services market by the $10,000 minimum in 1960 can today, when $10,000 is worth less than a third as much, litigate their modest claims in federal court. The virtually complete abolition of the amount-in-controversy requirement in federal-question cases, by statutes passed in 1976 and 1980, should also be mentioned; however, the effect on demand has been small because of the many federal jurisdictional statutes that did not require any minimum amount in controversy and that together covered most of the ground of the general federal-question jurisdictional statute.[25] Another form of indirect pricing of federal judicial services is the requirement of justiciability in Article III of the Constitution, a requirement alluded to in Chapter 2. Since 1960 the elements of justiciability, notably mootness and standing to sue, have been progressively relaxed, allowing more claims of federal right to be litigated in federal court.[26]

A most important development in the pricing of judicial services has been the greatly expanded availability of lawyers for indigent claimants, especially criminal defendants, as a joint result of Supreme Court decisions expanding the right to counsel in criminal cases, the funding of lawyers for poor people through the Legal Services Corporation (appropriations for which peaked at $321 million in 1981 and are now running at about $241 million a year), and, above all, the funding of lawyers for indigent federal criminal defendants under the Criminal Justice Act of 1964, for which appropriations are running at the rate of better than $20 million a year.[27] It is estimated that 47,000 appointments were made under the Act in 1983, 2,709 of them in courts of appeals.[28] Legal representation is an important, often a vital, input into the production of judicial services. The fall in the price of that input—from prohibitive to zero—for a large class of federal litigants is the economic equivalent of a dramatic drop in the price of the services themselves.

This raises the question of whether the great increase in the number of lawyers[29] has reduced the price of judicial services to nonindigent federal claimants. The answer is that this is unlikely. It is true that supply could outrun demand, and if that happened lawyers' fees would fall

25. See Charles Alan Wright, *The Law of Federal Courts* 179–181 (4th ed. 1983).

26. See, for example, *id.* at 60–67.

27. Although this figure may seem small relative to that for the Legal Services Corporation, it must be remembered that Criminal Justice Act funds are earmarked for federal criminal proceedings, which represent a very small fraction of the nation's legal business.

28. *1982 AO Ann. Rep.* 498.

29. According to estimates presented in Clark, supra note 1, at 95–96 (table 3), the increase was from 285,933 in 1960 to 557,556 in 1980.

and litigation would therefore rise. But there is no indication that this has happened; the increase in the supply of lawyers appears to have lagged behind rather than led the litigation explosion. Between 1940 and 1960, according to Census data,[30] the increase in the number of lawyers was moderate—from 182,000 to 213,000, or about 15 percent. This is not enough to explain a litigation explosion beginning in 1960. By 1970 the number of lawyers had risen to 273,000, an increase of about 30 percent over 1960.[31] But the big growth spurt occurred in the 1970s. The number of lawyers doubled—perhaps in response to,[32] but surely not causing, the litigation explosion that began in a short period centered around 1960. Of course only a small fraction of the nation's lawyers are engaged in federal trial or appellate practice. Nevertheless, incomplete data suggest that a similar boom in litigation was occurring in the state courts at the same time; and the expansion in legal rights that fueled the federal and state litigation booms must also have increased the demand for legal counseling and other nonlitigation services.

While some developments of the last two decades have reduced the price of litigating a federal claim in federal court, others have increased the number of potential claims by expanding the number of federal rights, thus shifting the demand curve for federal judicial services outward. The last quarter-century has seen much legislative and particularly judicial creation of federal rights. Probably the most important federal statute of this period in caseload impact was Title VII of the Civil Rights Act of 1964,[33] which created private remedies for discrimination, primarily racial and sexual, in employment. But more important than any single statute has been the fact that since the early 1960s (accelerating with the replacement of Justice Frankfurter by Justice Goldberg in 1962, decelerating only slightly since 1969, the period of the "Burger Court"), the Supreme Court, through broad interpretations of the Bill of Rights, the due process and equal protection clauses of the Fourteenth Amendment, the Habeas Corpus Act of 1867,[34] and section 1 of the Ku Klux Klan Act of 1871,[35] and through willingness to create

30. The only data available for the period; not comparable to Clark's data. See *id.* at 95 nn.111–112.

31. Clark's data show a smaller increase, about 25 percent. See *id.* at 95 (table 3).

32. See B. Peter Pashigian, "The Market for Lawyers: The Determinants of the Demand for and Supply of Lawyers," 20 *J. Law & Econ.* 53, 71 (1977) (table 5, variable 8, defined in chart I, in *id.* at 70); B. Peter Pashigian, "The Number and Earnings of Lawyers: Some Recent Findings," 1978 *Am. Bar Foundation Research J.* 51, 72.

33. 42 U.S.C. § 2000e.

34. Now 28 U.S.C. §§ 2241 *et seq.*

35. Now 28 U.S.C. § 1983.

private rights of action under federal statutes and the Constitution it-self, has in a series of landmark cases whose names are household words, at least to lawyers—*Baker v. Carr*,[36] *Bivens*,[37] *Roe v. Wade*,[38] *Monroe v. Pape*,[39] and many others—enormously enlarged the number of rights upon which a federal court suit could be founded.

I turn now to quantitative analysis of the causes of federal caseload growth. Table 3.9 presents the percentage growths between 1960 and 1983 of case filings in the various categories and subcategories of earlier tables. This table also contains what I call, with poetic license, "appeal rates" for the various types of cases, but what could more accurately be called "appeal potentials." These are not true appeal rates but merely the ratios of filings in the courts of appeals to filings in the district courts; and relatively few cases initiated in the district courts in 1960 or in 1983 were appealed the same year to the court of appeals. My reason for using this very crude method of estimating appeal rates will be given later in this chapter, and I will present an alternative procedure there.

The first entry in Table 3.9—the 27 percent increase in criminal fil-ings between 1960 and 1983—is a good illustration of the fact that caseload is not a simple function of broad social aggregates, or even of measures of the underlying activity giving rise to a federal claim. Al-though the amount of federal criminal activity has grown substantially since 1960, this growth is not reflected in federal criminal proceedings. As a matter of fact, the number of federal criminal prosecutions has fluctuated around 30,000 for the last 50 years.[40]

Some of the changes in Table 3.9 are more easily explained than others. Since the number of federal prosecutions has remained largely unchanged for a great many years, since the federal prison population has grown only slightly,[41] and since counsel is generally not appointed for convicted prisoners as distinct from accused defendants, the 234 percent increase in proceedings brought by federal prisoners to attack their convictions collaterally (that is, not by direct appeal but by a later, separate proceeding in the nature of habeas corpus) probably reflects in the main the increased number of federal rights that a federal prisoner

36. 369 U.S. 186 (1962) (reapportionment).
37. Bivens v. Six Unknown Named Agents of Fed. Bur. of Narcotics, 403 U.S. 388 (1971) (tort suits for violation of constitutional rights by federal officers).
38. 410 U.S. 113 (1973) (abortion).
39. 365 U.S. 167 (1961) (tort suits for violations of constitutional rights by state offi-cers).
40. The number rose from 31,301 in 1982 to 35,872 in 1983, but only time will tell whether the substantial increase in 1983 is the beginning of a long-term trend.
41. From 17,134 in 1960 to 22,169 in 1981 (U.S. Department of Commerce, Bureau of the Census, *Statistical Abstract of the United States 1982–1983*, at 191).

Table 3.9. Appeal rates and sources of growth of case filings, 1960 and 1983

Type of case	Percentage of growth, district courts	Percentage of growth, courts of appeals	Appeal rate, 1960 (%)	Appeal rate, 1983 (%)
Criminal	27	669	2.2	13.4
Civil	372	823	4.3	8.4
U.S. Civil	360	639	3.8	6.1
Condemnation	− 9	54	3.0	6.0
FLSA	−32	114	1.8	5.7
Contract	467	582	0.4	0.5
Tax	166	202	10.0	11.4
Civil rights	7,350	N.A.	N.A.	36.7
Postconviction	234	603	13.7	28.9
FTCA	130	892	4.0	17.2
Forfeiture and penalty	46	967	0.5	3.7
Social security	3,682	N.A.	N.A.	4.9
Private	381	927	4.6	9.9
Diversity	237	388	4.3	6.3
Admiralty	42	279	3.2	4.1
Antitrust	437	634	20.6	28.9
Civil rights	6,256	6,816	15.7	17.1
Intellectual property	273	115	10.7	6.2
FELA	92	157	2.7	3.7
Postconviction	2,929	3,566	12.7	15.4
Jones Act	53	642	1.4	7.0
LMRA	1,148	561	19.9	10.5
RLA	168	231	19.1	23.6
Administrative appeals	—	316	N.A.	N.A.
Other	—	601	N.A.	N.A.
Average[a]	250	686[b]	3.5[c]	9.0[c]

a. Weighted average, all filings.
b. 789% in cases from district courts.
c. From district courts only.

can assert in a postconviction proceeding today. Similarly, the enormous increase in the number of state-prisoner postconviction proceedings and state-prisoner civil rights proceedings must be largely a function of the greater number of federal rights that state prisoners, whether challenging their convictions in habeas corpus proceedings or challenging the conditions of their confinement in civil rights proceed-ings, enjoy today. Particularly important are rights that facilitate suit, such as the right of a prisoner to have access to law library materials to help him prepare his habeas corpus and civil rights filings.

The increase in the number of state-prisoner filings probably is not entirely a function of an increase in rights. The state prison population has grown substantially since 1960. But it has not increased by 2,929 percent, as has the number of case filings, but only by 122 percent.[42] Most of the caseload growth must therefore be unrelated to the fact that the states are prosecuting more people and imprisoning them for longer periods of time. However, the longer a person's sentence, the greater will be his incentive to try to get out through postconviction proceed-ings. So longer prison sentences may explain some of the growth in the number of cases beyond the growth explained simply by the effect of longer sentences on the size of the prison population.

The great increase in civil rights cases must also be a product in large part of new law—statute law, notably Title VII, and judicial reinterpre-tations of the Reconstruction civil rights statutes, such as 42 U.S.C. § 1983—though additional factors must have played a role too: increased judicial hospitality to discrimination claims and increased awareness of legal rights by victims of discrimination. The growth of America's for-eign trade over the past quarter-century implies greater use of our ports,[43] and this may explain the modest increase in admiralty and Jones Act (seaman-injury suits) cases. But railroad employment fell by almost 50 percent in this period,[44] yet FELA suits (railroad workers' personal injury suits) climbed faster than admiralty and Jones Act suits. The large increase in the number of suits under the Railway Labor Act, which provides remedies for violations of railroad collective bargaining contracts, is less mysterious; the steep decline in railroad employment, implying frequent layoffs and discharges, has been a fertile source of disputes over job-protection provisions in such contracts.

The tremendous increase in the number of cases under the social se-curity laws (the percentage of increase cannot be determined because there were too few such cases to be reported as a separate category in 1960, but obviously it has been phenomenal) must be due in part to the fact that three-fourths of these cases involve social security disability insurance and that between 1960 and 1983 the total number of recipi-ents of federal disability insurance grew almost sixfold, from 445,000 to

42. From 148,989 in 1960 to 330,998 in 1981. *Id.*

43. America's waterborne foreign trade almost tripled, in tons, between 1960 and 1977. See H. David Bess and Martin T. Farris, *U.S. Maritime Policy: History and Prospects* 92 (table 5.8), 137 (table 8.4) (1981).

44. From 793,000 to 469,000 workers. *Statistical Abstract, supra* note 41, at 626.

2,528,000.[45] The relationship between the growth of the welfare state and the rise of the federal judicial caseload is—at least in the social security area—inescapable. But since the increase in cases has been much steeper than the increase in the number of social security recipients, the expansion of the welfare state is not the whole story even with regard to the welfare cases on the docket. Indeed, it is apparent that the Reagan administration's well-publicized efforts to trim the social security disability rolls have been responsible for most, and maybe all, recent increases in social security cases. The early 1970s were a time of very rapid increase in the number of social security cases filed in the district courts—from 1,792 in 1971 to 10,355 in 1976. But 1976 turned out to be the peak year (until President Reagan took office), and by 1980 the number of cases filed had actually fallen, to 9,043. They then began a very rapid rise, to 9,780 in 1981, 12,812 in 1982, and 20,315 in 1983. Almost all of this growth has been in disability cases, which increased from 5,771 in 1980 to 18,764 in 1983. Without this increase the total number of social security cases filed in the district courts would have continued to fall, from 9,043 in 1980 to 7,322 in 1983. At least in the near term, deregulation can have as dramatic an effect on federal caseloads as regulation.

Other areas of docket growth are extremely puzzling. While the growth of the federal government may explain why the number of government contract and federal tax suits has risen, it cannot explain the magnitude of the rise: the number of contract suits has risen more than fourfold. The more than doubling of suits under the Federal Tort Claims Act is also mysterious. Although I can find no statistics on the number of accidental injuries caused by federal employees, I find it hard to believe that the number has doubled, especially since the number of federal employees has grown by only about 25 percent.[46] The statute was amended in 1974 to bring some intentional torts within its reach for the first time,[47] but these changes have not produced many suits. There have also been statutory changes in the federal laws concerning intellectual property (patent, copyright, and trademark law), but it is unlikely that these changes would have caused a more than threefold increase in the number of lawsuits. Private suits under the antitrust laws have been an area of growth for many years, though there

45. See Charles W. Meyer, *Social Security Disability Insurance: The Problems of Unexpected Growth* 48 (1979) (table 15); *Social Security Bull.*, October 1983, at 1.

46. See *Statistical Abstract*, supra note 41, at 265; U.S. Office of Personnel Management, "Federal Civilian Workforce Statistics: Monthly Release," December 1982, at 7.

47. See 28 U.S.C. § 2680(h) (intentional torts committed by law enforcement officers in the course of searches or arrests).

has been some leveling off in recent years and it now appears that the peak was reached well before 1982. Nevertheless, even for a specialist in antitrust law, as I used to be, the tremendous increase in case filings is perplexing. It is true that the 1960s were a time of great judicial hospitality to antitrust claims, but the 1970s and 1980s have not been; and it is not at all plausible to think that antitrust violations are simply more common today than they were in 1960. Also perplexing is the enormous increase in suits under section 301 of the Taft-Hartley Act (enforcement of collective bargaining contracts);[48] the number of workers who belong to unions has grown by only about 12 percent since 1960.[49]

One of the most interesting figures in Table 3.9 is the increase in the number of diversity suits, which have more than tripled. This cannot be a result of any change in federal law; the rights asserted in diversity suits are rights under state law. The decline in real terms in the minimum stake required to file such suits must explain a part of the 237 percent increase in these cases; but if 1958 is a reliable guide, even if the minimum amount in controversy had been increased to take account of inflation the number of diversity filings would have risen by only 127 percent.[50] In a further effort to predict the effect of a change in the minimum amount in controversy on the diversity caseload, I have reviewed the diversity cases in which I have written the majority opinion since I became a federal court of appeals judge in order to see how many would have been within the federal jurisdiction if the minimum had been raised to keep pace with inflation—if it had been raised, that is, to $35,000. Of the 18 cases, one was dismissed because the amount in controversy was less than $10,000 and in another the amount in controversy, though evidently more than $10,000, is not otherwise indicated. In 4 of the remaining 16 the amount in controversy was less than $35,000, although in one of these it was $27,000, which is sufficiently close to $35,000 that the case might not have been thrown out even if the jurisdictional minimum had been $35,000: the test for jurisdiction is only whether the plaintiff has a good-faith expectation of winning more than the minimum if he does win. In another one of the 4 cases the amount in controversy appears to have been between $10,000 and $35,000; and in the remaining 2 cases it was $23,000 and $20,000, respectively, and since these were contract claims it probably could not have

48. 29 U.S.C. § 185.

49. *Statistical Abstract*, supra note 41, at 408–409 (tables 680, 682).

50. This assumes that raising the minimum amount in controversy from $10,000 to $35,000, the increase necessary to offset inflation, would have the same percentage effect on the number of diversity cases filed in district court as the 1958 increase (slightly smaller in percentage terms) from $3,000 to $10,000 had.

been jacked up much higher. So about 25 percent of my cases (4/17) probably would not have been brought in federal court if the diversity minimum were $35,000.

Not only is this sample both a nonrandom and a small one, but it is a sample of court of appeals rather than district court cases, and cases with modest stakes are less likely to be appealed than those with large stakes. This perhaps explains why the estimate for my sample (25 percent) is much lower than that for district court filings (33 percent), which is based on what happened between 1958 and 1959. But since the caseload crisis is more acute in the courts of appeals than in the district courts, the former level may be the more pertinent one at which to study the effects of raising the minimum amount in controversy.

Turning to other possible reasons why diversity cases have increased so substantially, I very much doubt that state courts have been deteriorating relative to federal courts or becoming more prejudiced toward nonresidents; probably the opposite is true (the last column in Table 2.3 provides some support for this conjecture). And although it appears that the waiting period for a civil trial in the state courts grew significantly in this period,[51] while the federal trial queue grew only a little,[52] greater relative delay in state court actions would make the federal courts less attractive to defendants at the same time that it was making them more attractive to plaintiffs. So it is not clear that there would be a large net effect on diversity litigation. If there were, the ratio of diversity cases removed to the federal courts to the number originally filed in those courts should be falling; yet since 1970 (the first year for which data are available) the ratio has risen, from 17 to 24 percent, which suggests that federal courts are becoming more attractive to diversity defendants.

Probably the most important reason for the growing diversity caseload that does not have to do with the interaction of inflation with an unchanged amount-in-controversy requirement has been an expansion of plaintiffs' rights under state law, paralleling the expansion of plaintiffs' rights under federal law. Comprehensive state court statistics are unavailable, but it has been estimated that between 1977 and 1981, civil filings in state trial courts rose by 22 percent and criminal filings by 31 percent, and appeals rose by 30 percent.[53] These figures are comparable

---

51. The Institute of Judicial Administration's Calendar Status Study, 1954–1971, indicates that the waiting period grew about 50 percent between those years, but this is a very rough estimate.

52. See Clark, supra note 1, at 80–81, and Table 4.1 in the next chapter.

53. See Victor E. Flango and Mary E. Elsner, "The Latest State Court Caseload Data: An Advance Report," 7 State Ct. J. (Winter 1983), at 16, 20 (table 2), 22 (table 4). From National Court Statistics Project, State Court Caseload Statistics: Annual Report 14 (1979),

to those for diversity filings in the same period, and make it hard to resist the inference that the great growth in federal litigation since the early 1960s is part of a larger, and poorly understood, national phenomenon.

In this connection it is interesting—and sobering—to speculate about what the caseload of the federal district courts would be today if the federal courts had not enlarged the rights of state and federal prisoners, if Congress and the courts had not enlarged the rights of people claiming violations of their civil rights, and if Congress had adjusted the minimum-amount-in-controversy requirement for diversity cases to keep pace with the falling value of the dollar. The adjustments implied by these assumptions—namely, subtracting the total increase in civil rights and prisoner cases and 33 percent of the increase in diversity cases—yield an estimate of district court filings in 1983 of 210,034 cases, which is more than 75 percent of what the filings actually were and more than two and a half times what they were in 1960.

I shall now try to account for the growth in the caseload of the courts of appeals. The 316 percent increase in the number of administrative appeals shown in Table 3.9 seems at first glance an obvious symptom of the growth of the administrative state and hence easy to explain; but this is only partly true. In 1960 two agencies, the Tax Court and the National Labor Relations Board, accounted for three-quarters of these appeals. (There were 737 appeals in all; 203 came from the Tax Court and 348 from the Labor Board.) But the Tax Court is not really an administrative agency but rather an Article I court for deciding tax cases. In 1983 the Tax Court and the Labor Board continued to be major sources of administrative appeals, with 375 and 755 cases respectively; but together they accounted for less than 40 percent of the total. With the addition of one other agency, the Immigration and Naturalization Service, the second biggest source of administrative appeals that year after the Labor Board, the aggregate percentage rises to 50 percent. The remaining cases are scattered across a large number of agencies.

---

and U.S. Department of Justice, Bureau of Justice Statistics, *Special Report: State Court Caseload Statistics* (February 1983), I calculated that between 1975 and 1981 the increase in appeals filed in state courts was 53.5 percent. Data for longer periods are not available, at least on a nationwide basis, though it is at least suggestive that the number of judges in major state trial courts almost doubled between 1966–1967 and 1978–1979 (from 3,679 to 6,930); see Council of State Governments, *Book of the States 1982–1983*, at 254-55 (1982). Finally, incomplete data suggesting large increases in state appellate caseloads since 1960 are reported in Paul D. Carrington, Daniel J. Meador, and Maurice Rosenberg, *Justice on Appeal* 4-5 (1976), and in Stephen L. Wasby, Thomas B. Marvell, and Alexander B. Aikman, *Volume and Delay in State Appellate Courts: Problems and Responses* 13 (1979). And see *id.* at 17–22 for useful references to other studies of state appellate caseloads.

But to look only at administrative review proceedings brought directly in the courts of appeals is to miss a good deal of the impact of the growth of the administrative state on those courts. Many administrative review proceedings are brought in the district courts in the first instance, with a right of appeal by the losing party to the court of appeals. In 1960, 160 cases got into the courts of appeals by that route. No total figure is obtainable for 1983, but the two most important subcategories—social security cases and environmental cases—are listed and together accounted for 1,081 appeals. If Tax Court cases are subtracted in both years, and administrative review proceedings originating in district courts added, the increase in administrative agency cases in the courts of appeals between 1960 and 1983 is 421 percent (from 724 to 3,775 cases). In fact this understates the true figure, since some appeals from district court administrative review proceedings are not listed separately in the 1983 statistics.

I want to look more carefully at one component of this increase, the 141 percent rise in the number of cases from the Labor Board. Although there have been some significant changes in the statutes administered by the Board during this period, none is fundamental, and the unionized sector has been declining as a fraction of all workers; even in absolute numbers it has increased only moderately. Yet between 1960 and 1980 the number of complaints of unfair labor practices committed by employers made to the Board quadrupled.[54] Either employees have become more prone to complain or, as Professor Weiler argues, employers have become more prone to violate the National Labor Relations Act.[55] Whatever the explanation, it cannot be a change in law or the growth of the underlying activity. This is further evidence that the caseload would have grown faster in the past quarter-century than in the preceding one even if Congress and the courts had not been active in creating new rights, though not so much faster. The rate of increase in the number of appeals in Labor Board cases is much lower than the increase in the total number of administrative appeals (141 percent versus 421 percent); the "excess" growth probably reflects the expansion of existing agencies, the creation of new ones, and the judge-made ex-

54. See Paul Weiler, "Promises to Keep: Securing Workers' Rights to Self-Organization under the NLRA," 96 *Harv. L. Rev.* 1769, 1780 (1983) (table II, based on data from NLRB annual reports).

55. See *id.* at 1780 n.34, indicating that the fraction of complaints found to be meritorious has increased despite the tremendous increase in the number of complaints. Further evidence for Weiler's conjecture is that the percentage of NLRB orders enforced in full by the courts of appeals rose from 43.2 percent in 1960 to 63.9 percent in 1981, and the percentage set aside fell from 16 to 13.8 percent. *NLRB Ann. Rep. 1960,* at 199 (table 19); *NLRB Ann. Rep. 1981,* at 224 (table 19A).

pansion in the concept of who is an "aggrieved" person with standing to complain about administrative action, rather than merely an increased propensity to complain about violations of law.

With regard to appeals from the district courts to the courts of appeals, any change in caseload can be viewed as the product of two factors: change in the district courts' caseload—of which no more need be said—and change in the appeal rate from the district courts. If the appeal rate rises, the court of appeals caseload will rise faster than the district court caseload; if the appeal rate falls, the court of appeals caseload will rise more slowly or will fall. This makes the appeal rate of considerable interest; but unfortunately, the Administrative Office of the U.S. Courts does not compute appeal rates. The reason is understandable: the denominator of an appeal rate is the number of appealable orders, and this number is hard to come by. Although the general rule in the federal system is that only final decisions are appealable from the district courts to the courts of appeals, the concept of "finality" is exceedingly complex, and many nonfinal orders are appealable while many final orders (for example, dismissal pursuant to a settlement) are not. Criminal cases provide additional complications.

A better approximation to the real appeal rate than the one used in Table 3.9 is presented in Table 3.10. Since criminal defendants who plead guilty or *nolo contendere* cannot as a rule appeal their convictions, and since the government rarely appeals an adverse determination in a criminal case, I use the number of defendants convicted in 1983 after a trial as the denominator in computing the criminal appeal rate in Table 3.10, and the number of criminal appeals filed in the courts of appeals in 1983 as the numerator. Since the notice of appeal, which formally commences the appeal, must be filed within 60 days of the final judgment in a criminal or other government case and 30 days in a private case, the use of district court termination and court of appeals commencement figures in the same year is a defensible procedure. For civil cases I use district court terminations involving some action by the court, thus eliminating the significant fraction of cases that are dismissed by agreement of the parties. I would have preferred to use contested terminations, but unfortunately the Administrative Office stopped collecting the necessary information after 1960; for 1960 I subtracted dismissals by consent to get an approximation to the number of cases in which there was some court action. Contested terminations would be a much better proxy for civil appealable orders and would produce a higher estimate of the appeal rate—for 1960, 25 percent rather than 8.8 percent. Consistently with this method of estimation, Professor Jerry Goldman found in an unpublished study that the appeal

Table 3.10. Appeal rates, 1960, 1982, 1983 (in percentages)

Type of case	1960	1982	1983
Criminal	25.1	98.1	94.5
Civil	8.8	18.0	17.6
U.S. Civil	5.9	18.7	17.2
Condemnation	N.A.	N.A.	N.A.
FLSA	3.0	6.9	9.3
Contract	0.5	1.6	3.0
Tax	24.1	20.7	22.0
Civil rights	N.A.	61.2	58.9
Postconviction	21.6	34.0	34.2
FTCA	7.6	23.5	25.4
Forfeiture and penalty	1.7	7.0	9.0
Social security laws	N.A.	9.7	9.6
Private	12.4	17.8	17.8
Diversity	10.7	12.4	12.5
Admiralty	13.0	17.7	8.6
Antitrust	66.2	41.1	43.1
Civil rights	24.6	32.9	30.8
Intellectual property	22.6	21.5	14.9
FELA	11.6	5.1	6.0
Postconviction	13.3	18.8	20.2
Jones Act	6.7	8.5	9.1
LMRA	58.2	19.4	20.5
RLA	N.A.	N.A.	N.A.
Total[a]	10.3	21.4	20.9

a. Weighted average.

rate from district courts to the courts of appeals rose from 19 percent in 1951 to 23 percent in 1960, and then (with a very slight deceleration) to 28 percent in 1970.[56] Unfortunately his study did not extend beyond 1970, and there are no data on which to base a comparable estimate for the present.

Although the appeal rates in Table 3.10 are naturally much higher than those in Table 3.9, the proportionate relationships both between

56. Jerry Goldman, "Measuring a Rate of Appeal" 8 (Fed. Judic. Center, October 9, 1973, unpublished) (table II). Carrington, supra note 1, at 1102 found 1,730 appeals in a sample of 10,800 final judgments in U.S. civil cases in 1972, which translates into an appeal rate of 16 percent, slightly lower than the 1982 and 1983 figures in Table 3.9.

years and across subject-matter categories are similar. (I added another year, 1982, to Table 3.10 to see whether the figures might fluctuate sharply from year to year; generally, as can be seen, they did not.) Although Table 3.10 comes closer to the "real" appeal rates, if only we could measure them, both tables suggest that the key to understanding why the court of appeals caseload has grown by an astonishing 789 percent (excluding administrative appeals), while the district court caseload grew by "only" 250 percent, is that the appeal rate was rising (from 10.3 percent to 20.9 percent in Table 3.10) at the same time. We must explain *that* increase in order to discover why the court of appeals caseload has risen so much more rapidly than the district court caseload.

The explanation is clear only for the increase in the rate of criminal appeals, from 25 percent in 1960 to almost 95 percent in 1982. This increase must be largely a product of the Criminal Justice Act of 1964, which funds several thousand annual appointments of counsel in the courts of appeals and has made it possible for every federal criminal defendant to appeal his conviction—and almost every one does. Otherwise the increase in the appeal rate (in civil cases, from 8.8 to 17.6 percent) is quite mysterious. The increase is very broadly based: the rate rose in nine and fell in six subject-matter areas, and among those in which it rose steeply are several largely (though not entirely) untouched by the legal ferment of the last quarter-century—federal contract actions, federal tort claims suits, Jones Act (maritime personal injury) cases, and federal forfeiture and penalty suits. The appeal rate increased by about 20 percent in diversity cases even though Congress's failure to raise the minimum amount in controversy meant that the average stakes in diversity suits probably were smaller in real terms in 1983 than in 1960. It is not very plausible to suppose that the appeal rate has increased because district judges are committing more frequent errors. Perhaps, being more harried, they are; but the courts of appeals do not perceive this—as we have seen, the reversal rate has fallen dramatically. Thus the benefits of appealing do not seem to be rising; at the same time the costs of an appeal do not seem to be falling. It is not as if the appeal were a new institution, so that it would take some time for people to catch on to its potential; the courts of appeals were 69 years old in 1960. Perhaps what is happening is that the law is becoming more uncertain, and therefore less predictable, as a result of increasing complexity and, possibly, increased judicial activism (about which more in Chapter 7). A lawyer who loses in the trial court may know that reversal rates have fallen, but he may think he has a good chance of getting a reversal in *his* case—a better chance than he really does. If these mistakes are more common then they used to be—and there is every reason why they should be—this would explain a higher appeal rate in the face of a higher reversal rate.

I turn finally and briefly to the Supreme Court. In 1960 almost half the applications for Supreme Court review came from the federal courts of appeals; by 1982 the proportion had risen to almost 70 percent. The rest came from state appellate courts. We do not know how many cases were terminated at the final appellate level in the state courts in either year, but we do know the numbers for the federal courts of appeals. Terminations after argument or after submission without argument would be the principal candidates for application for Supreme Court review, and if we assume that all the applications came from these categories, then applications were filed in 33 percent of court of appeals cases so decided in 1960 and in only 26 percent in 1982. This decline may reflect the reduction in the probability that the application would be granted—from 15 percent in 1960 to 7 percent in 1982—which lowered the expected value of seeking Supreme Court review.[57] The decline in the rate of applying to the Supreme Court supports the economic model but highlights the question why the decline in the court of appeals reversal rate during the same period should not have dampened the enthusiasm for appealing district court decisions to the courts of appeals; the expected value of such appeals also fell.

Although the rate of applying for Supreme Court review fell, the absolute number of applications to review federal court of appeals decisions rose markedly—from 870 in 1960 to 2,841 in 1982. The dampening effect exerted by the reduced probability that certiorari would be granted was overwhelmed by the enormous increase in the pool of decisions from which certiorari could be sought.

To conclude, my analysis of the causes of the caseload growth in the federal courts since 1960 provides, I am afraid, only an insecure foundation for attempting to predict future changes in the caseload.[58] The causality is complex and not fully understood. The only legislation on the horizon that would greatly expand federal rights is a proposal to allow both prosecutors and defendants to appeal the length of a federal criminal sentence; the implications for the workload of the courts of appeals are staggering. The Supreme Court and lower federal courts continue to create new federal rights, though less enthusiastically than in the 1960s and the early 1970s. It is possible that there is a temporary glut of lawyers, which could result in an increase in litigation as they

57. McLauchlan, supra note 1, at 60 (figure 3.12) has a detailed chart of this decline.
58. For a pessimistic view of caseload forecasting in general, see the useful survey *Forecasting the Impact of Legislation on Courts,* supra note 1.

lower their fees in an attempt to compete for business. These are only a few of the factors affecting the caseload picture. All that is clear is that the federal caseload cannot be allowed to grow for long at the extraordinary rates of the past quarter-century without putting an end to the federal court system in its present form. At an annual rate of growth of 5.6 percent—the average rate of growth of the district courts' docket since 1960—it will take only ten years (from 1983) for their annual case filings to amount to almost 500,000, and by the year 2000 they will be 700,000. The corresponding figures for the courts of appeals, based on their average annual growth rate since 1960 of 9.4 percent, are 73,000 and 136,236, and for the Supreme Court, based on its rate (3.6 percent), 5,983 and 7,664. Of course, these are entirely mechanical extrapolations. Since we do not have a very clear idea of the causes of caseload growth, we cannot predict future growth with any confidence.

4

Consequences

THIS CHAPTER will trace the effects, so far as they are visible, of the caseload explosion.[1] Volume alone lacks policy significance; but volume can have profound consequences for the effective performance of a court system.

THE EXPANSION OF THE FEDERAL COURT SYSTEM

In a private market, an unexpected rise in demand has two effects (provided the producers are operating at capacity), as illustrated in Figure 4.1. In the short run, when (by definition) producers are unable to expand their productive capacity, price rises to ration demand to the existing fixed supply. In the long run, when producers can expand their capacity, supply will increase to accommodate (in part anyway) the higher demand and price will fall, though not necessarily to its level before demand rose. However, the federal court system's response to the steep and unexpected rise in the demand for its services that began in about 1960 (a rise approximated by the increase in case filings) has not followed this conventional pattern. Although the fee for filing a pleading in the district courts has risen from $15 to $60, which is more than the rate of inflation, it remains too low to have any appreciable effect in limiting demand. The filing fee in the courts of appeals is also trivial and has not even increased enough to offset inflation (it was $25 in 1960 and is $65 today)—and this despite the fact that demand has

1. For excellent previous studies on the consequences of the caseload explosion, now unfortunately somewhat out of date, see Paul D. Carrington, Daniel J. Meador, and Maurice Rosenberg, *Justice on Appeal* (1976); Henry J. Friendly, *Federal Jurisdiction: A General View* (1973); Paul D. Carrington, "Crowded Dockets and the Courts of Appeals: The Threat to the Function of Review and the National Law," 82 *Harv. L. Rev.* 542 (1969).

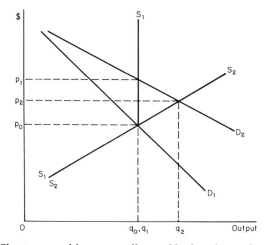

Figure 4.1 Short-run and long-run effects of higher demand on prices.

risen much faster in the courts of appeals than in the district courts. The fee for filing a petition for certiorari has doubled, from $100 to $200, again not enough to offset the nearly threefold increase in the price level. And the many indigent suitors pay no fee in any court.

The price of access to all federal courts has been allowed to fall as a result of the impact of inflation on the minimum amount in controversy required in diversity cases, unchanged since 1958, and (of much less importance) the abolition of the requirement in federal-question cases. The usual method of nonprice rationing of a good or service—the queue—has not been used to any appreciable extent either, though it is a time-honored method of equilibrating the supply of judicial services to the demand for them, and one that is apparently in use in the state courts. As shown in Table 4.1, federal court queues are only trivially longer today then they were 23 years ago (note particularly the last row in the table), when the caseload of the federal courts was much lighter.

Thus, without ever clearly acknowledging their policy, the people who control the federal court system (congressmen, executive branch officials, judges, and judicial administrators) have acted consistently over this period as if they had an unshakable commitment to accommodating any increase in the demand for federal judicial services without raising the price of those services, directly or indirectly, in the short run or in the long run. In terms of Figure 4.1, it is as if policymakers were committed to maintaining price p_0 no matter how far to the right D shifted. The political appeal of this response is evident: it shifts the

Table 4.1. The federal court queue, 1960 and 1983 (in months)

Court	Queue	1960	1983
District	Filing to disposition of cases tried	17.8	19.0
Court of appeals	Notice of appeal to disposition	8.3	11.1
Court of appeals	Filing in district court to disposition in court of appeals	23.4	24.8

costs of dealing with the increase in the demand for federal judicial services from the current users (realistically, the trial lawyers as well as the actual litigants)—who could be expected to protest vociferously if they had to pay more for using the federal courts, whether in the form of explicit user fees, queues, or restrictions on the federal courts' jurisdiction—to a diffuse group consisting of the taxpayers who have to pay for a larger federal court system, future litigants, and (in the end) all who are subject to the laws administered in the federal courts.

Two types of cost of responding to increased demand by increasing supply but not price should be distinguished. One is the direct monetary cost, which is relatively small; although the budget of the federal courts has grown very rapidly in recent years, it is still a drop in the bucket by the standards of modern American government. The other and greater cost is the reduction in the quality of federal judicial services. This cost of expanding the federal court system to whatever size is necessary to meet the demand for its services, at no increase in price to the users, is widely diffused and can be deferred for a time, though the time may be running out. The focus of this chapter will be on the second type of cost, the potential degradation in quality of the federal courts.

Figure 4.1 supplies a helpful framework for the analysis. The vertical slope of the short-run supply curve (S_1) reflects the difficulty (for clarity, impossibility is assumed) of expanding output in the short run, when productive capacity is fixed, assuming that capacity is being fully utilized when the unexpected surge in demand hits. In the longer run new production capacity can be added and costs will fall. But some of the inputs needed for this new capacity may be in permanently short supply. If so, the effort of producers to bid inputs away from alternative users will drive up price, and as a result the industry's costs at its new level of output will not fall back to their level before the industry expanded. If new increments of demand could instead be accommodated by adding productive units—new factories, say—having identical costs to the old ones, then the long-run supply curve (S_2) might be flat. In that event the price of the product at the new long-run equilibrium of demand and supply would be the old price even though output was much greater.

At first glance it might appear that the second model of supply (infinite supply elasticity in the long run) better describes the federal (or any) judicial system than the first. The argument runs as follows. Increases in demand can be accommodated, with a short lag, simply by adding judges, the basic productive unit of the system—the basic judicial "factory." Judges are not interchangeable, but since the present system of appointment is not primarily a merit system, there is no reason why an expansion in the number of judges should result in a lowering of their quality. If the attractiveness of a judgeship is reduced by increasing the number of judges, as beyond some point it would be, the effect can be offset by an increase in salary, with minimal budgetary consequences.

This, however, is *not* the model that has guided the federal court system in responding to the crisis of demand. No effort has been made to expand the number of judges in proportion to the increase in caseload. The number of district judges has not tripled, although it has doubled, so that at this level the increase in the number of judges has come closest to keeping pace with the increase in caseload. The number of court of appeals judges has not increased eightfold; it has not quite doubled. Thus, in both the district courts and the courts of appeals the caseload per judge has risen sharply since 1960, as shown in Figure 4.2. And of course the number of Supreme Court justices has not increased at all. Nor have the salaries of federal judges risen disproportionately to offset any diminution in status resulting from the large number of federal judges; their salaries have fallen, in real terms, since 1960.

The principal method of accommodating the caseload increase has been to expand the number of supporting personnel in the federal court. Not only do the hundreds of federal bankruptcy judges have more powers than their predecessors, the referees in bankruptcy; but the period since 1960 has seen the creation of a new and important federal judicial officer called a magistrate, of whom there are now almost 500 (about half are full-time), operating as a kind of junior district judge. There has also been a big expansion in the number of law clerks, and the creation of a kind of floating law clerk called a staff attorney. Many district judges and court of appeals judges now also use "externs," who are law students working as junior law clerks in exchange for course credit from their law schools; this practice was unknown in 1960.

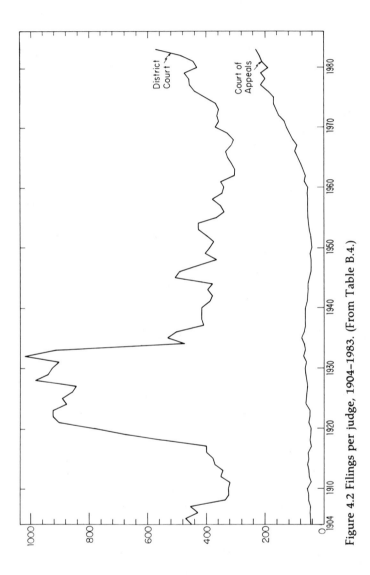

Figure 4.2 Filings per judge, 1904–1983. (From Table B.4.)

There are two reasons, I conjecture, why the increased demand for federal judicial services has not been met simply by increasing the number of judges in proportion to the increase in caseload. The first, and I think less important, is that it is politically impossible to raise federal judges' salaries to a level that would attract high-quality candidates, in the number required, in the relatively unattractive conditions of employment that would exist if there were as many federal judges as the caseload increases in recent years would justify. The problem would be particularly acute at the court of appeals level. There were 68 circuit judgeships in 1960; there are 132 today; there would be 517 if the number of judges had kept pace with the caseload. The individual judge's influence and status would be significantly diminished by such numerosity, and it is not very likely that Congress would respond by substantially increasing judicial salaries. Court of appeals judges are already among the highest paid officials in the federal government, and if their salaries were raised substantially, many other federal salaries would have to be raised as well. The public—a public increasingly disenchanted with government—probably would not stand for it. Of course, as there are more than 600,000 lawyers in the United States it would in principle be easy to find 132 highly qualified lawyers to serve as federal court of appeals judges. But when political criteria are taken into account, it is not so easy to fill all of these jobs with highly qualified persons at existing salaries; it will be harder when there are four times as many jobs to fill.

The other and more important reason why the number of judges has not been increased in proportion to the caseload increase takes us back to Chapter 1. A judicial system that has a law-creation as well as a dispute-resolution function is a pyramid; as the base expands, it becomes larger and larger relative to the apex, which in this case is the Supreme Court and which we may take to be fixed in size. It is essential that the intermediate appellate courts maintain a reasonable quality and uniformity of federal law in order to minimize the occasions on which the Supreme Court must intervene. But expanding the courts of appeals is difficult, too: one cannot just add judges to each of these courts, because beyond a certain point there are too many judges to deliberate effectively. Although the judges sit in panels of three, the full court must, in order to prevent different panels from deciding cases inconsistently, maintain a credible threat to rehear a case en banc if the panel deviates from the law of the circuit; and that threat becomes less credible when the number of judges reaches the level, conventionally taken to be nine, beyond which the deliberations of a court come increasingly to resemble those of a legislature.[2] If nine is the maximum feasible number of judges in each of the 12 courts of appeals (ignoring the Federal Circuit), that would imply an upper limit of 108 circuit judges. There are already 132 (ignoring vacancies, on the one hand, and senior judges, on the other).[3]

It might seem that this problem could readily be overcome by dividing existing circuits to create new ones, as was done two years ago in creating the Eleventh Circuit out of the Fifth. But it is doubtful how much more the device can be used. There is first the lumpiness in the demand for federal judicial services. If the Ninth Circuit, the largest in number of circuit judgeships with 23, were divided into two circuits, one limited to California, the California circuit would still have 18 circuit judges. And it would not be a good idea to have a circuit coterminous with a single state. This would impair the perspective that judges obtain by mingling with judges and lawyers from states other than their own, would reduce the ability of federal courts to transcend local prejudices and parochial outlooks, and would give disproportionate power to the senators (more likely, one of the senators) of a single state; they would largely control the staffing of an entire federal circuit. Even more important, increasing the number of regional circuits beyond the existing 12 would, by increasing the number of conflicts between circuits, increase the workload of the Supreme Court—the ultimate bottleneck in the federal court system.

An alternative approach is to reduce the number of judges who participate in en banc rehearings. This is done automatically today to a certain extent, because many circuits rely heavily on the services of visiting judges, who are ineligible to participate in rehearings en banc. But

2. See Reports of Proceedings of the Judicial Conference of the U.S. 15 (1964); Carrington, Meador, and Rosenberg, supra note 1, at 161–163; Allen Betten, "Institutional Reform in the Federal Courts," 52 Ind. L.J. 63, 78–79 (1976); Carrington, supra note 1, at 584; Daniel J. Meador, "The Federal Judiciary—Inflation, Malfunction, and a Proposed Course of Action," 1981 Brigham Young U.L. Rev. 617, 643–644. See also Justice Story's reaction in 1838 to the enlargement of the Supreme Court to nine justices, quoted in John R. Schmidhauser, Judges and Justices: The Federal Appellate Judiciary 118 (1979). Granted, there has been no systematic analysis of the difference between a 9-man and an 11-man court (the objection to an even number is obvious), though there is an interesting literature on the psychology of small-group interactions that might be consulted. See, for example, Bobby R. Patton and Kim Griffin, Problem-Solving Group Interaction 86–88 (1973); Robert T. Golembiewski, The Small Group: An Analysis of Research Concepts and Operations 146–149 (1962). But the fact that no one proposes to enlarge the Supreme Court beyond nine is pretty good evidence that a greater number is unwieldy for judicial deliberation.

3. On the serious problems of maintaining intracircuit uniformity in the courts of appeals under present-day conditions, see Stephen L. Wasby, "Inconsistency in the United States Courts of Appeals: Dimensions and Mechanisms for Resolution," 32 Vanderbilt L. Rev. 1343 (1979).

the heavy use made of visiting judges by the courts of appeals is itself one of the costs of the overloading of those courts. In 1983 visiting judges (mostly senior judges, and most of those senior district judges) sat on 10.9 percent of court of appeals panels.[4] (There are no statistics for 1960.) And this figure is misleading, because visiting judges rarely are used on cases that are not orally argued (that is, the less important cases). In my sample of published court of appeals opinions (see Table 3.6), visiting judges sat on 31 percent of the panels in 1983, compared to 22 percent in 1960. (These figures exclude en bancs.) Another study of court of appeals opinions, employing a much larger sample, found, surprisingly, that visiting judges sat on 47.3 percent of all the panels between 1965 and 1969.[5]

Although some use of visiting judges is entirely appropriate,[6] the extent of that use is a matter of concern. In a court with nine or more active members and heavy use of senior and visiting senior judges, almost every panel will be different, and the difficulty of maintaining some reasonable uniformity of law within the circuit correspondingly increased. But if the number of judges in each circuit were enlarged to the point where the services of visitors were no longer needed, the en banc procedure would be even more unwieldy than it is. For several years senior circuit judges were not allowed to participate in rehearings en banc, even to review decisions of panels of which they had been members in their own circuits. The law was changed in 1982 to allow seniors to participate in those en bancs.[7] There is no indication that in making this change (which restored a former practice) Congress gave any thought to the effect, slight though it might be, that the change would have on the utility of the en banc procedure in maintaining uniformity of decisional law within the larger circuits.

It might not be a terrible idea, though I hesitate to call it a good idea, to confine eligibility to participate in en bancs to the nine most senior judges of the circuit in active service; the remaining judges would become eligible as they acquired seniority. But no doubt there would be violent objection to constituting a corps of "second-class" active circuit

4. Administrative Office of U.S. Courts, *Federal Court Management Statistics 1983*, at 14. With only isolated exceptions, the only active judges who currently sit as visiting judges on courts of appeals are either district judges of the same circuit or circuit judges of the new Federal Circuit.

5. Justin J. Green and Burton M. Atkins, "Designated Judges: How Well Do They Perform?" 61 *Judicature* 358, 363 (1978).

6. Green and Atkins, supra note 5, found no statistical indications that visiting judges were not performing adequately in the period studied.

7. See Federal Courts Improvement Act of 1982, § 205, 96 Stat. 53, amending 28 U.S.C. § 46(c).

judges. The Ninth Circuit has adopted a democratic version of this idea by providing for rehearing by special panels consisting of the chief judge of the circuit and 10 active judges chosen at random from the remaining 22.[8] The random drawing is repeated for each new case and a further rehearing by the entire court is possible. The procedure is too new for a definitive evaluation. But ingenious as it is, it suffers from the same deficiency as the proposed Intercircuit Tribunal (discussed in the next chapter)—a lack of intrinsic authority. If the special panel divides closely, the parties and indeed the judges will attribute the decision to the luck of the draw rather than to the superior authority of the special panel over the original three-judge panel. Allowing the circuits to grow willy-nilly and instituting quasi-en-banc procedures is not the answer to the caseload problem of the courts of appeals. And this, coupled with the infeasibility of simply multiplying circuits, is a good reason why, even though the number of federal district judges has been allowed to rise almost as fast as the caseload and the number of court of appeals judges has been allowed to rise well above the optimum number, still most of the accommodation to the increased caseload, especially at the appellate level, has taken the form of adding parajudicial personnel. And the most important such personnel for the law-creation function of the federal courts are the law clerks and the staff attorneys.[9]

THE RISE OF THE LAW CLERK

The hiring of distinguished recent law school graduates to serve as federal judges' law clerks for a year or two became general in the 1930s. Supreme Court justices and circuit judges each had one in those days (district judges got theirs in the 1940s). The justices were each given a second clerk in 1947. In 1965 the district judges got a second; in 1970 the circuit judges got a second and the justices a third; in 1978 the jus-

8. See Judicial Council and Court of Appeals of the Ninth Circuit, "Report to Congress on the Ninth Circuit's Implementation of Section 6 of the Omnibus Judgeship Act of 1978 and Other Measures to Improve the Administration of Justice within the Ninth Circuit" 24–27 (June 1982, unpublished).

9. And constitutionally the least problematic. No one seems to think that the use of law clerks violates Article III, even though they do in a practical sense exercise a part of the judicial power of the United States yet are not, of course, Article III judges. But Congress's effort to expand the powers of bankruptcy judges created under Article I was struck down as contrary to Article III in Northern Pipeline Construction Co. v. Marathon Pipe Line Co., 102 S. Ct. 2858 (1982), and there are also challenges afoot (as yet unsuccessful) to some of the powers exercised by federal magistrates. I shall not consider any of these constitutional issues.

tices got a fourth, and in 1980 the circuit judges got a third.[10] In the 1970s the courts of appeals began hiring "staff attorneys," who are law clerks not permanently assigned to individual judges; they have raised the current ratio of law clerks to circuit judges to approximately four to one.[11] Thus, since 1960, the approximate beginning of the caseload explosion, the number of law clerks in the district courts and the Supreme Court has doubled, while the number of law clerks in the courts of appeals (including staff attorneys, who in the federal system are limited to those courts) has quadrupled. The difference parallels the greater increase in the caseload of the courts of appeals than of the district courts and the Supreme Court; a relationship between caseload growth and law-clerk growth seems plain.

I am going to discuss with somewhat more candor than is usual for a sitting judge the cost of the heavy reliance on law clerks that is implied by the high ratio of clerks to judges in today's federal courts. But I hope I will not be misunderstood as criticizing this reliance. There are a great many judges who would like nothing better than to do their own research and writing—who *did* their own research and writing before the workload pressures became overwhelming. The problem is that, except in the Supreme Court, which controls the major part of its workload (the hearing and decision of the cases that it accepts for plenary review), the caseload per federal judge has risen to the point where very few judges, however able and dedicated, can keep up with the flow without heavy reliance on law clerks, staff attorneys, and sometimes externs too. My desire is not to deplore a practice that seems forced on the judges by circumstances but to highlight a major cost of the caseload explosion.

Nor do I mean to suggest that the law clerk is merely a necessary evil. I shall come back to this important point, but for now I shall concentrate on the negatives, beginning with the difference that it makes to a judge (I am thinking particularly of circuit judges) how many law clerks he has.[12] If he has only one or two, problems of supervision and delegation are unlikely to be serious. But if he has three or four clerks, a significant amount of his time must be spent in supervising and coordinating their work. Additional secretarial assistance also becomes necessary; the judge now finds himself presiding over a staff. As more of his time becomes taken up with supervision and coordination, leav-

10. See John Bilyeu Oakley and Robert S. Thompson, *Law Clerks and the Judicial Process: Perceptions of the Qualities and Functions of Law Clerks in American Courts* 20 n.2.53 (1980).
11. See 1981 AO Ann. Rep. 69–70.
12. See Carrington, Meador, and Rosenberg, supra note 1, at 45–46.

ing less time for his conventional judicial duties, more of his judicial responsibilities must be delegated to the law clerks. The increase in delegation, by making the selection of new law clerks a more consequential decision, in turn requires the judge to spend more time on that selection. All of this comes at a time when the nondelegable judicial duties of circuit judges—reading briefs, hearing oral arguments, conferring with other judges to decide the cases heard—are increasing apace as part of the caseload explosion. The only real leeway is in the time the judge devotes to the actual preparation of his opinions; it is here that the greatest delegation of judicial responsibilities to staff can be expected to occur.

The process of delegation to law clerks (and staff attorneys) has not reached the point where the decisional function itself has been delegated. But as the ratio of law clerks to judges has grown, the tendency has been for more and more of the initial opinion-drafting responsibility to be delegated to law clerks, transforming the judge from a draftsman to an editor. Judging from the length and scholarly apparatus of Supreme Court opinions in recent years, the transformation is all but complete there. This is not altogether surprising; not only do the justices have more clerks, but the ratio of law clerks to opinions is much higher in the Supreme Court than in the courts of appeals. In the 1982 term the average justice wrote 17 signed majority opinions,[13] for which he had the assistance of four law clerks, if he wanted (one justice, Rehnquist, takes only three clerks, and another, Stevens, only two). This is a ratio of 4.25 opinions per clerk. In the same period the average circuit judge wrote almost 42 signed majority opinions (as noted in Chapter 3) and had the assistance of at most three law clerks (a few circuit judges take only two clerks). This is a ratio of 14 opinions per clerk. True, the justices write far more concurring and dissenting opinions than the circuit judges: 23 versus about 10.[14] But I shall argue in Chapter 8 that the writing of separate opinions by the justices, especially concurring opinions (of which each justice wrote an average of 8), is to some extent optional; if they were really the victims of a crushing workload they would write fewer.

The many differences between the two types of courts make any quantitative comparison problematic. The Supreme Court justices have a big screening function to perform, which the circuit judges do not, and the Supreme Court's cases are substantially more difficult on aver-

13. "The Supreme Court 1982 Term," 97 Harv. L. Rev. 1, 295 (1983) (table I).

14. The figure for the Supreme Court justices is from "The Supreme Court," supra note 13, at 295 (table I); the figure for the circuit judges is based on Table 3.6 in this book.

age than those of the courts of appeals. On the other hand, the justices have the benefit of a previous appellate opinion in every case; the luxury of choosing which cases to hear (which enables them to steer clear of many messy cases, having multiple issues or long trial records, that the courts of appeals cannot refuse to hear); the pick of the law clerks, almost all fortified in addition by a year's clerking in a lower court; and, on average, better briefs and better-prepared oral arguments, because lawyers take a case in the Supreme Court more seriously than one in a court of appeals. Moreover, the figure I gave for court of appeals opinions refers only to signed, published opinions, and an equal or greater number of cases are disposed of today without a published opinion but often with an unpublished order nearly as elaborate and as time-consuming to prepare. Also, many Supreme Court cases are difficult not because they are analytically complex but because the premises of decision are so uncertain that their outcome is indeterminate; such cases are not necessarily time-consuming to decide. Finally, and in sharp contrast to the situation in the courts of appeals, the major component of the Supreme Court's workload, the hearing and decision of argued cases (as distinct from deciding which cases to hear), is controlled by the Court itself and thus need not grow at all—and in fact has not grown as fast as the number of clerks per justice has grown. The increased delegation of the judicial function does not have the same inevitability in the Supreme Court as in the courts of appeals, and provides therefore a juster focus of criticism.

Although for a long time the polite fiction was maintained that law clerks were merely "go-fors" and "sounding boards," that time is past; the role of law clerks in opinion writing is now discussed openly, as it should be in a government that claims to rule by consent rather than by mystery. But more than an increase in candor is involved. Although no one has precise or comprehensive information on the subject, there is little doubt that law clerks do more of the opinion writing today than they did 20 or 30 years ago (this is apparent from talking with judges who have been active over this span and with former law clerks). The judges have heavier workloads and more law clerks, and opinion writing is the most time-consuming of the delegable judicial tasks. Moreover, as legal practice itself becomes more bureaucratic, fewer judges come to the bench with recent writing experience. They were supervisors in practice, and they slip easily into the role of being judicial supervisors.

Almost 10 years ago a state supreme court justice wrote: "Opinion writing by law clerks is certainly so widespread today that no symposium devoted to the duties of law clerks would be complete without some discussion of the subject."[15] Archibald Cox wrote recently of the "increasing use of law clerks who write opinions to justify their Justices' votes," and added: "Because each Justice has a number of law clerks and typically none serves more than one or two years, a heroic effort by a Justice would be required to impart unity of philosophy and authorship to the law clerks' drafts."[16] Professor Philip Kurland says that "more and more [Supreme Court] opinions are written by the law clerks rather than their Justices,"[17] and Professor Joseph Vining that Supreme Court clerks "routinely now say in private that they were the ghostwriters of one or another important opinion and that it was published with hardly a change."[18] And when circuit judges had only two law clerks, District Judge (now Circuit Judge) Alvin Rubin asked: "What are these able, intelligent, mostly young people doing? Surely not merely running citations in Shepard's and shelving the judge's law books. They are, in many situations, 'para-judges.' In some instances, it is to be feared, they are indeed invisible judges, for there are appellate judges whose literary style appears to change annually."[19] Judge Rubin is also the coauthor of the Law Clerk Handbook, which states that "the appellate court clerk's function, in its simplest terms, is to research the issues of law and fact in an appeal and to draft a working opinion for the judge, pursuant to his directions."[20] And recently Judge Wald, a very able member of the Court of Appeals for the District of Columbia Circuit, stated that court of appeals judges must use law clerks to assist in opinion drafting; she believes that the cases in her court today are so difficult and complex that a judge could draft only 12 opinions a year personally, and hence cannot do his or her job without delegating considerable opinion-drafting responsibility to law clerks.[21]

The fact that a law clerk writes an opinion draft does not by itself enable one to measure the clerk's impact on the opinion as eventually published. There is not only the judge's contribution as editor to be considered, but also the marching orders that he gives the law clerk be-

15. George Rose Smith, "A Primer of Opinion Writing for Law Clerks," 26 Vand. L. Rev. 1203 (1973).

16. Archibald Cox, Freedom of Expression 88 (1981).

17. Philip B. Kurland, Book Review, 47 U. Chi. L. Rev. 185, 197–198 (1979).

18. Joseph Vining, "Justice, Bureaucracy, and Legal Method," 80 Mich. L. Rev. 248, 252 (1981).

19. Alvin B. Rubin, "Views from the Lower Court," 23 U.C.L.A. L. Rev. 448, 456 (1976).

20. Anthony M. DiLeo and Alvin B. Rubin, Law Clerk Handbook: A Handbook for Federal District and Appellate Court Law Clerks § 1.200 (Fed. Judic. Center 1977).

21. See Patricia M. Wald, "The Problem with the Courts: Black-Robed Bureaucracy, or Collegiality under Challenge," 42 Md. L. Rev. 766, 777–778 (1983).

fore the latter sits down to write. The structure, the ideas, even the style of the opinion may be the judge's even though much of the actual drafting is the law clerk's. But it is generally true that whoever does the basic drafting of a document—a judicial opinion or anything else—will have a big impact on the final product.

Opinions drafted by law clerks tend to differ from opinions written by judges in several ways.

Style. Although, as Judge Rubin has said, delegation of opinion drafting to law clerks may result in a change of literary style with every change of law clerks, the dominant effect is stylistic uniformity rather than variety. The greater variance between opinions of the same judge is more than offset by the smaller variance among opinions of different judges. For judges draw their law clerks from a pool that is far more homogeneous than the pool of judges. The vast majority of law clerks are young, academically gifted, recent graduates of the nation's leading law schools, which provide a pretty uniform educational experience. The strongly marked individuality that traditionally characterized English and American judges and that makes the opinions of a Holmes, a Cardozo, or a Learned Hand instantly recognizable as their author's personal work is becoming a thing of the past. The result is not just a loss of flavor but a loss of information. A judge's style conveys a sense of the judge that can be used to help piece out his judicial philosophy from his opinions.

The standard opinion style that has emerged is the style of the student-written sections of the law reviews—which is not surprising when one considers who the law clerks are. The style tends to be colorless and plethoric, and also heavily given to euphemism. Thus, discrimination against men—which seems, at first glance anyway, rather an odd thing for a busy legal system to be worrying about—is called (along with discrimination against women, a more appropriate object of the law's concern) "gender-based discrimination." The rights that the current Supreme Court thinks particularly worthy of constitutional protection are called "fundamental rights," though most of them, like the right not to be discriminated against because you are a bastard (a word never used any more in judicial opinions), are not fundamental in the sense of underlying or being logically anterior to other rights. The question whether 15-year-old girls should be allowed to get abortions without having to tell their parents is put as a question of the rights of "minor women." People are not fired; they are "terminated" or "discharged." They are not sentenced to prison but "receive a sentence of incarceration." Discrimination against blacks is not forbidden; it is subject to "strict scrutiny." Discrimination against women is not disfavored; it is subject to "intermediate scrutiny." Prison inmates are "residents" and are assisted not by jailhouse lawyers but by "lay advocates." Instead of using language to highlight the things being discussed, the standard style draws a veil over reality, making it harder to see exactly what the judge is doing.

Length. Opinions written by law clerks tend to be longer than opinions written by judges. This is partly because the law clerk has more time to write than the judge (since there are more law clerks than there are judges and since the judges have many demands on their time that law clerks do not have), and partly because as a recent and academically distinguished student the law clerk may write more easily than the judge; but it is mainly because the law clerk does not know what he can leave out. Not being the judge, he is unsure what facts and reasons are essential and he naturally tends to err on the side of inclusion. And since he is not an experienced lawyer, many things are new and fresh to him that are old hat to his judge, other judges, and other readers of the opinion. However, prolixity is a very old judicial problem. As Wigmore observed years before law clerks played a significant role in opinion drafting, "The opinions often give the strong impression of being discoveries by the judges—discoveries, that is, of what *they* never knew before. The opinion exhibits conscientiously the mental lucubrations experienced in making this discovery. The lengthy opinions redundantly quote well-settled platitudes from earlier opinions—reproving old truths, which are apparently new and therefore interesting to the writers."[22] Nineteenth-century Supreme Court justices sometimes wrote opinions of staggering prolixity. Nevertheless, as we shall see, opinions today would probably be shorter if there were fewer clerks.

Candor. Almost every appellate case worth deciding in a published opinion involves some novelty and hence cannot be decided by a mere recitation of authority. But 200 years after Blackstone described the judges of the common law as "the living oracles" of the law,[23] which is to say mere transmitters, timid jurists still pretend that there is no such thing as a new case, a case of first impression—just new applications of settled principles. Law clerks usually are timid jurists (and we can be thankful for that). They do everything they can to conceal novelty and to disguise imagination as deduction—hence the heavy reliance in opinions drafted by law clerks on string citations for obvious proposi-

22. 1 John H. Wigmore, *A Treatise on the Anglo-American System of Evidence in Trials at Common Law* § 8a, at 244 (3d ed. 1940). The same language appears in a 1915 supplement to the second edition. See John H. Wigmore, *A Supplement to a Treatise on the System of Evidence in Trials at Common Law* vii (1915).

23. 1 William Blackstone, *Commentaries on the Laws of England* 69 (1765).

tions (where they are superfluous) and novel propositions (for which they are inaccurate); on quotations (too often wrenched out of context) from prior opinions; on canons of statutory construction that were long ago exploded as clichés; on truisms; on redundant adjectives and adverbs ("unbridled discretion," "inextricably intertwined," "plain meaning"); and on boilerplate of every sort.

Prolixity and lack of candor are not mere inelegances in judicial opinions. They increase the time required for reading an opinion—and most of the readers of judicial opinions are people whose time is valuable—and they reduce the opinion's usefulness as a guide to what the judges are likely to do in future cases. In this regard the heavy use in judicial opinions of quotations from other opinions seems an especially questionable practice. It is impossible to write a judicial opinion without a few general propositions in it, but to take one of those propositions and apply it in a totally different context, as so often is done, is to make the case from which it is quoted speak to an issue that almost certainly was not in the contemplation of the judges who decided that case. General statements with which no one disagrees do not decide difficult cases.

The underlying problem is that many law clerks feel naked unless they are quoting and citing cases and other authorities. They do not yet fully understand that in any case involving a novel issue (and if it is not novel, why write an opinion at all? Why not just cite the controlling cases?), the most important thing is not the authorities, which by definition do not determine the outcome of the case, but the reasoning that connects the authorities to the result. An opinion that is a string of facts, quotations, citations, and conclusions conceals the author's reasoning.

Research. Although opinions drafted by law clerks often make an ostentatious display of the apparatus of legal scholarship—string citations, copious footnotes, abundant references to secondary literature—such opinions (other than in the Supreme Court, where the ratio of law clerks to opinions is so high) may actually be less thoroughly researched than opinions written by judges. The time required to write the opinion presses on the time that the clerk would otherwise have to do research. If a circuit judge divides up the initial drafting of all his 60-odd published and unpublished opinions among three law clerks, the bulk of each clerk's time will be taken up with opinion writing. And it is not to be supposed that while this is going on the judge is sitting hunched over a LEXIS or WESTLAW terminal doing the original research for the opinion; he is busy supervising and editing. If the law clerks do not do the original research none will get done. If they lack the time they will have to depend on the briefs; and at least at the district court and court of appeals levels this will mean, all too often, dependence on inadequate research by the lawyers.

Even research is not fully delegable to law clerks. It is one thing (though itself not without perils) to rely on a law clerk to find the relevant precedents, and another to delegate to him the reading of them as well. A judge who relied for his knowledge of cases entirely on what the parties' briefs, and the opinions that his law clerks drafted for him, told him about the cases could end up with only a meager knowledge of the law.

Credibility. The less that lawyers and especially other judges regard judicial opinions as authentic expressions of what the judges think, the less they will rely on judicial opinions for guidance and authority. No doubt a brilliant opinion written by a law clerk and acknowledged as such by the judge in the first footnote of the opinion would have a certain authority by virtue of its intrinsic quality, in the same way that some books and law review articles have authority with judges. But this kind of authority is different and normally less weighty than the authority of an opinion known to reflect the thinking of the people who are doing the deciding and will continue to do so after this law clerk has left. The more the thinking embodied in opinions is done by law clerks rather than by judges, the less authority opinions will have.

I may be able to make this point clearer by distinguishing two senses of the term "holding." In a narrow sense it means the minimum rule that can be extracted from an opinion. In this sense the holding of Justice Douglas's opinion for the Supreme Court in *Griswold v. Connecticut*[24] is that states may not forbid married couples to use contraceptives. But the term is also used more broadly to describe the rule implied by whatever reasoning the court thought essential to its decision. In this sense the holding of *Griswold* is that the Bill of Rights, read as a whole, protects the rights of individuals to make certain intimate choices—including, of course, but not necessarily limited to, a right of married people to decide whether to engage in sexual intercourse for reproduction or for pleasure—which the state may not interfere with.

The broader holding depends critically on the structure, texture, and tone of the opinion itself, as distinct from the narrow holding, which, in the limit, depends on just the facts and the outcome. So the more it is sensed that an opinion is the work of the law clerk, the less attention judges and lawyers will pay to the broad holding. This will reduce the authority of judicial decisions as sources of legal guidance and will increase uncertainty and litigation.

24. 381 U.S. 479 (1965).

Greatness. It is a curious feature of the American legal system that a handful of famous judges should have made a contribution to the law so greatly disproportionate to their number.[25] But it is true; and it would be sad to think there will never be another great American judge. Yet one wonders whether an editor can be a great judge. It is not just a failure of imagination, I think, that makes me unable to visualize Oliver Wendell Holmes coordinating a team of law clerks and secretaries and polishing the drafts that the clerks submitted to him. The sense of style that is inseparable from the idea of a great judge in our tradition is unlikely to develop in a judge who does not do his own writing. People are not born great writers; they become great writers by hard work—as writers, not as editors. And the struggle to compose a coherent opinion provides a more searching test of the soundness of one's ideas than performing an editorial function does. It is all too easy to glide over the smoothly written product of an able assistant without searching out the stresses and weak joints. To write novels and to edit novels written by others are on different planes of creativity, and I think there is a similar difference in judicial creativity between writing one's own opinions and reviewing opinions written by one's law clerks.

The average appointment to the federal bench is not inferior to what it was formerly. Indeed, it is probably superior, because of the screening done by the American Bar Association; and even the upper tail of the distribution is probably no smaller than it used to be. But one wonders how many judges starting out today with equal promise to that of judges of former days will turn out to be quite so good. Most will feel they just do not have the time to do their own opinion writing; they will conceive their role from the outset as an editorial and supervisory one.

I must say a word about staff attorneys. It used to be the practice at federal administrative agencies to have centralized opinion-writing staffs rather than for each individual commissioner to have his own law clerks. The practice was much criticized,[26] and these staffs have tended in recent years to be replaced with law clerks on the judicial model. With lovely irony this movement has intersected a contrary movement in the state and federal appellate courts: the growth—called

25. It is related to the fact that, provided judicial opinions are substitutable one for another, as of course they are to some extent, a judge who is even just a little better than average will be cited disproportionately and called "great." See Sherwin Rosen, "The Economics of Superstars," 71 *Am. Econ. Rev.* 845 (1981).

26. See, for example, Louis J. Hector, "Government by Anonymity: Who Writes Our Regulatory Opinions?" 45 *A.B.A.J.* 1260 (1959). Much of Hector's discussion is applicable to the federal courts today. For example: "A paraphrase of another man's thought must always be a pallid substitute for the original thinking" (*id.* at 1263).

Table 4.2. Average length of federal appellate majority opinions

Year[a]	Supreme Court			Courts of appeals		
	Length (words)	Footnotes (no.)	Citations (no.)	Length (words)	Footnotes (no.)	Citations (no.)
1894	2,500[b]	—	—	—	—	—
1914	2,400	—	—	—	—	—
1934	2,600	—	—	—	—	—
1954	2,600	—	—	—	—	—
1960	2,500	15.2	39.3	2,300[c]	3.8[d]	12.1,[d] 12.4[e]
1969	2,000	—	—	—	—	—
1973	4,200	—	—	—	—	—
1975	4,200	—	22.7[f]	3,400[g]	—	13.8[h]
1976	3,000	—	—	—	—	—
1978	4,000	—	—	—	—	—
1980	4,100	—	—	—	—	—
1983	4,700	19.9	61.9	3,100[i]	7.0[d]	24.7[d]

a. Fiscal year for courts of appeals (ends June 30); term for Supreme Court (begins about October 1).

b. Estimates in this column are from Casper and Posner, *The Workload of the Supreme Court* 80 (1976) (table 4.7), updated using the same method, except for 1960, which is estimated from volume 363 U.S. (as are the Supreme Court footnotes and citations for that year). Supreme Court footnotes and citations in 1983 are estimated from volume 457 U.S. 1975 refers to 1974 term, and 1983 to 1982 term, for Supreme Court data.

c. Based on volume 279 F.2d. The estimate from Table 3.6, for signed opinions only (that is, excluding per curiams), is 2,900.

d. From Table 3.6.

e. From Landes and Posner, "Legal Precedent: A Theoretical and Empirical Analysis," 19 *J. Law & Econ.* 249, 257 (1976) (table 2) (1974–1975 sample).

f. From *id.* at 258 (1974–1975 sample).

g. Based on volume 517 F.2d.

h. From Landes and Posner, supra note e, at 256 (table 2) (1974–1975 sample).

i. Based on volume 701 F.2d. Estimate from Table 3.6 is 4,000.

"cancerous" in a recent article by Wade McCree[27]—of central staffs composed of what are called staff attorneys or staff law clerks.[28] Although staff attorneys have other assignments besides opinion drafting (such as assisting the judges with motions matters), and although most of their drafting is of unpublished opinions, today a significant number of published court of appeals opinions are drafted by a staff attorney rather than by a judge or one of his law clerks.

27. Wade H. McCree, "Bureaucratic Justice: An Early Warning," 129 *U. Pa. L. Rev.* 777, 787 (1981).
28. See Daniel J. Meador, *Appellate Courts: Staff and Process in the Crisis of Volume* (1974).

Several of the problems that I discussed in connection with opinion writing by law clerks are aggravated when opinion writing is done by staff attorneys, even when the staff attorneys are just as good as the regular law clerks. Since the staff attorney is not selected by the individual judge, he owes his loyalty to the court as a whole (perhaps too indistinct an entity to command much loyalty) rather than to the individual judge to whom he is from time to time assigned. There can be no assurance that the staff attorney will share the outlook and values of that judge, and he will not have a chance to acquire that outlook and those values, or at least to understand them sympathetically, by working continuously with the same judge for a substantial period of time. The staff attorney will therefore be less able to perform effectively as the judge's alter ego for opinion writing than the law clerks whom the judge picks himself and works with on a continuous rather than intermittent basis.

Table 4.2 investigates statistically the possible impact of the rise of the law clerks and staff attorneys on the output of opinions of federal appellate judges by presenting a variety of estimates of the average length of, and number of footnotes and citations in, majority opinions in the courts of appeals and Supreme Court at different times. The characteristics of the average opinion do not tell the whole story, however. Both Supreme Court justices and court of appeals judges are writing more opinions. Table 4.3 therefore presents figures on the opinion outputs and total word outputs of the average Supreme Court justice and average court of appeals judge. All signed Supreme Court opinions—majority, dissenting, plurality, and concurring—are included, except opinions in chambers and opinions (increasingly frequent) dissenting from denials of certiorari. For the courts of appeals, with their much larger output of opinions both published and unpublished, the data are harder to come by. The first two columns give the numbers of opinions and of words, respectively, but only for signed majority opinions.[29] The last column includes not only published per curiam and unpublished opinions but also an estimate of concurring and dissenting opinions (published only) based on the figures in Table 3.6.[30]

Tables 4.2 and 4.3 reveal a sharp increase in the number of both

29. Recall that for 1960 the number of opinions had to be estimated. The figure for total words in 1975 is an extrapolation from the figure in note g to Table 4.2, based on the ratio of the figures for number of words in Table 3.6 to the figures in notes c and i to Table 4.2.

30. For the number of published per curiam and unpublished opinions in 1960, I used the number in 1966, the first year for which these data are published. I used the 1960 percentage of separate opinions (15 percent) for all years up to 1975, and the 1983 percentage (19 percent) for the remaining years.

Table 4.3. Output per federal appellate judge

| Year[a] | Supreme court | | Courts of appeals | | |
	Opinions	Words (thousands)	Published majority opinions	Words in those opinions (thousands)	All opinions
1894	23	60	—	—	—
1914	32	77	—	—	—
1934	21	54	—	—	—
1954	16	34	—	—	—
1960	31	63	30	86	48
1964	23	46	—	—	—
1969	26	42	29	—	55
1972	45	116	33	—	74
1973	41	122	32	—	74
1975	39	111	37	160	68
1976	46	95	39	—	77
1978	40	112	38	—	78
1980	40	111	32	—	78
1983	39	146	42	169	95

a. 1960 is 1959 term, 1975 is 1974 term, and 1983 is 1982 term, for the Supreme Court.

opinions and words per justice or judge. For the Supreme Court, the period between 1969 and 1972—the period during which the justices each became entitled to a third law clerk—was the turning point: the number of opinions increased by about 50 percent and the number of words tripled. However, the substantial growth in the number of citations per case came later, perhaps with the addition of the fourth law clerk in 1980, although this cannot be determined from the limited data in Table 4.2. For the courts of appeals I have no estimates of the word lengths of any opinions other than signed, published majority opinions. But since it is apparent from Table 4.3 that the number of other opinions has grown much faster (from about 18 in 1970 to about 53 in 1983), the increase in total word output must be at least as great as that per Supreme Court justice, and the increase in average number of footnotes and citations has been significantly greater. This is consistent with the greater increase in the ratio of law clerks (including staff attorneys) to judges in the courts of appeals than in the Supreme Court during the period 1960 to 1983. But there does not appear to be any turning point for the courts of appeals comparable to the 1969–1972 turning point in the Supreme Court.

The figures in these two tables are quite remarkable when set against the background of the tremendous caseload growth since 1960. The growth has far outpaced the increase in the number of circuit judges, as we have seen, and there has been no increase at all in the number of Supreme Court justices. One might have thought that an increase in caseload per justice or judge would have led to a reduction in the average length of opinions, average number of footnotes and citations per opinion, and number of concurring and dissenting opinions—certainly not to an increase in any of these quantities. Although the law has become more complicated and difficult over this period—some evidence of this can be seen for the courts of appeals in Tables 3.6 and 4.6, and for the Supreme Court one has only to note the rapidly shrinking ratio of applications for review that are accepted to all applications—an increase in the difficulty of the average case simply aggravates the workload effects of an increase in caseload, and therefore should make an extravagant use of footnotes and citations even less feasible. Yet extravagant it remains. No one who reads many Supreme Court and court of appeals opinions, whether written in 1960 or 1983, can be persuaded that either court, at either time, has been economical, let alone parsimonious, in its use of footnotes and citations; or that most federal judicial opinions are, or were, tightly written. In particular, as a court of last resort, bound only by its own decisions—and rather tenuously bound, at that—the Supreme Court has no need to embellish its opinions with numerous citations. The ratio of citations and footnotes in Supreme Court to court of appeals opinions is more likely to be related to the different ratios of law clerks to opinions in the two courts (roughly 1 : 10 versus 1 : 30) than to the difference in judicial roles.

Tables 4.2 and 4.3 attest to the growth of bureaucracy in the federal court system. I do not mean "bureaucracy" in its social-scientific sense of an organization (usually governmental) that does not sell its output in a market;[31] by this test the judges themselves, even if they had no law clerks, would be bureaucrats. I mean "bureaucracy" in its popular sense of a large, unwieldy organization tenuously held together by paper. The basic response to the federal courts' caseload crisis has been to surround the judges with a corps of paper-wielding bureaucrats (fortunately, industrious and highly intelligent ones)—that is, the law clerks, who are the proximate cause of the enormous increase in the federal judicial output of separate opinions, footnotes, citations, and above all words. The law clerks have time to write and to write at

31. See, for example, Ludwig von Mises, *Bureaucracy* 47 (1944); William A. Niskanen, Jr., *Bureaucracy and Representative Government*, chaps. 1–4 (1971).

length, and they have a fondness for the apparatus of scholarship—
footnotes and citations—natural in those who have just emerged from
the academy.[32]

We have become so accustomed to the bureaucratization of government and other large institutions, and to the usages of a ghostwriting
society that run the gamut from politicians' speeches to the reading of
network television news from teleprompters by highly paid anchormen
with every appearance of spontaneity, that it may seem, and more important may be, quixotic to complain that federal judicial opinions are
increasingly the product of the judiciary's own ghostwriting bureaucracy. This development is not only the natural, but considering the alternatives an intelligent, adaptation to the caseload explosion. I only
want its costs to be understood.

In addition to the costs I have already mentioned, there is a threat to
the quality of appointments to the federal bench. Fifty years ago a federal circuit judge knew that if he was unable or unwilling to write—
himself—the opinions in the cases assigned to him, he would not be
able to hold his head up among his fellows. Now a circuit judge or Supreme Court justice who selects competent law clerks can churn out
competent judicial opinions without personal effort. The situation is
different in the district courts. A district judge cannot hide behind his
law clerks in the actual conduct of a trial. He must rule on most matters
on the spot, and if he is incompetent this will show up much faster than
incompetence on the appellate bench.[33] The bureaucratization of the
federal judiciary has also made a federal judgeship less attractive to
some of the lawyers most qualified for it. The caseload is such that few
judges can keep up with it without heavy reliance on law clerks and
staff attorneys. Many lawyers do not aspire to be editors of opinions
and supervisors of law clerks.

In emphasizing the costs of our present heavy reliance on law clerks,
I do not mean to suggest that the sole *raison d'être* of law clerks is to assist judges in coping with an impossible caseload. Law clerks would be
invaluable even if they were not necessary. Because they are generally
picked on a purely meritocratic basis while judges are not, the law clerk
system enables judges to hire assistants who in many cases have better

32. See Erwin N. Griswold, "Cutting the Cloak to Fit the Cloth: An Approach to Problems in the Federal Courts," 32 *Catholic U. L. Rev.* 787, 799 (1983). Of course I am not the
first to have discerned the growing bureaucratization of the federal court system. See
Owen M. Fiss, "The Bureaucratization of the Judiciary," forthcoming in *Yale Law Journal;*
McCree, supra note 27; and references in these articles.

33. One circuit judge is reported to have said many years ago, "Any solemn chump
can get away with being an appellate judge, but it takes an honest-to-God he-man to be a
good trial judge." Quoted in Calvert Magruder, "The Trials and Tribulations of an Intermediate Appellate Court," 44 *Cornell L.Q.* 1 (1958).

legal analytic capabilities, as well as being fresher and more energetic, than the judge himself. Moreover, a law clerk is the only person with whom a judge can discuss a case with complete freedom. There continue to be excellent judges who by rigorous direction and supervision of their law clerks manage to infuse their opinions with their own distinctive insights, thereby marrying mature wisdom to youthful brilliance. The institution can be a splendid one, but its expansion, inevitable though it may be, is bureaucratizing the federal courts. This is one of the major costs of the caseload explosion.

Although I am not alone in expressing concern with the proliferation of law clerks and staff attorneys,[34] the concern is by no means universally shared. Judge Harry Edwards, a distinguished member of the Court of Appeals for the District of Columbia Circuit, has in two recent articles mounted a spirited defense of the system.[35] The essential point he makes is that "careful judges will not allow an opinion to issue in their name until the words constituting the opinion precisely reflect their views on the proper disposition of the case."[36] I do not find this very reassuring. The qualification implicit in the adjective "careful" is surely important; and Judge Edwards does not address the temptation to judicial carelessness that comes from having a staff of eager young assistants quite willing to take responsibility from the judge's shoulders. More important, adoption is not creation. If it were, contemporary opinions would have the same feel as opinions written in the days when most judges wrote their own opinions. They do not.

It may be more than a coincidence that Judge Edwards is a member

34. For an unusually outspoken expression of this concern, see John G. Kester, "The Law Clerk Explosion," 9 *Litigation* (Spring 1983), at 20. The opening of Kester's article conveys the flavor: "Law clerks have invaded the judicial system, affecting the law, the profession, the judiciary, and the public. Law clerks have spilled over into every layer of the courts. They have changed the way the courts function by coming between the judge and the advocates. At their worst, they allow the weak judge to appear able, and they substitute a bureaucracy for the direct human quality on which justice depends. Once an institution that supplied mentors to instruct bright graduates, the clerkship has grown into a corps of post-adolescent mandarins, Judges for a Year after the fashion of *Queen for a Day*. It is one of the most disquieting changes in litigation to occur in the lifetime of most of us at the bar. Yet it is being accepted with virtually no analysis and no protest." Kester is a member of a leading Washington, D.C., law firm and a former president of the Harvard Law Review and former Supreme Court law clerk. Against his negative assessment must be set the literature, some of it downright hagiographic, referenced in Lana Caswell Gareia, "The Role and Experiences of Supreme Court Law Clerks: An Annotated Bibliography," 70 *Law Library J.* 338 (1977).

35. See Harry T. Edwards, "A Judge's View on *Justice, Bureaucracy, and Legal Method*," 80 *Mich. L. Rev.* 259 (1981); Harry T. Edwards, "The Rising Work Load and Perceived 'Bureaucracy' of the Federal Courts: A Causation-Based Approach to the Search for Appropriate Remedies," 68 *Ia. L. Rev.* 871, 882–889 (1983). See also his colleague Judge Wald's article, supra note 21.

36. *Id.* at 888.

Table 4.4.   Opinion length, footnotes, and citations, per case, D.C. Circuit, 1960 and 1983, compared to all circuits

Year	Sample	Length		Footnotes	Citations
		Pages	Words		
1960	All	3.8	2,863	3.8	12.4
1960	D.C.	2.2	1,664	3.5	7.9
1983	All	5.4	4,020	7.0	24.7
1983	D.C.	13.8	10,339	44.7	52.1

of the D.C. Circuit. In no other court has the transformation from an individual to an institutional opinion-writing style gone further. Table 4.4 depicts this transformation, comparing the D.C. Circuit cases in the two samples used in Table 3.6 with the complete samples.[37] If these results are reliable, the judicial opinion as traditionally understood has given way in the D.C. Circuit to the 10,000-word, 45-footnote, 52-citation essay—eclipsing in all but number of citations the Supreme Court itself (see Table 4.2). True, the D.C. circuit judges produce, as one would expect, fewer majority opinions than the average for the entire federal court of appeals system—only 22 per judge in 1983. But if the figures in Table 4.4 are representative, this still translates into upwards of 200,000 words per judge per year (and this excludes concurring and dissenting opinions). One can imagine (with some difficulty) one person writing this much—the equivalent of about a 400-page book—every year, year in and year out; but it is more than difficult to imagine the same person finding 200,000 words written by law clerks that exactly express his views. And while the cases that the D.C. Circuit decides today are substantially more complex on average than those it decided 23 years ago (in part because the circuit lost its local jurisdiction during this period, and in part because administrative regulation,

37. Because of the very small size of the D.C. Circuit subsample in the 1983 sample—four cases—I added the rest of the D.C. Circuit cases in the volume of F.2d (698) that I used to construct that sample. That gave me seven D.C. Circuit cases for 1983, compared to eight for 1960. Obviously these two samples are still too small to permit confident inferences to be drawn. Gordon Bermant, Patricia A. Lombard, and Caroll Seron, "The Cases of the United States Court of Appeals for the District of Columbia Circuit" 33 (Fed. Judic. Center 1982) (table 18), found an average of 37.1 citations in a sample of 48 D.C. Circuit opinions from fiscal 1980. This is lower than my figure, but the authors counted a case cited more than once as one citation (see *id.* at 18), whereas I would have counted it as a separate citation every time it was cited. Their study also reports length of opinions in pages (see *id.* at 33, table 18)—but without making clear how long the pages are (see *id.* at 49).

which now supplies the bulk of the cases that the D.C. Circuit reviews, has become more complex), the growth in complexity cannot explain all or even most of the growth in the length and scholarly appurtenances of the opinions. Much of it must be a result of the transformation in the character of the judicial opinion that the fourfold increase in law-clerk and staff-attorney assistants per judge has brought about.

On one point, however, Judge Edwards and I agree: further increases in the number of law clerks and staff attorneys per judge would be counterproductive.[38] The federal judicial caseload will continue to grow, and increasing the ratio of assistants to judges has been the principal means by which the system has coped with the caseload growth of the last two decades; it is widely agreed that we can no longer meet future growth in the same way.

OTHER CONSEQUENCES

The change in the judge's role brought about by the great expansion in the corps of law clerks and staff attorneys is only one consequence of the caseload explosion and the concomitant determination of the people who control the federal court system to meet every increase in demand for federal judicial services with a corresponding increase in supply. I have already mentioned the difficulty of maintaining reasonable uniformity of federal decisional law in the face of a large increase in the number of judges, which has made en banc review of panel decisions increasingly difficult and has reduced the Supreme Court's ability to supervise law creation by the lower federal courts. Still another consequence has been the curtailment of both the length and the frequency of oral argument. Although the Supreme Court still hears oral argument in most of the cases that it decides on the merits, the length of the standard argument has been chopped in half since 1960—from an hour to a half-hour per side. Naturally the curtailment of oral argument has been even more drastic in the courts of appeals. Once virtually all appeals were argued orally; now fewer than a third are.[39] The length of the average oral argument has declined precipitously; today it is under 20 minutes per side. (In 1960 it was 45 minutes to an hour per side.)

Although the average quality of oral argument in federal courts (including the Supreme Court) is not high, the value of oral argument to judges is high. This is not just because it gives the judge a chance to ask

38. So at least I read 68 *Ia. L. Rev.* at 889–890, though these pages can alternatively be read as allowing room for a modest further increase in judicial staffs.
39. Estimated from 1982 AO Ann. Rep. 84 (table 5), 87 (table 8).

questions of counsel, though this is very important, but also because it provides a period of focused and active judicial consideration of the case. The longer the argument, the more time the judge has to think about the case. Of course there are diminishing returns to oral argument, and judges should not hesitate to terminate an argument when they no longer find it productive. But the imposition of extremely short and stringent time limits, and the elimination of oral argument altogether in many cases where it would be productive (not all: oral argument in most pro se cases, that is, cases where the appellant is not represented by counsel, is a waste of the judges' time) have been costly if perhaps inevitable adaptations to the caseload explosion.

The curtailment of oral argument is closely associated with another adaptation: the unpublished opinion. Perhaps because an unargued case is thought less likely to be decided well than an argued one, unpublished opinions have become the usual method of disposing of appeals that are not orally argued—and a common method of disposing of argued cases as well. The unpublished opinion is both a consequence of the caseload explosion and a symptom of the effect of the explosion on quality. It deserves careful attention as a symptom of the overload of the federal courts today.[40]

It used to be that all opinions in federal court of appeals cases were published by the West Publishing Company in the *Federal Reporter*, or its successor, *Federal Reporter, Second* ("F.2d"), though some of these opinions were "one-liners" merely announcing the outcome of the appeal. With the rapid increase during the 1960s in the number of appeals, both absolute and relative to the number of judges, the practice of universal publication began to be questioned. Under prodding by the Judicial Conference of the United States, all the circuits adopted during the 1970s rules limiting publication to opinions meeting various criteria that are intended to identify an opinion likely to have precedential significance.[41]

These rules are sometimes defended on the ground that before they were promulgated, too many unimportant opinions were being published. How likely is it that this belief is correct? One mark of an unimportant opinion is that it is never cited in another judicial decision, so one way of estimating the incidence of unimportant opinions is by de-

40. The considerable—and almost entirely critical—literature on unpublished federal appellate opinions is well illustrated by Carrington, Meador, and Rosenburg, supra note 1, at 35–41; William L. Reynolds and William R. Richman, "An Evaluation of Limited Publication in the United States Courts of Appeals: The Price of Reform," 48 *U. Chi. L. Rev.* 573 (1981); Daniel N. Hoffman, "Nonpublication of Federal Appellate Court Opinions," 6 *Justice System J.* 405 (1981).

41. See Reynolds and Richman, supra note 40, at 577–579.

Table 4.5. Percentage of court of appeals opinions that had never been cited by 1976

Decade	Percentage
1890s	21
1900s	23
1910s	29
1920s	25
1930s	23
1940s	17
1950s	19
1960s	16

Note: These figures refer to signed opinions only.

termining what percentage of all opinions are never cited afterward. Table 4.5 presents estimates of these percentages for each decade of the federal courts of appeals through the 1960s, the last decade before the adoption of limited-publication rules.[42] If those rules had been motivated by concern that an increasing fraction of unimportant opinions were being published, this would imply that the 1960s were a period when a higher than average fraction of all opinions issued by the courts of appeals turned out never to be cited. But as a matter of fact the fraction of never-cited cases was lower for this decade than it had ever been—even though, since fewer years have elapsed in which cases decided then could have been cited than in which cases decided in earlier decades could have been cited, the number of never-cited cases from the 1960s is overestimated in Table 4.5. Still, even if the fraction of unimportant cases was lower in the 1960s than it had ever been, the courts of appeals were issuing more opinions than ever before, so the absolute number of unimportant cases may have been greater; this would be a reason for wanting to reduce the number of published opinions in such cases.

If the only practical consequence of the limited-publication rules

42. The source of these data is the "precedent project" of the Law and Economics Program of the University of Chicago Law School. This project, which is under the direction of Professor Jerry Goldman of Northwestern University's Political Science Department, Professor William Landes of the University of Chicago Law School, and myself, has compiled data on citations (in subsequent cases) to a random sample of 75 court of appeals opinions rendered in each year from 1891 to 1975, and also of citations (to earlier cases) in those opinions. On the study of judicial citation practices generally, see William M. Landes and Richard A. Posner, "Legal Precedent: A Theoretical and Empirical Analysis," 19 J. Law & Econ. 249 (1976).

were not publishing the old "one-liners," the rules would not be worthy of comment, especially since the information that the one-liners contained is still published; all unpublished opinions are reported in tables in F.2d that give the name of the case and the outcome of the appeal. What is new is that many appeals that formerly would have been decided with a full opinion—a per curiam or even a signed opinion—are now decided with an unpublished opinion. These are not frivolous appeals; one-line treatment would be inappropriate. They call for an opinion and they get it, but it is not published. Although these are not secret opinions, they may not (except in the Tenth Circuit) be cited by counsel as precedents in the circuit that issued them. Except in the Second Circuit there is no rule against citing them in another circuit, and this is occasionally done—though why a circuit should pay attention to the unpublished opinions of some other circuit, when it does not to its own, is hard to fathom. If the no-citation rule makes sense, each circuit should amend its rule to forbid the citation of unpublished opinions from other circuits as well as its own.

Despite the term "limited publication," the real significance of an unpublished opinion is that it is not citable as precedent. It is this that makes it not worth publishing; if unpublished opinions were citable as precedents, someone would publish them even if the federal courts got the West Publishing Company to agree not to. So when I say, following the conventional terminology, that the issue is whether to have limited or universal publication, I mean, more fundamentally, that the issue is whether there should be a class of federal appellate opinions that cannot be used as precedents. (In fact, publishers of specialized law reports, in areas such as patent, securities, and antitrust law, do include some unpublished opinions even though they still are not citable in the circuit of origin.)

The argument for publishing all opinions (other than one-liners) has several strands.

1. The unpublished opinions are not as carefully prepared as the published ones. The judge knows that an unpublished opinion will not be thrown back in his face someday as precedent for deciding a subsequent case, and that it will be largely immune from professional criticism because there is little interest in opinions that are not published and not citable. So nonpublication encourages judicial sloppiness.

2. The criteria for when an opinion shall be published are, as in the nature of the problem they must be, imprecise and nondirective; they amount to little more than saying that an opinion should not be published unless it is likely to have value as a precedent. But judges often will not know whether an opinion is likely to have such value. Hence

significant precedents—opinions whose precedential value outweighs the printing and reading costs to lawyers and other judges of having an opinion published—may be accidentally suppressed.

3. Almost by definition, all opinions have some actual or potential precedential value, because if the appeal involved no element of novelty whatsoever it could be disposed of in one line, or perhaps with a citation to a previous case or a statute. The total information value of the unpublished opinions—if they were published, and usable as precedents—would therefore not be negligible and might well outweigh the costs (in more volumes of F.2d to buy, and in more cases to retrieve and read) of publishing those opinions. No one has made a cost-benefit analysis, but there is no convincing basis for presuming that the additional costs of universal publication would exceed the benefits. A subscription to F.2d is currently $450 a year. Since unpublished opinions are shorter on average than published ones, and about 50 percent of all federal appellate opinions are unpublished, we are probably talking about $200–250 a year more per subscriber—for a good deal of information. But of course there are costs of absorbing as well as of purchasing information.

4. Despite the vast number of published opinions, most federal circuit judges will confess that a surprising fraction of federal appeals are difficult to decide, not because there are too many precedents but because there are too few on point. The increase in the number of published opinions is in major part a result of the creation of new fields and subfields of law rather than of the repeated decision of the same point. The major exception is the criminal field, where most appeals have no merit and where a smaller fraction of opinions could be published than are being published today with no great loss of information to the bar and district judges. But in civil cases greater publication would impart useful information to bench and bar—provided objection 1 could be overcome.

5. The unpublished opinion provides a temptation for judges to shove difficult issues under the rug, in cases where a one-liner would be too blatant an evasion of judicial duty.

Each strand in the above argument is impressive, but the argument as a whole has an internal contradiction. If point 1 is true—that is, if unpublished opinions, precisely because they are not going to be published, are not prepared with the same care as published opinions[43]— then points 2 through 4 are likely to hold true only if a practice of pub-

---

43. Reynolds and Richman, supra note 40, at 628, present some evidence supporting this proposition.

lishing all opinions would lead to improving the quality of opinions that are not now published. But it would do so only if point 1 were remediable—and if it were, limited-publication rules would probably not have developed. If the judges just do not have enough time to prepare a careful opinion in every nonfrivolous appeal, points 2 through 4 are greatly weakened. No one wants careless opinions to be published and to be citable as precedents; their information value would be slight— maybe even negative.

Given the workload of federal court of appeals judges today, the realistic choice is not between limited publication on the one hand, and, on the other, improving and then publishing all the opinions that are not published today; it is between preparing but not publishing opinions in many cases and not preparing opinions in those cases at all. It is a choice, in other words, between giving the parties reasons for the decision of their appeal and not giving them reasons even though the appeal is, by hypothesis, not frivolous. The latter alternative would be more attractive than it is if the preparation of unpublished opinions required a lot of a judge's time that could be reallocated to other areas of his work. But we are back to the first argument against the limited-publication system: the unpublished opinions are less carefully prepared because the judges put less time into them, not because they are lazy but because they are trying to use their limited time as productively as possible. Since the preparation of unpublished opinions is delegated to law clerks and staff attorneys, the question whether to have such opinions is a question of the opportunity costs not of judges' time but of law clerks' and staff attorneys' time. I shall not try to evaluate the trade-off between giving litigants reasons (albeit law clerks' and staff attorneys' reasons) and freeing up law clerks' and staff attorneys' time to do more work on other, and presumptively more important, cases; I am content to argue that this is the relevant trade-off and that the conventional argument against limited publication is flawed because it fails to recognize this point.

But it should be clear by now that the defense of limited publication against the arguments for universal publication depends precisely on the acknowledgment that unpublished opinions are in general inferior to published ones. The federal courts of appeals have adapted to the caseload explosion in part by reducing the quality of their output. This is an inevitable cost of the commitment to accommodate all increases in the demand for federal judicial services without raising the direct or indirect price of those services (except that a reduction in quality is a form of indirect price increase). If the caseload continues to grow in the years ahead, the quality of the federal courts will continue to decline unless major changes are made in the system.

Table 4.6. Capital stock of court of appeals precedents, 1973–1983

Year	Number of published opinions	Capital stock at end of year
1894–1973	141,188	63,839
1974	3,201	66,906
1975	3,583	67,528
1976	3,783	68,316
1977	3,686	68,978
1978	3,492	69,426
1979	3,564	69,925
1980	4,224	71,034
1981	4,752	72,603
1982	5,016	74,359
1983	5,544	76,547

Sources: William M. Landes and Richard A. Posner, "Legal Precedent: A Theoretical and Empirical Analysis," 19 *J. Law & Econ.* 249, 282 (1976) (table 6); Admin. Off. of U.S. Courts, *Federal Court Management Statistics* (various years).

Even if, contrary to what I have said so far, the federal courts could effortlessly upgrade their unpublished opinions to publishable quality, there would still be a problem with universal publication. Earlier I brushed off too quickly the costs of absorbing information, by focusing on the time and money costs of practitioners only. The time costs to the judiciary must also be considered. Granted, it is a mistake to add up all the cases that have ever been decided and conclude that it is an impossible job to sift through them all in search of the apt precedent. It is possible, thanks to the immense resources devoted to legal indexing; and it is actually less difficult than it seems, because precedents depreciate—that is, they lose their information value over time. One can measure this loss, if only very roughly, by seeing how the number of citations to a case decline with the passage of years. Professor Landes and I once used this method to estimate that the annual depreciation rate of federal court of appeals cases as precedents in these courts was 4.2 percent for the entire "capital stock" of precedents. And using this rate we then estimated that, although between 1894 (ignoring the first few years of the courts of appeals, when few decisions were rendered) and the end of 1973 those courts issued (another estimate) 141,188 published opinions, the undepreciated portion of this total stock at the end of the period was only 63,839 cases.[44] As shown in Table 4.6, where

44. See Landes and Posner, supra note 42, at 282 (table 6).

tnis estimate is brought up to date by adding to the stock at the end of 1973 the number of signed majority opinions issued in 1974, depreciating the sum by 4.2 percent, and repeating the entire process each year until 1983, the stock increased by roughly 20 percent in just ten years. One can imagine how it would have increased if all the unpublished opinions issued during that time had been published, adding greatly to the stock of precedents.

Obviously the estimates in Table 4.6 are very rough; among many other problems, the depreciation rate used is a historical rate that may have changed in the last ten years. Still, the table has some value in conveying a sense of the information overload that threatens the federal courts, and it reinforces earlier intimations that the task of decision, and not merely the number of cases, has increased. Limited publication may have more to commend it than the problems of quality that are also a consequence of unprecedented caseload pressures.

One aspect of the current nonpublication practice deserves more critical attention than it has received: the practice of routinely granting requests to publish unpublished opinions. It is questionable not only because it can lead to publication of substandard opinions but also because it can lead to bias in the creation of precedents. Institutions with recurrent litigation in particular areas—government agencies, insurance companies, railroads, and so forth—sometimes find it worth their while to review unpublished opinions systematically and request publication of those that favor their litigation interests. Unless their opponents are also repeat litigants with an interest in precedent, an unrepresentative sample of unpublished opinions will be given precedential status through publication, and the weight of precedent in particular areas will be distorted.

Another, if ambiguous, symptom of a decline in opinion quality due to the caseload explosion is the surprising persistence of the published per curiam opinion. A per curiam opinion is one not signed by any judge. Since a judge's identification with an opinion is greater when he is listed as the author than when he is one of three members of a panel none of whom is identified as the author, a judge's decision not to sign an opinion but to issue it as a per curiam opinion implies a lesser commitment to that opinion than to the opinions he does sign—implies, in other words, that the opinion, for whatever reason, is not so carefully crafted, so reliable and in a sense authentic, as his signed opinions. At a time when the less carefully prepared opinions are not published at all, the question arises why there should still be any published per curiam opinions.

In the days of universal publication, there were several reasons for per curiam opinions.

1. An opinion might be labeled per curiam as a signal to the reader not to expect a significant precedent; this was the most common reason for the per curiam label.
2. The writing of the opinion was shared by two or more members of the panel.
3. The court wanted the world to know that it was speaking with absolutely a single voice. Thus *Cooper v. Aaron*,[45] a stern rebuke to segregationist states, was signed by each of the justices.
4. The court felt it necessary to rebuke the district judge whose decision was before it on appeal but did not want his wrath to be concentrated on one member of the panel.
5. The judge assigned to write the opinion did not have the time to prepare the kind of opinion that he wanted posterity to judge him by.
6. The authoring judge thought it would seem immodest to be taking public credit for a short and insignificant piece of work.

Reasons 2 through 4 are as valid today, in the era of limited publication, as they were in the old days, but singly and in the aggregate they account for only a very small fraction of all published per curiam opinions. Reasons 1, 5, and 6 should have been made obsolete by the practice of not publishing an opinion which is not expected to have significance as a precedent or which has not evoked a substantial personal input from the judge assigned to write it. And since, as I have suggested, reason 1 alone probably explained most of the per curiam opinions in the days of universal publication, I would expect published per curiam opinions to be a sharply lower fraction of all published opinions today than 20 years ago. They are indeed a lower fraction but not sharply lower, as a comparison of volumes of F.2d chosen at random from 1962 and from 1982 reveals. In 300 F.2d (1962), 21 percent of the opinions were per curiams; in 669 F.2d (1982), the figure was 16 percent.[46] (One-liners—tables in 669 F.2d—were excluded from the comparison.) With reasons 1 and 6 of diminishing significance, it is possible to speculate that some opinions are being published today even though the judges have misgivings about the care devoted to the preparation of the opinion.

45. 358 U.S. 1 (1958).

46. The Administrative Office of the U.S. Courts does not collect data on the number of per curiam opinions, but has in recent years collected (though not published) data showing the number of appeals disposed of by various types of opinion, including per curiams. (There are more appeals than opinions, because often more than one separately filed appeal will be disposed of in a single opinion.) From these data it is possible to estimate that in 1983, 15 percent of the total of signed and per curiam published opinions were per curiams, but that as recently as 1978 the figure had been 22 percent.

Another possible consequence of the caseload explosion is the apparent growth in the number of "nonreasoned" separate opinions. I have avoided the more literate "unreasoned" to make clear that the adjective is intended to carry a technical, nonpejorative meaning. By a nonreasoned opinion I mean an opinion that does not attempt to provide reasons for its results; and I confine myself to separate opinions—that is, to concurring or dissenting opinions, or opinions that are part one and part the other—because a nonreasoned majority opinion in the sense in which I have defined the term is rare unless the case is frivolous, and in that event the reasons behind the result are obvious and do not need to be stated. It is rare in part because of the practice in many circuits of deciding all nonfrivolous cases with reasons, though not necessarily publishing the reasons. But the nonreasoned separate opinion is common, even if the opinion is published.

The limiting case I have in mind is the separate opinion that states simply "I dissent" or "I concur in the judgment." Most separate opinions are a little more elaborate than this, but many separate opinions, in the federal courts of appeals at least, consist of a short paragraph which announces a conclusion but merely hints at the reasoning process behind it (and sometimes there is not even a hint). I also classify as nonreasoned those separate opinions that simply adopt by reference the reasoning of the lower court, and thus make no effort to answer the reasons the majority gave for not adopting the reasoning of the lower court.

The only satisfactory explanation I can think of for the nonreasoned separate opinion is, once again, the time pressure that caseload growth has placed on federal judges. In an ideal world, it would be a most unsatisfactory method of discharging the judge's responsibilities.[47] It cannot be defended on the ground that the judge's reasons for dissenting, or for concurring without joining the opinion of the majority, are obvious (the justification for the one-liner); the other judges on the panel thought his position not only nonobvious but wrong. It cannot be defended on the ground that the judge cannot give reasons for his refusal to join the majority. Appellate judges in our system are supposed to base their judgments on reasons rather than intuition—or if this dichotomy seems too stark, on grounds capable of being rationally explained and defended even though their basis may be intuitive and their validity not fully demonstrable by rational processes. The nonreasoned opinion would not only be indefensible except for the

47. As has occasionally, though not as far as I know recently, been remarked. See Richard S. Miller, "The Work of the Michigan Supreme Court during the Survey Period: A Statistical Analysis," 11 *Wayne L. Rev.* 1, 12, 14 (1964); Alexander Simpson, Jr., "Dissenting Opinions," 71 *U. Pa. L. Rev.* 205, 211 (1923).

lack of time, it would be rather unseemly; it amounts to saying, "I disagree with you but I won't say why," thereby denying the obligation of the appellate judge to give public reasons for his judgments.

But before the practice is condemned the alternatives must be considered. If I am right that the pressures of time rather than some spirit of perversity lie behind the practice of the nonreasoned separate opinion, then it is unrealistic to imagine that the solution is for the judge to write a reasoned opinion every time he is unable to join in the majority opinion. The realistic choice is not between nonreasoned and reasoned separate opinions but between more and fewer separate opinions. The practical alternative to writing a nonreasoned separate opinion is to swallow one's doubts and join the majority opinion. The problem with this alternative is that it suppresses potentially valuable information; it gives a false impression of unanimity and thus makes an opinion seem a stronger precedent than it really is. The effect can be dramatic if, as is common today in most of the circuits, many appellate panels include a judge who is not a regular judge of the circuit. It makes a difference in how an opinion is received whether it reflects the view of two of the judges of the circuit, or it reflects the view of one and the other's view is to the contrary. I do not want to exaggerate the difference, however. It is not true that a 2 to 1 vote with the two circuit judges in the three-judge panel split gives no information about how the circuit as a whole feels about the question decided. *Stare decisis* applies even if the swing judge was not a regular member of the circuit, and *stare decisis* has a lot more weight than some "legal realists" think. Moreover, a reasoned majority opinion will have more intrinsic authority than a nonreasoned dissent or concurrence.

To sum up, I hope that by now I have convinced the reader that the model of judicial supply shown in Figure 4.1 is more accurate than a model which assumes that the supply of federal judicial services is infinitely elastic. We are long past the point where new increments of demand for federal judicial services could be met, with no impairment of quality, simply by adding more judges at existing salary levels. It has proved necessary to add many (but not enough) judges, to create a large judicial bureaucracy (with all the negative things this entails), to curtail oral argument drastically, to reduce the average quality of judicial opinions (the premise, I have argued, of the limited-publication rules), and in these and other ways to lower the quality of federal justice. Combined with unremitting caseload growth, the commitment of the federal court system to accommodating all increments of demand without increasing the price of access to the system has forced the system to operate in a region of sharply increased costs, of which the purely budgetary dimension is the least significant.

5

Palliatives

THE MOUNTING caseload of the federal courts has given rise, as one would expect, to many ameliorative proposals. Those that consist simply of more of the same—more judges, more law clerks and staff attorneys, more circuits, fewer and shorter oral arguments, publication of fewer opinions—need not detain us; nor will I discuss those few proposals that are so eminently sensible that they are universally endorsed yet are blocked by mysterious political forces, such as the perennial proposal to eliminate the remainder (in practice, just a vestige) of the Supreme Court's obligatory jurisdiction. Some proposals that are predominantly substantive rather than institutional in character, such as curtailing the federal courts' habeas corpus jurisdiction, will be discussed in the next chapter. There remains a rich menu of institutional proposals to discuss, from which I shall pick just five on the basis that they are the most far-reaching proposals that have some prospect of adoption, partial or (in some instances) complete, in the foreseeable future.[1] They are as follows: raising the price of access to the federal courts; limiting or abolishing the diversity jurisdiction; moving toward a system of specialized federal appellate courts; reforming administra-

1. Among the politically infeasible proposals that deserve serious attention is the abolition of the jury in civil cases—a course that the rest of the civilized world took long ago, but that would require, in the federal system, repealing the Seventh Amendment. Abolition would have a substantial effect on the workload of the federal district courts. The average federal civil jury trial in 1983 lasted 4.48 days, compared to 2.21 days for the average nonjury trial. If the difference is multiplied by the number of jury trials, and then divided by the number of district judges, this yields a time saving (if all jury trials were converted into nonjury trials) of 22 days per judge per year. Not all of this time would be saved, however: in cases not tried before a jury, Rule 52(a) of the Federal Rules of Civil Procedure requires the judge to prepare written findings of fact and conclusions of law. But there would undoubtedly be a considerable time saving.

tive review; and creating a kind of junior Supreme Court to assist the Supreme Court in assuring a reasonable uniformity of federal decisional law. The first two proposals are demand-limiting, the last three supply-expanding. I call all of them "palliatives" rather than solutions because none of them either is based on a radical rethinking of the role of the federal courts or would be likely to have more than a limited and temporary effect on their caseload.

UPPING THE ANTE

At present, little effort is made to ration access to the federal courts by anyone having a claim within one of the substantive categories of federal jurisdiction. Filing fees are nominal. Minimum-amount-in-controversy requirements have virtually disappeared except in diversity cases—where, however, the $10,000 requirement, set 25 years ago, has shrunk by about 70 percent in real terms because of inflation. Standing and related doctrines designed to limit the federal courts to the decision of actual cases have been liberalized. And there is still no general requirement that a losing party must reimburse the winner's attorney's fees. It is true that many federal attorney-fee-shifting statutes, covering particular subject-matter areas, have been enacted in recent years, and there are now more than a hundred. But their net effect has actually been to reduce the costs of suing in federal court. Some of the statutes allow only winning plaintiffs to get their attorney's fees reimbursed, which encourages suing; and many others, which do not, have nevertheless been interpreted to create a strong presumption in favor of awarding a winning plaintiff his fees and against awarding a winning defendant his fees,[2] so that they are much like the first group of statutes. And many legal questions involving the interpretation of attorney-fee statutes have arisen (for example, what is a "prevailing party"? What is a "reasonable" attorney's fee?) that have required, and continue to require, litigation to answer.

Chapter 1 presented the theoretical economic objection to charging stiff user fees in order to ration demand for federal judicial services: the courts, especially the appellate courts, provide a benefit to nonusers— to the consumers, as it were, of the precedents they produce. To encourage the users to produce this external benefit, we let them shift some of their costs to the community that comprises the external beneficiaries. Or to put it differently, we subsidize litigation by making the

---

2. As in the most important of the modern fee-shifting statutes, the Civil Rights Attorney's Fees Awards Act of 1976, 42 U.S.C. § 1988. See Hensley v. Eckerhart, 103 S. Ct. 1933, 1937 (1983); Hughes v. Rowe, 449 U.S. 5, 14–15 (1980) (per curiam).

taxpayers rather than the litigants bear some litigation costs, namely the costs of the judicial system itself, on the theory that the taxpayers as potential litigants benefit from the forensic exertions of the actual litigants.

There is nothing wrong with the theory; the interesting question is what the optimum subsidy is today. With user fees accounting for a tiny fraction of the current federal judicial budget,[3] and with the amount of federal litigation rapidly rising and seriously threatening the quality of the federal judiciary's output, the subsidy is far too great. Indeed, we may have reached the point where any further increase in litigation, far from benefiting potential litigants by clarifying the law, will harm them by making the law more uncertain, through the effect of additional litigation in reducing the quality of the judiciary's output. In either case we ought to stop encouraging federal litigation; and realistic user fees are a natural and attractive method of doing so with regard to civil litigation between nonindigents. Stiff fees, charged to the plaintiff if he files in federal court and to the defendant if he removes to federal court a case originally filed in state court, would tend to divert cases with small monetary stakes from the federal court system to more suitable dispute-resolution processes, since a fixed user fee would constitute a higher percentage tax on such cases than on cases with large stakes. There would thus be a shift in the composition of the nonindigent civil docket toward litigants who have a big stake in the outcome of their lawsuit—and they are the best kind of litigants to have in a court system. I do not say this out of snobbishness (and anyway there is a difference between a rich litigant and a litigant who has a big financial stake in the outcome of his case); it is just that if great cases and hard cases make bad law, financially significant cases make good law. The bigger the financial stakes in a case, the greater are the legal resources that will be expended on the case; and the more informed the judge is

---

3. As a matter of fact, it is not reported as part of the federal judicial budget (an absurd procedure, which deprives the administrators of the federal court system of any incentive they might otherwise have to get the fees increased); nor have I been able to find it anywhere in the published appendices to the Budget of the United States. However, I am informed by the Treasury Department that an account in the Treasury Department Receipt Account Trial Balance for Fiscal Year 1983, captioned "Fees for Legal and Judicial Services, Not Otherwise Classified" (Account Symbol 0869), contains the federal courts' income for fiscal 1983 from filing fees. The total amount shown in the account is $36,-367,169.93, which if it represented just filing fees would equal about 5 percent of the federal courts' expenditures; but I am almost certain that it includes other receipts.

The basic filing fee is the $60 fee for filing a case in federal district court. Even if all of the 240,000 civil complaints filed annually were accompanied by payment of the fee, which they are not since many of the plaintiffs are indigent, the total amount collected would be only $14 million, which is less than 2 percent of the federal judicial budget.

on the law and the facts as a result of the parties' efforts, the more likely he is to render a sound decision. This is the only justification for minimum-amount-in-controversy requirements. User fees are similar but more flexible. To require a minimum amount in controversy bars some suits absolutely but affects all other suits—where the amount in controversy exceeds the minimum, however slightly—not at all. A nontrivial fixed user fee would operate as a tax on all suits, and, appropriately, as a proportionately diminishing tax as the stakes rise. A $1,000 fixed fee would be a 10 percent tax on a case worth $10,000 to the plaintiff, but only a 1 percent tax on a case worth $100,000. (There is also an argument, which I shall not pursue, for placing a percentage fee on top of the flat fee; this would discourage plaintiffs from making excessive demands for damages in their complaints, and by doing so would make it easier to settle damage cases.) Flat user fees are cheaper to administer than minimum-amount-in-controversy requirements (though they do involve some collection costs) because the court does not have to determine whether the stakes come up to some minimum level. User fees also yield both government revenue and information about the demand for judicial services; minimum-amount-in-controversy requirements do neither.

Two objections to moving to a system of stiff user fees spring to mind. First, the system cannot be applied to indigent litigants, who constitute a large, and under a user-fee system would constitute a larger, fraction of the total users of the federal courts; the composition of the federal courts' docket would thus be altered in a way that might dismay a number of federal judges. Second, there are those who feel that it is "unfair" to ration access to a court system by willingness (which presupposes ability) to pay, especially perhaps access to the federal courts by those having federal claims. Regarding this objection, the following observations are in order. (1) The question is not one of denying access to the courts but of shifting litigants from one court system (the federal) to others (the state court systems) which are forbidden by the Constitution to close their doors to persons wanting to litigate federal claims in state court.[4] (2) The principle of using money to ration access to particular courts is implicit in the diversity jurisdiction's minimum-amount-in-controversy requirement, and until a few years ago there was a minimum-amount requirement in many classes of federal-question cases. (3) Many federal claims—for example, a state criminal defendant's federal defenses to the criminal charges—must be litigated in state courts, and indeed the federal courts had no general

4. See Charles Alan Wright, *The Law of Federal Courts* §§ 45–46 (4th ed. 1983).

federal-question jurisdiction until 1875. (4) Supreme Court review would remain available in all state cases involving federal claims or defenses. (5) An equal number of people having federal claims of small value may benefit as may lose if size of claim is used, directly or indirectly, to ration access to the federal courts. The rules the federal courts lay down are rules for big and small claims alike, even if the latter claims are litigated in state courts—but applying federal law—rather than in federal courts. The larger the stakes in the case (or cases) in which the rule is established, the more likely it is to be a sound one; and many holders of small as well as large federal claims will benefit if the edifice of federal judge-made law is well built.

Although shunting cases from one overcrowded court system to another may seem unfair, if not to the litigants, then to the second system, there is a fundamental difference between the overcrowding problems of the federal court system and those of the state court systems. Because of the great disparity in size between the federal judiciary and the judiciary of the states considered as a whole, the same percentage reduction in the federal caseload and shift to the states will cause a much smaller percentage increase in state caseloads. The caseload figures in Chapter 2 imply that a 10 percent reduction in the federal courts' caseload would cause less than a 1 percent increase in the caseload of the state courts—assuming that all of the federal cases were refiled as state cases. And the assumption is unrealistic; some of the federal cases would be shunted to private arbitration, especially if the states followed the lead of the federal government and raised their court filing fees. Admittedly, if they did, there would be a danger of overdiscouraging litigation, especially by persons just above the indigence level. But this is not an imminent danger; and even if some state courts begin to charge stiff filing fees, others—small claims courts, for example—will not.

It is possible, of course, that a state judicial system might be so saturated that even a 1 percent increase in its business would cause it serious problems. Moreover, the effect of redistributing judicial business from the federal courts to the states might be concentrated in a few states and lead to increases much larger than 1 percent in those states. I have not studied these problems, though I cite in the next chapter a study that concludes that the state courts could absorb the whole of the federal diversity jurisdiction (about 20 percent of the caseload of the federal district courts) without undue strain. But the fact that the federal courts are so much more powerful than the state courts suggests, however offensive the suggestion may seem coming from a federal judge, that attending to the quality of the federal court system is a more urgent priority than attending to the quality of the state systems—which anyway is something that only the states can do effectively.

A full analysis of redistributing caseload from the federal to the state courts would also consider the relative quality of the two types of courts. It is widely believed that the federal courts are better on average than the state courts because the conditions of federal judicial employment are better. If this is so, there may be a reduction in the quality of adjudication if cases involving federal claims are shunted to state courts. But some redress of the balance of power between federal and state courts is long overdue, and would be worth a small reduction in the average quality of decisions. More important, if reducing the caseload of the federal courts (or, more realistically, the rate of caseload growth) increases the quality of their decisions, those federal claimants who remain in the federal court system will experience a higher quality of justice, and their gain will offset the loss suffered by those litigants who are induced by higher user fees to litigate in state courts. And for some types of claims, private arbitration will provide an attractive alternative.

Another possible problem in redistributing caseload to the state courts should be mentioned. If fewer cases involving issues of federal law are litigated in federal courts and more in state courts, there will be fewer conflicts (inconsistent determinations of federal law) between circuits but more conflicts between states; and since there are almost four times as many states as there are circuits, the potential for conflicts that only the Supreme Court can resolve will be greater. But how much greater is uncertain; and the problem would not exist with respect to those reallocated cases that were diversity cases.

The impact on federal judges' job satisfaction of increasing the fraction of indigent cases by raising user fees is not quite so petty and selfish a point as it may sound. Since a large part of the rewards of being a federal judge today are nonmonetary, since federal judges like other people must be assumed to be motivated primarily by considerations of self-interest, although not a narrowly monetary self-interest, and since the political system seems unwilling to increase the real salaries of federal judges substantially, it would endanger the quality of the federal judiciary to alter the composition of the federal caseload in the direction of greater monotony. But the point would have bite only if really stiff user fees were imposed, which seems in any event politically infeasible. The practical reform would simply be to raise the existing, and absurdly inadequate, fees to a higher, but not astronomically higher, level.

A recent study by the RAND Corporation estimates the federal budgetary cost of the average tort case filed in federal court to be $1,740, but in certain kinds of tort case the figure rises to $15,028 if there is a jury trial.[5] It is not to be supposed that the $60 federal district court filing fee is about to be raised to either of those levels for any sort of case, but if it were raised, say, to $500 this would be a big increase and would eliminate at least a few of the trivial tort cases that are filed in federal district courts today. Similar increases would also be justified in many other areas of federal civil (excluding indigent) litigation. If we moved just a little way toward placing the federal court system on a user-supported basis, the political costs would be small and the benefits in reduced caseload, though also small, would be welcome. And we would learn something about the elasticity of demand for various types of federal judicial services, and hence something about the likely effectiveness of other demand-limiting measures. In a period of renewed interest in placing more of the costs of government on the users of government services,[6] an economically more realistic user-fee structure for the federal courts than we have is worth more attention than it is receiving.

Rather more attention has been paid to another method of rationing access to the federal (and state) courts: fee shifting—that is, forcing the losing litigant (defendant *or* plaintiff) to bear the winner's legal fees.[7] In force everywhere in the civilized world except the United States and Japan, fee shifting could help solve the problem of excessive federal court caseloads. Fee shifting penalizes excessive optimism, which I suggested in Chapter 1 is a *sine qua non* for a case being tried rather than settled in advance of trial; and it discourages litigation by risk-averse litigants because it makes the costs of defeat greater than under the present system.[8]

5. James S. Kakalik and Abby Eisenshtat Robyn, *Costs of the Civil Justice System: Court Expenditures for Processing Tort Cases* xviii, xix (RAND Institute for Civil Justice 1982). And for an extension to several other types of federal cases, see James S. Kakalik and R. L. Ross, *Costs of the Civil Justice System: Court Expenditures for Various Types of Civil Cases* (RAND Institute for Civil Justice 1983).

6. See, for example, Judy Sarasohn, "User Fees a Major Issue: Railroad, Trucking, Barge Industries Renew Old Battles," 39 *Cong. Q. Weekly Rep.* 2185 (1981); William J. Lanouette, "Critics Seek Big Bucks from Big Trucks to Repair Damage to Interstate Roads," 13 *Nat'l J.* 2122 (1981).

7. For a good recent discussion with many references to the literature, see Thomas D. Rowe, Jr., "The Legal Theory of Attorney Fee Shifting: A Critical Overview," 1982 *Duke L.J.* 651.

8. See Richard A. Posner, *Economic Analysis of Law* 452 (2d ed. 1977); Steven Shavell, "Suit, Settlement, and Trial: A Theoretical Analysis under Alternative Methods for the Allocation of Legal Costs," 11 *J. Legal Stud.* 55 (1982). See also George L. Priest, "Regulating the Content and Volume of Litigation: An Economic Analysis," 1 *S. Ct. Econ. Rev.* 163 (1983), and other studies cited there.

Because so much of federal law is highly uncertain at the level either of doctrine or of application of doctrine to particular facts—where our continued heavy reliance on juries introduces an additional element of unpredictability—increasing the costs of the loser may seem unfair. And indeed the uncertainty of our law may explain why we have clung to rules that in effect distribute the risks of litigation. But it is also unfair to make the winning party bear his costs of suit; and between the two parties, the one whose rights were vindicated has a better claim for reimbursement of his attorney's fees than the other party does. Moreover, there are other people's interests to be considered besides just those of the immediate parties to the suit. Litigation imposes a cost on prospective litigants by making them wait longer in the court queue and possibly also by preventing the judge from giving full and careful consideration to their cases; and the cumulative caseload pressures to which every lawsuit contributes its little bit may well be hurting society as a whole by reducing the quality of the rules that federal courts make for the guidance of the society.

As with user fees, fee shifting will have no effect on litigation brought by or against, and lost by, indigents; and a rule that allows the indigent to get his attorney's fees reimbursed if he wins but does not penalize him if he loses will, like the statutes mentioned earlier that allow only prevailing plaintiffs to get their fees reimbursed ("one-way" fee shifting, as in section 4 of the Clayton Act, governing attorney's fees in private antitrust damage suits), encourage litigation. Even two-way fee shifting is ambiguous in its implications for the volume of litigation. It discourages a person who thinks he may lose from litigating. But at the same time it encourages a person who thinks he has a very strong case (claim or defense) to litigate rather than to be fobbed off with a nominal settlement offer (if he is the plaintiff) or (if he is the defendant) to buy off the opponent with a generous settlement offer; for he has something additional to gain from victory in court—his costs of suit. Moreover, in complex litigation, deciding whether and to what extent a party has prevailed, and what a reasonable fee for his litigation efforts would be, are themselves litigable—and frequently litigated—issues. Nevertheless, it is generally believed that two-way fee shifting reduces the amount of litigation.[9] We could easily experiment with two-way fee shifting in particular areas to see whether this is a correct prediction.

Fee-shifting statutes apart, there is a limited form of fee shifting in

9. See, for example, Herbert M. Kritzer, "Fee Arrangements and Fee Shifting: Lessons from the Experience in Ontario" 21–22 (Working Paper 1983-3, Disputes Processing Research Program, University of Wisconsin, Madison, Wisconsin, unpublished).

the federal (as in the state) courts today by virtue of the common law doctrine, increasingly invoked, that allows the winning party to get a fee award by showing that his opponent was litigating in bad faith.[10] The standard today is variously phrased: frivolousness, bad faith, without reasonable cause, done purely for delay. All these terms imply the same thing: a purpose in litigating not to win—the litigant knows he has no case (or defense)—but to obtain some collateral advantage from litigation, normally delay but sometimes discouragement of a competitor or even the breaking up of a personal relationship. There are also many cases in which no ulterior motive appears or can be inferred but in which the claim or defense is totally, hopelessly, lacking in merit. Because of the connotations of bad faith that cluster around the word "frivolous" in its legal sense, judges are reluctant to shift fees in cases where the worst that can be said of a litigant is that he or his lawyer was too stupid to realize the hopelessness of their cause. It might therefore be an improvement over the present situation to make generally applicable to federal court litigation the approach of the Equal Access to Justice Act, which allows a private party litigating with the United States to recover a reasonable attorney's fee if the government was not "substantially justified" in its litigating position.[11] Under this standard the government must pay its opponent's fees if the government's position, although not frivolous in the sense implying bad faith, lacks a solid basis in law or fact.[12] This is an interesting halfway house to complete fee shifting, and it might be well to experiment with it in private litigation before going all the way.

I want to suggest another experiment (again one that would require a statute): fee shifting in diversity cases. The diversity jurisdiction is embattled, and rightly so; the case for its abolition, explored in the next section of this chapter, is a powerful if not quite conclusive one. The weaker the case for retention of a branch of federal jurisdiction, the weaker must be the objection to a measure calculated to reduce the occasions on which the jurisdiction is invoked. We could see how fee shifting works in diversity cases and use the experience gained from that experiment to decide whether to move more generally toward its adoption for the federal court system.

The easiest of all pricing methods to implement, since it requires nothing more than inaction, would be to allow the queue for federal trials to grow significantly. The effect of a court queue is to reduce the

10. See, for example, Overnite Transport, Co. v. Chicago Indus. Tire Co., 697 F.2d 789 (7th Cir. 1983). To similar effect are 28 U.S.C. § 1927 and Fed. R. App. P. 38.

11. 28 U.S.C. § 2412(d)(1)(A).

12. See, for example, McDonald v. Schweiker, 726 F.2d 311, 316 (7th Cir. 1983).

present value of the plaintiff's claim, thus increasing the probability that the case will either be settled or be shunted off to an alternative system of dispute resolution, such as the state courts or private arbitration. The problem is that delaying litigation results in decay of evidence, thus reducing the accuracy of the litigation process, and in uncertainty of legal obligation. These are high prices to pay for limiting the caseload.

Finally, jurisdictional minimum amounts in controversy could be reintroduced into federal-question cases; but for reasons stated earlier, higher user fees seem preferable.

LIMITING OR ABOLISHING DIVERSITY JURISDICTION

Diversity cases account for 20 percent of the district courts' current caseload and 14 percent of the courts of appeals' caseload (see Table 3.2), though almost none of the Supreme Court's. The Court does from time to time consider jurisdictional issues in diversity cases, and so it cannot ignore completely the applications it receives to review diversity decisions, but those applications are not numerous.[13]

To gauge the effect of abolishing the diversity jurisdiction on the workloads of the district courts and courts of appeals requires adjusting the raw caseload figures for the difficulty of diversity cases relative to that of other components of the courts' dockets. Table 3.5 in Chapter 3, a subject-matter classification of the cases in my sample of signed, published majority opinions, provides an implicit weighting of court of appeals cases by difficulty. Only 8 percent of the 1983 opinions in the sample were diversity cases. This suggests that, at least at the court of appeals level, diversity cases are below average in difficulty; it also suggests that eliminating diversity jurisdiction might have a smaller impact on the workload of the courts of appeals than is implied by the fact that 14 percent of the cases appealed to those courts in 1983 were diversity cases.

Table 5.1 adjusts for the relative difficulty of diversity cases in the district courts by presenting a subject-matter breakdown of trials in those courts in 1983, the assumption being that trials place the greatest demand on the time and energy of federal district judges. There are a number of interesting differences between Tables 5.1 and 3.5 but the one to note for now is that diversity cases are overrepresented among trials—24 percent versus 20 percent among cases filed. This suggests

13. See Gerhard Casper and Richard A. Posner, *The Workload of the Supreme Court* 52 (1976) (table 3.12).

Table 5.1. Breakdown of federal trials, 1983

Type of case	Percentage of trials (N = 18,664)[a]
Criminal	35.6
Civil	64.3
U.S. civil	10.9
Condemnation	2.3
FLSA	0.3
Contract	0.9
Tax	1.3
Civil rights	1.0
Postconviction	0.3
FTCA	2.3
Forfeiture and penalty	0.7
Social security laws	0.1
Private	53.4
Diversity	24.3
Admiralty	1.2
Antitrust	0.8
Civil rights	11.4
Intellectual property	1.4
FELA	1.4
Postconviction	4.9
Jones Act	2.3
LMRA	0.8
RLA	N.A.

Sources: 1983 AO Ann. Rep., tables C4, C5B (condemnation), C8 (criminal).

a. This figure is lower than the corresponding figure in Table 3.3 (number and length of trials) because the figure in Table 3.3, which is from table C8 in the 1983 AO Ann. Rep., includes preliminary-injunction and other evidentiary hearings as well as full-fledged trials, whereas table C4, which I used as my source of civil trials for the present table (because C4 has a finer subject-matter breakdown than C8), does not.

that abolishing the diversity jurisdiction would markedly decrease the workload of the district courts—perhaps by a quarter.

Interestingly, the same result is suggested by the most recent "time and motion" study of federal district judges.[14] The study assigned a weight of 1.2192 to diversity cases, which means that the average di-

14. 1979 Federal District Court Time Study (Fed. Judic. Center, October 1980). Results are summarized in 1980 AO Rep. 295 (table 49).

versity case is 22 percent more demanding than the average case on the district courts' docket as a whole. This in turn implies that the weighted share of diversity cases in that docket is not 20 but 24 percent—the same weighted share obtained by computing the fraction of federal trials that are diversity trials.[15]

In sum, eliminating diversity jurisdiction would have dramatic effects on the district courts' caseload (though, as I have stressed, this is the most manageable of all components of the federal courts' overall caseload); a smaller though still significant effect on the courts of appeals' caseload, where the caseload crisis is most acute; and trivial effects on the Supreme Court's caseload. Abolition would not be a panacea for the caseload problem, but it would provide measurable relief, and the case for it has to be considered seriously.[16]

The most common argument for abolition postulates that the purpose of the diversity jurisdiction, as authoritatively announced by Chief Justice Marshall in *Bank of the United States v. DeVeaux*,[17] is to protect nonresident litigants from local bias; points out that sectional bias has greatly declined since 1789; and concludes that the jurisdiction is therefore unnecessary. This argument does justice neither to the case for nor the case against abolition. The emphasis on bias is misplaced for a variety of reasons unrelated to the alleged secular decline in sectional bias (and anyway, the relevant question is not whether sectional bias has declined, but what its current level is). To begin with, bias played a smaller role in the creation of the diversity jurisdiction than is assumed today, as can be seen from the way in which the jurisdiction was configured in the first Judiciary Act, and still is. The plaintiff can sue a defendant of diverse citizenship in federal court even if the plaintiff is the resident, and the defendant the nonresident, of the state in which the suit is brought, or even if they are both nonresidents. And any defendant can remove a diversity case filed in state court to federal court as long as no defendant is a citizen of the state in which the suit was brought; there is no requirement that the plaintiff himself be a citizen of that state.

15. Professor Shapiro's poll of federal judges produced a similar estimate of the workload accounted for by diversity cases at the district court level, 21.8 percent. See David L. Shapiro, "Federal Diversity Jurisdiction: A Survey and a Proposal," 91 *Harv. L. Rev.* 317, 335 (1977) (table B). However, his estimate of the court of appeals diversity workload— 11.9 percent (*id.*)—is higher than mine. But his study relates to a period some years earlier than mine, so there is no necessary inconsistency.

16. The literature pro and con abolition is enormous. See the references in Wright, supra note 4, § 23. The most formidable opponent of the jurisdiction is Judge Henry J. Friendly. See his *Federal Jurisdiction: A General View*, pt. VII (1973).

17. 9 U.S. (5 Cranch) 61, 87 (1809).

In a 1928 study of colonial court records, Judge Friendly (as he now is) concluded that colonial courts were not prejudiced against nonresidents; and from his study of the legislative history of Article III he concluded that the principal motive for diversity jurisdiction was not fear of sectional bias but the concern of commercial interests that state courts were pro-debtor, and a related but more general concern, again held mainly by commercial interests, that state courts were of poor quality and very political.[18] Presumably these commercial interests did not much fear the courts of their own states, where their own political weight would be felt, but they did fear the courts of other states, and they wanted access to a more professional tribunal; this may be why the Judiciary Act allowed two nonresidents to litigate in federal court. Moreover, if sectional bias were the main problem, the diversity jurisdiction would be only part of the solution. Federal district judges must by law be residents of the districts in which they sit, and invariably at the time of their appointment they are long-time residents (there is of course more geographic diversity of judges on the courts of appeals); and no district crosses state lines.[19] Jurors in a federal trial are drawn from one federal district, and though in rural areas a district will be larger than a county, which is the usual area from which a state jury is drawn, the difference often is not very important from the standpoint of reducing regional or sectional bias. Moreover, federal district courts often draw juries from less than the whole district—from the division (which may consist of just one or two counties) in which the court sits.

If, as I have been doing recently, you discuss with lawyers whose clients have access to the federal courts under the diversity jurisdiction, either as plaintiffs or as removing defendants, what factors make them choose federal or state courts in particular cases, sectional bias rarely appears on the list—less because it is not thought to exist than because it is not thought to operate much less in federal courts. Nor does the matter of relative quality of state and federal courts show up on the list, for the excellent reason that lawyers do not care about the quality of a tribunal per se but about its likely disposition toward their client. One very important consideration in the lawyer's choice, at least among the lawyers I have talked to, is what judge he is likely to get. Another is the relative length of the state and federal court queues—lawyers who want fast action will opt for the federal court. The different procedures in state and federal court also play a role. A big factor today is that most federal civil jury trials are before 6-man juries, whereas most of the states retain the 12-man civil jury. This makes a difference to the risk-

18. "The Historic Basis of Diversity Jurisdiction," 41 *Harv. L. Rev* 483 (1928).

19. Like almost all general statements about law and legal institutions, this one is imprecise. See Wright, supra note 4, at 8 n.3.

averse defendant because extreme verdicts are likelier with smaller juries, constituting as they do smaller and therefore less representative samples of the population. Finally, lawyers sometimes will steer a case to the court system with which they happen to have more experience.

Speaking of small and unrepresentative samples, I am quick to confess that my sampling of trial lawyers' opinions on the diversity jurisdiction has been completely unsystematic. But I take comfort from the broad correspondence between my findings and those of a large and careful mail survey conducted by Kristin Bumiller.[20] Although she found that what she calls "local bias" is a factor in the choice to litigate diversity cases in federal court, it is significant only in the rural districts in her survey. And her conclusion was that lawyers in rural areas fear bias in favor of local interests rather than prejudice against nonresidents of the state.[21] In a sparsely populated county, either the plaintiff or the defendant may well be a personal or professional (often political) acquaintance of the county judge or of jurors drawn from the county. The federal district that embraces the county will usually be much larger, and the probability of such connections therefore less. But in an urban area, county and federal district are likely to be coterminous or nearly so, and the probability of personal or professional acquaintance between a party and court personnel is likely to be small in either state or federal court. While local bias may thus explain the preference of many lawyers to retain the diversity jurisdiction, retention provides a very limited solution. The problem exists if one party is local and the other is from another part of the state—but in that case there is no federal diversity jurisdiction.

Apart from local bias, the Bumiller survey found, consistently with my informal survey results, that lawyers generally choose to litigate diversity cases in federal court either because they are more familiar with federal procedure or because they prefer the generally shorter trial queues of the federal courts. Whether these are good reasons for retaining the diversity jurisdiction may be doubted. Bumiller also found, contrary to my impressions, that lawyers often elect to proceed in federal court because they think federal judges are better than state judges. But there may not be any real inconsistency between her results and mine. The entry "judges of superior caliber" in her questionnaire was the closest in meaning to "judge more likely to rule in my favor." Lawyers who chose the first may have meant the second (which was not listed as a possible choice).

Although to a hard-nosed practicing lawyer the quality of the pre-

20. Kristin Bumiller, "Choice of Forum in Diversity Cases: Analysis of a Survey and Implications for Reform," 15 *Law & Soc'y Rev.* 749 (1980–1981).
    21. *Id.* at 761.

siding judge is not a basis of consistent preference, it is widely believed that federal judges are, on average (an important qualifier), of higher quality than their state counterparts. If this is true, it would not be surprising. As we saw in Chapter 2, the terms of employment of federal judges generally are better than those of state judges; and for this and perhaps other reasons there is more competition for federal judgeships and also more elaborate screening of candidates for federal than for state judgeships. But whether the federal courts are actually better is not for me to say; and I should certainly not like to be understood as suggesting that it is seemly (though maybe it is inevitable) that federal district judges should, in exercising federal habeas corpus jurisdiction, review the decisions of the supreme court of the states in which they sit (as they do). I note also Professor Bator's recent argument for regarding state supreme courts as equal in quality to federal courts of appeals—a forceful argument, though I disagree with his assertion that state supreme court justices are on average paid as well (if it can be called that) as federal circuit judges.[22]

There is some indirect but interesting evidence that the federal courts really are of somewhat higher average quality than state courts. Even in the years since the *Erie* decision eliminated or, more realistically, confined their creative lawmaking role in diversity cases, the federal courts have made a disproportionate contribution to the shaping of the common law—at least as measured by the choices made by casebook editors and treatise writers of what common law cases to include in their works, and by certain other indices of quality and influence.[23] The effect of the *Erie* decision on the law-creation function of federal courts in diversity cases has been exaggerated; the picture of the federal judge as ventriloquist's dummy[24] is overdrawn. Especially in a period when only about half of all federal court of appeals decisions are published, and given the deference (sometimes excessive)[25] that those courts pay to the interpretation of state law by district judges, the reported court of appeals diversity cases tend to be ones in which the state law is unclear, so that decision must be rested on general principles of common law rather than on slavish adherence to established state precedents. Such decisions are necessarily creative.

22. See Paul M. Bator, "The State Courts and Federal Constitutional Litigation," 22 *Wm. & Mary L. Rev.* 605, 630 (1981). My Table 2.3 indicates that federal circuit judges are on average paid significantly more than state supreme court justices.

23. See William M. Landes and Richard A. Posner, "Legal Change, Judicial Behavior, and the Diversity Jurisdiction," 9 *J. Legal Stud.* 367, 380–382 (1980). See also Shapiro, supra note 15, at 326.

24. In Judge Jerome Frank's phrase. Richardson v. Commissioner, 126 F.2d 562, 567 (2d Cir. 1942).

25. As argued persuasively by Wright, supra note 4, at 375–376.

Table 5.2. Percentage of state court citations in federal court of appeals
diversity opinions

Year	Percentage
1933	34
1934	36
1935	55
1936	16
1937	23
1938[a]	35
1939	67
1940	56
1941	69
1942	48
1943	59
1970	43
1971	47
1973[b]	40
1974	35
1975	43

a. Year of *Erie* decision.

b. 1972 is omitted because the required information was inadvertently not collected
for that year's opinions.

Thus there would be some loss to the development of the common
law from abolition of the diversity jurisdiction; and there would also be
a diminution in the variety of the federal judge's docket, though perhaps of a welcome sort. There is also an economic case, developed in
the next chapter, for retaining at least a fragment of diversity jurisdiction—a case related to but distinct from concern with sectional bias.
Against these factors must be weighed the benefits of significantly reducing the caseload pressures on the federal courts (other than the Supreme Court). The loss to state common law might be a gain to federal
law. There is also the curious fact that federal courts of appeals in diversity cases seem to prefer citing their own previous diversity decisions rather than state court decisions,[26] even though the latter are more
authoritative. This tendency is confirmed by some data from the University of Chicago Law School's precedent project, mentioned in the
preceding chapter. Table 5.2 shows the percentage of state court cita-

26. See Landes and Posner, supra note 23, at 374–375.

tions in federal court of appeals diversity opinions in the five years before and the five years after *Erie* was decided, and in the five most recent years in the sample. In the wake of *Erie* the federal courts began as one would expect to cite state court decisions much more frequently than they had been doing before. But in recent years the ratio of state court to federal court citations has fallen almost to what it was before *Erie* was decided. The growing apart of state and federal courts in the decision of questions of state law suggests that the problems of legal uncertainty and federal judicial usurpation that characterized the era of *Swift* v. *Tyson* may be returning.

The balancing of all these factors is difficult and leads me to suggest, as many others have done, that we begin by curtailing the diversity jurisdiction. Let us by all means not only restore the minimum amount in controversy to where it was in real terms 25 years ago—which would require raising it from $10,000 to (in round numbers) $35,000—but also move it up another notch, to $50,000, and see what the effects are. I am less certain about whether we should limit diversity jurisdiction to cases where sectional bias is a possible factor in the choice of federal court. This would be an irrational mode of curtailment if I am correct that sectional bias is not an important factor in diversity jurisdiction, and may never have been. To readers who disagree with this and think that sectional bias is the only valid basis for retaining diversity jurisdiction, I will point out that according to a study done by the American Law Institute in 1969, if residents of the state of suit, and corporations doing business in a substantial way in that state, were forbidden to invoke the diversity jurisdiction (as the ALI proposed), the number of diversity cases would fall by almost 60 percent.[27] No data have been collected that would enable the ALI's estimate to be updated to the present. It is possible, however, to calculate from unpublished data collected by the Administrative Office of the U.S. Courts how many diversity cases would be eliminated from the federal courts by adopting a slightly more limited proposal, whereby a diversity suit could be brought only by a nonresident against a resident and removed only by a nonresident sued by a resident. No other combinations (resident suing nonresident, or nonresident removing suit by nonresident) engage the concern with bias in favor of residents. The results of this calculation, which appear in Table 5.3, are dramatic: half the diversity jurisdiction would be eliminated.

27. American Law Institute, *Study of the Division of Jurisdiction between State and Federal Courts* 465–467 (1969). Unpublished statistics of the Administrative Office of the U.S. Courts show that only 20 percent of the diversity cases filed in 1967 were brought by a resident of the state in which the suit was filed either against a nonresident individual or against a nonresident corporation not doing business in the state.

Table 5.3. Effect of limiting diversity jurisdiction (based on 1983 data)

Cases brought by res. against nonres.	Cases brought by nonres. against nonres.	Removed by nonres. or sued by nonres.	Other cases[a] (%)
20,354	3,905	577	24,270 (49.9)[b]

a. Cases brought by nonresidents against residents, and cases brought by residents against nonresidents and removed.

b. The surprising number of cases (more than 10 percent) in which both parties resided in the same state are excluded in making this calculation; one hopes these were dismissed early in the litigation. Also excluded were the small number of cases where a resident defendant removed; a resident may not remove a diversity case. See 28 U.S.C. § 1441(b).

It is evident that adopting the modest proposal on which these results are based, in combination with raising the minimum amount in controversy to $50,000, would have dramatic effects on the diversity jurisdiction.

SPECIALIZED FEDERAL COURTS

Since the caseload crisis is most acute in the courts of appeals, the movement to create specialized federal courts of appeals may seem irresistibly attractive.[28] Specialization would eliminate many of the problems associated with indefinitely multiplying the number of federal appellate judges. There are far more fields of federal law than there are plausible regions for separate federal courts of appeals, so there could be many more federal courts of appeals, each of smaller size, in a system of specialized courts. And of course the subject-matter and regional methods of organization could be combined—and would have to be in the busiest fields such as criminal law. The multiplication of courts organized on subject-matter lines would not create any conflicts in federal law between courts, because each court would have a monopoly of its subject matter.

The new Court of Appeals for the Federal Circuit, described in Chapter 2, is a portent, though a slightly ambiguous one, of increased specialization in the federal judicial system. A merger of existing specialized courts, the new court will actually be less specialized than either of its predecessors. But it will be much more specialized than any

28. For illustrative discussions see Paul D. Carrington, Daniel J. Meador, and Maurice Rosenberg, *Justice on Appeal* 168–184 (1976); Ellen R. Jordan, "Specialized Courts: A Choice?" 76 *Nw. U.L. Rev.* 745 (1981).

of the regional courts of appeals, and its jurisdiction is being enlarged at their expense.

Like many who have written on this topic before me,[29] I have serious reservations about the idea of specialized federal appellate courts. Some of what I say may have implications for specialization at the trial level as well, but I will not try to draw them out; there are different trade-offs, which might warrant a different degree of specialization at the two levels, as we have today in court of appeals (generalist) review of Tax Court (specialist) decisions.

In evaluating the advantages and disadvantages of appellate specialization, I shall take as given the existing structure of the American legal system onto which any additional specialized courts would be grafted. That is, I shall assume that the methods of educating lawyers, appointing judges, and conducting trials will remain fundamentally as they are today. This assumption is important because it is possible to conceive of the creation of a specialized judiciary as part of a more far-reaching reorganization of the American legal system. In Europe the judiciary is much more specialized than it is in this country,[30] and I am not prepared to assert that this is a bad thing, given the very different structure of the Continental system.

I also shall not consider the kind of specialization that consists of rotating judges among specialized divisions of their court, as is done, for example, in the circuit court of Cook County, Illinois. There have been proposals to do this in the federal courts of appeals.[31] I am also going to assume that everyone knows what a specialized court is—and thereby conceal a significant ambiguity in the concept. The Tax Court, conventionally, is a specialized court; the National Labor Relations Board, conventionally, is an administrative agency. But an important method of increasing judicial specialization would be simply to reduce the

29. See, for example, Commission on Revision of the Federal Court Appellate System, *Structure and Internal Procedures: Recommendations for Change* 28–30 (1975); David P. Currie and Frank I. Goodman, "Judicial Review of Federal Administrative Action: Quest for the Optimum Forum," 75 *Colum. L. Rev.* 1, 68–74 (1975); Henry J. Friendly, "Averting the Flood by Lessening the Flow," 59 *Cornell L. Rev.* 634, 639–640 (1974); Patrick E. Higginbotham, "Bureaucracy—The Carcinoma of the Federal Judiciary," 31 *Ala. L. Rev.* 261, 268 (1980); Simon H. Rifkind, "A Special Court for Patent Litigation? The Danger of a Specialized Judiciary," 37 *A.B.A.J.* 425 (1951).

30. There is an excellent description in Daniel J. Meador, "Appellate Subject Matter Organization: The German Design from an American Perspective," 5 *Hastings Int'l & Comp. L. Rev.* 27 (1983).

31. See Daniel J. Meador, "The Federal Judiciary—Inflation, Malfunction, and a Proposed Course of Action," 1981 *Brigham Young U.L. Rev.* 617, 645–646; Daniel J. Meador, "An Appellate Court Dilemma and a Solution through Subject Matter Organization," 16 *U. Mich. J. Law Reform* 471 (1983).

scope of judicial review of agency action. The Labor Board is close to being a court already (what obscures recognition of this fact is the board's partisanship). Because the board's prosecutorial arm, the General Counsel, is independent of the board's members, and because the board has rarely used its power of explicit rule making, the principal function of the board's members has become appellate review of the decisions of administrative law judges, the trial judges of the system. If the board members had the same terms that judges of the Tax Court have (14 years instead of 5 years), the Labor Board would be a Labor Court. Yet the example of the Tax Court suggests that there would still be a perceived necessity to allow judicial review in the courts of appeals. Still, the narrower the scope of that review, the greater is the implied delegation of judging to specialized tribunals and the bigger the role of the specialized judiciary relative to the generalist judiciary. Indeed, so potentially significant is this method of reducing the caseload of the Article III courts that I shall give it separate consideration in the next section of this chapter.

Finally, I accept unreservedly that our judges are specialized—to judging. Familiar as this point is, it is hardly inevitable. Federal judging could be a part-time occupation; federal regulatory commisioners, some federal magistrates, and most arbitrators are part-time judges. I assume the main reason that federal judging is not part-time[32] is a concern with real or apparent conflicts of interest; a secondary reason, important today, is that many more judges would be needed, which would make it more difficult to maintain a minimum coherence of federal law.

The functional specialization of federal judges has two implications for the question whether more subject-matter specialization would be a good idea. First, it is a partial answer to the doubts of those nonjudges—practitioners, or law professors, specializing in one or at most two fields of law—who, reflecting on their own ability to master additional fields, dismiss out of hand the possibility that a federal judge could have an adequate working knowledge of even a significant fraction of the fields in which he is required to decide cases. A federal appellate judge spends essentially all of his professional time deciding appeals. The distractions that reduce the amount of time which the successful practitioner or law professor spends reading and writing and thinking about law to a fraction of the working day—travel and committee work and dealing with clients or with students—are matters from which federal judges are largely free, with the important—poten-

---

32. Except that federal judges are allowed to do part-time teaching and writing.

tially, the devastating—exception of time spent supervising and coordinating a staff of legal and clerical assistants. With rare exceptions, no
federal judge will know an area of substantive law as well as its fore-
most practitioners and scholars, but he will know more than busy practitioners and scholars think he could know when they imagine trying to
cram more study time into their crowded days. And he will have a skill
at judging that comes from long practice in evaluating arguments of
counsel, decisions of trial judges, and trial records and that is a legitimate fruit of specialization in the function of appellate judging.

Another implication of specialization of function concerns job satisfaction, and in turn the caliber of people willing to accept appointment
to the federal courts of appeals. One does not have to be a Marxist,
steeped in notions of anomie and alienation, to realize that monotonous
jobs are unfulfilling for many people, especially educated and intelligent people, and that the growth of specialization has given to many
white-collar jobs a degree of monotony formerly found only on assembly lines. I have said that all a federal court of appeals judge does, essentially, is decide appeals; this means reading briefs and records,
hearing oral arguments, conferring with other judges after the argument, preparing opinions, reviewing opinions prepared by the other
judges on the panel, voting on petitions for rehearings—and little else.
The activities I have just mentioned, repeated over and over again, have
about them an element of the monotonous. This is one reason that most
of the courts of appeals and the Supreme Court continue to take a
summer recess. But for many judges the recess would not save the job
from being monotonous if the subject matter were uniform. It is not an
adequate reply that most lawyers today are specialists. I repeat my distinction between specialization of function and specialization of subject
matter. The antitrust lawyer specializes in one field of law, but his daily
rounds are more varied than those of the appellate judge—sometimes
he is trying (more likely pretrying) a case, sometimes he is arguing an
appeal, sometimes he is counseling a client.

How much variety would the average federal judge require to make
him happy? Too much can induce a well-merited sense of inability to
cope. Many federal judges would be content to hear no criminal cases;
many would be content to hear no diversity cases, knowing they would
still have a large common law jurisdiction, both federal and state. The
new Federal Circuit court is only a semispecialized court; its jurisdiction spans several unrelated fields. The problem of job satisfaction may
not be very serious even if the federal courts are moved a fair way toward becoming specialized courts.

Moreover, even if a specialized (or semispecialized) federal appellate judiciary would attract on average somewhat less able lawyers than our generalist judiciary does, it does not follow that greater specialization would be bad. A person who does only one job may perform better than an abler person who divides his time among several jobs, none of which he learns to do really well. But I question whether this insight can be transferred to appellate judging from the industrial, technical, and academic fields where it is conventionally articulated. It is easy to understand what is meant by someone who is a specialist in engineering or orthopedic surgery or ancient Greek dialects, but what is a specialist in an ideology? It is a fact, if perhaps an unfortunate one, that many areas of our law, especially federal law, have a strong ideological cast. To say, for example, that Laurence Tribe or Gerald Gunther or Philip Kurland or John Ely is a "specialist" in constitutional law has rather a special meaning: they are specialists in the sense that they know constitutional law much better than most scholars or practitioners; but few people, even those who take seriously the idea of dividing the Supreme Court into a constitutional and a nonconstitutional branch, would also want to fill the constitutional branch with people like Tribe, Gunther, and so on *because* they are specialists in constitutional law. A real specialist is not just someone who knows a lot about a subject; he is someone to whom we are willing to entrust important decisions that affect us, and we are willing because we think the specialist is objective—that is, his judgment is independent of his personal values, which are values that we may not share. This is not a sense that most people have about experts in constitutional law.

To take a less dramatic example, but one closer to my own professional experience, consider the implications of creating a specialized court to decide antitrust appeals. Antitrust is a forbidding field to the noninitiate. Its practitioners are experts, but are they objective? Antitrust theorists are divided today into three warring camps. One of them thinks that among the important values that the antitrust laws are designed and should be interpreted to promote are social or political values having to do with decentralizing economic power and equalizing the distribution of wealth.[33] Between it and the two other camps, which are united in believing that the only proper goals of antitrust laws are economic, there is no common ground. As yet there is no objective method of choosing between the economic and noneconomic approaches. And within the economic camp there is a "Harvard School," prone to find monopolistic practices, and a "Chicago School," which

33. See, for example, Robert Pitofsky, "The Political Content of Antitrust," 127 *U. Pa. L. Rev.* 1051 (1979).

believes the same practices to be for the most part procompetitive;[34] and again there is as yet no agreed-upon method for deciding which view is correct.

These cleavages, reflecting deep and at the moment unbridgeable divisions in ethical, political, and economic thought, would not be eliminated by committing the decision of antitrust appeals to a specialized court; on the contrary, they would be exacerbated. A "camp" is more likely to gain the upper hand in a specialized court than in the entire federal court system or even in one circuit. The reason is not only that most appointments to the specialized court would be made from the camps but also that experts are more sensitive to swings in professional opinion than an outsider, a generalist, would be. The appearance of uniform policy that would result from domination of the specialized court by one of the contending factions in antitrust policy would thus be an illusion; a turn of the political wheel would bring another of the warring camps into temporary command. If antitrust were the domain of a specialized court there would have been a greater expansion in the scope and intrusiveness of antitrust policy in the 1960s and 1970s than in fact occurred, followed by a more radical contraction in the 1980s than has occurred. The history of the Federal Trade Commission, which in part is a specialized antitrust court, provides some evidence of this.

Judge Friendly has raised similar questions about proposals to create a federal court of criminal appeals.[35] Inevitably such a court would become an arena of struggle between the "law and order" and the "criminals' rights" advocates—between those who believe the paramount concern of courts interpreting criminal law and procedure should be the public safety and those who think it should be the protection of criminal defendants' rights. The work of such a court would be closely monitored by congressional committees and private watchdog groups, and the court would become a focus of criticisms that today are diffused across the many generalist federal courts that decide criminal cases as part of a much broader jurisdiction.

Antitrust, criminal, and constitutional law are not the only areas of contemporary federal law that are divided into warring camps. Another is patent law, which is riven by a deep cleavage, paralleling the cleav-

---

34. For a description of the two "economic camps" see Richard A. Posner, "The Chicago School of Antitrust Analysis," 127 *U. Pa. L. Rev.* 925 (1979). See also Bickel, "The Antitrust Division's Adoption of a Chicago School Economic Policy Calls for Some Reorganization: But Is the Division's New Policy Here to Stay?" 20 *Houston L. Rev.* 1083 (1983).

35. See Friendly, supra note 29, at 639–640.

ages in antitrust law, between those who believe that patent protection should be construed generously to create additional incentives to technological progress and those who believe that patent protection should be narrowly construed to accommodate the procompetitive policies of the antitrust laws. Social security disability law is divided between those who emphasize the humane and remedial objects of the law and those who worry about fostering dependence and depleting the federal budget. These fields are divided over questions of value, which cannot be answered by consulting an expert observer, neutrally deploying his value-free knowledge. Indeed, that is why we call them questions of value.

It is remarkable in how few fields of modern American law there is a professional consensus on fundamental questions. One such area is trusts and estates, which has somehow avoided getting entangled in the myriad social tensions of the day. It is only a matter of time, however, before some enterprising radical legal scholar takes it upon himself to assault this traditional bulwark of the wealthy; and already there is ideological struggle over the issue of "social responsibility" in the investment of trust assets. Federal tax law is another consensus field. This fact, in combination with the difficulty nonspecialists have with questions of tax law, provides a strong argument for creating a federal court of tax appeals,[36] though such a court would provide only limited relief to the other courts of appeals (there were only 843 tax appeals from the district courts and Tax Court in 1983). But torts, for example, traditionally an area of state law but increasingly one of federal law as well, is, like antitrust, a field of ideological combat between those who favor contracting liability and those who favor expanding it. Bankruptcy is divided between pro-debtor and pro-creditor camps. Not even contract law and property law have escaped ideological conflict: consider the debate over unconscionability in contract law, and over tenants' rights in property law. The fierce divisions in administrative law, labor law, corporation and securities law, civil rights law, and federal jurisdiction and procedure require no comment. There is little fruitful communication across most of these divides.

Thus, whatever drawbacks there are to a specialized judiciary are unlikely to be offset by gains from greater specialization; in most areas, indeed, there will be no such gains. Vocational monotony is the least of these drawbacks, for it can probably be avoided by giving each court a cluster of special fields. A greater drawback, at least to those who believe in the value of judicial independence from the partisan political pro-

36. As forcefully argued in Friendly, supra note 16, at 461–471.

cess, is that a specialized court can be controlled by the executive and legislative branches of government more effectively than a generalist court can be. It is easier to predict how someone will decide cases in his specialty than how he will decide cases across the board; therefore, if courts are specialized, the officials who appoint judges will be better able to use the appointments process to shape the court, and Congress will find it easier to monitor, and through the appropriations process to control, the court.

Now it is true that the less independent the courts are from the other branches of government, the less they can be expected to carry out the will of an earlier legislature, as embodied in the statutes which that legislature enacted; and the less durable therefore are the "deals" that special interest groups can make with the legislature.[37] The choice is therefore between two types of federal judicial independence—independence from the constellation of political interests that at any given time is dominant in Congress and the White House, and independence from the will of an earlier Congress as expressed in its legislation. Although I hesitate to give an opinion on which type of independence is "better," the former probably reduces the power of interest groups— the "factions" about which Madison wrote in *Federalist* No. 10—in shaping public policy.[38] The ability of legislators to project their will into the future through legislation that must be interpreted by judges is limited anyway by the fact that in performing their interpretive function the judges, however conscientious they are about ascertaining and carrying out the will of the enacting Congress, are largely limited to public materials—the language of the statute, committee reports, and other conventional aids to interpretation—in ascertaining that will. And since the public materials invariably seek to disguise rather than to flaunt the extent to which the real aim of the legislation is to advance the selfish interests of one group in the society, the process of statutory interpretation by judges tends to give legislation a more public-spirited cast than the legislators actually intended. This is no more than a tendency, though. The judges easily may overlook compromises, and thus impart greater thrust to a piece of legislation than the legislators agreed to.

In suggesting that the judiciary would be less independent from the

37. See William M. Landes and Richard A. Posner, "The Independent Judiciary in an Interest-Group Perspective," 18 *J. Law & Econ.* 875, 885–887 (1975).

38. The abolition of the Commerce Court (a specialized appellate court for review of orders of the Interstate Commerce Commission) after only three years of existence, in major part because it was thought to have been "captured" by the railroads, illustrates this point. See Felix Frankfurter and James M. Landis, *The Business of the Supreme Court: A Study of the Federal Judicial System* 153–174 (1928).

other branches of government if it were specialized by subject matter, I am obviously associating the generalist federal judiciary with the constitutional idea of the separation of powers. This association has another aspect. The idea that the judiciary is a check on the other branches of government derives not only from the power of the courts to invalidate legislation as unconstitutional but also, as emphasized by Hamilton in *Federalist* No. 78, from the judiciary's role as an intermediary between the coercive powers of the state and their application to the individual citizen. The federal courts play their role as a buffer between the political branches (and any interest groups that dominate them) and the citizen more effectively when they are composed of generalists. A generalist court provides some insulation; a specialist court is apt to be a superconductor. Specialists are more likely than generalists to identify with the goals of a government program, since the program is the focus of their career; they may therefore see their function as one of enforcing the law in a vigorous rather than a tempered fashion. In this respect the case for a generalist federal judiciary resembles the case for the jury—not despite, but because of, its lack of expertness.

An earlier qualification must be repeated: the generalist court will be more faithful to the original spirit of an enactment, the specialist court to the current legislative and executive will. But these fidelities are of a different order. The specialist is more faithful to the current goals of a program than the generalist because he is subject to greater control by the political branches. There is no mystery about *his* incentives. But the generalist judge, if faithful to the original goals of a statutory program at all, is so as a matter of conscience rather than compulsion. A desire to temper the harshness of the law, to make legislation more civilized, or sometimes even to thwart the popular will is, rightly or wrongly, a part of many judges' consciences; and it operates to blunt the impact of interest groups on the law.

The examples of the Tax Court and the Federal Trade Commission show that it is not inevitable that a specialist court will be a monopolist of its field. But it is highly probable, other than in vast fields such as criminal law. The more confined the jurisdiction of a court, the fewer judges are needed to man it; and if only a few judges are needed, economies of specialization will be sacrificed by having more than one court. The monopoly will not be complete, because the court's decisions will be subject to review by the Supreme Court. But the Supreme Court will be handicapped in reviewing the work of a specialized court. The specialized court can be expected to evolve a distinctive legal culture that will be hard for any generalist body to fathom; and the Supreme Court will not have the benefit of competing judicial answers to choose among when deciding questions within the domain of the specialized court. The problem is general; judicial monopoly reduces diversity of ideas and approaches—what in other contexts has been called "yardstick competition."[39] Although the federal courts of appeals do not compete directly with each other any more than the state supreme courts do, they compete indirectly by providing varied responses to common problems. If two circuits disagree on a question, other circuits benefit from the clash of views. The circuits as well as the states are laboratories for judicial experimentation, and a judicial monopoly of a field of federal law eliminates competition in that field.

Judicial monopoly also concentrates government power. The federal court system is extremely diffuse, notwithstanding the supremacy of the Supreme Court; the more than 600 other Article III judges also play a role in administering such national programs as Medicaid, Title VII, and antitrust. Specialization by subject matter would bring about a greater concentration of judicial power even if the individual judges of a specialized court had the identical incentives and outlook of the average generalist judge.

A related point is that specialization reduces the geographic diversity of the federal judiciary. We think of the federal court system as a unitary national system, but it is very rare that someone is appointed to the district court who is not a resident, usually a long-time resident, of the district, or that someone is appointed to the court of appeals unless he is a resident not only of the circuit but of the particular state of the circuit to which the judgeship has been informally allocated. Specialized federal appellate courts, in contrast, would be Washington courts. There are not enough antitrust appeals to justify a specialized court of antitrust appeals in every district, every state, or even every circuit. The way to make specialization pay is to broaden the judicial "market," to make it nationwide. It is not logically necessary, merely overwhelmingly likely, that the site of a national court will not be Akron, or Janesville, or Miami, but Washington, D.C. This means that the members of specialized federal courts will be appointed with much less attention to regional diversity than are the members of the generalist federal judiciary. And because there are marked political differences among the nation's states and regions, a departure from geographic diversification as a principle of federal judicial selection implies once again an increase in the concentration of governmental power.

Judicial specialization would also reduce the cross-pollination of

39. See, for example, Clair Wilcox and William G. Shepherd, *Public Policies toward Business* 528 (5th ed. 1975).

legal ideas. Those who think that the basic concepts of antitrust law are totally different from those of tort law will not be troubled by this. But those who think, like Holmes, that there is a general legal culture that enables those broadly immersed in it to enrich one field with insights from another will see this as still another drawback of specialization:

> Every group, and even almost every individual when he has acquired a definite mode of thought, gets a more or less special terminology which it takes time for an outsider to live into. Having to listen to arguments, now about railroad business, now about a patent, now about an admiralty case, now about mining law and so on, a thousand times I have thought that I was hopelessly stupid and as many have found that when I got hold of the language there was no such thing as a difficult case. There are plenty of cases about which one doubts, and may doubt forever, as the premises for reasoning are not exact, but all the cases when you have walked up and seized the lion's skin come uncovered and show the old donkey of a question of law, like all the rest.[40]

Yet sometimes it is the generalist rather than the specialist who suffers from tunnel vision—for example, the generalist who in deciding a tax case does not look beyond the particular subsections of the Internal Revenue Code that the parties cite to him and thus never understands the statutory design.

Specialization is a potential source of serious boundary problems. Cases that have to do with review of administrative action involve, almost by definition, single issues or at least issues within a single branch of law—the branch administered by the agency in question. You cannot join to a request for social security disability benefits a tort claim against the person who disabled you. But in many areas of law, complaints cutting across a variety of fields are the norm rather than the exception, and those cases are difficult to deal with in a system of specialized courts: either one specialized court is assigned the whole case, producing underspecialization with respect to those issues that come from a different field of law, or the case is split between different courts and judicial economy is lost.

Finally, a generalist judiciary can cope better with unforeseen changes in the caseload mix than a specialized judiciary can. It is a

---

40. Letter to John C. H. Wu (May 14, 1923), reprinted in *Justice Oliver Wendell Holmes: His Book Notices and Uncollected Letters and Papers* 163–164 (Harry C. Shriver ed. 1936).

mathematical law that the federal appellate caseload as a whole changes less from year to year than the components of that caseload. Hence if each component were assigned to a separate court it would be more difficult to match supply to demand, as shown in Table 5.4. An unexpected increase in the number of social security appeals in one year does not subject the courts of appeals to unbearable strain, because the other components of its caseload are increasing more slowly, and some are actually decreasing. But if there were a separate social security court of appeals, a sudden big increase in the number of social security appeals could put a big strain on that court because there would be no compensating decreases, while a sudden big decrease could leave its judges underemployed. And altering the number of judges is not a feasible method of coping with short-term caseload fluctuations. The process of creating new federal judgeships and then of filling the newly created vacancies is a painfully slow one. Reducing the number of federal judges is a very slow process too; it can be done only through attrition, because of the tenure provisions of Article III. (I leave aside the constitutional question of whether, if Congress abolished an entire court—for example, the Seventh Circuit—it would still have to pay the judges their salaries.) The process is slow even in Article I courts, because judges of those courts are appointed for long fixed terms. No one has suggested yet that a good way to match supply to demand is to lay off judges when their services are not needed, like factory workers or airline pilots, and recall them when demand picks up.

The problem of matching supply to demand is not merely theoretical. A widespread perception that the judges of the Court of Claims and

Table 5.4. Changes in selected components of the federal appellate caseload, 1982–1983

Category	Percentage change from previous year in cases filed (+ or −)
Antitrust	− 9
Civil rights	+ 7
Labor	+16
Tax	+10
Postconviction[a]	+10
Social security	+27
Environmental	−28
All civil cases	+ 8

a. Including prisoner civil-rights cases.

the Court of Customs and Patent Appeals did not have enough work to do, at least as measured by current norms of judicial busyness, was an unspoken reason behind giving the new Federal Circuit court a broader jurisdiction than its constituent courts had had. At the same time, it is clear that the bankruptcy judges are heavily overloaded because of the unexpectedly large increase in the number of bankruptcy filings in the last several years (they have more than doubled since 1979). The problem of supply-demand imbalance has been less serious in the courts of appeals because of the diverse character of their caseload.

Although the drift of thinking in the profession seems to be toward greater judicial specialization, as one would expect in light of the caseload pressures, I want to end this section with a brief glance at a very interesting proposal, related to my point about geographic diversity, that goes against the grain. This is the proposal to alter the venue provisions of statutes granting rights to judicial review of federal administrative decisions to make it more difficult to get such decisions reviewed in the Court of Appeals for the District of Columbia Circuit.[41] Over the years this court has become almost a specialized court of administrative agency review[42]—55 percent of its cases in 1983 were administrative appeals—and its location in Washington, D.C., a place unrepresented in the Senate, has increased the presidential appointive power over the court. Dealing as it does with more controversial subject matter than the Tax Court or the former Court of Claims and Court of Customs and Patent Appeals, this court can be thought of as an experiment in changing the federal judiciary into a series of specialized courts, located, one would expect, mainly or entirely in Washington. Consistent with what I have suggested is a tendency of specialized courts, the D.C. Circuit has—by its own report—defined its responsibility in relation to the administrative agencies it reviews as being not to act as a buffer between the agencies and the citizens they are trying to coerce, but to spur the agencies to regulate more effectively; it is not holding the horses back but lashing them forward.[43] Thus one can understand not only

41. For a critical discussion of the proposal, see Cass R. Sunstein, "Participation, Public Law, and Venue Reform," 49 U. Chi. L. Rev. 976, 990–1000 (1982).

42. For a good discussion see Patricia M. Wald, "Making 'Informed' Decisions on the District of Columbia Circuit," 50 Geo. Wash. L. Rev. 135 (1982). See also Gordon Bermant, Patricia A. Lombard, and Carroll Seron, The Cases of the United States Court of Appeals for the District of Columbia Circuit (Fed. Judic. Center July 1982).

43. See, for example, Adams v. Richardson, 480 F.2d 1159 (D.C. Cir. 1973) (en banc) (per curiam); Calvert Cliffs Coordinating Comm. v. AEC, 449 F.2d 1109, 1111 (D.C. Cir. 1971); Environmental Defense Fund, Inc. v. Ruckelshaus, 439 F.2d 584 (D.C. Cir. 1971); Greater Boston Television Corp. v. FCC, 444 F.2d 841, 850–851 (D.C. Cir. 1970); Antonin Scalia, "Vermont Yankee: The APA, the D.C. Circuit, and the Supreme Court," 1978 S. Ct. Rev. 345; Cass R. Sunstein, "Deregulation and the Hard-Look Doctrine," 1983 S. Ct. Rev. 177, 181–184, 209–210.

why, as noted by Professor Sunstein,[44] environmental activists strongly oppose the proposed venue changes, but also why it is possible to mobilize an interest group on a seemingly technical issue of federal jurisdiction in relation to the D.C. Circuit. This would be more difficult to do in regard to the other circuits, with their more diverse "clientele."

For all the reasons I have given, I am reluctant to endorse any proposals for new federal specialized courts except a court of tax appeals. And there is another reason: I conjecture that the practice, curious to non-lawyers, of judges employing as their law clerks fresh graduates of law school rather than seasoned practitioners is related to the generality of the federal jurisdiction and the specialized character of the modern practice of law. A lawyer who knows one field of federal law well but the others not well at all is of less value to a federal judge than a less experienced lawyer who knows many fields of federal law pretty well. Only recent graduates are likely to fill this bill, for once they have practiced for a few years they will have forgotten much of what they learned in law school outside of the particular field in which they happen to be specializing as practitioners. Therefore I would predict that if we moved to a system of specialized courts, we would tend to see a different type of law clerk—a more experienced practitioner, functioning more like an assistant judge than a judicial assistant. We would see, in other words, the emergence of a more conventionally bureaucratic judicial system—carrying us still further away from the traditional Anglo-American conception of judging.

The conception itself has not served us so well that it should be immune from reexamination; but anything so fundamental would be beyond the scope of this chapter, and indeed of the book. And despite the negative tone of this section I do not deny that specialized appellate courts have benefits—in reducing the number of intercircuit conflicts and hence the workload of the Supreme Court, in lessening legal uncertainty both by reducing conflicts and by making judicial decision making more predictable through reducing the number of decision makers in each field of law, and in enabling whatever potential gains there are from judicial specialization to be realized. Nor could one say with any confidence that the costs that I have so emphasized really outweigh these benefits; we are dealing with imponderables.

RETHINKING ADMINISTRATIVE REVIEW

We saw in the last chapter that much of the federal caseload, especially at the court of appeals and Supreme Court levels, consists of the review

44. See Sunstein, supra note 41, at 987–990.

of administrative agency decisions. I believe that some of the review function could be drawn inside the agencies, thus lightening the judicial caseload. The problem today is that although there is appellate review within most agencies, the review function very often is performed in so perfunctory and unconvincing a manner that the review has little credibility with many federal judges and has to be repeated by them. A good example is provided by the burgeoning field of social security disability review. If an applicant is denied the benefits he is seeking, he can demand a trial-type hearing before an administrative law judge of the Social Security Administration followed by an appeal to an obscure body within the Administration called the Appeals Council. I have read many administrative law judges' decisions in social security disability cases, all of which the disappointed applicant had asked the Appeals Council to review (as he had to do, before he could begin judicial review proceedings), but I can remember only one occasion on which the Appeals Council wrote an opinion, even when the administrative law judge's decision raised difficult questions. The situation in the National Labor Relations Board is similar, though less extreme. Decisions by administrative law judges are appealed to the Board, which invariably issues some type of opinion. But usually the opinion is a paragraph of boilerplate with at most a footnote making one or two minor modifications in the adminstrative law judge's decision. As a result of this perfunctory administrative review process, federal judicial review of Labor Board decisions means, in the vast majority of cases, federal judicial review of decisions of administrative law judges—to whose decisions the principles of administrative review require the courts of appeals to give as much and maybe more deference than to decisions of federal district judges. I realize that the Board's members have a far heavier caseload than any federal appellate judges do, but it would be easier and cheaper for Congress to establish within the Board a tier of credible appellate judges who would write opinions in all but frivolous cases than to continue expanding the federal courts so that they can keep up with a rising workload of administrative-review cases.

With the appellate process within the agencies strengthened, the scope of federal appellate review of administrative decisions could be reduced. In the case of social security disability benefits, maybe it could be eliminated altogether; and certainly there would be no need for the two tiers of judicial review that we now have—review in the district court with a right of appeal to the court of appeals. What I am describing, of course, is a kind of specialized appellate review; and the caveats emphasized in the preceding section of this chapter must therefore be kept in view. But as I said there, the principle of specialized adjudication is firmly ensconced in the administrative process. I now suggest a modest expansion that will relieve the federal courts of appeals of some of their burdens without transforming *them* into specialized courts.

A SECOND SUPREME COURT?

More than a decade ago a study group headed by Professor Paul Freund recommended the creation of a new federal appellate court between the courts of appeals and the Supreme Court.[45] At the time the number of cases filed in the Supreme Court was about 3,700 a year; it is now moderately higher (4,200). The specific recommendation was for a permanent court that would both screen petitions for certiorari for the Supreme Court and decide, on reference from the Court, cases involving conflicts between circuits. The recommendation has been hotly debated in the intervening years and many variants proposed,[46] but it seemed to be getting nowhere until Chief Justice Burger in 1982 proposed the beguiling variant of a temporary court, limited to deciding intercircuit appeals on reference from the Supreme Court. This proposal[47] has picked up a good deal of support, and if it comes to grief it will probably be over the political issue of who is to appoint the judges.

I shall put to one side any possible constitutional problem arising from the fact that Article III ordains the creation of *one* Supreme Court by noting that the Supreme Court would retain its supremacy because it could review decisions of the Intercircuit Tribunal (as the court proposed by the Chief Justice would be known), though it is anticipated that the occasions for such review would be rare. I turn directly then to the soundness of the proposal as a matter of policy. The strongest reason in favor of it was indicated in Chapter 4: with the growth in the number of federal court of appeals judges per circuit, number of circuits, and number of court of appeals decisions, the potential for, and almost certainly the actual number of, intercircuit conflicts has grown, while the Supreme Court's capacity to deal with them has declined with the growth in the number of applications.

But it would be hasty to conclude from this that an Intercircuit Tribunal would be a good thing. It would be a good thing only if the Supreme Court could not readily increase the number of intercircuit conflict

45. See Federal Judicial Center, *Report of the Study Group on the Case Load of the Supreme Court* (AO, December 1972).

46. See references in Casper and Posner, supra note 13, at xi n.2; Note, "Of High Designs: A Compendium of Proposals to Reduce the Workload of the Supreme Court," 97 *Harv. L. Rev.* 307 (1983).

47. As embodied in S. 645, 98th Cong., 1st Sess., March 1, 1983. For an excellent analysis see Arthur D. Hellman, "Caseloads, Conflicts, and Decisional Capacity: Does the Supreme Court Need Help?" 67 *Judicature* 28 (1983).

cases that it hears—which I shall assume—and, in addition, if the Supreme Court ought to be resolving more intercircuit conflicts than it now is doing. This is not so clear.[48] Conflicts that do not involve subjecting the same person to inconsistent legal obligations are not intolerable, and most intercircuit conflicts, including most that the Supreme Court resolves, are of this type. (I do not count the United States as a "person," since it can usually adapt pretty well to different rules in different circuits.) Most procedural conflicts are of this type, and so are most conflicts of any sort in the field of criminal law. When a conflict does not subject the same person to inconsistent legal obligations, there is a presumption that it should be allowed to simmer for a time at the circuit level. An issue that provokes a conflict among the circuits that is not immediately eliminated by one circuit's receding from its previous position is likely to involve a difficult legal question; and a difficult question is more likely to be answered correctly if it is allowed to engage the attention of different sets of judges deciding factually different cases than if it is answered finally by the first panel to consider it. After most circuits have spoken to a question, and if the circuits are closely divided, it is then time for the Supreme Court to step in and resolve the conflict. The proposition that federal law ought to be the same everywhere in the country is not persuasive. If uniformity is desirable (as it is), so are diversity and competition. Federal law is so pervasive today that much of the role that the different states played in the past in the development of legal doctrine through competition among the courts of the different states must be played today, if it is to be played at all, by the federal circuits.

But it can be argued that even if there is no need to resolve any more intercircuit conflicts than the Supreme Court is resolving today, the Court is so overworked that the Intercircuit Tribunal would, by taking over the Court's function of resolving intercircuit conflicts, improve the Court's performance. In the 1982 term, about 30 of the roughly 150 cases that the Court decided by signed opinion were intercircuit conflicts—20 percent. But despite much lore to the contrary, it is not obvious that 150 cases is too many for a court of nine members, sitting en banc, to decide in a term. This averages out to fewer than 17 majority opinions per justice, which is far less than at the court of appeals level. Of course the Supreme Court's cases raise more difficult questions on average, but it does not follow that these cases are more time-consuming to decide and write up. Indeed, there is practical evidence that they

48. For divergent views on this question compare Casper and Posner, supra note 13, at 85–92, with U.S. Commission on Revision of the Federal Court Appellate System, supra note 29, at 16–19, 76–168.

are not: a court in which the average judge writes more concurring and dissenting opinions than signed majority opinions (23 versus 17 in the 1982 term), and in which many opinions are almost suffocated in footnotes and other parade of learning, is not a court lacking for time. The Court's opinion caseload has risen and fallen over the years, and no one has ever found any correlation between the number of cases that the Court decides each year and the quality of its decisions. The justices could write more, but briefer and simpler, majority opinions, and fewer concurring and dissenting opinions.

Moreover, I do not accept the premise that underlies all I have said in this section—that the Supreme Court is deciding the minimum number of intercircuit conflicts. It may well be deciding too many—and this is not just the biased opinion of a circuit judge! Observers of the Court's work, including an occasional Supreme Court justice, have long been struck by the number of unimportant cases that the Court decides each year—while complaining about its intolerable caseload.[49] My favorite recent example of a case that does not seem to belong in the nation's highest court is *Walter v. United States.*[50] A pornographer shipped 12 packages containing a total of 871 boxes of film, each film depicting obscene homosexual activities, to a female associate of his nicknamed Leggs. He addressed the packages to "Leggs, Inc." at her place of work. The packages were misdelivered to "L'Eggs Products, Inc.," the manufacturer of women's hosiery. Employees of L'Eggs opened the packages and found the boxes of film, which revealed their contents through explicit verbal descriptions and suggestive drawings. The employees took the packages to the FBI, which opened the boxes of films and ran the films on a projector to verify their obscene character. Walter and others were convicted of federal obscenity charges, and they challenged their convictions on the ground that the FBI had committed an illegal search of the boxes of films. The Supreme Court sustained this contention, though no single opinion commanded majority support. If the Court were really busy, it would have passed up the chance to wrestle with this freakish case.

49. See, for example, William J. Brennan, Jr., "Some Thoughts on the Supreme Court's Workload," 55 *N.Y. State Bar J.* (May 1983) at 14–15; Friendly, supra note 16, at 51; Henry J. Friendly, "Indiscretion about Discretion," 31 *Emory L. J.* 747–758 n.35 (1982); Milton Handler, "What do Do with the Supreme Court's Burgeoning Calendars?" 5 *Cardozo L. Rev.* 249, 262 (1984); John Paul Stevens, "The Life Span of a Judge-Made Rule," 58 *N.Y.U. L. Rev.* 1, 17 (1983). But cf. Arthur D. Hellman, "The Supreme Court, the National Law, and the Selection of Cases for the Plenary Docket," 44 *U. Pitt. L. Rev.* 521, 630–634 (1983); Arthur D. Hellman, "Error Correction, Lawmaking, and the Supreme Court's Exercise of Discretionary Review," 44 *U. Pitt. L. Rev.* 795, 866–872 (1983).

50. 447 U.S. 649 (1980).

I conclude that, even putting aside the fact that the Court's caseload is to a significant extent a product of feedback from its own earlier decisions expanding the reach of federal law, it would seem that the problems for which the Chief Justice is seeking the succor of an Intercircuit Tribunal have been to a significant extent created by the Supreme Court itself. But the circuit judges as well as the Supreme Court justices hold keys to the solution. The problem of unresolved conflicts between circuits would be ameliorated if each circuit adopted a policy of automatically deferring, other than, perhaps, in cases of great significance, to the resolution of any issue of law by three circuits, so that if the first three circuits to consider an issue agreed on how it should be decided the remaining circuits would consider themselves bound by the decision. Of course, the first three circuits might get the issue wrong; but the probability is sufficiently small to be outweighed by the benefits to judicial economy from deeming the matter closed.

There is finally the question how good the Intercircuit Tribunal is likely to be. The very thing that makes the idea politically attractive at the moment—its temporary feature—seems inconsistent with the new court's being able to function optimally. It is to be composed of judges from each circuit who will serve on a part-time basis and then return full-time to their circuits. It is possible, but I think unlikely, that its members may, either consciously or unconsciously, view themselves as circuit representatives, in which event the resolution of an intercircuit conflict would depend more on the circuit origins of the members of the panel that decided the particular case than on the merits of the case. The more serious problem is that since the court will be composed of the same personnel as the courts of appeals, randomly sampled with regard to quality, the average quality of the court's decisions may be no higher than that of the decisions it is reviewing. Because of the greater care given the selection of Supreme Court justices than of circuit judges, and because of the unique nationwide perspective that membership on the Supreme Court affords, the Supreme Court is a better court than the average (maybe than any) court of appeals; and when it resolves a conflict between two circuits it is therefore more likely than not to resolve it correctly. (But it could save itself some time by sometimes just adopting the opinion of the circuit it agreed with.)[51] There can be no similar expectations of the Intercircuit Tribunal: it would cut

51. I have my doubts, for example, whether it was necessary for the Supreme Court to write an opinion affirming Judge Friendly's magnificent opinion in Leist v. Simplot, 638 F.2d (2d Cir. 1980), aff'd sub nom. Merrill Lynch, Pierce, Fenner & Smith v. Curran, 456 U.S. 353 (1982), rather than simply adopting his opinion as the decision of the Supreme Court.

off some conflicts prematurely, resolve others incorrectly, deflect attention from the real causes of the Supreme Court's problems, increase the
workload of circuit judges (by reducing the number actually sitting in
the courts of appeals), and delay federal litigation.

III

RETHINKING THE

FEDERAL JUDICIAL

PROCESS

6

The Role of Federal Courts

in a Federal System

THE DIFFICULTY of solving the federal courts' caseload problems by the measures considered in the last chapter invites a different kind of approach, explored in this and the next two chapters—a more general reconsideration of the federal judicial process. Of course, such reconsideration may have value apart from its contribution to alleviating the caseload crisis; but the crisis gives this kind of fundamental analysis an urgency it would otherwise lack.

In this chapter the role of federal courts in our system is reexamined, from the ground up. Maybe it is wrong to take even the broad outlines of the federal courts' present jurisdiction for granted; maybe the heart of their problems is that their jurisdiction is far too extensive. Fundamental changes in jurisdiction are, of course, much more difficult to bring about than the incremental changes discussed in the last chapter, and much that will be discussed here will strike the practical-minded reader as excessively academic. But American public policy is so volatile that today's radical speculations may easily become the conventional wisdom of just a few years from now. And in any event, consideration of fundamental reform may reinforce the case for incremental reforms, as in the case of the diversity jurisdiction, to which I return again in this chapter.

FEDERALISM AND FEDERAL COURTS

The most fundamental question is, why have separate state and federal court systems? This is not an inevitable concomitant of a federal system. Canada, for example, a federation of ten provinces corresponding roughly to the states of the United States, has only traces of a dual court system. The principal courts—the Supreme Court of Canada, and the Court of Appeal and Superior Court for each of the provinces—have jurisdiction over both provincial and federal cases, but they are not provincial courts exercising federal as well as provincial jurisdiction; they are federal courts also exercising provincial jurisdiction, their judges being appointed, and the costs of the courts defrayed, by the national government.[1] Giving *our* federal courts a general and exclusive jurisdiction over state as well as federal cases is out of the question; it would be tantamount to the destruction of our federal system because American courts are so much more powerful than Canadian courts, the latter being close to the English model discussed in Chapter 2. But that still leaves as an option, though in the end I believe an unsound one, doing away with our lower federal courts (that is, all but the Supreme Court) and letting the state courts handle federal litigation at the trial and intermediate appellate levels.[2]

Whether there should be a dual system of courts in a federal system requires consideration of the theory of federalism, that is, of the allocation of responsibilities between the national government and regional or local governments. The literature on federalism began on a very high plane with the *Federalist*,[3] and distinguished judges such as John Marshall, Oliver Wendell Holmes, Louis Brandeis, Felix Frankfurter, and (the fullness of time may reveal) William Rehnquist have enriched it. Lately the subject has begun to attract the attention of social scientists, notably economists.[4] Although my discussion too will be in a scientific

1. See Gerald L. Gall, *The Canadian Legal System* 180–181 (2d ed. 1983).

2. A related possibility—designating state judges to serve also as federal judges—would require a constitutional amendment, because the individuals in question would lack the guarantees of independence that Article III requires that federal judges be given.

3. For some later examples, illustrating the diversity of the literature, see 1 Alexis de Tocqueville, *Democracy in America* 158–172 (Henry Reeve trans., rev. ed. 1899); Kenneth Clinton Wheare, *Federal Government* (4th ed. 1964); Henry J. Friendly, "Federalism: A Foreword," 86 *Yale L.J.* 1019 (1977); Paul A. Freund, "The Supreme Court and the Future of Federalism," in *The Future of Federalism* 37 (Samuel I. Shuman comp. 1968); American Law Institute, *Study of the Division of Jurisdiction between State and Federal Courts* (1969); Harry N. Scheiber, "Federalism and Legal Process: Historical and Contemporary Analysis of the American System," 14 *Law & Soc'y Rev.* 663 (1980); Paul M. Bator, "The State Courts and Federal Constitutional Litigation," 22 *Wm. & Mary L. Rev.* 605 (1981); Michael E. Solimine and James L. Walker, "Constitutional Litigation in Federal and State Courts: An Empirical Analysis of Judicial Parity," 2 *Hastings Constitutional L.Q.* 213 (1983).

4. See, for example, Tiebout, "A Pure Theory of Local Expenditures," 64 *J. Pol. Econ.* 416 (1956); George J. Stigler, "The Tenable Range of Functions of Local Government," in Staff of Joint Econ. Comm., 85th Cong., 1st Sess., *Federal Expenditure Policy for Economic*

spirit, I acknowledge that the relationship between the states and the federal government cannot be regarded solely as an expedient one, designed to promote liberty or efficiency or other values and alterable from time to time as circumstances, or the values themselves, change. The states retain whatever powers the Constitution did not grant to (or are not being exercised by) the federal government. The issue is not for us, as it is for example for the British or the French, simply whether it would be better to have more or less centralization of government— unless we are prepared to alter the Constitution in the most fundamental way imaginable.

But having entered this caveat about treating the allocation of responsibilities between the state and federal courts (and more broadly between the states and the federal government) as a question of expediency, I shall in the remainder of this chapter do just that for the sake of analytical clarity. And since good analysis is cold-blooded, I shall give no weight to the pieties of federalism that have adorned so many judicial opinions of the last decade. One is told in *Schlesinger v. Councilman,* for example, that "under Art[icle] VI of the Constitution, state courts share with federal courts an equivalent responsibility for the enforcement of federal rights, a responsibility one must expect they will fulfill."[5] For purposes of this chapter I deny that one *must* expect them to do any such thing. One is told in *Stone v. Powell* that "state courts, like federal courts, have a constitutional obligation to safeguard personal liberties and to uphold federal law."[6] State judges do have that obligation—it is imposed by Article VI—but I shall not assume, without a stronger reason than an oath, that state judges understand and fulfill the obligation as federal judges do. And here is a passage from *Sumner v. Mata:* "State judges as well as federal judges swear allegiance to the Constitution of the United States, and there is no reason to think that because of their frequent differences of opinions as to how that docu-

---

Growth and Stability 213 (Comm. Print 1957); Richard A. Posner, *Economic Analysis of Law,* chap. 26 (2d ed. 1977); Robert P. Inman and Daniel L. Rubinfeld, "The Judicial Pursuit of Local Fiscal Equity," 92 *Harv. L. Rev.* 1662 (1979); *The Economics of Federalism* (Bhajan S. Grewal, Geoffrey Brennan, and Russell L. Mathews eds. 1980); Susan Rose-Ackerman, "Does Federalism Matter? Political Choice in a Federal Republic," 89 *J. Pol. Econ.* 152 (1981); Frank H. Easterbrook, "Antitrust and the Economics of Federalism," 26 *J. Law & Econ.* 23 (1983); J. Robert S. Prichard (with Jamie Benedickson), "Securing the Canadian Economic Union: Federalism and Internal Barriers to Trade," in *Federalism and the Canadian Economic Union* 3, 15–27 (Michael J. Trebilcock et al., eds., 1983); Jerry L. Mashaw and Susan Rose-Ackerman, "Federalism and Regulation" (Columbia Law School, Center for Law & Econ. Studies, Working Paper no. 1, September 1983).
5. 420 U.S. 738, 755–756 (1975).
6. 428 U.S. 465, 493 n.35 (1976).

ment should be interpreted, all are not doing their mortal best to discharge their oath of office."[7] For present purposes, "frequent differences of opinions" is a more interesting part of this passage than the reference to the oath, or the unwillingness to infer from frequent differences of opinion that the state judges are not "doing their mortal best to discharge their oath." The theory of federalism that I shall expound, borrowing from the recent social scientific literature, is built on the assumption that people, including judges, act in accordance with their rational self-interest, whose promptings are not solely those of conscience, though conscience plays a role. This assumption is consistent with the well-known realism of the framers, who, though they did require that state judges take an oath of allegiance to the Constitution, plainly did not regard it as a sufficient guarantor of faithful adherence to the Constitution.

In considering the allocation of responsibilities between the state and federal courts that a theory of federalism implies, it can make a difference whether one looks upon the two court systems as they are in fact, with systematically different conditions of employment, or as they might be abstractly conceived—identical in every respect except their jurisdictions. As we saw in Chapter 2, the conditions of employment of federal judges have from the beginning been superior, on average, to those for state judges, notably in the matter of length of tenure. Lifetime tenure increases judicial independence in two ways: directly, by protecting the judges from retribution for unpopular decisions, but also indirectly, because by allowing them to remain fully employed until death it makes alternative employment less attractive. Judicial independence is threatened by the carrot as well as by the stick.

Are the differences in the conditions of employment between state and federal judges merely accidents that should not influence one's thinking about the ideal allocation of responsibilities between them? I believe not, not only because these differences have been so persistent but also because they are themselves implied by the theory of federalism. State governments have less monopoly power than the federal government. If a person did not like Huey Long's Louisiana, he could move to Alabama or Texas or any of the other (then) 47 states; but it was and is much more costly to emigrate from the United States altogether. The fact that the ability to vote with one's feet is much greater at the state than at the federal level produces a greater competitive check on the abuses of governmental power at the state level.

7. 449 U.S. 539, 549 (1981). This rhetoric is very old. In 1884 the Court wrote in Robb v. Connelly, 111 U.S. 624, 637, "Upon the State courts, equally with the courts of the Union, rests the obligation to guard, enforce, and protect every right granted or secured by the Constitution of the United States."

The federal government's potential monopoly power was much in the thinking of the framers of the Constitution, and one of the checks they set up against it, as we are told in *Federalist* No. 78 (Hamilton), was the independent judiciary with its lifetime tenure and secure (except for inflation) compensation. This costly check—it *is* costly to have a body of officials insulated from the usual incentives to efficient performance—would have less social value at the state level, where the power to be checked is not nearly as great. So it is not a surprise that the terms of employment of state judges (most of whom are elected) are indeed less conducive to judicial independence than those of federal judges. Since we thus have a body of judges, the federal judges, who—not adventitiously but for reasons derivable from the theory of federalism—have more secure and attractive employment conditions than do state judges and therefore have greater independence from political influences, we should in deciding how to allocate responsibilities between state and federal judges take the federal judges' greater independence into account. It is a factor intrinsic to the theory.

While the independent federal judiciary is an important check on the abuse of political power by the federal legislative and executive branches, it is no more a complete substitute for political competition than public utility regulation is a complete substitute for economic competition. There is thus an argument, much emphasized in the literature of federalism, for vesting governmental functions to the extent possible at the local or regional level. Those governments compete to keep taxpayers—on whom they depend for their revenues—from moving out of the jurisdiction; national governments, except to a very limited extent, do not. But the competitive benefits of state as opposed to federal provision of public services can be overstated. It is true that if a faction or, as it is called today, an interest group takes control of a state government and uses its control to try to redistribute wealth to itself, at some cost in efficiency analogous to the efficiency loss caused by monopoly in the economic marketplace, its power to exploit will be limited by the threat that those whom it is trying to exploit will move to another state. The threat of "exit" in the case of the federal government's being taken over by a faction would be, as I have said, much feebler. But we must also ask which government—state or federal—is more likely to be taken over by a faction, and here the answer that *Federalist* No. 10 (Madison) gave, and the modern literature repeats, is state government. The larger the polity, the higher are the costs of putting together a coalition that will dominate it. So even though monopoly achieved is a much more serious problem at the federal than at the state level, the probability that it will be achieved is less. It is therefore unclear at what level the *expected* cost of monopoly is higher. But notice that even if the expected cost of monopoly were exactly the same at both the state and the federal levels, the potential consequences of monopoly would be much greater at the federal level in the (less likely) event that it occurred there. Since most people are risk-averse with regard to large stakes, and since this particular risk is impossible for most people to insure against, the monopoly danger may well be greater in an expected-utility, even if not an expected-cost, sense at the federal than at the state level.

But all this shows is that the argument based on competition for preferring (where feasible—an important qualification taken up later) state to federal government is plausible; it does not prove that the argument is correct, because the costs and probabilities and attitudes toward risk on which the argument depends are unknown. However, there is another and more familiar argument for preferring to locate governmental responsibilities, where possible, at the state rather than the federal level. This is the argument made by Holmes and Brandeis when they described the states as laboratories for public-policy experimentation.[8] They were pointing out an important advantage of decentralization in government, as in other activities: it provides valuable information about the provision of public services, because diverse polities naturally come up with different solutions to common problems and the results of these different solutions can be compared. This is another form of "yardstick competition."[9]

Decentralization has another dimension, this one related to costs of production. Beyond a certain point, which probably was reached some time ago in the case of American government, further centralization in the provision of goods or services leads to diseconomies of scale that reduce efficiency. The parceling out of governmental responsibilities among the 50 states and the federal government allows us to avoid a gigantic bureaucracy which, even if not tyrannical, would probably be highly inefficient. Imagine what a brontosaurus a single national court system having 30,000 judges would be!

But the argument for localizing government is not absolute. If either the benefits or the costs of a governmental action are experienced outside the jurisdiction where the action is taken, and the costs of negotiations between governments are assumed, for reasons I cannot begin to go into here, to be very high, then there is an argument for assigning

8. See, for example, Truax v. Corrigan, 257 U.S. 312, 344 (1921) (Holmes, J., dissenting); New State Ice Co. v. Liebmann, 285 U.S. 262, 311 (1932) (Brandeis, J., dissenting). For a skeptical view see Susan Rose-Ackerman, "Risk Taking and Reelection: Does Federalism Promote Innovation?" 9 J. Legal Stud. 593 (1980).

9. See Chapter 5, note 39.

responsibility to a higher level of government. On the benefits side, national defense is the classic illustration; but a more pertinent one is the setting by one state of generous welfare benefits which attract people from other states, so that a benefit is conferred on people outside the jurisdiction. The costs side has many good examples: the industry in one state that pollutes the headwaters of a river that runs through another; the state that taxes a good which is sold mainly out of state and for which demand is inelastic, so that the incidence of the tax is borne largely out of state; and the automobile accident in which a state resident injures an out-of-stater (though we shall see that it may make a difference whether the accident occurs in or out of the state). All these are examples of cost and benefit "externalization," to use the economist's useful term.

THE OPTIMAL SCOPE OF FEDERAL JURISDICTION

The theory of federalism just described can be used to derive an ideal allocation of lawmaking responsibilities between the states and the federal government, an allocation that would resemble, but of course would not be identical to, the allocation we actually observe today. And whenever the theory would assign substantive lawmaking responsibility to federal rather than state government, there is an argument for assigning jurisdiction (whether exclusive or concurrent is an issue I defer for the moment) to federal courts. Since state judges can be expected to be less independent of state political forces than federal judges when both are residents of a state adversely affected by federal regulation, a state court may be an unsympathetic tribunal in a case where a federal right has been created in order to correct an interstate externality. Thus, if the federal government has decided to regulate water pollution because interstate externalities deprive states of enthusiasm for this task, it is logical to assume that state judges, identifying more than federal judges with the dominant political interests in the state, also would lack enthusiasm in enforcing the federal statute.

Even where substantive lawmaking power remains with the states under the ideal division of lawmaking responsibilities—and thus even in diversity cases, for example—there is a role for the federal courts. For example, because the costs and benefits of automobile and other accidents that occur in a state are felt largely within that state, the optimal (and of course the actual) responsibility for tort law is mainly the state's rather than the federal government's. Yet sometimes a state resident's tort victim is a nonresident, and then there is a possible cost externalization. I emphasize "possible": the state (or more precisely some and perhaps most residents of the state) is the loser, along with the nonresident, if people are deterred from traveling in the state because its tort rules as applied are stacked against nonresidents. But the state court may not have a state-wide perspective, or its judges may be elected for such short terms that they lack incentives to give due consideration to the long-run welfare of the state's residents. However, since these conditions hurt residents as well as nonresidents, the externalization is only partial and the argument for federal diversity jurisdiction is therefore weakened. And in the case of disputes over contracts between residents and nonresidents, there should be no cost externalization at all. Any unequal application of state law to bargains with out-of-staters will be nullified for the future by adjustments in the terms of the bargains to reflect the probability of such application. This is true even if the state court has a strictly local, strictly short-term perspective, provided the contracts are not so long-term that it will be many years before rebargaining occurs. The same is true of torts between parties having a preexisting relationship with each other.[10]

This analysis suggests a rationale for some part of the diversity jurisdiction of the federal courts, but much less than we now have or would have even if the jurisdiction were confined to cases where a nonresident who is suing (or being sued by) a resident seeks to bring the case in (or if he is the defendant remove it to) a federal court. In all contract and many tort cases the theory of federalism implies that local rules will be applied equally to nonresidents, because those nonresidents are economically linked with residents. But if the nonresident is a tort victim of a resident and the parties were strangers before the accident, the theory predicts that the resident will receive favored treatment from the courts of his state. On this view the rationale for diversity jurisdiction is similar to that for using the commerce clause of Article I of the Constitution to prevent the states from establishing tariff-like obstacles to interstate commerce.

Although the suggested ground for diversity jurisdiction is of limited reach, it is also independent of the degree to which a state's residents are xenophobic. Even if they have no particular hostility to nonresidents, their economic self-interest will give them and their agents, including their judges, an incentive to apply the laws unequally to residents and nonresidents in some types of case. Of course it can be argued that the framers of Article III, in creating the diversity jurisdiction, wanted to reduce interstate hostility and not just to overcome ex-

10. See the classic treatment of externalities in Ronald H. Coase, "The Problem of Social Cost," 3 *J. Law & Econ.* 1 (1960).

ternalities; that they wanted to create a nation, not just a common market. But today, when increased education, better transportation and communications, and greater interstate mobility have lessened the parochialism that the framers worried about, it is significant that there is a rationale untouched by concern with parochialism for retaining at least a part, though probably a very small part, of the diversity jurisdiction.

The concept of externalities can be used to justify other areas of federal jurisdiction: for example, the federal government's insistence, as in the Federal Tort Claims Act,[11] on confining suits against it to federal courts. If a postal van runs down someone and the victim can sue the Postal Service in his own state's court, then the judge, to the extent he considers himself an agent of the state rather than of an impersonal "law," will have an incentive (of which he may be quite unconscious) to resolve doubtful questions of fact and law against the Postal Service. The costs of any judgment against the Postal Service will be borne by the federal taxpayer and thereby spread throughout the nation, but the benefits will be concentrated in the state.

The theory of federalism can be used to justify many of the federal criminal laws, and their enforcement in federal courts. The federal regulatory laws that happen to carry criminal sanctions, and federal statutes punishing such distinctively federal crimes as murder in a federal prison or counterfeiting, are not problematic at all; but what of the federal statutes that punish such crimes as fraud, extortion, embezzlement, theft, kidnapping, and trafficking in narcotics or pornography, ostensibly because of a supposed and usually minor impact on trade among the states or because an interstate instrumentality such as the mail is used? In some of these cases a clear externality exists that justifies federal regulation. Examples are the production of pornography in one state for sale in another; fraud against a bank whose depositors are insured by the federal government, with the result that much of the cost of the fraud is borne out of state even if all of the depositors are residents;[12] and criminal activity that takes place in many states, such as an interstate network of narcotics importers, distributors, and dealers, so that no one state bears the full costs of the activity, and coordination of different state law enforcement authorities would be costly.

A distinct justification for many of the federal criminal statutes is unrelated to externalities but has rather to do with another facet of the theory of federalism, the greater vulnerability of states than of the fed-

11. 28 U.S.C. §§ 1346(b), 2671 et seq.

12. There would be no externality if the insurance premium were tailored to the risk of loss of the individual bank ("experience rating"), but it is not; a uniform nationwide insurance premium is charged.

eral government to control by factions. One aspect of this is the greater vulnerability of state law-enforcement agencies, including courts, to domination by corrupt elements. The theory of federalism predicts, as we have seen, that federal authorities will be less corruptible, and this provides an argument for using them to police, with the aid of their own courts, certain basically local problems. I am thus suggesting an analogy between a part of the federal criminal jurisdiction and the Constitution's guarantee to the states (in Article IV) of a republican form of government.

There is great overlap between federal and state criminal laws, and my analysis may provide some answers to the question of how to allocate law-enforcement responsibilities in the area of overlap.[13] For example, although bank robbery is both a state and, if the bank is federally insured (as almost all banks are), a federal crime, the federal government no longer prosecutes most bank robbery cases, but it does prosecute most bank fraud cases. I suggest the following explanation. A robbery is a breach of the peace; it inflicts tangible and immediate harm, in the form of fear for bodily safety, on residents of the state in which the robbery occurs; the financial consequences are usually secondary and often small. The motive for state prosecution is clear. But the costs of a bank fraud are often borne largely out of state, and this reduces the incentive for state prosecution. Moreover, bank fraud may undermine confidence in the nation's entire banking system. For both reasons, the optimal investment in punishing bank fraud is greater than any state would think worthwhile in order to protect its own local interests.

Another ground for federalizing an area of government responsibility is the existence of economies of standardization; this is the basis for the federal admiralty jurisdiction. The distinguishing feature of maritime law is that a ship's owner may be sued in tort or contract in any port where the ship calls, through the venerable fiction that the ship is the wrongdoer.[14] This is a useful device for making shipowners answerable for wrongdoing in courts convenient for their victims. But as a modest quid pro quo for having to defend themselves in courts all over the world, shipowners have from time immemorial demanded access to the national courts of the countries at which their ships call. To require a company that has casual and intermittent contacts with many different countries to become knowledgeable about the local courts in those countries—not only about the personnel and procedures, but about the

13. On which see Richard S. Frase, "The Decision to File Federal Criminal Charges: A Quantitative Study of Prosecutorial Discretion," 47 U. Chi. L. Rev. 246, 284–290 (1980).
14. See Oliver Wendell Holmes, Jr., The Common Law 28–30 (1881).

law they apply—would increase the cost of international trade unduly. The solution is to have one set of courts apply a common body of law in each country. As we saw in Chapter 2, this is the historical, as well as functional, explanation for federal admiralty jurisdiction.

This explanation does raise some questions, though. One is its applicability to incidents involving purely domestic uses of navigable waterways—a collision between two domestic carriers hauling iron ore between Great Lake ports, or an accident on a pleasure craft, again domestic, on the Mississippi River. Both accidents would be within the federal admiralty jurisdiction, and it is hard to see why. The argument that admiralty is a specialized field that state courts could not administer competently is pretty thin when applied to river or lake accidents occurring in federal circuits that have little experience with admiralty law because there is no major port in the circuit.

My explanation suggests that the admiralty jurisdiction may be underinclusive as well as overinclusive. There was a time when ocean shipping was the only major international business, but it is no longer. A company that manufactures a product shipped all over the world, and that under modern, expansive notions of personal jurisdiction is amenable to suit in a multitude of local courts for the consequences of an accident caused by the product, can argue as persuasively as any shipping line that it should not only have access to the national courts of each country (which it can get in the United States by virtue of the "alienage" jurisdiction in Article III, a counterpart to the diversity jurisdiction), but also be subject to a uniform national body of law, equivalent to admiralty law, administered in those courts.

Although the theory of federalism can explain much of the existing jurisdiction of the federal courts—may even, as I have just suggested, point to the expansion of that jurisdiction in some directions—it cannot, at least at the point to which I have carried it thus far, explain anything like the whole of it. Consider the rights conferred by the Bill of Rights and made applicable to the states by the Supreme Court's very liberal interpretation of the due process clause of the Fourteenth Amendment, and the rights independently conferred against state action by the equal protection and due process clauses of the Fourteenth Amendment. Few if any of these rights can be derived from a concern with externalities. The right recognized in *Shapiro v. Thompson*[15] to collect state welfare benefits no matter how recent one's arrival in the state actually created an externality—an external benefit, to nonresidents, that might lead states to reduce welfare benefits to their own residents. Most

15. 394 U.S. 618 (1969).

Fourteenth Amendment rights, however, simply are not related, or are related only tenuously, to externalities. Consider the oppression of blacks by the southern states after Reconstruction. Unless one treats moral outrage as a cost—a step that pretty much erases the distinction between internal and external costs—the costs of that oppression were borne mainly by the southern rather than the northern states (though one can argue, rather speculatively as it seems to me, that southern oppression drove blacks to northern cities where they proceeded to impose heavy costs on the welfare and criminal justice systems). Even more clearly, rights against age discrimination, sex discrimination, cruel and unusual punishment, double jeopardy, ineffective counsel in criminal cases, and similar rights that occupy much of the attention of the federal courts today have little to do with interstate spillovers.

Is there any justification in the theory of federalism for making such rights enforceable in federal rather than state courts—any reason to expect state judges to be less sympathetic than federal judges to claims of denial of counsel, for example, given that the unfairness and errors caused by such denials will be experienced overwhelmingly by state residents rather than outsiders? The answer may lie in an earlier point, that federal judges are likely to be more independent from the electoral branches of government than state judges. The theoretical grounds for that independence are unrelated to the enforcement of any rights against state governments. But since we have this corps of highly independent judges, there is an argument for giving them responsibility for enforcing such federal rights as are likely to be asserted by people who are politically disfavored in state courts not because they are nonresidents—most of them are residents—but because they lack effective political power in the state.

We must distinguish, however, between rights that are unpopular because they are unreasonable or have no basis in the Constitution, and rights characteristically asserted by politically weak groups; it is only the latter for which a case for federal enforcement can be made. Moreover, many federal rights are popular, or at least are asserted by members of politically influential groups. An example is the federal statutory right against age discrimination.[16] The aged in our society are strong politically at the state as well as the federal level. The fact that they have been able to obtain federal legislation in their favor does not imply that state judges, if given exclusive responsibility for enforcing the legislation, would not do so sympathetically. The case for federal jurisdiction over cases arising under such legislation is not clear.

16. Age Discrimination in Employment Act of 1967, as amended, 29 U.S.C. §§ 623 *et seq.*

The discussion to this point has suggested that the present scope of federal jurisdiction exceeds the ideal scope derived from the theory of federalism. This in turn implies that it would be beneficial to cut back on federal jurisdiction, but specific benefits have yet to be identified. There would be some, however. One would be a reduction in the dangers of political monopoly, a reduction brought about by shifting governmental power, here exercised by judges, to the most local level possible, consistent with efficiency. Another would be a reduction in the diseconomies of scale that are, as we have seen in previous chapters, seriously harming the federal court system. True, reducing your workload by increasing someone else's is not a dependable formula for increasing efficiency. But because of the enormous disparity in the number of state and federal judges, a proportionately large reduction in the caseload of the federal courts would (even after correction for differences in the average difficulty of state and federal cases) translate into a proportionately very small increase in the caseload of the state courts.[17] Even so, a small decrease in the efficiency of each state's judiciary, when multiplied 50 times, might offset the large gain in efficiency that the federal courts might obtain from a reallocation of caseload. But if I am right in my previous suggestion that the work of the federal courts is more vital to the nation's welfare than that of the state courts, the gain could still exceed the loss, when both gain and loss are viewed in broad social terms. The gain clearly would exceed the loss if state court systems are not yet operating in the region where small increments in demand generate diseconomies of scale.

SPECIFIC CASELOAD IMPLICATIONS

Table 6.1 collects data from earlier tables on the workload of the federal district courts and courts of appeals today. Almost half the workload (nearer a third in the courts of appeals, if case filings are used to measure workload), consisting of federal criminal cases and cases to which the federal government is a party, would be largely unaffected by even a rigorous application of the principles of federalism. No longer are many criminal cases prosecuted in federal court that could just as well be handled in state courts. The increase in the incidence of federal

17. Some concern has been expressed that abolishing the diversity jurisdiction would aggravate the congestion of state courts in some large cities. This concern is rebutted effectively in Robert J. Sheran and Barbara Isaacman, "State Cases Belong in State Courts," 12 *Creighton L. Rev.* 1, 61–68 (1978). See also Bernard S. Meyer, "Justice, Bureaucracy, Structure, and Simplification," 42 *Md. L. Rev.* 659, 674 and n.71 (1983), and studies cited there.

Table 6.1. Caseload-workload of the lower federal courts, 1983, broken down by subject matter

Subject matter	District courts		Courts of appeals	
	Cases filed[a]	Trials[b]	Cases filed[c]	Opinions[d]
Criminal	12.9	35.6	16.2	20.0
Civil	87.1	64.3	68.3	64.0
U.S. civil	34.6	10.9	19.7	23.0
Condemnation	0.3	2.3	3.2	1.0
FLSA	0.3	0.3	0.2	0.0
Contract	17.0	0.9	0.8	1.0
Tax	1.5	1.3	1.6	0.0
Civil rights	0.7	1.0	2.4	4.0
Postconviction	1.6	0.3	4.3	6.0
FTCA	1.0	2.3	1.7	1.0
Forfeiture	1.3	0.7	0.4	0.0
Social security	7.3	0.1	3.4	4.0
Private	52.5	53.4	48.6	41.0
Diversity	20.1	24.3	12.2	8.0
Admiralty	2.0	1.2	0.8	3.0
Antitrust	0.4	0.8	1.2	2.0
Civil rights	6.4	11.4	10.3	5.0
Intellectual property	2.0	1.4	1.1	4.0
FELA	0.8	1.4	0.3	0.0
Postconviction	9.5	4.9	13.8	7.0
Jones Act	1.5	2.3	1.0	1.0
LMRA	1.5	0.8	1.4	3.0
RLA	0.1	N.A.	0.1	1.0
Administrative appeals	—	—	10.4	14.0
Other	—	—	5.1	2.0

a. From Table 3.2.

b. From Table 5.1.

c. From Table 3.2. Percentages are of all cases, not just (as in Table 3.2) cases appealed from district courts.

d. From Table 3.5 (sample of 100 signed, published majority opinions, which is why there are no fractional percentages).

crimes in recent years has far outpaced any increase in the resources allocated to federal criminal prosecutions, with the result that most federal crimes that state courts and criminal justice authorities can deal with effectively under state statutes punishing the same criminal activity are being dealt with that way. Therefore any big reduction in the burden that federal criminal prosecutions place on the federal courts will have to come from reforms that are beyond the scope of this book to evaluate, such as repealing criminal prohibitions of some activities. Regarding civil cases to which the federal government is a party either as plaintiff or as defendant, not just tort-claims cases but condemnation, contract, and tax cases—in fact, every category of U.S. civil cases—there is a strong *prima facie* case for federal jurisdiction since, if brought in state court, these cases would invite (as we have seen) "rational prejudice" against the federal government. The cost of its losing such a case is diffused throughout the nation, but the benefits are concentrated within the state.

This leaves the half of the docket that consists of private civil cases, including appeals from administrative agencies. Diversity is a major candidate for reducing the federal caseload even if the diversity jurisdiction is not abolished altogether, since the part that would survive under principles of federalism would be only a small fraction of the present jurisdiction. The scope of the admiralty jurisdiction could be reduced somewhat, but I do not know how much; I do not know what fraction of admiralty cases are purely domestic, and many that are probably are also within the diversity jurisdiction. On the other hand, federal administrative appeals cannot be moved to state courts. And with regard to the last two rows under private civil cases in Table 6.1—private cases under federal labor statutes—there is a powerful objection, once again rooted in the concept of externalities, to handing cases over to state courts. It is the same objection which, at a more fundamental level, explains why labor law is a field almost exclusively of federal law. On the whole and despite the countercurrent introduced by the Taft-Hartley Act, the policy of federal labor law is to promote unions,[18] a policy that would have only limited effectiveness on a sectional basis. If New York State, for example, favors unions and as a result wages rise there, industry will move—though not all of it, of course, and not all at once—to states which do not favor unions and in which as a result wages are lower. Such a shift in the center of gravity of American industry has, of course, occurred. Section 301 of the Taft-Hartley Act,[19] which gave the federal courts jurisdiction over suits to enforce collective bargaining contracts and is the principal source of the labor cases filed in federal district courts, can be viewed as a compromise in which companies were given enforceable rights in labor con-

18. See, for example, 49 Stat. 449, § 1 (preamble to Wagner Act); S. Rep. No. 573, 74th Cong., 1st Sess. 2, 4, 6 (1935); 78 Cong. Rec. 9888 (1934) (remarks of Representative Connery); Richard A. Posner, "Some Economics of Labor Law" (forthcoming, *University of Chicago Law Review*).

19. 29 U.S.C. § 185.

tracts[20] but were not allowed to enforce those rights in accordance with state law. On this view, the Supreme Court was right to hold as it did in the much-criticized *Lincoln Mills* case[21] that courts in section 301 suits had to apply a federal common law of labor contracts rather than state labor-contract law. To allow states to develop their own law of collective bargaining contracts would have enabled the anti-union states to attract still more business away from the pro-union states.

Although the area of labor relations is a good example of the general point that federal court jurisdiction sometimes is warranted in order to deal with a problem of interstate spillovers, the same cannot be said for federal jurisdiction to enforce the Federal Employers Liability Act,[22] a tort statute for railroad workers that explicitly allows suits to be brought in either state or federal court. There is no apparent reason of contemporary significance for the alternative federal venue. The statute is pro-worker, if it is anything (since wages are not regulated, workers may in effect give back in wages what they gain in accident benefits from FELA). And whatever may have been true when the railroads were the most powerful industry in America, no one believes that state courts today are biased in favor of railroads in deciding tort suits against them. Putting aside the even more fundamental question of why accidents to railroad workers should be governed by federal law but accidents to travelers at railroad crossings by state law—a question of substantive law reform—I can think of no reason why state courts cannot be trusted to enforce the FELA. Concern with prejudice against railroads cannot explain the alternative federal venue, since a railroad is not permitted to remove to federal court an FELA case filed in state court.

Bodies of law such as antitrust and intellectual property that create commercial rights pose acutely the question of why a dual system of courts is needed. If Congress wants to create remedies against banks for nondisclosure of credit terms to borrowers, or remedies against securities brokers for misleading their customers, or against cartelists, or against thieves of intellectual property, why not trust state courts to administer the laws in an even-handed fashion? With respect to some federal statutes that create private rights, I cannot think of any answer at all. I cannot imagine why, for example, Truth in Lending cases, odometer-tampering cases,[23] or securities fraud cases involving the securities

---

20. Unions got the same rights but did not particularly want them. They viewed the strike rather than the lawsuit as the most effective method of enforcing collective bargaining contracts in the union's favor.

21. Textile Workers Union v. Lincoln Mills, 353 U.S. 448 (1957).

22. 45 U.S.C. §§ 51 *et seq.*

23. See Motor Vehicle Information and Cost Savings Act, 15 U.S.C. §§ 1981–1991 (1976).

of small, local, closely-held corporations should be tried in federal rather than state courts. Whatever the possible merits of the statutes under which these cases are brought, they do not involve interstate externalities.

I have more sympathy for the argument that some federal statutes, well illustrated by the antitrust and intellectual property (patent, copyright, and trademark) statutes, involve a high level of analytical difficulty that would baffle many state courts and lead to many erroneous decisions—as antitrust, for example, has done (and frequently, too) even in the federal courts. If the superior employment conditions of federal relative to state judges can be assumed to make the federal courts of higher average quality than the state courts, these reasons supply in turn a ground for giving the federal courts exclusive jurisdiction over especially complex federal law. Another factor is the interest in national uniformity of legal obligation when, as is frequently the case in such fields as antitrust and intellectual property (and in securities cases involving publicly traded companies), a single business activity affects many states and so would bring the actor under the potential jurisdiction of many different state court systems if the states were permitted to exercise jurisdiction. For example, if a company planning to develop a product that will require patent protection in order to be profitable has to predict the reactions of many states' courts nominally applying the same, but by assumption complex and difficult, federal statute, the costs of the company's planning will be multiplied. The Supreme Court will not have the time to iron out all the differences among the states. True, by the same token assigning exclusive jurisdiction to the federal courts will not ensure complete uniformity, for reasons explored in Chapter 4. But there will be more uniformity than if enforcement is committed to 50 different state court systems.

Notice that I was speaking in the last paragraph of *exclusive* federal jurisdiction. Normally, federal jurisdiction is concurrent. The plaintiff can sue in state court if he wants, and usually the defendant can then remove the case to a federal district court (though sometimes, as in FELA cases, he cannot) if he wants. It makes sense to give the parties their choice of court systems provided the state court is thought competent to cope with the issues. If not, there is the danger that the state court will create bad law. But the danger is slight, as long as the defendant has a right to remove to federal court. For usually one of the parties will think itself better off in the competent tribunal, and if so either the plaintiff will file its case in the federal court or the defendant will remove the case to that court. If both parties are content to remain in state court, that court probably is competent to decide the case. The argument for exclusive federal jurisdiction in such cases, and therefore generally, is weak.

Since much federal statute law is vague or complex or deals with inherently complex subject matter—or all three at once—there is a presumption in favor of giving federal courts jurisdiction, though just concurrent jurisdiction, to enforce private rights under federal statutes dealing with commercial matters. But where the federal right has close counterparts in familiar common law concepts such as fraud and deceit, or regulates local activities (such as odometer tampering by used-car dealers), the presumption is reversed. There is no reason to make consumer deception by local sellers a concern of federal courts.

Potentially the largest area for federal jurisdictional reform motivated by principles of federalism, but an area about which I can say little in this book without changing its focus entirely, is in regard to postconviction (including civil rights) cases brought by state prisoners, and to other private (always in the sense of non-federal-government) civil rights cases. Together these categories account for almost a third of the private civil cases on the district courts' docket and almost a sixth of their total docket (but less than a fourth of the courts of appeals' total docket—and only half of that if just signed, published majority opinions are counted).

The system of federal postconviction rights consists mainly of habeas corpus proceedings brought by state prisoners complaining that they were convicted in violation of federal constitutional law, and of section 1983 suits brought by properly convicted state prisoners complaining that the conditions of their confinement violate their federal constitutional rights by constituting "cruel and unusual punishment." This jurisdiction is premised on distrust that state courts will protect the federal civil rights of criminal defendants and convicts. To evaluate the premise, it is necessary to distinguish between two types of criminal rights. The first consists of rights intended to minimize the probability of convicting an innocent person, and is illustrated by the traditional rule, given constitutional status by the Supreme Court in interpreting the due process clause of the Fourteenth Amendment,[24] that the state must prove a defendant's guilt of each of the elements of the crime beyond a reasonable doubt. Since the reasonable-doubt standard stops well short of certainty, it implies to the unknowledgeable that a significant if small fraction of innocent people are convicted, which if true would warrant additional tiers of judicial review. But the danger of an

---

24. See In re Winship, 397 U.S. 358 (1970); Patterson v. New York, 432 U.S. 197 (1977); Jackson v. Virginia, 443 U.S. 307 (1979).

innocent person's being convicted under the American system of criminal justice, whether state or federal, is actually much smaller than the reasonable-doubt standard implies (though not zero),[25] mainly because other rules of criminal procedure prevent the jury from even considering a great deal of highly probative evidence of guilt. (The danger is especially small if "innocent" is construed to mean that the defendant did not do the criminal act of which he was accused; that is, if state-of-mind questions are put to one side.)[26] To prove guilt beyond a reasonable doubt on the basis of legally admissible evidence is no mean feat. And if 20 years ago there were areas of the South in which there was a significant danger that a black person might be convicted for a crime he had not committed, today the state courts in all areas of the country can, I believe (I do not pretend I can prove this), be trusted to protect the innocent of whatever race, creed, national origin, or income, with exceptions too few and isolated to justify federal judicial intervention. *Jackson v. Virginia*, which holds that a federal court in a habeas corpus proceeding must vacate the petitioner's conviction if no rational tribunal could have found him guilty beyond a reasonable doubt, probably came too late to do much good. But it has imposed heavy burdens on the federal courts.[27]

Most of the rights that the federal courts have applied in state criminal proceedings in the name of the Constitution, some with more and some with less basis in the constitutional text, have nothing to do with protecting the innocent. Examples are the right to be free from cruel and unusual punishments, which comes into play only after the defendant is lawfully convicted, and the right to exclude from a criminal trial illegally seized, but usually reliable, evidence of guilt. In most states the rights of the guilty enjoy little political favor, and it is therefore quite possible that in the absence of effective federal judicial review, many state judges would give those rights less protection than the Constitution, as interpreted by the Supreme Court, tells them to. And though it is also quite possible that the Court has interpreted the Constitution too broadly in the area of criminal rights, if one lays that possibility aside and takes for granted the scope of federal criminal rights as declared by the Supreme Court and the lower federal courts, the argument for giving the holders of those rights access to the federal courts is a powerful

25. See Hugo Adam Bedau, *The Courts, the Constitution, and Capital Punishment* 67 (1977).

26. For an interesting discussion of the difference see Charles L. Black, Jr., *Capital Punishment: The Inevitability of Caprice and Mistake* 57–64 (2d ed. 1981).

27. A recent study found that 22.4 percent of federal habeas corpus petitions attack the sufficiency of the evidence to convict the petitioner in his state trial. Karen M. Allen, Nathan A. Schachtman, and David R. Wilson, "Federal Habeas Corpus and Its Reform: An Empirical Analysis," 13 *Rutgers L.J.* 675, 759 (1982).

one.[28] But my discussion does imply that federal courts should not be required to determine whether a rational jury could have found the petitioner (the defendant in the state trial) guilty beyond a reasonable doubt. There is no reason consistent with the principles, or the present-day realities, of federalism for the federal courts to worry lest states convict their innocent citizens.

With regard to many, though not all, noncriminal civil rights cases, the argument for federal jurisdiction is also weak. It is no longer true that blacks or Jews or Orientals or even American Indians constitute "discrete and insular minorities"[29] despised by a politically, economically, and socially dominant majority of white Protestants—there is no such dominant majority—or that these groups lack political power and representation in the judiciary. Title VII cases probably would not be decided much differently today in state than in federal courts. The time may have come to stop thinking in terms of stereotypes that, however descriptive of the attitudes of some state officials decades ago, ignore the peaceful but profound social revolution that has occurred since the mid-1960s.

Furthermore, many civil rights cases do not involve discrimination of any sort. Most cases, other than prisoner cases, are brought either by businessmen complaining that the state deprived them of property without due process of law or by state employees complaining that the state fired them without a hearing.[30] It is a mystery to me why such cases should be litigable in federal courts. Local businessmen are not powerless or despised members of their communities, and public employees are an effective political interest group in all states. Even accepting unprotestingly that the Fourteenth Amendment is violated when a local school board discharges a tenured teacher without a hearing, I am at a loss to understand why state courts cannot be trusted to enforce the teacher's Fourteenth Amendment right, especially when the issues involved in such cases are of a kind familiar to state courts; the teacher's case, though nominally a constitutional case, is essentially a breach of contract action. The principal argument against giving state

28. However, Solimine and Walker, supra note 3, present some interesting empirical evidence against this conclusion. See id. at 242 (table III). Their article also contains a very thorough review of the literature pro and con the proposition that state courts should be considered equally reliable forums with the federal courts for the enforcement of federal rights.

29. United States v. Carolene Products Co., 304 U.S. 144, 152 n.4 (1938).

30. See, for example, Board of Regents v. Roth, 408 U.S. 564 (1972); Baer v. City of Wauwatosa, 716 F.2d 1117 (7th Cir. 1983). A public job with tenure is considered "property" within the meaning of the Fourteenth Amendment's due process clause.

courts exclusive jurisdiction in such cases is that if one views a state's judiciary as just another state agency, it means allowing the state to adjudicate disputes to which it is a party. Because the separation of powers is weaker at the state than at the federal level, there is some merit to the argument, but probably not much. The Eleventh Amendment to the Constitution, which the Fourteenth Amendment did not repeal, allows the states to confine the litigation of disputes between a state resident and the state itself to its own courts, even if the plaintiff is asserting a federal claim against the state; and this system is accepted with little protest of which I am aware. And when a state officer violates the constitutional rights of a citizen of the state, often he is violating state law as well, in which event he may get no sympathy from any organ of state government.

But against this perhaps too sunny view must be raised the sensitive and therefore seldom discussed issue of variations in quality among the courts of the different states. In some states today it would be quite wrong to impute to the state courts any prejudice against persons asserting federal rights; in others one is not so sure. Yet it is unthinkable that the jurisdiction of the federal courts should vary from state to state depending on someone's assessment of the quality of the state (and federal) judges in those states. Severely aggregative judgments seem unavoidable, which greatly complicates the difficulty of fixing the appropriate boundaries between state and federal jurisdiction.

It should be growing clear to the reader that the principles of federalism may not, after all, have revolutionary implications for reallocating federal judicial business to the state courts. If the theory were applied rigorously, perhaps 20 percent of the federal district courts' cases, and 21 percent of the courts of appeals' cases, would be reassigned to state courts.[31] The resulting relief of federal caseload pressures, though welcome, would only postpone the ultimate crisis a few years. Moreover, rigorous application of the theory would involve reassigning some, perhaps many, cases from state to federal courts. Advances in transportation and communication are increasingly making the nation (and for many products the whole world) a single market, thus magnifying the problem of interjurisdictional externalities. I mentioned earlier the ex-

31. These figures were obtained by assuming that two-thirds of the diversity cases, half the admiralty, Jones Act, and private civil rights cases, 10 percent of the state prisoner cases, and all of the FELA cases on the docket of federal district courts and courts of appeals, as shown in Table 6.1, would be reassigned to state courts. If trials (district courts) and opinions (courts of appeals) are used instead of cases filed, the figures in text become 24 percent and a disappointing 9 percent, respectively.

ample of the products liability of a manufacturer who ships worldwide. Consider now a domestic manufacturer shipping nationwide. Tort liability for defective or unduly dangerous products is an area of law that has thus far been left to the states. But suppose that some state's courts consider a particular design feature of a rotary lawnmower unduly dangerous, and it is cheaper for the manufacturer, who sells nationwide, to change the feature on all the lawnmowers he produces than just on those that are to be sold in the state in question. Then the state is indirectly but effectively imposing costs on nonresidents. I am not advocating a national products liability law, but merely emphasizing by this example that it is unlikely that the theory of federalism always points to shifting regulatory responsibilities from the federal government to the states rather than in the opposite direction.

A somewhat related example of how one might argue for expanding federal jurisdiction in some areas consists of the whole set of cases in which a federal question first appears in a defense to the plaintiff's complaint. Under present law the defendant is not allowed to remove the case to federal court just because he has a federal defense (a right he would have if the complaint were based on federal law), although if the same federal issue were the basis of a claim made by him he could sue in federal court.[32] The distinction is not quite so arbitrary as it sounds. It would be a serious mistake to make all cases in which a federal defense was asserted removable as a matter of right. In many the federal defense would have little merit—would, indeed, have been concocted purely to confer federal jurisdiction—yet this fact might be impossible to determine, with any confidence, without having a trial before the trial. Of course, frivolous federal claims are also a problem when only plaintiffs can use them to get into court, but a less serious problem. If the plaintiff gets thrown out of federal court because his claim is frivolous, and must start over in state court, he has lost time; and the loss may be fatal if meanwhile the statute of limitations has run. But the defendant may be delighted to see the plaintiff's case thrown out of federal court when the court discovers that the federal defense is frivolous. This is why it would not be a complete answer to the problem of the frivolous federal defense to allow removal on the basis of a federal question first raised by way of defense but give the district court discretion to remand the case back to the state court. (There would be an analogy to the well-recognized discretion of a federal district court to dismiss a state law claim even though it is so closely related to the

32. See Franchise Tax Bd. v. Construction Laborers Vacation Trust, 103 S. Ct. 2841 (1983).

plaintiff's federal claim that it is within the court's pendent jurisdiction.)[33]

Reference to removal and to pendent jurisdiction brings up the interesting question of the case that raises issues of both state and federal law. An alternative to the federal habeas corpus jurisdiction as a method of deciding federal questions in state criminal cases would be to allow criminal defendants to remove their prosecution from state to federal court if they had federal defenses. The habeas corpus jurisdiction involves a duplication of effort (both state and federal courts must pass on the defendant's federal defense) that removal would not. But by shifting most criminal litigation from state to federal courts, removal would bring about a much bigger displacement of state authority into federal courts than does the federal habeas corpus jurisdiction even in its expansive modern form. The implicit balancing of federalism and judicial economy tips against economy in this instance. In the case of pendent jurisdiction, which allows a plaintiff to join a nonfederal claim with his federal claim in the interest of judicial economy, the balance tips the other way, especially since more than judicial economy is involved: if the federal claimant had to bring two cases rather than one to get complete relief, he would find it more costly to litigate his federal claim if there were no pendent jurisdiction. The additional cost to the state criminal defendant of having to litigate his federal constitutional claims twice, first in the state trial and then in the federal habeas corpus proceeding, is not a detriment to the average criminal defendant. Quite the contrary, it gives him two bites at the apple—and probably he will not have paid for the apple.

In concluding this section, I want to return once more to the assumption that state judges are on average less independent from political influences and (a closely related point) of somewhat lower average quality than federal judges. I hope that any state judges reading this book are not too offended by this assumption or outraged by my self-serving complacency as a federal judge in giving voice to it. The assumption may of course be wrong, and in any event the words "on average" conceal enormous variations both among states and among judges within any given state. But the interesting point is this: even if the assumption is indulged to the fullest, my analysis has yielded the conclusion that the federal courts' jurisdiction should in all likelihood

33. On the modern contours of the judge-made "pendent jurisdiction" of the federal courts, which allows a federal court to adjudicate a state-law claim over which the court would not have jurisdiction, provided the claim is closely connected to a claim over which it does have jurisdiction, see United Mine Workers v. Gibbs, 383 U.S. 715 (1966). And on discretion to remand a case that has been removed, see 28 U.S.C. § 1441(c).

be curtailed relative to that of the states. Those who reject my assumptions about the superior independence and quality of the federal courts will no doubt be led to even more drastic conclusions. But it is right for me, in proposing reforms that many proponents of the alleged "juster" justice of the federal courts will instinctively resist, to adopt these proponents' assumptions about the relative quality and independence of federal and state courts. Proceeding with me from common assumptions in that regard, they may be more willing to reexamine their views of the proper scope of federal jurisdiction in light of my analysis.

FEDERALISM AND SUBSTANTIVE DUE PROCESS

I have said that the theory of federalism has implications for substantive law that I do not want to pursue in this book. But I do not want to leave them out of account altogether. One of these implications, moreover, illustrates a facet of federalism that I have not yet considered.

In an opinion for the Supreme Court in *Missouri v. Holland*, Justice Holmes, talking about the framers of the Constitution, said: "It was enough for them to realize or to hope that they had created an organism; it has taken a century and has cost their successors much sweat and blood to prove that they created a nation. The case before us must be considered in the light of our whole experience and not merely in that of what was said a hundred years ago."[34] One might have thought that the Constitution did create a nation, and wonder what the reference to "sweat and blood" means. The "blood" is the blood shed in the Civil War, in which Holmes served for three years and was wounded seriously three times. Before the Civil War it was not certain that the United States really was a nation, and not just a confederacy, an alliance among sovereign nations. It took the blood of the Civil War to extinguish the idea that states had a right to secede.

The Civil War taught a lesson about the instrument the framers had drafted, the original Constitution: that they had made a mistake in putting the social institutions of the states almost completely beyond the reach of the federal judicial power. The Constitution conferred few judicially enforceable rights against the states other than in areas of conduct (such as trade among the states, governed by the commerce clause) that were "purely" economic. The grant of power to Congress in Article I was broad enough (though perhaps not so understood in those days) that, if Congress had wanted, it could have intruded itself into the social and political arrangements of the states. But it did little, apart from helping slaveowners to recover runaway slaves. The Civil War showed

34. 252 U.S. 416, 433 (1920).

that there cannot be an American nation if the states are totally free to go their own way in the matter of social arrangements. Some minimum homogeneity of social institutions is necessary if people are to consider themselves Americans first and Georgians or New Yorkers second.[35]

When Lincoln said " 'A house divided against itself cannot stand.' I shall believe this government can not endure, permanently half *slave* and half *free* . . . It will become *all* one thing, or *all* the other,"[36] he was expressing the unbearable tension that had been created because the South had slavery and the North did not. The abolitionists' passionate hostility to the institution made southerners fearful for its future and determined to hold on to a big enough fraction of the Senate to block any movement for restrictive legislation or constitutional amendment. This determination was reflected in pressure to extend slavery to the territories, and Lincoln's resistance to this pressure so greatly identified him with opposition to slavery that his election was the signal for secession.

The enactment of the Thirteenth Amendment at the end of the Civil War eliminated slavery in form but not in substance. Southern states enacted "Black Codes" that placed the new freemen in the same serflike state that freed blacks had occupied in the South before the Civil War. The main purpose of the Fourteenth Amendment—as is clear not only from its background but from its little-read sections 2 through 4—was to complete the emancipation of the Negro. But with that purpose I have no direct concern here. My interest is in the open-ended provisions of section 1, in particular the due process clause.

I have described this provision as open-ended, but this is not a universally accepted position. Some would limit it, in accordance with its language, to the protection of procedural rights; others to a narrow subset of such rights.[37] I do not want to enter the debate over whether the due process clause is open-ended. I shall assume it was intended to give the Supreme Court broad discretion to invalidate state laws, and having made that assumption shall ask how the discretion should be guided and offer an answer based on the history just recounted.

The usual answer to the question of how to guide judicial discretion in interpreting open-ended constitutional provisions, including the due process clause, is summed up in the words "natural law."[38] This term

35. "A certain uniformity of civilization," as Tocqueville put it. See 1 *Democracy in America*, note 3 supra, at 169.

36. "A House Divided": Speech at Springfield, Illinois, June 16, 1858, in 2 *Collected Works of Abraham Lincoln* 461 (Roy Prentice Basler ed. 1953) (paragraph breaks omitted; emphasis in original).

37. See Frank H. Easterbrook, "Substance and Due Process," 1982 *Sup. Ct. Rev.* 85.

38. See, for example, Edward S. Corwin, "The Supreme Court and the Fourteenth Amendment," 7 *Mich. L. Rev.* 643 (1909).

refers to a body—not necessarily the same body—of transcendent principles: principles not embodied in any conventional source of law, such as a constitutional or statutory text or judicial precedents, but available to fill in the contours of broad grants of judicial power, such as I am assuming the due process clause contains. Liberty of contract, for many years the judicial touchstone in applying the due process clause to state regulation of business, is a natural law concept and so is the concept of privacy that judges invoke when applying the due process clause to state regulation of contraception and abortion.[39]

I offer in a speculative spirit the following alternative to natural law as a possible guide to the application of the due process clause: a law that deprives a person of life, liberty, or property in violation of a fundamental social norm *held by most of the nation* denies due process. If Indiana adopted the Islamic code of punishment, or Florida authorized torture in police interrogation, or New Mexico decided to censor its newspapers, or California abolished the right to trial for crimes, these states would be violating the due process clause. In contrast, the position of two Supreme Court justices (Brennan and Marshall) that capital punishment is always and everywhere unconstitutional would be unacceptable under the view of due process that I am proposing, because the national consensus is in favor of, not against, capital punishment.

Notice that I am using as my index of consensus state legislation. I am not suggesting that the content of the due process clause should change with the latest public opinion polls. But then, you may ask, what if all states enacted the Islamic code of punishment? Would the federal courts be helpless, under my view of the due process clause of the Fourteenth Amendment, to strike down this affront to our conception of civilized criminal justice? They would; but we must imagine how our ideas about civilized criminal justice would be different from what they are today if all or even most states had adopted the Islamic code.[40] The code could not gain adoption in 50 states, or even in 26 states, unless there were a profound revolution in thought; and who are the judges to try to stop such revolutions?

Obviously my view is incompatible with the idea that the due process clause "incorporated" any provision of the Bill of Rights *in toto*. That idea attributes to those who framed and enacted the due process clause of the Fourteenth Amendment truly revolutionary intentions. The Bill of Rights was intended to weaken the federal government; apply the Bill of Rights to the states through the due process clause and you

39. See Richard A. Posner, *The Economics of Justice,* chap. 11 (1981).
40. Cf. Paul Gewirtz, "The Jurisprudence of Hypotheticals," 67 *A.B.A.J.* 864 (1981).

weaken the states tremendously by handing over control of large areas of public policy to the federal judges, whose interpretations of the Bill of Rights are (short of constitutional amendment) conclusive of its meaning. It is hard to believe that this was intended by all the state legislators whose votes were necessary to ratify the amendment.

I anticipate the objection that if a policy commands a national consensus, Congress can be trusted to deal with the deviant states, and therefore my approach would have no application. But this is incorrect. The modern theory of legislation teaches (what is, after all, familiar enough from common observation) that interest groups often can manipulate the legislative process to thwart the popular will.

My concept somewhat resembles the idea expressed by Justice Cardozo in *Palko v. Connecticut*,[41] and much emphasized in the jurisprudence of Justice Frankfurter, that the due process clause embodies a notion of "ordered liberty," or "notions of justice of English-speaking peoples,"[42] distinct from the specific provisions in the Bill of Rights. But it differs in anchoring the concept of "ordered liberty" in the idea of national consensus.[43] This anchor limits the subjective, ad hoc character of the concept; the judge is not free to set his personal views against the views embodied in the public policy of a majority of the states. Although this idea has never commended itself to federal judges in the uncompromising form in which I have stated it, there are approaches to it not only in several Frankfurter opinions,[44] but in several recent opinions dealing with the constitutionality of the death penalty.[45]

It is a necessary condition of unconstitutionality under this approach that the challenged state practice be followed in only a minority of the states. But it is not a sufficient condition. The goal is not to stifle experimentation but to prevent deviations from the national consensus that are so extreme, so shocking, that they threaten national unity. No doubt, though, this approach would prevent some experimentation; for it is hard to distinguish the first experiment from the shocking deviation. But this is not such a bad thing. Most new ideas are bad, and the

41. 302 U.S. 319, 324–325 (1937).

42. Adamson v. California, 332 U.S. 46, 67 (1947) (Frankfurter, J., concurring). See also Rochin v. California, 342 U.S. 165, 172 (1952).

43. An idea with roots in eighteenth-century and early nineteenth-century jurisprudence, as argued in William E. Nelson, "The Eighteenth-Century Background of John Marshall's Constitutional Jurisprudence," 76 *Mich. L. Rev.* 893 (1978).

44. See, for example, Carpenters & Joiners Union v. Ritter's Cafe, 315 U.S. 722, 728 (1942) (Frankfurter, J., concurring); Haley v. Ohio, 332 U.S. 596, 602 (1948) (Frankfurter, J., concurring).

45. See, for example, Furman v. Georgia, 408 U.S. 238, 385 (1972) (Burger, C. J., dissenting); *id.* at 436–443 (Powell, J., dissenting); Enmund v. Florida, 102 S. Ct. 3368, 3372–74 (1982).

new ideas that are good, or at least that reflect powerful forces in the society, will hang on tenaciously until the courts realize that they reflect dominant views. The Supreme Court was unperceptive when in the late nineteenth and early twentieth centuries it struck down state experimentations in social and economic regulation that now command a national consensus. Nothing in the suggested approach would help a judge to be far-sighted, but it would at least keep the judges' hands off institutions that a majority of the states approve—capital punishment being a notable example—more securely than the natural law approach has done.

As should be obvious from my historical remarks, I base this suggested view of due process on the idea that the great shift in power from the states to the federal courts that was brought about by the Fourteenth Amendment had as its purpose—apart from the obvious one of emancipating the Negro—to help prevent the reemergence of dangerous sectional tensions. But what is the evidence that the framers of the Fourteenth Amendment held this view of what they were doing? I shall answer this question indirectly by quoting another passage from Holmes's opinion in *Missouri v. Holland*. It is the sentence that directly precedes the passage I quoted earlier, and reads: "When we are dealing with words that also are a constituent act, like the Constitution of the United States, we must realize that they have called into life a being the development of which could not have been foreseen completely by the most gifted of its begetters."[46] A constitutional provision is an act of government rather than just a text for interpretation. As such, it brings about social changes that may prevent its being reinterpreted in a way that greatly changes what has come to be its accepted meaning, even if the reinterpretation would make the text conform more closely to the original meaning. It may be too late in the day to limit the Fourteenth Amendment to matters of race or its due process clause to a narrow sense of process. But the natural law approach to the clause is not so entrenched, so accepted, that it must be deemed part of the text. And although that approach has some support in the background and legislative history of the Fourteenth Amendment,[47] it so curtails the power of the representative branches of government in the states that the people who voted for the Fourteenth Amendment in Congress—and especially the state legislatures that voted to ratify it—

46. 252 U.S. at 433.

47. See Edward S. Corwin, "The Doctrine of Due Process of Law before the Civil War (II)," 24 *Harv. L. Rev.* 460, 477–479 (1911); Charles Fairman, "Does the Fourteenth Amendment Incorporate the Bill of Rights? The Original Understanding," 2 *Stan. L. Rev.* 5, 36 (1949).

could not have intended to authorize the courts to adopt such an approach.

Although not directly supported by the language or legislative history of the clause, the consensus approach that I am proposing does less violence to the intentions of the framers of the Fourteenth Amendment and is consistent with the dominant fact behind the amendment—the Civil War. If the Fourteenth Amendment did anything more than emancipate the Negro (not that this wouldn't have been achievement enough), it gave the Supreme Court the power to prevent the growth in the states of new social institutions that would be so obnoxious to dominant national feeling that they might kindle sectional passions of the sort that had led to the Civil War.

Although sectional differences and hostilities still exist in this country, they are much less intense than they used to be. The proper role of the due process clause as a force for national unity is therefore smaller today, so it is surprising to find the Supreme Court less tolerant of regional differences than formerly. Capital punishment, control of pornography, education of aliens, regulation of contraception—matters to which the due process clause of the Fourteenth Amendment can hardly be said to speak with a clear voice—are some examples of social questions that could be left to the states to work out without any danger to national unity, but that instead are being resolved by the federal courts.

The suggested approach to "substantive due process" questions has judicial workload implications, of course, but, as with the other suggestions made in this chapter, its merit does not lie mainly there. The values of federalism are independent of the contribution that it can make to the current problems of the federal courts. In fact, as I noted earlier, unflinching application of the theory of federalism could result in expanding the federal courts' jurisdiction in significant areas.

7

Judicial Self-Restraint

GREATER SELF-RESTRAINT would seem a natural prescription for a court system suffering from acute overload, especially since its opposite, "judicial activism," continues, even in an era of conspicuous judicial activism, to be a premier term of judicial opprobrium[1] (thus illustrating the definition of hypocrisy as the tribute that vice pays to virtue). But, like federalism, judicial restraint has a significance that transcends the current problems of the federal courts. Indeed, the question of judicial restraint is not limited to the federal courts. But it is a more urgent question for them than for the state courts, because the federal courts are more powerful; the temptations to activism are headier.

A question that will occupy me a great deal in this chapter is whether judicial self-restraint has or can be given any definite meaning; perhaps it is just one of those hopelessly shopworn expressions in which the judicial vocabulary abounds—"chilling effect," "facial overbreadth," "strict scrutiny," and "fundamental rights" being some other examples.[2] And if the term is meaningful, can the concept it denotes be

---

1. A few recent examples: "Today's decision is a conspicuous exercise in judicial activism," Engle v. Isaac, 102 S. Ct. 1558, 1576 (1982) (dissenting opinion); "judicial activism run rampant," Madison Consultants v. FDIC, 710 F.2d 57, 68 (2d Cir. 1983) (dissenting opinion); "In a land weary of . . . judicial activism," Joy v. North, 692 F.2d 880, 898 (2d Cir. 1982) (dissenting opinion).

2. My least favorite is the standard judicial expression for the Supreme Court's abortion decisions: "*Roe* and its progeny," referring to Roe v. Wade, 410 U.S. 113 (1973), and the cases following it. For examples of this usage see City of Akron v. Akron Center for Reproductive Health, Inc., 103 S. Ct. 2481, 2487 n.1 (1983); Harris v. McRae, 448 U.S. 297, 312 (1980); Murillo v. Bambrick, 681 F.2d 898, 904n.11 (3d Cir. 1982); Baird v. Department of Public Health, 599 F.2d 1098, 1099 (1st Cir. 1979). The pun in *"Roe"* may be inescapable, but there are many alternatives to "progeny" that would not call to mind inappropriate—or perhaps too appropriate—images. This is the situation, discussed by Orwell in a classic essay, where "the writer is not seeing a mental image of the objects he

shown to be a good thing? I shall approach these questions by first considering what "principled" (as distinct from "result-oriented") adjudication is and whether it is possible for either restraint or activism to be a valid principle of adjudication.

PRINCIPLED ADJUDICATION

In the most famous sentence in American legal scholarship, Holmes wrote: "The life of the law has not been logic; it has been experience."[3] And he continued, "The felt necessities of the time, the prevalent moral and political theories, intuitions of public policy, avowed or unconscious, even the prejudices which judges share with their fellow-men, have had a good deal more to do than the syllogism in determining the rules by which men should be governed."[4] Holmes did not say whether it was a good or a bad thing that law (he was speaking of judge-made law, the common law) had been shaped more by felt necessities, intuitions of public policy, and so forth than by logic. But it is pretty clear that he thought it inevitable, and—being a Social Darwinist[5]—not a bad thing; for among other things he was constantly putting the syllogism down (it couldn't wag its tail,[6] and so on). Yet this is the same man who said that the Fourteenth Amendment had not enacted a particular theory of political economy, that of laissez-faire; and what he meant, of course, was that it was wrong for the justices to read that theory into the Constitution.[7]

"The Path of the Law" contains the most compact expression of

---

is naming." "Politics and the English Language," in 4 *Collected Essays, Journalism and Letters of George Orwell* 127, 134 (Sonia Orwell and Ian Angus eds. 1968 [1946]).

3. Oliver Wendell Holmes, Jr., *The Common Law* 1 (1881).

4. *Id.*

5. See Oliver Wendell Holmes, Jr., "Herbert Spencer: Legislation and Empiricism," in *Justice Oliver Wendell Holmes: His Book Notices and Uncollected Letters and Papers* 104, 107–109 (Shriver ed. 1936); Robert W. Gordon, "Holmes' *Common Law* as Legal and Social Science," 10 *Hofstra L. Rev.* 719, 739–740 (1982). "Social Darwinism" is sometimes used as a synonym for laissez-faire capitalism, but it has a broader meaning in Holmes's thought, as the idea that the Darwinian model of struggle resulting in the survival of the fittest provides an apt description of human society. When Social Darwinism is so understood, war, the trade-union movement, the market of ideas, and legislation are all seen to be aspects (along with conventional economic competition) of the Darwinian process in human society. It is only by defining the term narrowly that Professor Donald Elliott is able to conclude that Holmes was not a Social Darwinist; see "Holmes and Evolution: Legal Process as Artificial Intelligence," 13 *J. Legal Stud.* 113, 126 n.57 (1984).

6. Letter to John C. H. Wu, in *The Mind and Faith of Justice Holmes: His Speeches, Essays, Letters and Judicial Opinions* 419 (Max Lerner ed. 1943).

7. See Lochner v. New York, 198 U.S. 45, 75 (1905) (dissenting opinion). Although I am skipping around in Holmes's long professional life, his thinking was pretty much of a piece throughout it, and any ambiguity in his thought cannot be dispelled by dating.

Holmes's thinking on the role of policy in law: "I think that the judges themselves have failed adequately to recognize their duty of weighing considerations of social advantage. The duty is inevitable, and the result of the often proclaimed judicial aversion to deal with such considerations is simply to leave the very ground and foundation of judgments inarticulate, and often unconscious . . . When socialism first began to be talked about, the comfortable classes of the community were a good deal frightened. I suspect that this fear has influenced judicial action both here and in England."[8] From the tone of this passage, and much else besides, we know that Holmes thought it wrong that judges should allow a fear of socialism to influence their decisions. But on his terms, why? The essay continues:

> I think that something similar has led people who no longer hope to control the legislatures to look to the courts as expounders of the Constitutions, and that in some courts new principles have been discovered outside the bodies of those instruments, which may be generalized into acceptance of the economic doctrines which prevailed about fifty years ago . . . I cannot but believe that if the training of lawyers led them habitually to consider more definitely and explicitly the social advantage on which the rules they lay down must be justified, they sometimes would hesitate where now they are confident, and see that really they were taking sides upon debatable and often burning questions.[9]

The first sentence in the passage just quoted suggests a theory of constitutional interpretation, to which I shall return later; the second, however, amounts to saying little more than that judges ought to be better informed than they are. If, having read widely, a judge became convinced that socialism was really a bad thing or a good thing, there is no basis clearly expressed in Holmes's writings for regarding the judge as acting illegitimately if he decided—though only when precedents and other formal sources of law, including a constitutional text that invites free interpretation, did not yield a determinate outcome—to embody his political preferences in his judicial decisions. Hamilton tried to persuade his fellow New Yorkers to ratify the Constitution by arguing that life-tenured federal judges would protect the interests of the "comfortable classes" against the mob.[10] Holmes would think this bad, as would most modern judges, but the question is why.

8. 10 *Harv. L. Rev.* 457, 467 (1897).
9. *Id.* at 467–468.
10. See *Federalist* No. 78, in *The Federalist Papers* 226, 227, 231–232 (Roy P. Fairfield 2d ed. 1981); and note 15 infra.

The legal tradition against which Holmes was rebelling has come to be called formalism. It is the idea that the judge has no will, makes no value choices, but is just a kind of calculating machine, or even "a logical automaton, a phonograph repeating exactly what the law had definitely declared."[11] The idea had received naive expression in Blackstone's metaphor of the judges as the "living oracles" of the law[12]—that is, as passive transmitters rather than creators. When Holmes wrote *The Common Law* and "The Path of the Law," Blackstone's intellectual descendants were no longer speaking of oracular utterance but of logical deduction.[13] The judge got the principles of the law from his predecessors, from custom, from judges of higher courts, from legislatures, and from the Constitution, and deduced from those principles the correct outcome in each case before him: "So judicial dissent often is blamed, as if it meant simply that one side or the other were not doing their sums right, and, if they would take more trouble, agreement inevitably would come."[14]

Formalism is often thought to be hypocritical and wrong. But this depends on the period. If all the judges agree on the premises for decision, which was closer to being true in Blackstone's time than in Holmes's, formalism may describe the judicial process with considerable, though not complete, accuracy;[15] for the premises will strike the

11. Morris R. Cohen, *The Faith of a Liberal* 43 (1946).

12. 1 William Blackstone, *Commentaries on the Laws of England* 69 (1765). The idea is much older than Blackstone—at least as old as Cicero. See John Dickinson, "The Law behind Law," 29 *Colum. L. Rev.* 113, 115 n.8 (1929). Hamilton said much the same thing in *Federalist* No. 78, supra note 10, at 227: "The judiciary . . . can take no active resolution whatever. It may directly be said to have neither Force nor Will, but merely judgment." And Chief Justice Marshall: "Courts are the mere instruments of the law, and can will nothing." Osborn v. Bank of United States, 22 U.S. (9 Wheat.) 738, 866 (1824).

13. See, for example, Christopher Columbus Langdell, *A Selection of Cases on the Law of Contracts* viii (2d ed. 1879); 2 Charles Warren, *History of the Harvard Law School and of Early Legal Conditions in America*, chap. 43 (1908). Cf. Mauro Cappelletti, "The Law-Making Power of the Judge and Its Limits: A Comparative Analysis," 8 *Monash U. L. Rev.* 15, 20–22 (1981). Of Langdell's contracts casebook, supra, Holmes wrote in an anonymous review, "There cannot be found in the legal literature of this country, such a *tour de force* of patient and profound intellect working out original theory through a mass of detail, and evolving consistency out of what seemed a chaos of conflicting atoms. But in this word 'consistency' we touch what some of us at least must deem the weak point in Mr. Langdell's habit of mind. Mr. Langdell's ideal in the law, the end of all his striving, is the *elegantia juris*, or logical integrity of the system as a system. He is, perhaps, the greatest living legal theologian." 14 *Am. L. Rev.* 233 (1880).

14. Holmes, supra note 8, at 465.

15. In a previous note I quoted Hamilton's statement from *Federalist* No. 78 that the judiciary has no "will." But just a few pages later he says, "It is not with a view to infractions of the constitution only that the independence of the judges may be an essential safeguard against the effects of occasional ill humours in the society. These sometimes extend no farther than to the injury of the private rights of particular classes of citizens, by unjust and partial laws. Here also the firmness of the judicial magistracy is of vast im-

judges as axioms, and the specific case outcomes will be deducible from them. Judges today agree less on the premises of decision than they did even in Holmes's time. This is so even though statutes bulk larger in the law today than when Holmes wrote, and they may seem to invite deductive treatment more than common law principles do, and thus to reduce the scope for judicial creation of law. But many issues of statutory interpretation cannot be answered deductively, at least once the "canons of construction" are recognized for what they are—fig leaves covering decisions reached on other grounds, often grounds of public policy. And some statutes do little more than provide an initial impetus to the creation of bodies of frankly judge-made law (as in antitrust). That is why the federal courts of appeals, even though they do not exercise a general common law jurisdiction, find that a great many of the issues they are called upon to decide are common law issues in the practical sense that the application of a body of judge-made law is required to decide them. Furthermore, the decline of pure common law has been matched by the rise of a style of constitutional law that is ever less anchored in the text of the Constitution and therefore ever more like common law.[16] Though in part this is the judges' fault and therefore not a good reason for their acting unconstrained by the text, it is inevitable that as the date of enactment of a constitutional provision recedes, interpretation will—it must—become freer, if the language allows.

Yet the formalist idea dies hard. In part it survives as a judicial defense mechanism[17]—a way of shifting responsibility for unpopular decisions to other people, preferably dead people such as the framers of the Constitution, whose graves provide a convenient place for the buck

---

portance in mitigating the severity, and confining the operation of such laws. It not only serves to moderate the immediate mischiefs of those which may have been passed, but it operates as a check upon the legislative body in passing them; who, perceiving that obstacles to the success of an iniquitous intention are to be expected from the scruples of the courts, are in a manner compelled by the very motives of the injustice they meditate, to qualify their attempts . . . Considerate men, of every description ought to prize whatever will tend to beget or fortify that temper in the courts" (supra note 10, at 231–232). What is this but an invitation to judges to set their own sense of justice against that embodied in legislation, and in the guise of interpretation to make legislation more civilized in application than it was in intention? This is not a formalist recipe; it suggests (and approves) a concept of judicial decision making similar to that described by Holmes. Of course, the *Federalist* is advocacy; but Hamilton would not have made the argument I have just quoted if his readers would not have thought it presented a respectable conception of the judicial function.

16. See Henry P. Monaghan, "Our Perfect Constitution," 56 *N.Y.U.L. Rev.* 353, 391–395 (1981).

17. Wittily described in Alexander M. Bickel, *The Least Dangerous Branch: The Supreme Court at the Bar of Politics* 84–98 (1962).

to stop. But formalism is also widely believed, especially by good law professors. Consider the argument in Henry Hart's famous article, "The Time Chart of the Justices,"[18] that the trouble with the Supreme Court is that the justices do not have enough time to discuss the cases with one another and that if they discussed them more they would disagree less. This diagnosis implicitly conceives the process of judicial deliberation as a search for technical answers to technical questions, for, as noted in a reply to Hart, debating questions of value may simply harden the disagreements among the debaters.[19] Yet the vastness and complexity of American law, its extension into all sorts of politically controversial areas, the lack of disciplined legislative processes, the amazing diversity of ethical and political opinion in the society, and the political character of the judicial appointing process (all of these to some extent, of course, related rather than independent factors) make it inevitable that many judicial decisions will be based, at least in part, on value judgments, rather than wholly on technical, professional judgments. Decisions so made are by definition not scientific, and therefore not readily falsifiable or verifiable either—and as a consequence not always profitably discussable.

Critical though he was of formalism, Holmes believed, as do most contemporary legal thinkers, that some considerations ought to be out of bounds to the judge even in cases where the conventional legal materials give out—cases that no formalist could decide. The judge is not to decide even a very close case on the basis of which of the parties is the more sympathetic human being or which has the better or the nicer lawyer or more powerful friends in the news media or which belongs to the judge's own race, social class, or sex. A decision influenced by any of these factors is not "impartial," but this is just a conclusion. A decision is not impartial if factors that ought to be extraneous to the decision-making process influence it; we must ask why certain factors are extraneous and others—the "felt necessities of the time," for example—are not.

A common but superficial answer is that if judges based decisions on unacknowledged personal preferences, the law would be unpredictable. This assumes that judges would not declare the true grounds of decision in such cases. They would not, but only because decision ac-

---

18. 73 *Harv. L. Rev.* 84, 99–100 (1959). And for a thoroughly contemporary defense of formalism see Ronald Dworkin, *Taking Rights Seriously* (1977), especially chap. 4 ("Hard Cases"), which argues that judges should not use "policy," but only "principle" (distinguished in *id.* at 82–86), to decide even the hardest cases.

19. See Thurman Arnold, "Professor Hart's Theology," 73 *Harv. L. Rev.* 1298, 1312 (1960).

cording to personal preference is so widely thought to be wrong that no judge would dare admit that he was deciding cases on such a basis; and we have to consider why it is thought wrong. The reason is that it would make the judiciary too autocratic. If a judge did not like you or your friends or liked your opponent or his friends better, he might sit by and let you lose your property or liberty. He might, in effect, declare you an outlaw. We do not want judges to wield such power.

It is no answer that a judge would be appointed only if his preferences matched those of the appointing authorities, who may be assumed to represent the dominant political forces of the society. As pointed out in Chapter 2, ideology is not the dominant factor in most federal judicial appointments; even less important are the candidate's purely personal preferences and prejudices, which anyway are not likely to be well known to the appointing authorities. And although ideology does play a big part in appointments to the most powerful court, the Supreme Court, often the appointee's views are not well known to the President or the Senate, or they change after he becomes a justice. Moreover, the preferences of the appointing authorities may not reflect the popular will many years later, when the judges they appointed will still be in power. And even if they do, we do not want government to have as much power as it would if judges were perfect agents of the general will. It is also thought wrong for judges to base decisions on partisan political concerns, and for a similar reason: we do not want the political parties to have the power over our lives that they would have if the judges were their agents, even if the winning party is the authentic spokesman of majority opinion.

So far I am on pretty solid ground. No one will argue that a litigant's personal characteristics or party identity ought to influence the court's decision. A decision so influenced would be "result-oriented," a term that has a useful meaning if used to denote decision according to personal or partisan considerations that are generally agreed to be illegitimate. Of course, if this usage were accepted, we would encounter the term much less frequently in judicial opinions than we do,[20] but the respite would be welcome. The term has become debased by being used to announce disagreement with particular principles. This is un-

20. Two recent examples: "If ever a court was guilty of an unabashedly result-oriented approach, this case is a prime example," Plyler v. Doe, 102 S. Ct. 2382, 2409 (1982) (dissenting opinion); "Things have really reached the point where the result-oriented jurist will attain the result he desires whatever the words say that are to be construed," SCM Corp. v. United States, 675 F.2d 280, 286 (Ct. Cl. 1982) (dissenting opinion). See also McKaskle v. Wiggins, 104 S. Ct. 944, 959 (1984) (dissenting opinion); Connell v. Sears, Roebuck & Co., 722 F.2d 1542, 1551 (Fed. Cir. 1983).

derstandable, though; the line between "principled" and "result-oriented" is sometimes a fine one. Suppose it turned out that Judge A always voted against labor unions when they were parties to cases before him. If he did this because he disliked unions we could properly describe his decisions as result-oriented, but if the consistency of his votes resulted simply from the fact that he had formulated and was applying a principle that determined these outcomes, the label "result-oriented" would be inappropriate.

I suggest the following practical, though only partial, test for distinguishing a principled from a result-oriented decision: a decision is principled if and only if the ground of decision can be stated truthfully in a form the judge could publicly avow without inviting virtually universal condemnation by professional opinion. If the only "principle" that explained a judge's decisions in tax cases was that he thought tax collection communistic or satanic, his tax decisions would be unprincipled, because he would never admit publicly—not in this society, not today—what his ground of decision was. The same would be true with deciding labor cases on the basis of a dislike for unions. The "unprincipled" and the "result-oriented" are simply those grounds that at the particular historical moment are so generally rejected that they would never be announced as the true grounds of decision.

However, to be a principled adjudicator means more than just being willing to state publicly the true ground of decision; it also means being consistent. To take an extreme example, it would be unprincipled to decide all discrimination cases between black and white males in favor of blacks on the basis of one principle, and all discrimination cases between a black man and a white woman in favor of the woman on the basis of another principle, if the two principles were inconsistent with each other. Decision according to principle, then, is decision according to a (1) publicly stated ground that is (2) consistent with the grounds the judge uses to decide other cases.

Notice that I have spoken of principle, not "neutral principle." But all that Professor Wechsler's famous article[21] seems to have meant by "neutrality" was consistency, the second part of my test for principled decision making—and a part satisfied by all sorts of ridiculous rules of decision. A rule that in a lawsuit between a black and a white, the white must always win (or always lose) would be neutral; it would consistently abstract from all the particulars of the litigants and their dispute

---

21. Herbert Wechsler, "Toward Neutral Principles of Constitutional Law," 73 *Harv. L. Rev.* 1 (1959).

except the one made relevant by the rule, and would thus be internally consistent. My suggested "publicity test" makes the concept of principled adjudication less empty.

But perhaps not much less. Deciding antitrust cases on the premise that the antitrust laws are intended to promote economic efficiency is principled and so is deciding them on the premise that the laws are intended to limit economic power. Deciding criminal cases on the premise that the public safety is the paramount good to be served by the criminal justice system is principled and so is deciding them on the premise that the paramount good is to protect defendants' rights. Deciding cases under the National Labor Relations Act on the premise that its purpose (even with the Taft-Hartley amendments) is to foster the cartelization of labor is principled but so is deciding such cases on the premise that the National Labor Relations Board has gone too far in shifting the balance of power from companies to unions. In short, a commitment to principled adjudication does not enable a choice among competing principles; it does not mean that the judge will choose the best, or even defensible, principles, though it may make it more likely. While "unprincipled" is a severe criticism to make of a judge's work, "principled" is only a tepid compliment.[22]

For it is not true that as long as a judge is principled, he is entitled to apply any principles he chooses. The terms of the statute he is applying, or precedent, or the other sources of authoritative guidance to judicial decision making may dictate the application of a particular principle in a particular case. It is only when the springs of authoritative guidance run dry that the judge enters the area of legitimate judicial discretion. But nothing I have said so far provides a reason against a judge's allowing his fear of socialism, or his hatred of big business, to influence decision in cases (which may be few or many) where he finds the law in its application to the case to be unclear or in equipoise even after conscientious and skillful study of conventional legal materials. After all, "fear of socialism" is just a pejorative term describing a principled belief in economic individualism, and "hatred of big business" a pejorative term for a principled belief in populism. It would hopelessly muddle the term "principled" to confine it to grounds we agree with or think sound.

To summarize very briefly, I have suggested that there is an area in which a judge cannot decide cases simply by reference to the will of

22. See M. P. Golding, "Principled Decision-Making and the Supreme Court," 63 *Colum. L. Rev.* 35, 41, (1963).

others—legislators, or the judges who decided previous cases, or the authors of the Constitution. Within that area, the judge must bring in his own values and preferences in order to make decisions. But he must do so in principled fashion, "principled" implying not merely consistent but also enjoying sufficient public approbation that the judge is not afraid to state the principle in his opinions. Among these principles are activism and self-restraint, which will be the focus of the rest of this chapter.

THE MEANING AND CONSEQUENCES OF JUDICIAL ACTIVISM AND SELF-RESTRAINT

The term "judicial self-restraint" could be used in at least five different senses. (1) A self-restrained judge does not allow his own views of policy to influence his decision. (2) He is cautious and circumspect, and thus hesitant about intruding those views. (3) He is mindful of the practical political constraints on the exercise of judicial power. (4) His decisions are influenced by a concern lest promiscuous judicial creation of rights result in so swamping the courts in litigation that they cannot function effectively. (5) He believes that the power of his court system relative to other branches of government should be reduced.

The first definition is useless for present purposes because I am interested in exploring the possibilities of self-restraint in the open area of judging, where by definition a correct decision cannot be made without bringing in personal policy preferences. Definition 2 identifies what I shall call the "deferential" judge, to distinguish him from the judge who is self-restrained in the sense used in definition 5; as I shall argue later, the confusion of deference with the other sense has had unfortunate consequences. Definitions 3 and 4 identify what I shall call "prudential self-restraint," which I shall discuss briefly before turning to my principal focus, self-restraint as a substantive political principle used by judges in deciding certain cases in the open area (definition 5).

Prudential self-restraint has two aspects, the "political" (definition 3) and the "functional" (4). Most judges either practice the political version or would do so on a suitable occasion. There are limits beyond which even Supreme Court justices cannot go without provoking effective retribution from Congress or, as in the case of Chief Justice Taney's struggle with Lincoln over habeas corpus,[23] seeing their judgments sim-

---

23. See Carl Brent Swisher, 5 *Oliver Wendell Holmes Devise History of the Supreme Court of the United States: The Taney Period 1836–64*, at 847 (1974).

ply ignored. But I am not interested in exploring those limits here, in part because they are usually broader than the boundaries of the other sorts of restraint that I shall discuss.

The second kind of prudential self-restraint, the functional type, is based on recognition that decisions that create rights result in heavier caseloads, which can in turn impair the courts' ability to function (hence the word "functional"). The extremely serious caseload problems that beset the federal courts today make it a question of some urgency whether a judge legitimately may consider caseload effects when deciding a case. He surely may in areas such as jurisdiction and procedure where judicial economy is an accepted factor in judicial decision making (and, at least in close cases, I should think, in other areas as well). If the question is one of standing to sue, or whether judicial review of administrative action lies in the district court or the court of appeals in the first instance, or whether a federal court should abstain when a parallel suit is pending in state court, or whether pendent jurisdiction should be broadly or narrowly construed, and the answer is not dictated by precedent, judicial economy will inevitably, and justifiably, be one of the weights that the judge puts in the balance in making his decision. And it will be a heavier weight the heavier the caseload is. Those who were persuaded by the analysis in Part II of this book will have to agree that a failure to economize on federal judicial resources wherever possible may impose substantial social costs in the form of reduced federal judicial quality; and this is a legitimate consideration in any area of law where judicial economy is itself a legitimate consideration.

I am mainly interested in what I shall call "separation-of-powers judicial self-restraint," or less clumsily "structural restraint." By these terms, which describe judicial self-restraint in an accepted sense[24] that I should like to see become its exclusive sense in order to minimize ambiguity, I mean the judge's trying to limit his court's power over other government institutions. If he is a federal judge he will want federal courts to pay greater deference to decisions of Congress, of the federal administrative agencies, of the executive branch, and of all branches and levels of state government. Structural restraint is not a liberal or a conservative position, because it is independent of the policies that the other institutions of government happen to be following. It will produce liberal or conservative outcomes depending on whether the courts

24. See, for example, Alpheus Thomas Mason, "Judicial Activism: Old and New," 55 *Va. L. Rev.* 385 (1969) ("should it [the Supreme Court] stand aloof, exercise self-restraint, defer to legislature and executive, leave policy-making to the initiative of others?").

in question are at the moment more or less liberal than those institutions.[25]

Because separation-of-powers self-restraint implies a low judicial profile, it tends to produce outcomes similar to those produced by prudential self-restraint in either its political or its functional form. The forms of judicial self-restraint are related in another way. The federal courts—one has been told over and over again until the point has become thoroughly hackneyed—lack the power of purse or sword, lack the legitimacy conferred by an electoral mandate, yet have responsibility for countermanding the elected branches. They do this not only when enforcing the Constitution against state as well as federal legislative and executive action but also when enforcing federal statutes in accordance with the intent of the enacting rather than the current Congress. Hence, the argument continues, the courts are the weakest branch of the federal government and must conserve their political capital, which can be squandered not only by promiscuous countermanding of the other branches but also by the decline in professional respect for the courts' decisions that must accompany any sizable expansion in the number of judges or any relaxation of the traditional limitations on justiciability.

Yet the recent history of the federal courts suggests that it is not their political capital that is running out so much as their judicial capital. Although there are stirrings of revolt by the political branches against the self-aggrandizement of the judicial branch in the last two decades, nothing comparable to Franklin Roosevelt's court-packing plan is yet visible on the horizon.[26] This is in part because some of the groups on whose behalf the courts have been aggressive lately, notably women and blacks, are politically powerful, and protect the courts' vulner-

---

25. Those who doubt me should read Bernard Siegan's recent book and the admiring review of it by Mark Pulliam, which show that there is a movement afoot (among scholars, not as yet among judges) to make the majority opinion in *Lochner* the centerpiece of a new activist jurisprudence. See Bernard H. Siegan, *Economic Liberties and the Constitution* (1980); Mark Pulliam, Book Review, 18 *Wake Forest L. Rev.* 971 (1982). Compare Professor Epstein's suggestion for using the takings clause of the Fifth Amendment to limit redistributive taxation. Richard A. Epstein, "Taxation, Regulation, and Confiscation," 20 *Osgoode Hall L.J.* 433 (1982); see also Richard A. Epstein, "Not Deference, but Doctrine: The Eminent Domain Clause," 1982 *Sup. Ct. Rev.* 351, 360 n.19. Another recent contribution to the *Lochner* revival movement is Michael Conant, "Antimonopoly Tradition under the Ninth and Fourteenth Amendments: *Slaughter-House Cases* Re-Examined," 31 *Emory L.J.* 785 (1982), which begins: "This study concerns the possible revival of a sleeping giant, the common law and constitutional tradition barring governmental grants of monopoly in the ordinary trades."

26. Cf. Henry P. Monaghan, Book Review, 94 *Harv. L. Rev.* 296, 300–301 (1980).

able political flanks, and in part because the political branches are happy to shift responsibility for unpopular policies to the federal courts, which are a kind of lightning rod since the judges cannot be voted out of office. Indeed, since the courts are inherently weak yet seem to be getting away with a big "power grab" from the political branches, there is a presumption that these branches are cooperating in the shift of power—and with it responsibility—to the courts. Not the autonomy of the federal courts but their capacity to function effectively has been called into question—by a caseload crisis that is the result, at least in part, of these courts' self-aggrandizement. Against a background of caseload crisis, the hostility of the political branches, even if not great enough to give rise to restrictive legislation, can cause acute distress to the courts. If Congress and the President will not help the courts to solve their crisis—if indeed they decide to wage a kind of guerrilla warfare against the judges, as by denying them proper salary increases—the profligate expenditure of the courts' political capital in the last two decades may turn out to have serious adverse consequences on the federal court system after all.

It should be clear by now that the term "judicial self-restraint" can be used precisely, and not merely as a synonym for the behavior of the responsible judge, or for judicial circumspection in general or devotion to *stare decisis*—implying deference to other judges in the same judicial system—in particular. This is not to say that judicial deference is not a good thing, only that it is a different thing from judicial self-restraint in a useful sense. A decision overruling *Marbury v. Madison*[27] would be pretty wild stuff, but it would be self-restrained in my terminology because it would reduce the power of the federal courts vis-à-vis the other organs of government. Or, to speak of two real overrulings, *Erie R.R. v. Tompkins*[28] and *Mapp v. Ohio*,[29] both of which have been criticized as reaching out to decide important questions not adequately briefed or argued by the parties[30] (in *Erie*, not even raised), *Erie* is a self-restrained decision in my terminology because it reduced the power of the federal courts vis-à-vis the state courts, while *Mapp* is activist because it had the opposite effect.

27. 5 U.S. (1 Cranch) 137 (1803).

28. 304 U.S. 64 (1938), overruling Swift v. Tyson, 41 U.S. (16 Pet.) 1 (1842).

29. 367 U.S. 643 (1961), overruling Wolf v. Colorado, 338 U.S. 25 (1949), insofar as *Wolf* had held that the exclusionary rule in search and seizure was not applicable to the states.

30. On *Mapp* see 367 U.S. at 672–677 (Harlan, J., dissenting), and on *Erie* see the discussion (not a criticism) in "In Praise of Erie—and of the New Federal Common Law," in Henry J. Friendly, *Benchmarks* 155, 171–172 n.71 (1967). The issue of the continuing validity of *Wolf* had been raised by the petitioner in *Mapp*, but later abandoned.

Activism (which in my terminology is merely the opposite of restraint) is distinct not only from boldness but also from intrusiveness. When a court creates private remedies for enforcing a statute, or new defenses to the enforcement of contracts, it makes the judiciary a more intrusive presence in private activities. But unless the court is acting contrary to the will of the other branches of government, it is not being activist. It may be taking power away from private persons—and therefore may be enlarging the power and reach of government—but it is not taking power from the other branches of government. Some of the objections leveled against judicial activism can be leveled against judicial intrusiveness, such as that it draws down the courts' political capital too far; and what I earlier called functional self-restraint embraces the avoidance of intrusiveness as a special case. But nonintrusiveness in private affairs is not the same thing as judicial self-restraint in the separation-of-powers sense. If it were, *Lochner* would be an example of judicial restraint, and the term would be hopelessly muddled.

Whether history will commend a judge's choice of where to position himself on the activism-restraint axis will depend on the particular historical situation in which he finds himself. There is no inconsistency in arguing that it would have been a mistake for Chief Justice Marshall— the Marshall of *Marbury v. Madison* and *Gibbons v. Ogden*[31]—to have embraced judicial self-restraint and for Chief Justice Burger to have embraced judicial activism. If the courts are too miserly in using their powers to check the other branches of government, they might as well not be a part of the system of checks and balances, though the Constitution meant them to be.

In thus suggesting that judicial self-restraint is a contingent, a time-and-place-bound, rather than an absolute good, I may seem to be overlooking powerful arguments (in addition to the "political capital" argument already dealt with) that restraint is always the right policy for the federal courts. But a review of these arguments reveals a number of problems.

1. One can argue for judicial self-restraint from a general concern with the menace of powerful government discussed in the preceding chapter. But the argument can be parried by pointing out that any power that the federal courts gather to themselves in disregard of the counsels of self-restraint is, by definition, obtained at the expense of the other branches of government, federal or state.

2. One can argue that the framers of the Constitution envisaged a much smaller role for the federal courts than they have played almost

31. 5 U.S. (1 Cranch) 137 (1803); 22 U.S. (9 Wheat.) 1 (1824).

from the beginning. Even so, we do not know how loose a garment the framers meant to weave in the Constitution. The passages that I quoted in the last chapter from Justice Holmes's opinion in *Missouri v. Holland* indicate that he, though an advocate of structural restraint, thought that the Constitution had been meant to be a loose garment. True, my metaphor is ambiguous; Holmes used these passages in the *Missouri* case, as he used similar passages in so many other cases, to argue that the Constitution had not been meant to fasten a straitjacket on government. There is a principled difference between reading the Constitution broadly with regard to executive and legislative powers and broadly with regard to judicially enforceable rights against government—with regard, that is to say, to judicial powers. It is, indeed, the difference between restraint and activism. But to state the difference is not to determine the choice. As noted in Chapter 2, the framers of the Constitution gave the federal judges extraordinary guarantees of independence so that they would be fearless in protecting individual rights against encroachment by the other branches of government; and though the framers' thinking ran more to property rights than to what we call civil liberties,[32] the constitutional text is not so confined. The framers could not have foreseen how aggressive the federal courts have become, but neither could they have foreseen the expansion in the executive and legislative powers of government, against which the federal courts were intended to be a counterweight.

3. One can argue, on behalf of structural restraint, that the courts are less democratic than the other branches of government—and they are—but for this to be a telling point one must not only meet Professor Ely's defense of the Warren Court's activism as having made government more democratic,[33] but also show why we should have more democracy than we do. The standard syllogism—law in a democratic system is made by elected representatives; federal judges are not elected representatives; therefore lawmaking by federal judges is usurpative—overstates the framers' devotion to democracy.[34] The framers knew that judges did not always just find, but sometimes made, law— that the English judiciary had made most of the law of England. And they must have known that the Constitution (which they intended to be judicially enforceable) was not in every passage crystal clear. Yet they ordained an appointed federal judiciary with life tenure, on the English model: a nondemocratic branch. True, the judges were not to exercise

---

32. See, for example, Robert A. Dahl, *A Preface to Democratic Theory*, chap. 1 (1956).

33. See John Hart Ely, *Democracy and Distrust: A Theory of Judicial Review* 74 (1980).

34. See Dahl, supra note 32, chap. 1, on "Madisonian Democracy," and Irving Kristol, *Reflections on Neoconservatism*, chaps. 7–8 (1983).

the same free-wheeling legislative discretion as the elected representatives; the judicial power (Article III) cannot be identical to the legislative power (Article I). The difference is captured in the Holmes metaphor that I quoted in Chapter 1: the judge (but not the legislator) is "confined from molar to molecular motions." But as a motto of judicial self-restraint this suffers from the fact that the sum of a large number of molecular motions may be molar. The common law method of law creation is incremental, but the increments add up. And although the democratic principle has become more pervasive since the original Constitution (as illustrated by the Seventeenth Amendment, which abolished indirect election of senators), this cuts both ways. It makes the federal judiciary more anomalous, but it also makes it a more needed counterweight to the other branches of government, since a principal reason for the guarantees of judicial independence in Article III was distrust of a democratic legislature.

4. The preceding argument can, however, be recast as follows. Democracy is a means as well as an end: a means of resolving very difficult social and political questions in a way that minimizes strains to the essential social fabric. Decisions made by so unrepresentative, so isolated, indeed so oligarchic an institution as the federal judiciary lack legitimacy when the courts stray into areas, as increasingly they have been doing, where they cannot point either to an authoritative text or a national consensus to support their decisions. Nor, indeed, can the judges have any confidence that their decisions in these areas are "right" in any ultimate ethical sense. As they cannot claim any special competence, they might as well leave the decisions in such areas to the more overtly political branches.

5. A related argument is that the federal courts are not good at exercising this or that function that they have annexed from the other branches (running prisons, for example). They are not.[35] But too often this argument compares real courts, warts and all, with an ideal vision of other government institutions. American government is widely believed not to be performing well at any level these days—a point, however, that even if accepted can be turned by arguing that the federal courts have sapped other government institutions of their sense of responsibility and self-respect by taking away much of their authority.[36]

---

35. See Donald L. Horowitz, *The Courts and Social Policy* (1977); Donald L. Horowitz, "Decreeing Organizational Change: Judicial Supervision of Public Institutions," in *The Courts: Separation of Powers* 39 (Bette Goulet ed. 1983).

36. A classic exposition of this argument is James Bradley Thayer, "The Origin and Scope of the American Doctrine of Constitutional Law," 7 *Harv. L. Rev.* 129, 155–156 (1893).

To which the riposte is: prove it. In any event, this (like 4) is an argument about the here and now—not about restraint versus activism *sub specie aeternitatis.*

6. Self-restraint is a risk-averse strategy from the standpoint of the polity as a whole. The judiciary, unlike the legislature (unlike even the executive, with its large bureaucracy), lacks any internal checks and balances. A vote of five Supreme Court justices can have sudden and profound national consequences. Of course the Supreme Court is not all-powerful; I mentioned earlier some of the ways in which the other branches can keep it in check. But provided the Court takes care to secure its political flanks, which in recent years it has done very successfully, it can usually checkmate the efforts of the other branches to check it. Indeed, it is because the courts are so little restrained by the other branches that the issue is cast as one of *self*-restraint. But of course if self-restraint is carried too far the courts will cease to play their appointed role in the system of checks and balances.

Although self-restraint may not always and everywhere be the right policy for the federal courts, we surely need more of this commodity today, though I shall offer just two bits of evidence. The first is the overload of the federal courts itself. The second is a summary of Chief Justice Warren's judicial philosophy by a recent and on the whole admiring biographer:

> Warren's craftsmanship as a jurist was thus of a different order from that identified with enlightened judging by proponents of judicial restraint. Warren saw his craft as discovering ethical imperatives in a maze of confusion, pursuing those imperatives vigorously and self-confidently, urging others to do likewise, and making technical concessions, if necessary, to secure support. In believing his concessions on matters of doctrine to be "technical," Warren was defining his own role as a craftsman. It was a role in which one's sense of where justice lay and one's confidence in the certainty of finding it were elevated to positions of prominence in constitutional adjudication, and where craftsmanship consisted of knowing what results best harmonized with the ethical imperative of the Constitution and how best to encourage other justices to reach those results.[37]

Whatever this is, it is not judicial craftsmanship. To identify one's personal ethical preferences with natural law and natural law with consti-

37. G. Edward White, *Earl Warren: A Public Life* 229–230 (1982), quoted in Dennis Hutchinson's perceptive review, "Hail to the Chief: Earl Warren and the Supreme Court," 81 *Mich. L. Rev.* 922, 923–924 (1983).

tutional law is to make constitutional adjudication a projection of the judge's will. And as the courts move deeper into subjects on which there is no ethical consensus, judicial activism in the form attributed by Professor White to Chief Justice Warren becomes ever more partisan and parochial, lawless, and finally reckless.

At this point it is useful to recall the "publicity" test for a principle: a ground of decision that the judge is willing to state openly. Although many activist decisions contain principles (for example, "one man, one vote"), contemporary activism itself is not a principle, because no judge will espouse it (unless, as we shall see, he first redefines it to mean restraint). The activists and the restrained denounce activism with equal gusto.

APPLICATIONS OF THE ANALYSIS

I began by asking why Holmes was opposed to making hostility to socialism an element in judicial decision making, and the answer, it should now be clear, is that it would have been inconsistent with judicial self-restraint in its separation-of-powers sense—a more important part of Holmes's judicial philosophy, deeply rooted in his Social Darwinism and a skeptical habit of mind, than his dislike of socialism. In areas where considerations of judicial self-restraint were irrelevant, as they usually are when a judge is expounding private judge-made law as distinct from public law, Holmes decided cases (tort cases, for example) in accordance with the individualistic—anti-collectivist, even one might say anti-socialist—philosophy that came naturally to him but that he subordinated to considerations of judicial self-restraint when there was a conflict.[38]

My definition is also helpful in clarifying the relationship between judicial self-restraint and judicial personality. Self-restraint in the sense in which I am using the term does not, or at least need not, come from being a modest, deferential, timid judge—words inapt to describe Holmes, Brandeis, Frankfurter, and other leading judicial exponents of self-restraint. These judges had no lack of self-esteem or self-confidence, and no above-average reverence for precedent; they merely thought the courts ought to be deferring to the other branches of government more than they were doing, though with important exceptions—freedom of speech for Holmes and Brandeis, federal criminal procedure for Frankfurter. The exceptions are significant because they suggest that judicial self-restraint can no more constitute a complete

38. See, for example, United Zinc & Chem. Co. v. Britt, 258 U.S. 268 (1922) (the sulphuric acid attractive-nuisance case).

judicial philosophy than judicial activism can. Even in cases where the materials of decision in a narrow sense do not dictate the outcome of the case at hand, so that the judges' personal policy preferences or values have to be brought in to decide it, the policy of judicial self-restraint is not the only policy the judge ought to think about. Holmes was not necessarily inconsistent in wanting to restrict government regulation of speech and the press more than the courts were doing and regulation of wages and hours less. Although the language and history of the First Amendment did not dictate his position in free-speech cases, they at least offered a handhold.

Being timid could, of course, make a judge unwilling to challenge the other branches of government, and therefore self-restrained. But this is not inevitable; the timid judge might also be unwilling to reexamine his predecessors' activist decisions, or might be intimidated by his law clerks, by the law professoriat, by the media, or by a strong-minded activist colleague. So if it is wrong to equate restraint with timidity, it is equally wrong to equate activism with boldness. What is true, however, is that bold, self-confident judges are apt to write broader opinions than timid, insecure ones. And broad opinions (if we disregard for a moment their content) enhance the power of the judiciary, for they signify that the same number of cases will create more law than if the judges wrote narrow opinions, sticking close to the facts of each case. And the more judge-made law there is, probably the more power the judiciary will be taking from the other branches of government. Admittedly, bold judges might spend all their time establishing broad principles of judicial restraint, or regulating purely private conduct in areas that the other branches were not interested in regulating, as is true in many areas of tort and contract law. But all this means is that activism and boldness, as I have been at pains to stress, are not the same thing; they may still be positively correlated.

A quite different type of personal philosophy, skepticism, might also lead a judge to adopt a restrained posture—and did, in the case of Holmes and of Learned Hand. Skepticism may make a judge unenthusiastic about exercising power because he lacks confidence that it will do any good and is therefore unwilling to compete in the power arena with the other, thrusting branches of government. And judicial self-restraint has other sources besides personality and general outlook. It can arise from a straightforward concern with the overload on the court system (a natural concern for any federal judge today) or from fear of retribution by the political branches against an overactive judiciary. It can come from theory—from the "capital preservation" theory that I mentioned earlier, or from a theory of the separation of powers. And judicial self-restraint is often opportunistic—as, of course, judicial activism often is, too. The judge does not like his colleagues' policy preferences, but rather than saying so he takes the "neutral" stance that the courts ought to be doing less—of everything.

The distinction between embracing self-restraint as a principle and having a cautious personality shows what is wrong with the following argument frequently made by liberal commentators:[39] There are liberal and conservative (which the argument equates to restrained) judges. The former believe in interpreting judicial powers expansively in the service of the liberal political agenda, the latter in avoiding judicial innovation. Therefore a good liberal judge gives little weight to precedents that are not liberal, but the good conservative judge gives great weight to all precedents, liberal as well as conservative. In other words, "Although judicial restraint normally refers to a Court's recognition of and deference to the law-making functions of the legislative branch, it also includes a Court's upholding its predecessor's decisions. Indeed . . . the rule of *stare decisis* is fundamental to the philosophy of restraint."[40] If this view is accepted, and the judiciary is dominated by successive waves of liberals and conservatives, the law will necessarily grow more liberal even if the number of liberal and conservative judges is the same in the long run. This is a clue that the argument, with its built-in ratchet, is wrong. If a liberal judge is one who seeks to advance the liberal agenda, a conservative judge is one who seeks to advance the conservative agenda. A judge could be a timid liberal or a timid conservative, a bold liberal or a bold conservative. He could, along the less partisan axis that I have been discussing, be an activist judge who was deferential toward precedent or a restrained judge who was not.

Closely related to the confusion between judicial self-restraint and deference toward precedent are confusions between judicial self-restraint and legal formalism, and between judicial activism and legal realism. There is a sense in which formalism is a timid (when it is not merely a hypocritical) judicial philosophy because it denies the creative element in judging. But judicial self-restraint is not a correlate of timidity, and formalism is actually alien to its exercise. Formalism is not a usable method of deciding difficult cases in today's legal culture, but a

---

39. See references in Charles M. Lamb, "Judicial Restraint on the Supreme Court," in *Supreme Court Activism and Restraint* 7, 24 (Stephen C. Halpern and Charles M. Lamb eds. 1982), and in Grover Rees, "Cathedrals without Walls: A View from the Outside," 61 *Tex. L. Rev.* 347, 354 n.32 (1982). For a particularly clear recent example of the genre, see Floyd Abrams, "Supreme Court Justices: An Issue," *New York Times*, February 23, 1984, at 25, col. 1.

40. Lamb, supra note 39, at 24.

way of describing the judicial process falsely. The purpose of the false description is to conceal the exercise of power. The activist judge has need for such concealment: he is trying to enlarge the power of his court at the expense of other institutions of government, and some of them may resist the encroachment. Denying that he is exercising discretion—power—is part of his political rhetoric. But the practitioner of judicial self-restraint is trying to reduce rather than enlarge his power. It is in his interest to emphasize, as Holmes did,[41] the inescapable, though in the hands of a disciplined judge the limited, element of will—of value judgments—in judicial decisions. By thus demystifying the exercise of judicial power he advances *his* agenda, which involves reducing that power.

A corollary is that the practice of candor is more congenial to the restrained than to the activist judge. Candor requires admitting that the judge's personal policy preferences or values play a role in the judicial process. This admission promotes judicial self-restraint in its separation-of-powers sense by exposing judges as people who exercise political power rather than merely passively recording and transmitting (or perhaps amplifying just a bit) decisions made elsewhere in government. It is no surprise that a frequent defense of judicial activism is that it is not activism at all, but the opposite: the passive—and, the defender often adds, the fearless—carrying out of the commands of the Constitution, or the legislature, or a higher or a prior court.[42] The boldest counsel of uncandid activism is Professor Mark Tushnet's statement that if he were a judge, he would ask in each case "which result is, in

41. A theme of G. Edward White's recent study, "The Integrity of Holmes' Jurisprudence," 10 *Hofstra L. Rev.* 633 (1982). An example is Holmes's dissent in Olmstead v. United States, 277 U.S. 438, 470 (1928) ("We have to choose, and for my part I think it a less evil that some criminals should escape than that the Government should play an ignoble part").

42. See, for example, Frank M. Johnson, Jr., "The Role of the Judiciary with Respect to the Other Branches of Government," 11 *Ga. L. Rev.* 455, 474–475 (1977). Professor Bickel described one exemplar of this style of activism as follows: "It is not, then, that Justice Black would hide his own fundamental convictions from public view. It is just that he is in the happy position of being able to enforce as law, not merely his own convictions, but the literal constitutional text. For he ever returns us to the text and offers his results wrapped in its cellophane, with locked-in flavor, untouched by contemporary human hands" (Bickel, supra note 17, at 92). The passive pose is not a monopoly of liberal activists, of course. Here is the key passage from the decision that struck down the Agricultural Adjustment Act, an important New Deal statute: "It is sometimes said that the court assumes a power to overrule or control the action of the people's representatives. This is a misconception . . . When an act of Congress is appropriately challenged in the courts as not conforming to the constitutional mandate the judicial branch of the Government has only one duty—to lay the article of the Constitution which is invoked beside the statute which is challenged and to decide whether the latter squares with the former." United States v. Butler, 297 U.S. 1, 62 (1936).

the circumstances now existing, likely to advance the cause of socialism? Having decided that, I would write an opinion in some currently favored version of Grand Theory [in constitutional law]."[43] We have come full circle from the days when judicial activism was motivated by fear and loathing of socialism. But whatever the motivation, the need to clothe the naked beast is a constant.

I want to consider briefly the relationship between the concept of judicial self-restraint in its structural or separation-of-powers sense and the current debate over constitutional and (to a much lesser extent) statutory interpretation. The debate has raised such questions as: Should interpretation be "strict" or "loose"? Should we, indeed, abandon, as a contemptible fiction, the notion that a statute or a constitution can be interpreted?[44]

It may seem intuitive that the more loosely the Constitution is interpreted, the more activist the courts must be. But it seems so only because of the tendency to equate "loose" with "broad" construction, and there is only an empirical, not a logical, relationship between the two terms. If Congress abolished the right to jury trial in federal civil cases, it would take a very loose construction of the Seventh Amendment to avoid a declaration of unconstitutionality. In arguing that statutes should be declared unconstitutional only when their unconstitutionality was clear beyond reasonable doubt,[45] Thayer was asking that the Constitution be construed loosely when doing so would promote separation-of-powers self-restraint.

Confusion is compounded because strict *statutory* construction often, and maybe generally, promotes what I have called functional restraint. Suppose the question is whether to create a private damage remedy for the violation of some statute. The statute is silent on the matter, but the court is confident that creating the remedy would advance the legislators' purposes. The strict constructionist would tend nevertheless to hold back. That would reduce the power of the legislature by thwarting

43. "The Dilemmas of Liberal Constitutionalism," 42 *Ohio St. L. J.* 411, 424 (1981). For a contrasting ideological perspective see Lino A. Graglia, "Was the Constitution a Good Idea?" *National Rev.*, July 13, 1984, at 34. Professor Graglia's implicit answer—"no"—is based on his belief that "what the judges tell us in almost every case in which they invoke the Constitution—is simply not so" (*id.*). Professors Tushnet and Graglia are both perfectly respectable law professors, though one believes that the federal courts should be interpreting the Constitution so as to promote socialism and the other believes that constitutional review should be abolished. The gap between them illustrates the unprecedented political polarization of legal scholarship today.

44. For a witty discussion of "interpretivism" versus "noninterpretivism," see Philip B. Kurland, "Curia Regis: Some Comments on the Divine Right of Kings and Courts 'To Say What the Law Is,' " 23 *Ariz. L. Rev.* 581 (1981).

45. See note 36 supra.

its intentions because they were imperfectly expressed, and in the long run would reduce the business of the courts. For, in general, the more legislation there is, the busier the courts are. If through strict construction the courts make the legislatures work harder to produce legislation, they will produce less and the courts will have less work to do. Thus, strict statutory construction promotes judicial self-restraint in its functional sense but retards it in its structural or separation-of-powers sense.

RESTRAINT AND OTHER JUDICIAL VALUES

I have said that I do not think judicial self-restraint can be an adequate shorthand for good judging. This is not only because many questions that federal judges are called upon to decide do not raise an issue of restraint (even in constitutional cases: when courts adjudicate preemption issues under the supremacy clause, for example, they are arbitrating disputes between Congress and the states), but also because restraint is only one factor in responsible judicial decision making. Others are self-discipline (implying among other things due submission to the authority of statutes, precedents, and other sources of law external to the judge's own legal imagination), thoroughness of legal research, power of logical analysis, a sense of justice, a knowledge of the world, a lucid writing style, common sense, openness to colleagues' views, intelligence, fair-mindedness, realism, hard work, foresight, modesty, a gift for compromise, and a commitment to reason and relatedly to the avoidance of "result-oriented" decisions in the narrow sense in which I have used the term. Restraint is not everything. *Brown v. Board of Education*[46] was an activist decision, but a justifiable one.

The qualities I have mentioned are admired in the activist and the restrained alike. That is why I left out a quality I happen to admire very much in judges—candor. Candor is more likely to be cherished by admirers of judicial self-restraint, and the formalist style that is the opposite of candor by admirers of judicial activism. So to some extent one has to take one's stand on the question of restraint versus activism before being able to place a value on the balance between candor and formalism in a judicial opinion. But not entirely. Although complete candor is in any event inappropriate in public documents of government, a total lack of candor would make a judicial opinion flunk my "publicity" test of principled adjudication.

The first quality I have listed, self-discipline, provides a key to

46. 347 U.S. 483 (1954).

the proper role of personal policy preferences in judging. The self-disciplined judge does not try to evade the controlling decision of a higher court by misstating that decision or distorting the facts of his case. And when the legislature's purpose can be discerned, he decides the case in accordance with that purpose. He is the honest agent of others until the will of the principals can no longer be discerned, and then he perforce becomes a principal himself. The higher up on the judicial totem pole he is, the more often he has to depart from the honest agent's role. But a self-disciplined judge keeps to that role as long as it is possible to do so.

The open area is not fixed, but depends in part on how bold, on the one hand, or deferential, on the other, the judge is toward precedent. To decide cases within that area (broad or narrow) the judge will have to pick from a large menu of competing policies, of which activism and self-restraint are only one pair.[47] "Liberalism" and "conservatism" are another. Although one recoils from these terms because of their vagueness and their emotive and partisan overtones, they are neither irrelevant to judging nor meaningless—"liberalism" in its modern sense referring to the belief that there should be extensive regulation of economic life to promote equality, but little or no regulation of personal behavior; "conservatism" referring in some versions to the opposite weighting of social and personal regulation and in others to laissez-faire in both the personal and economic domains. Thus understood, the concepts of liberalism and conservatism are expressions of rival conceptions of human nature that go back to the dawn of Western civilization.

It does not detract from, and may even be an element of, Holmes's greatness that his belief in Social Darwinism infused many of his opinions, not only in the "hard" cases for which he is not widely admired today,[48] but also in his much-admired free-speech opinions. His concept of the marketplace of ideas,[49] which he used to expand the reach of the First Amendment, is Darwinian, and Social Darwinism appears to underlie his deference toward legislative experimentation; the dissent in *Lochner* is a Darwinian document. It should not matter to our assessment of Holmes the judge whether we think Social Darwinism a good thing or a bad thing, so long as we do not think it childish, vicious, idio-

47. The literature on the proper grounds of judicial decisions is vast; for a recent and highly pertinent contribution see John Bell, *Policy Arguments in Judicial Decisions*, chaps. 1 and 2 (1983).

48. Such as Buck v. Bell, 274 U.S. 200, 207 (1927) ("Three generations of imbeciles are enough").

49. See Abrams v. United States, 250 U.S. 616, 630 (1919) (dissenting opinion).

syncratic, or partisan in the sense in which his adopting the Democratic or Republican campaign platform of 1900 as his judicial *vade mecum* would have been partisan and therefore unprincipled, result-oriented. The effort of a powerful mind to bring the big ideas of his age into the law when judicial craft alone will not decide a case should not be deprecated. But the qualification is important. The element of will, of personal policy preference, is inescapable in the American judicial process; but the willful judge, the judge who makes will the dominant element of his decision making, is properly reprobated. Moreover, a preference may be too personal to be a legitimate ingredient of the judicial process. It is one thing for the judge to give expression to the big ideas of his age, and to recognize that they need not be—in our society, are unlikely to be—ideas that command universal support. But if they are idiosyncratic, the judge has no business using them to decide cases. That would make the law too quirky and unpredictable. Even in the open area the judge must remain impersonal to the extent of confining his policy choices to values that are widely, though usually they will not be universally, held.

8

The Judicial Craft

THIS CHAPTER deals with some of the eternal problems of judicial (especially appellate) technique[1]—the judge's institutional responsibilities, the writing of judicial opinions, the methodology of *stare decisis* (decision according to precedent)—as they present themselves in the federal courts today. These problems would, of course, exist, and have little diminished significance, even if there were no caseload crisis. But they have been aggravated by the crisis and their solution would go some way toward alleviating it. Poor judicial technique has consequences—delay, laxity in controlling the course of litigation, and above all legal uncertainty—that increase both the number of lawsuits (in the case of uncertainty) and the judicial resources devoted to each lawsuit.

The hard-headed will object, however, that poor judicial technique is just another name for the technique of poor judges, so that the problems I have just mentioned would solve themselves if the selection of federal judges were made more meritocratic (which is not likely to happen) and are insoluble otherwise. There is truth to this; you cannot make judges more intelligent, more learned, and more dispassionate by preaching to them. But it may be possible to improve judicial performance somewhat by persuading judges to alter their attitude toward

---

1. Two useful compendia of readings on the subject are Robert A. Leflar, *Appellate Judicial Opinions* (1974), and Ruggero J. Aldisert, *The Judicial Process: Readings, Materials and Cases* (1976). On opinion writing in particular see the many references in Kathleen Waits, "Values, Intuitions, and Opinion Writing: The Judicial Process and State Court Jurisdiction," *1983 U. Ill. L. Rev.* 917, 919–936. On the work of trial judges Judge Charles E. Wyzanski, Jr.'s, classic, "A Trial Judge's Freedom and Responsibility," *65 Harv. L. Rev.* 1281 (1952), though it precedes the current era of massive caseloads, remains well worth reading.

particular aspects of their jobs. Federal judges, indeed, may be more responsive to preaching than ordinary sinners are. As pointed out in Chapter 1, the conditions of federal judicial employment have been carefully designed to minimize the role in judicial decision making of some of the strongest incentives that motivate human action, such as the desire for wealth and promotion. Federal judges should therefore be more than ordinarily sensitive to other promptings, such as those of conscience, which can be stimulated by professional criticism.

Most of the observations in this chapter are more pertinent to appellate than to trial judges. Diffidence is not the main reason for my refraining from discussing the latter beyond a few general comments. Although I have never been a district judge and my experience sitting by designation in the district courts of our circuit has been limited to conducting seven trials, the position of a court of appeals judge provides a good vantage point for evaluating the work of district judges. But having reviewed more than 600 district court decisions since becoming a court of appeals judge, I find myself with few systematic criticisms of the federal district courts. Signs of haste are evident in the work coming out of these courts; but this is cause for commiseration rather than criticism.[2]

I cannot improve on Judge Friendly's "job description" of federal district judges: "disposing of cases by trial or settlement with fairness and with the optimum blend of prompt decision and rightness of result; they also have the responsibility of demonstrating the quality of federal justice to ordinary citizens—parties, witnesses and jurors."[3] He adds in a footnote: "Perhaps it may seem shocking thus to suggest there should ever be compromise in the goal of attaining perfection. But the nature of the tasks of trial courts sets limits on their abilities to achieve this. Rulings on the admissibility of evidence are the most obvious instance where quick decision is essential. Beyond that I do not believe the greatest district judges to be those who stew for months and then write a long opinion on a novel point of law concerning which they are almost certain not to have the last word."[4] Although most district

2. I shall not discuss the "hottest" current topic of discussion about federal district judges—their responsibilities in institutional reform litigation, on which see, for example, Donald L. Horowitz, "Decreeing Organizational Change: Judicial Supervision of Public Institutions," in *The Courts: Separation of Powers* 39 (Bette Goulet ed. 1983); Judith Resnik, "Managerial Judges," 97 *Harv. L. Rev.* 374 (1982). In my observation the district judges do as well as could be expected given the inherent limitations of judicial competence to perform managerial responsibilities. The problem is really an aspect of the issue of judicial activism versus judicial self-restraint, discussed in Chapter 7.

3. Henry J. Friendly, "The 'Law of the Circuit' and All That," 46 *St. John's L. Rev.* 406, 407 (1972) (footnote omitted).

4. *Id.* at 407 n.6.

judges adequately fulfill the role described by Judge Friendly, there are four areas of recurrent deficiency that might be improved by a change of attitude.

1. Some district judges are careless about verifying the existence of federal subject-matter jurisdiction when neither party challenges the court's jurisdiction. The unspoken attitude of these judges seems to be that if both parties want to litigate in federal court, the judge should let them. This position is wrong in its disregard of the limitations that the Constitution and Congress have placed on the exercise of the judicial power, and is especially irresponsible in a period of heavy caseloads.

2. District judges sometimes are (understandably) rather insensitive to the limitations of appellate jurisdiction and to the caseload pressures in the courts of appeals. The general rule in the federal courts is that only final judgments—judgments that wind up the lawsuit—are appealable.[5] There are many exceptions to this rule, but it would be disastrous if the exceptions were allowed to swallow it entirely; the courts of appeals would rapidly be overrun if an indefinite number of appeals were possible in a single lawsuit. Some of the important exceptions to the final-judgment rule, however, lie largely in the hands of district judges. Appeals from orders that would not otherwise be appealable final judgments—appeals under Rule 54(b) of the Federal Rules of Civil Procedure and section 1292(b) of the Judicial Code—require certification by the district judge; and some judges grant such certification too freely, being happy to see the case taken out of their hands for a time. They either neglect the limitations in the rules themselves, or in exercising their discretion give little weight to the burdens on the appellate court.

3. Some district judges delegate too much of their authority, not just to their law clerks (a problem at all levels of the federal judiciary) but to magistrates and externs. Some district judges' chambers are buzzing hives of judicial supernumeraries. The pressure to delegate comes directly from the caseload crisis, is acute and understandable, yet must be resisted. Even as a method of keeping the judge current with his docket, it can be self-defeating. For example, judges who delegate a lot tend to delegate to a magistrate the preparation of the pretrial order in cases that go to trial. Because the Federal Rules of Civil Procedure allow uninformative pleadings, the pretrial conference and the order that emanates from it are critical to the pace of the trial. If the pretrial order fails to narrow the issues for trial to the questions of fact and law

---

5. See 28 U.S.C. § 1291; Charles Alan Wright, *Handbook of the Law of Federal Courts,* chap. 11 (4th ed. 1983).

that are genuinely in dispute, the trial will be longer and more confused than it need be. Only the person who will conduct the trial—the judge (I put to one side cases tried by a magistrate with the agreement of the parties)—can hammer out an effective pretrial order; no one else has sufficient authority in the eyes of the parties.

4. Many judges do not exercise a firm enough hand in guiding pretrial discovery, the preparatory stage of litigation when the parties busy themselves with serving interrogatories and taking depositions in order to obtain leads for examination and cross-examination at trial. The judges' failure is understandable in light of their enormous workload, yet it was a problem when workload was much less. Most judges simply do not like to get involved in the preliminary stages of a case unless they are being asked to decide the case on a motion to dismiss or a motion for summary judgment. But a firm judicial hand is necessary to protect litigants from the use of discovery to embarrass, intimidate, or exhaust their opponents and thereby force unfair settlements. Amendments to the Federal Rules of Civil Procedure that took effect on August 1, 1983, impose increased managerial responsibilities on district judges and strengthen the sanctions for abusing the discovery process, but it remains to be seen how the judges will react to their new powers and responsibilities.

In limiting my criticisms of federal trial judges to rather minor areas of their performance, I do not want to seem unduly complacent about the district courts. The heavy and emotionally taxing workload (Table 6.1 showed that 40 percent of the trials in the federal district courts are of criminal, including postconviction, cases), the inadequate pay, and possibly a diminution in prestige caused by the substantial increase in the number of district judges in recent years are provoking resignations, making it harder to recruit highly qualified candidates, and reducing the quality of the district courts' performance. These developments should make anyone contemplating the future of these courts anxious. But the most serious deficiencies of judicial technique are not at the district court level; they are at the level of the courts of appeals and the Supreme Court.

THE INSTITUTIONAL RESPONSIBILITIES OF FEDERAL APPELLATE JUDGES

There is a difference between an appellate judge's thinking of himself as an individual who happens to do his work in committee and thinking of himself as a member of a court conceived of as something more than the set of judges who constitute it—a difference, in short, between an individualistic and an institutional judicial perspective.[6] The individualist judge acts as if he wanted to maximize his personal welfare, which includes such things (in different mixtures) as leisure, friendship, ego, and reputation as a jurist. The institutional-minded judge acts as if he wanted to maximize the social output or value of his court. I have used the "as if" formulation to emphasize that I am not suggesting, and do not believe, that judges think of themselves in these ways; judges do not have greater insight into their own motives than other people do into theirs. But if an observer had enough information about a judge's behavior, he could fit the judge into one of my two categories. It is, incidentally, because no one has full information about judges that reputation and social value can diverge. If everything were known, the judge who maximized the social value of his court would have the highest reputation.

The problem of institutional responsibility is not acute in the district courts because a district court is not a "court" in the same sense in which a court of appeals or the Supreme Court is. The judges who constitute a district court perform their functions as individuals with little collegial interaction. The position of chief district judge is a highly responsible one, but this is because many district courts have more judges and staff, bigger budgets, more courtrooms, and for all these reasons more administrative problems than courts of appeals do; there are, for example, twice as many judgeships in the Northern District of Illinois than in the court of appeals for the Seventh Circuit. Because the district court does not declare the law that its judges apply, it need not and usually does not speak with a single, an institutional, voice. But when each appellate judge speaks with a separate voice, there is judicial cacophony.[7]

Thus a sense of institutional responsibility is vital at the appellate level. But the structure of the federal appellate court system fosters individual self-assertion rather than institutional loyalty and cohesion. Life tenure and the divorce of compensation from performance not only reduce the impact of institutional malfunction on the individual judge (and thus make the problem of institutional responsibility more intractable in the federal than in state courts); they also make the position of chief judge (the Chief Justice in the case of the Supreme Court)

6. For some pertinent observations by a former solicitor general of the United States, see Erwin N. Griswold, "Cutting the Cloak to Fit the Cloth: An Approach to Problems in the Federal Courts," 32 *Catholic U. L. Rev.* 787, 796–800 (1983).

7. English appellate judges deliver individual opinions seriatim at the close of argument. For reasons too numerous to go into here, this is not a realistic model for American appellate courts.

inherently a weak one. He has few levers with which to move his colleagues in the direction of better judicial citizenship. Moreover, since chief judges of federal courts of appeals are not chosen but attain office through seniority, they take office with no presumption that anyone thought they had significant leadership qualities. Many do; but this is serendipitous. Because some do not, recently Congress limited the terms of chief judges to seven years.[8] This risk-averse strategy has a cost: it weakens the position of the chief judge, thus aggravating one leadership problem while alleviating another. Historically, judges of powerful intellect and character exercised informal leadership roles in the courts of appeals. But the opportunities for such leadership are declining as the number of judges on each court of appeals grows larger—which reduces interaction among the judges—and as each judge becomes busier, which leaves him with less time to confer with colleagues.

The leadership structure is better in the Supreme Court. The Chief Justice is appointed to that post; and his power to assign the majority opinion in the cases in which he is in the majority gives him a real lever for dealing with the other justices—provided he is not in dissent most of the time. The chief judges of the courts of appeals also assign the majority opinion when they are in the majority. But except in the First Circuit, which has only four circuit judges in regular active service, the chief judge will sit on only a fraction of the panels; and anyway in a panel of only three judges the assigning of opinions is more constrained than when there are nine. Each Supreme Court justice, moreover, is one of only nine members of an exceptionally powerful, controversial, and closely observed court; his behavior will have a nontrivial effect on the Court and through it on him and the whole federal court system. Even in a court of appeals of nine or fewer judges, the behavior of one will have relatively little effect on the court or himself, because a court of appeals is not the relevant unit for generating a feedback effect from its judges' actions. Congress tends to legislate uniformly with respect to the courts of appeals (except in regard to the number of judges). For example, all of the circuit judges are paid the same; and if one shirks his institutional responsibilities and thereby reduces the quality of his court, this is unlikely to provoke legislation affecting the courts of appeals in general or his court in particular. (In fact, it is unlikely even to be noticed.) Thus there is a more serious free-rider problem at the court of appeals level than at the Supreme Court level.

8. Federal Courts Improvement Act of 1982, 96 Stat. 52, amending 28 U.S.C. § 136 (a) (3) (A).

Among other things that impair the sense of appellate institutional responsibility is the practice of the signed opinion. As the only judicial act to which an individual's name is attached, the publication of an opinion in a significant case is more important to an appellate judge's reputation than any and perhaps all of his "little, nameless, unremembered acts" (with apologies to Wordsworth) on which the effective operation of an appellate court also depends. The reputation of the famous judges rests on their opinions, not their teamwork. Although the publication of some of Justice Brandeis's unpublished opinions[9] has afforded a rare glimpse of the hidden dimensions of appellate judging, where considerations of institutional effectiveness may require the suppression of an individual view, Brandeis's judicial reputation still rests on his published opinions rather than on the other contributions he made to the work of the Supreme Court. Few judges or justices can expect anyone to be interested in any dimension of their judicial output other than published opinions and public votes. I am not suggesting that we do away with the signed opinion; it is indispensable to making the threat of searing professional criticism an effective check on irresponsible judicial actions. But it has costs as well as benefits.

Another force working against the spirit of institutional responsibility among appellate judges is the importance quite properly attached to impartiality as a defining attribute of a good judge. It is easy to confuse impartiality with indifference, a tendency fostered by the modern usage of the word "disinterest" (which formerly meant impartiality—and still does to purists) as a synonym for lack of interest. To take an active interest in one's court as an institution—to be concerned with its effectiveness and not just with preparing for, voting on, and writing opinions in particular cases—is to risk appearing less detached, though it is perfectly consistent with detachment. The appellate judge's tendency to view his role as a passive one is reinforced by the way in which problems are presented to a judge for solution. The judge watches a procession of randomly sorted cases coming before him for decision; a pattern is difficult to discern; thus it is natural for him to think that his job is to deal with each case separately without worrying about the pattern or about the effects of his decisions taken as a whole on the health of the judicial system. Of course, this is a less serious problem for the Supreme Court, with its largely discretionary jurisdiction.

For district judges, from whose ranks about 40 percent of the circuit

9. Alexander M. Bickel, *The Unpublished Opinions of Mr. Justice Brandeis: The Supreme Court at Work* (1957).

judges come and who have additional importance in the work of the courts of appeals because district judges are the most frequent visiting judges on them,[10] there is the further problem of having to adjust to the very different audience of an appellate judge as opposed to a trial judge. The trial's judge's audience is in most cases pretty much limited to the parties and their counsel. But this is only a minute fraction of the appellate judge's audience: he is deciding cases and writing opinions for the guidance of the bar and the district bench and for the illumination of other appellate judges, law professors, and law students, and to do his job right he must be aware of the broader audience for his work. To this audience the institutional aspect of judging is the important one. The larger audience has very little interest in particular judges; it is interested in the law as declared by the *court*.

If what I have said so far is correct, the conditions of federal appellate judging make the development of an adequate sense of institutional responsibility on the part of the judges difficult at best. And the difficulty is growing with the increase in caseload. As the number of judges increases, the behavior of each has ever less impact on the performance of the court as a whole and hence, through a feedback effect, on the individual judge. Moreover, the time available to each judge for performing his institutional responsibilities diminishes as he becomes busier. Judicial activism, a strongly marked characteristic of modern federal adjudication, makes it all the harder for a court to maintain a sense of institutional responsibility, by multiplying occasions for disagreement.

In light of this analysis, it is not surprising that symptoms of institutional irresponsibility are increasingly evident in the performance of the federal appellate courts, and particularly in their opinions, which are the principal public dimension of appellate judging. True, some of these things (for example, the excessive length of opinions) are also symptoms of the rise of the law clerk, discussed in Chapter 4. But both the multiplication of law clerks and the decline in the courts' sense of institutional responsibility are due in part to the same thing—the caseload crisis.

To put it bluntly, many contemporary federal appellate opinions seem to be self-indulgent displays performed with little concern for the interests and needs of the audience for the opinions. A self-indulgent opinion is, among its other characteristics, much longer than it need be (the statistics in Table 3.6 are suggestive in this regard), the author having made no effort to prune it of facts, procedural history, and citations

10. Of 318 judges designated as visiting judges in the federal courts of appeals in 1982, 262 were active or senior district judges.

that are unnecessary to an understanding of the decision. Irrelevant procedural details (such as the substitution of a new cabinet officer as the nominal defendant in a case) are routinely and boringly recited, along with dates and places and names that are of no importance to the legal principles involved in the case, and strings of citations far too long to reflect the actual reading of the opinion's nominal author.[11] The audience for the opinion, consisting as it will of lawyers and judges professionally concerned with the subject matter of the opinion, will not be able to skip the boilerplate, because the court's essential reasoning may be buried somewhere in it. Therefore such an opinion is inconsiderate of the time of the busy professionals who must wade through it and of the clients who must pay for their time. At one level this is merely inept, a by-product of the ghostwriting society, judicial sector. But it is also irresponsible; it subordinates the judge's institutional obligations to his delight in self-expression, or more mundanely to his reluctance to make the effort necessary to curb the self-expressive ardors of his law clerks.

Notice, however, that I have not said that modern judicial opinions are longer than they could be; I said they were longer than they need be. If brevity is achieved by omitting issues that ought to be discussed, or by stating results without reasons, or by suppressing adverse facts, or by writing elliptically, the price is too high. There are opinions that, once the boilerplate of procedural details, supernumerary facts, and redundant or inapposite citations is stripped away, are actually too short; the analysis is missing. This is not to say that the opinion writer must discuss every issue presented, every argument made, by each party. Issues of no possible merit or general interest should not be discussed in a published opinion merely to reassure counsel for the losing party that the court did not overlook one of his contentions, for counsel is only a small part of the audience for a published appellate opinion.

One symptom of the prolixity of the modern federal judicial opinion[12] is the heavy use of footnotes, documented in Table 3.6. To footnotes that merely cite cases or other authorities the only objection is that they are unnecessary. Opinion writers discovered long ago that they could print the citations right in the text without disturbing the reader's concentration; the italicization of case names in modern case reports helps the eye of the reader so inclined to skip easily over case

11. And each court of appeals citation will be followed by "cert. denied" (if certiorari was applied for and refused), even though the Supreme Court has said time and again that denial of certiorari imports no view on the merits of the decision below.

12. Wonderfully illustrated by the 113 pages of opinions in Zweibon v. Mitchell, 516 F.2d 594 (D.C. Cir. 1975) (en banc).

names. The textual footnote, so common in contemporary opinion writing, is open to two graver objections. First, it retards reading speed and comprehension. The reason for this is not just that the eye has to glance to the bottom of the page, read what is written there, and then return to the place where the interruption occurred; it is also that the material in the footnote will not flow easily from the sentence from which the footnote was dropped and into the following sentence—otherwise the writer would not have placed the material in a footnote. The interruption is to the mind as well as the eye. Second, a lot of bad law is made in footnotes. The court's holdings are authoritative wherever they appear on the page; but often the opinion writer will have placed material in a footnote because he was not quite sure it was right and yet it seemed in some way necessary in order to complete his argument, or at least supportive of it.

The two objections are related. Writing with footnotes, other than purely bibliographic footnotes, is a lazy form of writing. (I say this who should not, since I have written a number of books—this book, for example—and many articles, with textual footnotes.) It enables the author to avoid having to decide whether a proposition is important enough to his argument to be integrated into it or sufficiently dubious or marginal to be discarded. Writing with textual footnotes leads to the retention of some propositions that are superfluous or questionable or both, and to the statement of others in a form that is difficult to relate to the author's argument. These are particularly serious shortcomings in legally operative documents intended to be read by busy professionals.

The principal appeal of the textual footnote is to the author: it spares him the pain of having to discard anything that he considers to have some value or interest, and it enables him to show, or at least pretend, that he is hard-working, learned, and scrupulous. I realize that some of our greatest judges, including Brandeis and Friendly, have used textual footnotes. So I do not anathematize their use completely. But they are being overused. They are particularly objectionable when they are written by law clerks and not carefully reviewed by the judge.

Another and increasingly common manifestation of excessive judicial self-assertion is the abuse—often shrill, sometimes nasty—of one's colleagues.[13] Nothing is less helpful, less convincing, or less edifying to the professional readers of judicial opinions (including other judges) than denunciations of a disagreeing colleague. Such criticisms figure ever more prominently not only in dissenting and concurring opinions

13. For a striking recent example see Franz v. United States, 712 F.2d 1428 (D.C. Cir. 1983).

but in majority opinions as well, now that it is the fashion for the author of the majority opinion, usually in footnotes, to attack the dissenting opinion (and sometimes even a concurring opinion). Judicial indignation fails as effective rhetoric for three reasons. The first is the jejune and unimaginative vocabulary of abuse in which judges express themselves. The same well-worn epithets—"result-oriented," "unprincipled," "disingenuous," "activist," "unreasoned," "glib," "novel and unjustified," "unilluminating," "absurd," "apocalyptic," "rhetorical," and so on—appear over and over again, with ever-diminishing impact.[14] Second, the rhetoric of judicial abuse is in many cases opportunistic: the first to cry "activist" is usually an activist; the unprincipled cries "unprincipled." Some dissenting opinions, indeed, invite the following paraphrase: "My learned brethren have misstated the facts, discarded precedent, twisted the language and ignored the purpose of the statute, thrown logic to the winds, quoted out of context, and disregarded the promptings of common sense. They have used all the techniques of judicial willfulness; now watch a real master use them!" Third, readers are not interested in the degree to which one judge has been upset by another judge, and anyway probably think the passion in judicial opinions feigned, as indeed it often is.

Judges' abuse of each other is institutionally irresponsible. The abusive dissent characteristically exaggerates and distorts the holding of the majority opinion, to the confusion of the bar and lower court judges. Abuse in opinions is not only a distraction to the reader but also lowers the reputation of the judiciary in the eyes of the public (the small public that reads opinions, the bigger public that reads newspaper accounts of opinions). If the reader agrees that the abuse is justified he will naturally think less well of the judge being abused; if he thinks the abuse is hyperbolic he will think less well of the abusing judge; quite often he will think the abuse merited but intemperate and think less well of both judges. I do not suggest that dissent be suppressed to conceal the faults of judges; but there is a difference between stating a disagreement and calling a colleague wrong, or unprincipled, or dishonest.

The printed abuse of colleagues is far more common in the Supreme Court than in any court of appeals (though in recent years the District of Columbia Circuit has run a close second). This is odd for two rea-

---

14. Sometimes one finds imaginative abuse; it is more effective, but less civil. See, for example, Dobbert v. Florida, 432 U.S. 282, 311 (1977) (dissenting opinion) (describing majority opinion as "an archaic gargoyle"); Railroad Retirement Bd. v. Fritz, 449 U.S. 166, 176 n.10 (1980) ("The comments in the dissenting opinion . . . are just that: comments in a dissenting opinion").

sons. First, the justices have to live together in a way that circuit judges do not; the justices sit all the time together, whereas circuit judges sit almost all the time on randomly sorted three-judge panels and may therefore sit with a particular colleague only a few times each year. And public abuse does not foster either personal friendship or professional cooperation. Second, since the average case the Supreme Court decides is difficult, one would think it easier for justices than for circuit judges to regard disagreement as just that—rather than as a stubborn refusal by one side to see reason, which is the tone in which many of these disagreements are registered. One is put in mind of Holmes's remark, quoted in the preceding chapter, about judges who think that if there is a dissent it means that someone hasn't done his sums right. The abuse of one's judicial colleagues is thus another sign that formalism lives, if only as a style. Maybe the justices speak in such tones of apodictic certainty because at some unconscious level they are afraid that if they lowered the temperature of the debate, the public would realize that many Supreme Court opinions are at bottom merely expressions of personal predilection on debatable questions of social policy.[15]

Since feelings do run high in some cases, the abusive dissent—at least the abusive dissent that conveys the judge's real emotions—is, if inexcusable, at least understandable. But the abuse *of* dissents, an ever more frequent feature of majority opinions of cases in which a dissent is filed,[16] is not even that. Victory should breed magnanimity. Having won the struggle with the dissenting judge for the minds and hearts of the other judges, the author of the majority opinion should not feel driven to abuse the loser. And, even when completely civil in tone, the majority opinion that takes issue with the dissent (usually in footnotes that begin, "The dissenting opinion incorrectly states . . .") is the quintessence of inconsiderate opinion writing. It is unreadable, because portions are explicitly intended to be read only after the reader has read the dissenting opinion, which he cannot do without reading the majority opinion since the dissenting opinion normally will presume acquaintance with the majority opinion.

Ideally, the author of the majority opinion should take the time to recast it so that it anticipates and meets the arguments of the dissent without referring the reader forward. Such a majority opinion is at once self-sufficient and responsive to the arguments of the dissenting opinion, and it is much easier to read than an opinion unchanged as a result

15. Cf. Robert A. Leflar, "Honest Judicial Opinions," 74 *Nw. U. L. Rev.* 721, 738 (1979).

16. For recent examples, see Pennhurst State School & Hospital v. Halderman, 104 S. Ct. 900 (1984); Federal Energy Regulatory Comm'n v. Mississippi, 456 U.S. 742 (1982).

of the dissent except by the addition of counterattacking footnotes. But it is also harder to write, because it requires revising the text of the majority opinion and not just adding footnotes. (The point is general: what is easier to read is harder to write, and vice versa.) I realize that the justices face severe time pressures in cases decided near the end of term, because of the Court's self-imposed rule (questioned in Chapter 1) of deciding every case before breaking for the summer recess. These pressures may make it irresistible to respond to a dissent by just adding some footnotes. It also makes life easier for the other justices in the majority, who must approve the revised majority opinion before it can be released; they can review it more easily if the only new matter is in footnotes.

If my concern with the style and tone of contemporary appellate opinions seems overly fastidious to some readers, I refer them to an article by a distinguished professor of tax law, in a journal designed to be read by tax practitioners, reviewing two recent tax decisions of the Supreme Court.[17] In a section of the article entitled "Distractive Footnotes," Professor Blum states:

> The opinion is, to put it mildly, loaded with footnotes that are distractive or puzzling or unduly suggestive . . . Many of the footnotes are efforts to rebut or undercut positions taken in the minority opinion. Some of these notes are lengthy and not a few are written in rather shrill language . . . My belief is that in tax litigation the Supreme Court's role, aside from resolving constitutional issues, is to settle the particular cases before it on the basis of general analysis of relevant statutory and judicial antecedents and to embody that analysis in words that will give maximum general guidance to tax practitioners, the IRS and lower courts confronted with related or similar questions. Long opinions (especially if overly technical or jurisprudential) do not contribute to this goal. Nor do heavy footnotes. And least of all footnotes that score debaters' points about minority opinions . . . The Court's main audience surely cannot place a high value on the thrusts and counter thrusts of the justices. These discourses add greatly to the burden of understanding the message of the court. Why force the readers to dis-

17. Walter J. Blum, "The Role of the Supreme Court in Federal Income Tax Controversies—*Hillsboro National Bank* and *Bliss Dairy, Inc.*," *Taxes*, June 1983, at 363. The two cases reviewed in the article were decided together *sub nom.* Hillsboro National Bank v. Commissioner, 103 S. Ct. 1134 (1983). See also Walter J. Blum, "Dissenting Opinions by Supreme Court Justices in Federal Income Tax Controversies," 82 *Mich. L. Rev.* 431 (1983).

cover just what material in these footnote forays is integral to the prevailing analysis and not merely criticisms of the minority? Another group of footnotes consists of references to things that have little or no bearing on the problems in controversy . . . Somehow I am reminded of the usual contents of the basic taxation course in law school. Serious tax people studying the opinion might well consider this type of footnote as an annoyance. Then there are abundant references to articles on various aspects of the tax benefit rule. I count four citations to commentators in the footnotes and an equal number in the text. Such displays of research are surplusage. Most readers doubtless are willing to assume that the Court has done its homework . . . Most troubling are footnotes that may be read as throwing into doubt long-standing tax results that have not been challenged in years.[18]

Such criticisms are frequently voiced, though rarely published.

I have taken for granted thus far that we are to have dissenting and concurring opinions as well as majority opinions. Dissenting and to a lesser extent concurring opinions have played so important a role in the development of the law that it would be a great error to suppress them;[19] it would actually make law less rather than more certain, by concealing from the bar important clues to the law of the future. But it does not follow that a judge should dissent (or write separately in concurrence) at the drop of a hat. The difference between the institutional and the individual perspective is important here. From a purely individual standpoint, a judge naturally wants to indicate to the world where he (or, increasingly, she) stands; he does not want to be put into the target area of criticisms directed at an opinion that he voted against. But suppose that although he thinks he is right and the majority wrong, he also thinks it unlikely that his or any other court will, or perhaps even should, reopen the question in the foreseeable future. The case may involve one of those frequent questions where it is more important that the law be settled than that it be got just right. In such a case a dissent will communicate a sense of the law's instability that is misleading; the decision is as solid a precedent as if it had been unanimous. From an

18. Blum, "Role of the Supreme Court," supra note 17, at 368 (paragraph breaks and footnotes deleted).

19. A few examples of highly influential concurring opinions are Justice Brandeis's concurrence in Ashwander v. TVA, 297 U.S. 288, 341 (1936); Justice Jackson's concurrence in D'Oench, Duhme & Co. v. FDIC, 315 U.S. 447, 465 (1942); and Justice Traynor's concurrence in Escola v. Coca Cola Bottling Co., 24 Cal. 2d 453, 461, 150 P.2d 436, 440 (1941), described as Traynor's greatest opinion in G. Edward White, Tort Law in America: An Intellectual History 197 (1980).

Table 8.1. Majority, dissenting, and concurring opinions, Supreme Court, selected years 1894–1982

Term	No. majority opinions[a]	No. dissenting opinions[b]	No. concurring opinions	Majority opinions as percentage of total
1894	188	18	0	91
1914	272	14	2	94
1934	168	13	7	89
1954	82	46	14	58
1959	135	111	30	49
1964	95	70	43	46
1969	105	85	48	44
1972	178	171	56	44
1973	171	145	54	46
1974	155	138	54	45
1975	156	117	86	43
1976	142	140	91	38
1977	135	143	81	38
1978	138	122	78	41
1979	149	156	79	39
1980	138	119	91	40
1981	167	135	95	42
1982	162	140	70	40

Sources: 1894–1974, Gerhard Casper and Richard A. Posner, *The Workload of the Supreme Court* 80 (1976) (table 4.7); 1975–1982, Supreme Court Note, *Harvard Law Review*, November 1976 through November 1983.
a. Signed and per curiam.
b. Including partial dissents.

institutional perspective it is better for the disagreeing judge not to dissent publicly in such a case, even though such forbearance will make it more difficult for someone to write the judge's intellectual biography.

As shown in Table 8.1, there has been a big increase in the past 50 years in the number of dissenting opinions in the Supreme Court. As late as 1934 only 13 opinions dissenting in whole or part were filed, but by 1959 this number had risen to 111. It peaked at 171 in 1972 and has since fluctuated between about 120 and 160. The standard explanation is that the greater difficulty of the average Supreme Court case (resulting from the declining fraction of applications for review that the Court can accept) and the Court's increasing involvement in areas of law where there is no value consensus (abortion being a prime example) make greater disagreement inevitable. There is a great deal of truth to this explanation, and it must also account in part for the even more dramatic increase in the number of concurring opinions in the Supreme Court (7 in 1934, 30 in 1959, 95 in 1981—the peak year). Many concurring opinions are the functional equivalent of dissents: the concurring judge disagrees with the majority's holding but adventitiously reaches the same result—affirmance, or reversal, or whatever—on a different ground. The difference between this type of concurrence and a dissent is that by depriving the author of the majority opinion of a vote for that opinion, the concurrence may cause the case to be decided by plurality opinion.[20] This is the automatic result if another judge on a three-judge panel has filed a dissenting opinion or if the vote is five to four in a Supreme Court case. In either case an alternative way of avoiding decision by plurality opinion is for the dissenting judge to withdraw his dissent or for the author of the plurality opinion to withdraw his and join the concurring judge's opinion. There is no obvious reason why it is the concurring judge who should yield—except where (as in the Supreme Court, and in a court of appeals when it sits en banc) the panel has more than three judges and there is a plurality opinion that is one vote shy of being a majority. One cannot expect the dissenting judge to switch over and give the plurality a majority. But the concurring judge—who at least agrees with the plurality's outcome, and can hardly expect to move all the members of the plurality to his own, as it were private, view of the case—has a responsibility to think long and hard before condemning the bar to the tedious labor of trying to extract a usable precedent from a decision in which no opinion commands a majority.

Justice Blackmun's concurrence in *Baldasar v. Illinois*[21] illustrates the problem of concurring opinions in cases where there is no majority opinion. The defendant was convicted of misdemeanor theft, but because it was the second such conviction he was punished as a felon. He had not had counsel in the first proceeding, and the question for the Court was whether his "uncounseled" conviction could be used to "enhance" his subsequent conviction from a misdemeanor to a felony conviction. In a per curiam opinion by five justices, the Supreme Court reversed "for the reasons stated in the concurring opinions." There were three concurring opinions. Two, more or less compatible with each other (leading one to wonder why they could not have been

20. On which see "Note: The Precedential Value of Supreme Court Plurality Opinions," 80 *Colum. L. Rev.* 756 (1980). The fraction of cases decided by plurality opinion in the Supreme Court has risen sharply in recent years. See Frank H. Easterbrook, "Ways of Criticizing the Court," 95 *Harv. L. Rev.* 802, 805 n.9 (1982).

21. 446 U.S. 222, 229–230 (1980).

melded into one), took the position that since the Constitution had been interpreted to require that counsel be supplied to an indigent defendant in a felony case and since Baldasar was, in effect, being punished as a felon for his first, nominally misdemeanor, theft, his punishment violated the Constitution. But these two opinions together commanded only four votes, making Justice Blackmun's concurrence the key to inferring a majority position. And he took a completely different tack from the other concurring justices, reasserting a position that he had taken (and that had been rejected) in a previous case to the effect that the defendant should have a right to counsel whenever the offense with which he is charged is punishable by at least six months' imprisonment. Since Baldasar's first theft conviction could have been so punished (though it was not), that conviction was invalid in Justice Blackmun's view and therefore could not support enhancement. On whether a valid "uncounseled" misdemeanor conviction could ever support enhancement of a subsequent misdemeanor conviction to felony status—the issue the other judges thought was presented by *Baldasar*—Justice Blackmun said nothing. By his silence he not only deprived the bar and the lower court judges of the guidance that a majority opinion would have provided, but made it impossible even to infer a "lowest common denominator" holding (beyond what was implicit in the outcome of the case) of the sort that sometimes can be extracted from a comparison of a plurality opinion with a concurring opinion or opinions; there was no common ground between him and the other concurrers. If he had gone on and addressed the issue considered by the other concurring justices, such a ground might have emerged.

Often a concurring opinion will purport to join the majority opinion as well as just the judgment, and is filed in order to (1) express the concurring judge's understanding of what the majority opinion means, (2) register a minor reservation, (3) suggest additional reasons for the result, or (4) criticize a dissenting opinion. All such concurring opinions show inconsiderateness—by the concurring judge (except type 3), and often by the author of the majority opinion—for those professionally obliged to read judicial opinions. A concurrence of type 1 casts a big shadow over the authority of the majority opinion. In a number of famous examples well known to lawyers,[22] the "understanding" expressed by a concurrence or concurrences whose judges' votes were essential to a majority was so at variance with the manifest import of the majority opinion as to make it really just a plurality opinion—the

22. See, for example, Commonwealth Coatings Corp. v. Continental Casualty Co., 393 U.S. 145, 150 (1968); Parratt v. Taylor, 451 U.S. 527, 544–545 (1981).

pretense that the concurring judges joined the majority opinion serving mainly to trip up the careless reader. A concurrence of type 2 casts a lesser, but often still long, shadow over the authority of the majority opinion. As for type 3, if the members of the majority think the additional reasons sound, or at least defensible, the author of the majority opinion ought to work those reasons into his opinion. Similarly, if the concurring judge has a good answer to an argument made in a dissent, the author of the majority opinion should adopt it, so that the reader is not required to read two opinions on the same side of the case.

In all of these cases the unspoken conventions of the judicial trade require the concurring judge to withdraw his opinion if the author of the majority opinion agrees to incorporate the substance of it in his own opinion. However, a few judges feel that a concurring judge has a proprietary interest in his ideas and that incorporating them into the majority opinion would unfairly deny the concurring judge public credit for them. This feeling illustrates the difference between the individualistic and the institutional outlook. What is important is not who gets the credit for an idea (which anyway will most of the time have originated not with the judge but with counsel or a law clerk or the author of a treatise or a law review piece), but that the idea be presented to the reader of the court's decisions in a readily understandable form.

More than economy of communication is at stake. A majority opinion is generally stronger when it has been recast to incorporate the suggestions of concurring judges. Edmund Burke wrote: "If I might venture to appeal to what is so much out of fashion in Paris, I mean to experience, I should tell you, that in my course I have known, and, according to my measure, have co-operated with great men; and I have never yet seen any plan which has not been mended by the observations of those who were much inferior in understanding to the person who took the lead in the business."[23] The author of the majority opinion may not think that a colleague's suggestions add a great deal, but if they are important to the colleague, an opinion recast to include them will have the additional strength that comes from a pooling of thoughts. I do not for a moment suggest that opinions should be drafted by committee. Committee drafting is as unsatisfactory in opinion writing as in any other drafting endeavor. The drafting ought to remain the responsibility of the authoring judge, a responsibility that the requirement of signing the opinion enforces; but the ideas in it should be the integrated expression of the thoughts of all the judges who subscribe to it.

I have said that some concurring opinions are the functional equiva-

23. Edmund Burke, *Reflections on the Revolution in France* 281 (1968 Pelican ed. [1790]).

lent of dissents. But, surprisingly, most are not. In the 1981 and 1982 terms of the Supreme Court, 61 percent of the concurring opinions purported to join the majority opinion in its entirety. The existence of so many opinions that could so readily be avoided by any court that had a lively sense of its institutional responsibilities gives rise to an inference that this sense is in decline. But maybe it was never very great, and just was masked by a scarcity of law clerks. The proliferation of law clerks has been a necessary although not a sufficient condition for the proliferation of concurring opinions; if there were fewer law clerks, the justices would have less time to crank out these opinions.

The number of concurring opinions is a sign of a deficient spirit of institutional responsibility in still another sense. The time that a judge spends on a concurring opinion is taken from the performance of his other responsibilities. The Supreme Court has, of course, a very important institutional responsibility in addition to deciding cases on the merits; it must screen the thousands of applications for review that it receives each year in order to pick between 100 and 200 cases to decide on the merits. This screening function is inherently very difficult to perform because of the enormous number of applications that the Supreme Court receives and the random sequence in which they are received. Yet we are told by Justice Stevens, confirming widespread impressions, that the justices give rather little personal attention to the screening function.[24] But they find time to write concurring opinions in great profusion—70 in the 1982 term, which was almost half the number of majority opinions (162).

In complaining about plurality and concurring opinions in the Supreme Court, I may seem to be neglecting Professor Easterbrook's elegant demonstration that no body—not even a court—that makes decisions by voting can be expected to produce consistent results unless the choice put to the voters is very simple.[25] One of Easterbrook's examples will indicate the nature of the problem.[26] Suppose that three justices believe the Constitution protects sexual freedom broadly; three believe it protects sexual freedom not at all; and three believe that it protects some forms of sexual freedoms but not others—specifically, that it entitles adults, but not children, to buy contraceptives. The first case to arise involves the right of adults to buy contraceptives, and the Court by a vote of six to three holds that there indeed is such a right. If the three justices who believe that the Constitution protects some but not all claims of sexual freedom join an opinion written by a justice

24. "Some Thoughts on Judicial Restraint," 66 *Judicature*, November 1982, at 177, 179.
25. See Easterbrook, supra note 20, at 811–832.
26. See *id.* at 819.

who believes (and states in the opinion) that it protects all such claims, they have—if they also believe in *stare decisis*—checkmated themselves; for the opinion will announce a principle that requires that the next case, where the right of children to buy contraceptives is the issue, be decided the same way. So they will be tempted to write separately—as will be the absolutists, if the opinion is assigned to a justice in the intermediate group; for if the absolutists go along with the intermediate approach, they will have no hope of prevailing in the next case. Thus, the unhappy choice is among (1) decision by plurality opinion, (2) refusal to stand by precedent, and (3) surrender by one group of justices of their convictions to a group no larger.

Plurality opinions, concurring opinions, shifting coalitions, frequent overrulings (many not acknowledged as such), inconsistent lines of precedent—in other words, the manifold institutional failings of appellate courts in general and the Supreme Court in particular—are, in Easterbrook's analysis, primarily consequences of the fact that a court is an electoral body; for the modern literature on public choice shows that electorates, and legislatures composed of elected representatives, cannot be expected to make rationally consistent decisions. This suggests that one possible way of taking Easterbrook's point is that if the Supreme Court acts like a legislature its decisions will resemble those of a legislature, not only in the character of each decision taken separately but in the relation of successive decisions to one another. And from that relation one will be able to infer whether the Court is in fact acting like a legislature—a body in which each member votes according to either his individual values and preferences or those of his constituents.

Although the nature of American law makes it inevitable that courts will *sometimes* make law like a legislature, and to that extent will resemble legislatures, it is possible as part of a general criticism of contemporary judicial activism to deplore the extent to which the Supreme Court has become a legislative body and to hope that the trend may someday be reversed. But Easterbrook's point goes deeper. Even if judges cast their votes on the basis not of personal value choices but of technical legal judgments (or what appear to be such—value choices may lie just beneath the surface), whenever they divide into two or more camps the court as a whole may find it impossible to establish and adhere to consistent doctrine. This can be seen by making the following substitutions in the example I gave earlier: for believers that the Constitution protects sexual freedom broadly, believers that the doctrine of pendent jurisdiction should be interpreted broadly; for believers that the Constitutions protects sexual freedom not at all, believers that the doctrine of pendent jurisdiction is unconstitutional; for believers that the Constitution protects some but not all forms of sexual freedom, believers that some but not all forms of pendent jurisdiction are proper. And then one makes the issue in the first case whether pendent party jurisdiction is proper when the 'main claim involves a federal question, and in the second whether it is proper when the main claim is a diversity claim.[27]

The public-choice model that generates Easterbrook's results assumes, however, that each judge is an individualist; he may consult with his colleagues before making up his mind, but once he does make it up he will do everything he can to make the law conform to it. And almost my entire point in this chapter is that the problems of our judicial system are, to a significant extent, a result of the judges' individualistic attitudes toward their role. If judges were more committed (emotionally, not just intellectually) to the idea of collective judicial responsibility; if—reminding themselves that judicial appointment is not meritocratic—they took themselves and their particular ideas and approaches less seriously; if they were more willing to give ground freely and to search for common ground in the way that a corporate task force might try to devise a marketing strategy for one of the corporation's products—then we would have a judicial system that generated less heat but more light.

I do not want to pretend, however, either that a revolution in attitudes is a feasible goal or that it would solve completely the problem that Professor Easterbrook has directed our attention to. The analogy to marketing is imperfect. The correctness or incorrectness of a marketing strategy can be determined rather straightforwardly by observing results in the marketplace, but it is much more difficult to verify the correctness of a legal position on an unsettled question, even if the question is technical and not emotion-laden. Part of the difficulty is that the information necessary to give a definitive answer will so often be unobtainable; and when people lack information they make guesses that are heavily influenced by their personal experiences and values, and their guesses will diverge if their experiences and values are divergent. Part of the difficulty is that most of the interesting questions in our law are not wholly technical. In the example I gave of the federal courts' pendent jurisdiction, a judge's attitude on almost all the questions that arise about this jurisdiction will be influenced by his attitude toward the highly political and emotive issue of federalism.

I turn now from the Supreme Court to the courts of appeals. Here the problems I have discussed are less acute. More of the work of these

27. Compare Hixon v. Sherwin-Williams Co., 671 F.2d 1005 (7th Cir. 1982), with In Re Oil Spill by Amoco Cadiz, 699 F.2d 909 (7th Cir. 1983).

courts really is technical. Because their jurisdiction is obligatory rather than discretionary, most of the appeals they get can be decided by the application of settled principles. Moreover, Supreme Court decisions bind the courts of appeals in a way in which they do not bind the Supreme Court itself, and therefore narrow considerably the scope for choice. Hence the institutional role is more easily played at the court of appeals level. Nevertheless, several types of institutional responsibility demand the attention of the court of appeals judges and do not always receive the attention they deserve. The first is avoiding undue delay in the disposition of appeals. It is very important that an appeal be decided as soon as possible after it is argued to the panel (or submitted to the panel without argument.). Sometimes other cases raising the same or similar issues are being held on the court of appeals' docket or on a district court's docket pending decision of the appeal, so that the effects of delay in handing down that decision are magnified. Moreover, prompt decision of the issue presented on appeal may head off a dispute or a lawsuit, or may provide helpful information to lawyers and judges in other circuits or to the Supreme Court. And because appeals often do not decide cases finally but are merely way stations to a final decision, delay in deciding an appeal may reduce the accuracy of the ultimate adjudication, as by causing evidence to become outdated. There is, of course, a trade-off between the costs of delay and the benefits of patient and exhaustive consideration; but in some cases too little weight is given to the interest in prompt disposition of the appellate court's business.

Another institutional responsibility that sometimes is slighted is that of protecting litigants from harassment by their opponents. The federal courts of appeals have broad powers to assess sanctions against lawyers who file frivolous appeals,[28] but impose them less frequently than they ought to, perhaps because the benefits from imposing sanctions redound to the court and the legal community as a whole rather than to the individual judge.

A related point has to do with the inclination of some appellate judges to remand a case for further proceedings rather than terminate it. Although there are many cases in which it would be quite irresponsible for the court of appeals to direct entry of judgment, no matter how grievous the district court's error, it is a great hardship to litigants and district judges to have a case sent back to the district court again and again, as happens all too often. If a case has been once before in the court of appeals, the court should make every effort to assure that its second coming is its last.

28. See Fed. R. App. Pro. 38; 28 U.S.C. §§ 1912, 1927.

An important part of an appellate court's function involves deciding whether to adopt a rule or a standard to decide a particular issue. In Chapter 1, I said that a rule is a statement of the form, if X, then Y, where Y is a particular legal outcome and X the constellation of facts that generates it. Here I want to use the word "rule" more narrowly, to describe the case where X is a single, mechanically or at least readily determinable fact; and "standard" to mean a rule in which ascertaining X requires weighing several (nonquantitative) factors or otherwise making a judgmental, qualitative assessment. The requirement of a more than $10,000 stake in diversity cases is a rule; if instead the requirement were that the stake be "substantial," you would have a standard. Negligence is a standard, strict liability a rule.[29]

The choice between rule and standard has profound institutional implications. Because a rule is more definite, the adoption of a rule will increase legal certainty and thereby reduce the amount of litigation; it will also make each lawsuit simpler and shorter. True, if the effect is to increase the scope of liability—as by substituting strict liability (liability based on cause rather than fault) for negligence (which requires proof of both cause and fault)—the amount of litigation may rise because there are more potential claims, even though there is less uncertainty about how to decide each claim. But generally rules reduce and standards increase the amount as well as the length of litigation, and in a time of acute caseload pressures these consequences make rules attractive. Yet courts seem to shy away from declaring definite rules. They prefer to avoid definitive decision by announcing a vague standard or, what amounts to the same thing, a multifactored test with equal weighting of each factor, leaving to the indefinite future the resolution of the uncertainties implicit in such an approach.

Sometimes this course is the better part of valor; the premature adoption of a rule may prevent the courts from obtaining the information they need to make a sound rule. But I think the tendency today is to be overly cautious about adopting rules. This tendency is particularly unfortunate in regard to jurisdictional questions, as an example will show. The Medicaid statute distinguishes between a determination by the Secretary of Health and Human Services that a state's Medicaid plan does not conform to the requirements of the statute, and a disallowance by the Secretary of a particular expenditure. The first type of determination (plan nonconformity) is directly reviewable in the court of appeals, and there only. A disallowance, by contrast, is by implication reviewable in the district court in the first instance, with a right of

29. See Isaac Ehrlich and Richard A. Posner, "An Economic Analysis of Legal Rulemaking," 3 *J. Legal Stud.* 257 (1974); Richard A. Posner, *Economic Analysis of Law* 424–425, 441–442 (2d ed. 1977).

appeal to the court of appeals; but clearly it is not reviewable in the court of appeals directly. It is therefore a matter of some importance to the states whether a particular determination is a determination of plan nonconformity or a disallowance. Unfortunately, it often is not clear.

The First Circuit, in *Commonwealth of Massachusetts v. Departmental Grant Appeals Board*,[30] adopted a standard to guide this determination. The standard involves a sequence of three inquiries. "First, we consider whether the matter might have fit comfortably within the statutory language ... as a determination of noncompliance [what I have called nonconformity], if the Secretary had chosen that route. Second, we ask whether it is of such a character, by reason of its generality and importance, as to point towards inclusion under the compliance rather than the disallowance rubric. And, last, we look at the Secretary's chosen procedures and labels—not as definitive but as entitled to some respect."[31] Apart from the uncertainty implicit in any multifactored test, the court's formulation is full of vague terms—"fit comfortably," "generality and importance," "point towards," "some respect." A state faced with such a standard will often be uncertain which court it belongs in and will therefore have to file two suits to be sure that the statute of limitations will not run on it if it turns out to have chosen the wrong court. Since nothing much turns on whether the court having the initial review jurisdiction is the district court or the court of appeals— either way the ultimate review jurisdiction will be in the court of appeals (subject only to review by the Supreme Court on certiorari)—this is a good example of a situation where it is more important to have a rule than to have the right rule, or a "righter" standard: more important, that is, to the proper discharge of the appellate court's institutional responsibilities.[32]

Multifactored tests exercise a strong fascination over modern judges. I recently came across an opinion in the Ninth Circuit, involving the award of attorney's fees under a statute, in which the court first reminded the district court of an earlier decision that had prescribed

30. 698 F.2d 22 (1st Cir. 1983).

31. *Id.* at 27.

32. For a simple alternative test to the First Circuit's, see Illinois Dept. of Public Aid v. Schweiker, 707 F.2d 273 (7th Cir. 1983). (I confess that this is a self-serving reference, since I wrote the Seventh Circuit's opinion.) A parallel example is provided by ICC orders; if they are for payment of money they are reviewable in the district court, otherwise in the court of appeals, and it is not always easy to classify an order—it may, for example, decree both payment and injunctive-type relief. Compare the "bright line" approach of Consolidated Rail Corp. v. ICC, 685 F.2d 687, 694 (D.C. Cir. 1982), with the much vaguer "impact" approach of Empire-Detroit Steel Division v. ICC, 659 F.2d 396, 397 (3d Cir. 1981).

twelve factors for the district courts to consider in making fee awards under the statute, and then for good measure added five more factors for the district courts to consider.[33] Since no weighting of the factors was suggested, the test is wholly nondirective and anyway the issue of attorney's fees is not important enough to justify making a busy district judge examine seventeen different factors before making his award.

STARE DECISIS

I said at the beginning of this book that judges in the Anglo-American tradition make law as well as decide disputes. More precisely, when in the course of deciding a dispute a court writes an opinion giving reasons for its decision, it is creating a precedent to guide decisions in future cases. The body of precedents is the judge-made law ("common law," broadly defined) and is a very large part of the law applied in federal courts. In Chapter 10 I shall consider how federal judges can come up with right principles of common law; here I shall discuss the methodology of decision by precedent.[34]

The weight of precedents in subsequent decisions is the critical issue here. One can imagine a system—it is the traditional Continental system—in which precedents are followed only if the court concludes after an independent analysis that they are right. Precedents would have no more inherent weight than law-review articles. The problem is that, with everything always up for reexamination, the body of precedents would provide very insecure grounds for predicting how judges would decide future disputes. The common law would not contain any definite commands and therefore would not regulate people's conduct effectively. Hence the doctrine of *stare decisis* ("stand by what has been decided"). In England the doctrine was once understood literally, to mean that a court would never overrule its decisions. *Stare decisis* in this strong sense was followed by the English courts between 1898 and 1966, when the House of Lords, England's highest court, rejected rigid *stare decisis* for itself.[35] But American courts have always felt themselves free to reconsider and discard a previous decision, either because on

33. Sapper v. Lenco Blade, Inc., 704 F.2d 1069, 1073 (9th Cir. 1983).

34. For some good discussions see James Hardisty, "Reflections on Stare Decisis," 55 *Ind. L.J.* 42 (1979); 1 Henry M. Hart, Jr. and Albert Sacks, *The Legal Process: Basic Problems in the Making and Application of Law* 587–588 (tent. ed. 1958); Edward H. Levi, "The Nature of Judicial Reasoning," in *Law and Philosophy: A Symposium* 263 (Sidney Hook ed. 1964), also 32 *U. Chi. L. Rev.* 395 (1965); Karl N. Llewellyn, *The Bramble Bush: On Our Law and Its Study* 64–69 (1960); A. W. B. Simpson, "The *Ratio Decidendi* of a Case and the Doctrine of Binding Precedent," in *Oxford Essays in Jurisprudence* 148 (Guest ed. 1961).

35. See Rupert Cross, *Precedent in English Law* 5 (2d ed. 1968); P. B. Kavanagh, "Stare Decisis in the House of Lords," 5 *N. Zealand L. Rev.* 323 (1973).

reflection it appears to have been decided incorrectly or because changes in law or society have made it obsolete.

Even though the issue is academic in our country, the question of whether inflexible adherence to precedent is a good or a bad idea has theoretical interest, and the answer is not certain. To the traditional and rather obvious arguments against it must now be added Professor Easterbrook's demonstration that it can result in substantive outcomes being determined by the order in which cases arise (this was one of the possible consequences in the sexual-freedom example in the previous section). The principal argument in favor of inflexible *stare decisis*, which will appeal to those who think modern courts overbold, is that it induces courts to make the narrowest possible rulings, knowing they can be changed only by statute (or, in the case of constitutional rulings, by constitutional amendment—a pretty conclusive reason against inflexible adherence to precedent in constitutional law). Some judges, of course, might be tempted to make their rulings as broad as possible precisely because the rigid rule of *stare decisis* would serve to project their rulings into the indefinite future. But they would resist the temptation, realizing that *stare decisis* in its rigid form would be rejected if the rigid form did not induce the courts to rule narrowly.

Although there have been many dramatic overrulings in American law, overrulings are rare in the day-to-day work of any appellate court, even the Supreme Court. One of the main purposes of law is regulatory—to induce people to behave in particular ways. It will fail in this purpose if it is constantly changing direction. If the judges do not follow precedent they might as well be arbitrators; and they cannot expect their successors to follow precedent if they do not. Of course to follow precedent slavishly is also confining, as the English courts discovered. But there is a happy medium, and it involves some although not frequent overruling.

An interesting variant of the problem is presented by the District of Columbia Circuit's recent decision in *Lorion v. Nuclear Regulatory Commission*.[36] The question in *Lorion* (a parallel question to that in the *Commonwealth of Massachusetts* case that I discussed earlier) was whether jurisdiction to review decisions of the Nuclear Regulatory Commission refusing to institute licensing proceedings lies in the district court, in the first instance, or in the court of appeals. Earlier decisions of the D.C. Circuit had held that it was in the court of appeals.[37] When the same issue arose later in the Seventh Circuit, that court expressed some

36. 712 F.2d 1472 (D.C. Cir. 1983), cert. granted *sub nom.* Florida Power & Light Co. v. Lorion, 104 S. Ct. 1676 (1984).

37. The principal case was Natural Resources Defense Council, Inc. v. Nuclear Regulatory Comm'n, 606 F.2d 1261, 1264 (D.C. Cir. 1979).

skepticism about the correctness of the D.C. Circuit's decision but decided to follow it in the interest of avoiding a conflict between circuits and uncertainty over which court had jurisdiction to review nuclear regulatory actions (or inactions) of this type.[38] In *Lorion* the D.C. Circuit, taking note of the Seventh Circuit's skepticism, overruled its own earlier decisions and held that the district court rather than the court of appeals has the initial review jurisdiction. But as I noted in discussing the *Commonwealth of Massachusetts* decision, it does not make a great deal of practical difference whether initial jurisdiction to review agency action is in the district court or in the court of appeals; the only really important thing is that people challenging agency action know what court to sue in. Although the D.C. Circuit's latest decision may be right (a question on which I shall offer no opinion, since the case is pending before the Supreme Court), it is hardly so clearly right as to warrant having thrown the question of jurisdiction into confusion. No one could be sure what the Seventh Circuit would do if the issue came up to it again: it might decide to follow the D.C. Circuit's latest twist in order to avoid a conflict between circuits, or it might decide to adhere to its previous decision in order to minimize jurisdictional uncertainty for persons seeking judicial review of the Nuclear Regulatory Commission in the courts of the Seventh Circuit. All this confusion is disproportionate to the importance of getting the jurisdictional issue just right. The Supreme Court has had to grant certiorari to resolve an unnecessary conflict between circuits.

A question of greater practical importance than whether a court feels free to overrule a previous decision is how broadly it interprets precedents. It is elementary, but sometimes overlooked, that a precedent is the joint creation of the court that decides the case which is later recognized as a precedent and the courts that interpret that case in the later cases. No part of the first opinion will be neatly labeled "precedent"; the precedent will be declared, and its scope delineated, in later cases that rely on the opinion. Of course the first court can try to demarcate once and for all the precise content and scope of the precedent latent in its opinion, but this approach carries its own danger. The strength of adjudication as a method of creating law comes from the fact that the court is able to focus on arguments and evidence developed in the setting of an actual dispute; there is an analogy to the physical law that the power of an electromagnetic beam is inverse to its breadth. But the narrowness of the court's focus limits its ability to rule intelligently on

---

38. Rockford League of Women Voters v. Nuclear Regulatory Comm'n, 679 F.2d 1218, 1220–21 (7th Cir. 1982).

factual situations remote from the one before it; and this in turn limits its ability to formulate sound rules of *general* application until the decision of many similar cases has shown that the same result ought to hold despite the factual differences among the cases. The second court to decide such a case will have the advantage over the first court of having both the previous decision and a new dispute before it, a dispute the first court could not have considered except in its imagination. It is therefore fitting that the second court should decide the breadth of the precedent created by the first.

This does not mean, however, that the first court must not speak to any facts beyond those immediately before it. What the first court has to say about the possible scope of the precedent that it has sired is of great interest. But the court should not try to make this part of its opinion be definitive. This is the part that a later court, having the benefit of greater experience, should feel freest to modify without thinking that it is disserving the principle of *stare decisis*. And it is not just a matter of narrowing the first decision; the first court is not entitled to set arbitrary limits to the precedent it thinks it is establishing. Although the life of the law has not been logic, it is unseemly for a court to say, in effect (and sometimes in words perilously close to these), "The logic of our reasoning would imply that a case which raised fact X instead of Y as in the present case should be decided the same way, but we do not desire to be so logical."[39] It should be left to the next court to decide, having the benefit of fact X before it, how far the logic of the first decision ought to be pressed. Consider, for example, *Briscoe v. LaHue*,[40] where the Supreme Court recently held that a police officer testifying at a trial has absolute immunity from federal civil rights liability based on his testimony. In a footnote the Court stated that it was expressly reserving the question whether its ruling extended to a police officer's testimony before a grand jury.[41] If the Court had suggested a possible distinction between the liability of a witness before the petit jury and the liability of a witness before the grand jury, the reservation of the issue would have been appropriate; but the Court did not. It should have said nothing and left it to a subsequent case to decide whether *Briscoe* had settled the issue of grand jury testimony.

The fact that a decision's precedential significance is tentative until the decision is interpreted and applied is the basis for the occasional suggestion that there is a fundamental distinction between decisions and statutes as sources of law, even in a regime where a court is forbid-

39. Cf. Elrod v. Burns, 427 U.S. 347, 353 (1976) (plurality opinion).
40. 103 S. Ct. 1108 (1983).
41. *Id.* at 1112 n.5.

den to overrule its prior decisions.[42] The suggested distinction is that the scope and meaning of the decision are determined not by the authors of the decision but by the authors of subsequent decisions, whereas (ignoring constitutional adjudication) a court has no power to modify the meaning of a statute. The distinction is real, but there is perhaps less actual difference than meets the eye. The draftsmen of a statute labor under much the same disadvantage as the author of an opinion in the first of a series of related but factually distinguishable cases—limited foresight. They can no more anticipate all the factual situations to which the statute might be applied than a judge can anticipate all the factual situations to which his decision might be applied. Necessarily, much must be left to the court faced with an unanticipated factual situation. Just as a decision means what a later court says it means, so a statute means what a court later says it means—a court that has had to apply it to facts unanticipated and therefore not provided for by the draftsmen.

I do not want to leave the impression that the later judges can make of the earlier decision anything they want to make of it, any more than they can make anything they want of a statute, and still be considered responsible judges. There is no higher form of the judicial art than determining the precedential significance to be given decisions cited to the judge in connection with a new case. The judge has to balance the benefits in certainty from interpreting the earlier decision broadly against the costs in a higher likelihood of an erroneous result if a decision is applied to a factual situation of which the earlier court was at best imperfectly aware.

The federal courts of appeals find themselves in a complicated situation in regard to *stare decisis*. Unlike the Supreme Court, which has only to decide how much weight and scope to give previous Supreme Court decisions, the courts of appeals (*Erie* problems to one side) have to consider how much weight and scope to give three different classes of decisions: decisions of the same circuit, those of other circuits, and those of the Supreme Court. It might appear that in relation to Supreme Court decisions, the issue for the court of appeals would not be *stare decisis* but obedience to higher authority. This is true in the sense that the courts of appeals are bound by the decisions of the Supreme Court; they cannot overrule the Supreme Court, and they can refuse to follow a Supreme Court decision only when it is apparent from intervening Supreme Court decisions that the Court would overrule its earlier deci-

42. See Simpson, supra note 34, at 165–167. For a contrasting view see H. L. A. Hart, *The Concept of Law* 123–124 (1961).

sion if the same case arose again.[43] But this does not settle the question whether to construe a particular Supreme Court decision broadly or narrowly. When *stare decisis* is divorced from the issue of overruling and viewed as a doctrine of interpretation rather than of power, its application to the relations between an inferior and a superior appellate court is manifest.

The present position—more accurately, tendency—with regard to *stare decisis* in the courts of appeals is that Supreme Court decisions and decisions of the same circuit are deemed authoritative and interpreted broadly, while decisions of other circuits are treated as no more than persuasive and interpreted narrowly. I am not sure how sensible this pattern is. The issue with regard to Supreme Court decisions can be posed most sharply as follows: should a court of appeals deem itself bound by dictum in a Supreme Court majority opinion? On the one hand, the law may be more certain if it does, because every sentence in such an opinion will then have the force of law; I say "may" rather than "will" because, since dicta in one opinion may conflict with dicta in another, certainty may not be increased on balance, not much anyway. On the other hand, to treat Supreme Court dicta as authoritative is to deprive the legal system of the benefits of creative thinking by the rest of the federal judiciary informed by actual disputes that could not have been present to the minds of the justices.[44] Thus, the fact that a dictum is deliberate and considered, rather than off the cuff, should not be enough to give it binding force, since the court did not have before it the facts to which the dictum relates—that is what makes it a dictum. Although Supreme Court justices may be abler on average than district and circuit judges (because more carefully screened for appointment) and have better staff and a superior perspective for formulating legal doctrine, the courts of appeals alone have 15 times as many judges as the Supreme Court. These judges have in the aggregate an important contribution to make to the formulation of legal doctrine—especially when dealing with factual situations that have never been before the Supreme Court and therefore have never been considered by the Supreme Court justices except possibly in their imagination.

This discussion has assumed that the distinction between holding and dictum is clear-cut and well-understood. But, remarkably—considering how fundamental the distinction is to a system of decision by

43. See, for example, Browder v. Gayle, 142 F. Supp. 707, 717 (M.D. Ala.) (three-judge court), aff'd per curiam, 352 U.S. 903 (1956); United States v. Girouard, 149 F.2d 760, 765 (1st Cir. 1945) (dissenting opinion), rev'd, 328 U.S. 61 (1946).

44. See Calvert Magruder, "The Trials and Tribulations of an Intermediate Appellate Court," 44 *Cornell L.Q.* 1, 5, 7 (1958).

precedent—the distinction is fuzzy not only at the level of application but at the conceptual level.[45] There is a nicely circular definition: whatever a later court does not feel bound by is dictum. Although it is possible to do a little better than that, the circular definition has the value of pointing us toward the practical considerations that should guide the use of the words "holding" and "dictum." If dictum is what can be ignored by a later court, then we should ask what it is that makes one part of an opinion more reliable than another. I have already given my answer: the reliable part is the part that is grounded in the facts of the case, and the unreliable part is the part that speculates about how other factual situations should be treated. Judges work under great time pressure and are deprived of many of the methods by which other decision makers inform themselves, but they do have one valuable source of information and that is an actual, concrete dispute. The parties' briefs and arguments will focus the judges on the facts of the dispute, and the decision the court comes up with is likely to be sensible in light of those facts. But it may not be sensible with regard to different facts, which were not before the court except as vague speculation (and often not at all). Moreover, despite the scholarly apparatus with which modern judicial opinions are adorned, few judges are scholars, and anyway they lack the leisure of scholars. So if a judge used an opinion as a vehicle for writing a treatise on some field of law, the treatise part would be entitled to no more—indeed, considerably less—weight than a law professor's treatise.

But if one goes to the other extreme and insists that a judicial opinion is authoritative only with respect to the exact constellation of facts that was before the judges who decided the case, the decision will have no utility as a precedent, because no two cases have exactly the same facts. This problem is somewhat alleviated automatically because the reader's access to the facts of a case is pretty much limited to what the court says the facts were, so that simply by leaving out some facts the court can expand the reach of its decision. Even so, the facts required to make the decision intelligible to the reader will often be so particular that another case just like it would be quite unlikely ever to arise. This is one reason why judicial opinions contain analysis and not just a statement of facts followed by announcement of the result; the analysis shows which facts are essential to the decision.

I am now prepared to define the "holding" of a case as simply a rule of the form described earlier: if X facts (something less than all the facts

45. See the excellent discussion in "Comment: Dictum Revisited," 4 *Stan. L. Rev.* 509 (1952).

of the case), then Y legal outcome. The holding can be explicit or implicit. If the latter, it may not be clear just what facts were essential to the decision, and therefore subsequent courts will be able to interpret the holding narrowly. This explains how it is that one can have a narrow and a broad holding in the same case. But what the later court cannot properly do (though it is done all the time) is to disregard precedent by substituting for the actual holding of an earlier case a narrower rule on which the earlier decision could have been but was not based.[46] If in our sexual-freedom example the court that decides the case involving the right of adults to use contraceptives states explicitly that the age of the user is irrelevant, a later court, faced with a case in which the user is a child, cannot say that the first court held just that adults have a right to use contraceptives. That is not what the first court held; it is not a rule that can fairly be inferred from its opinion. If the first court had said nothing about age, then depending on what it did say the second court might be able to limit the first court's holding to adults. But if it discards the rule on which the first case was decided and substitutes another, then it is overruling the first case, and should say so.

If dictum were simply everything that was not the holding, then by defining holding one would have defined dictum. But "dictum" is often used with pejorative overtones, to mean not merely what is not binding on a later court but what is superfluous in the first court's opinion. Because of these overtones it would be misleading to call the reasons a court gave for its result "dicta." True, the reasons are not the rule. The rule is the outcome given the important facts, the function of the reasons being to indicate which facts are important. Thus the reasons are vital; they just are not the same thing as the holding, the thing that binds the later court by the principle of *stare decisis*. For the sake of precision, the world "dictum" should be used only to denote the portions of the opinion that are not essential to extracting the holding.

To illustrate some of these distinctions, let us suppose that the question in a case is whether criminal trials must be public, and the court holds that they must be and gives as its reason that the public will lose confidence in the judicial system unless judicial proceedings are open to the public. If the particular trial in the case had been a burglary trial (a fact recited but not emphasized in the opinion), and later the issue arose as to whether the trial of a man accused of raping a child had also to be conducted in public, the statement about public confidence in the judicial system could not be dismissed as dictum. But the statement

46. See Henry J. Friendly, "In Praise of Erie—and of the New Federal Common Law," in *Benchmarks* 155, 157–158 (1967).

would not dictate the outcome of the second case, because it would not be the holding of the first case. It would just be a reason, an essential reason, perhaps, and therefore not a dictum, but a reason that might be outweighed by another reason that was not present in the first case because the facts were different. Now if the first court had also said, "And, by the way, we think that school board meetings should also be open to the public," that would be an example of dictum, because it would not be essential, in the court's own thinking, to its holding about criminal trials. It would also be a statement made without benefit of a concrete factual record, and probably without benefit of comment by counsel; it would therefore be intrinsically less deserving of weight in future cases.

Just how much weight dicta should be given, and just how broadly a holding should be interpreted when the scope of the holding is unclear, depend on a variety of factors, including the respect in which particular judges are held and the separation-of-powers concerns discussed in the previous chapter. Here I shall consider only how the current caseload crisis might affect the balance. On the one hand, the heavier the caseload pressures on the courts, the greater is the need for legal certainty, since uncertainty foments litigation. On the other hand, the same pressures, operating (to some extent indirectly) on the Supreme Court, have increased the dangers of relying on Supreme Court dicta. As the pool of lower court decisions from which the Court picks its cases expands, the average difficulty of the cases it decides increases. And the more difficult a case is, the less likely it is that the court that decides it can deal effectively not only with the particular facts before it but with other factual situations that are related but that may also be different in potentially critical ways. Moreover, the growth of the law-clerk bureaucracy, nowhere so pronounced as in the Supreme Court, has diminished the authenticity and hence the intrinsic authority of judicial opinions generally. As Supreme Court opinions become longer, more discursive, and more heavily footnoted, only the naive can continue to believe that everything in every opinion has been knowingly adopted by a majority of the justices; and federal judges are less inclined to take their cues from Supreme Court law clerks than from Supreme Court justices. Thus it is unclear on balance that the caseload crisis ought to make lower court judges interpret Supreme Court holdings more broadly, and weight Supreme Court dicta more heavily, than they would do if the crisis abated.

The greater weight that a federal court of appeal gives to its own decisions than to those of other courts of appeals is a potentially troubling feature of the practice of *stare decisis* in the courts of appeals. If those courts constituted a single court system, this disparate treatment would be totally unjustifiable. But the truth is that the 13 courts of appeals constitute at best a loose confederacy, brought under some semblance of unity only by their common subjection to the ultimate authority of the Supreme Court. For reasons discussed in earlier chapters, this is not a bad thing; we need some competition in the formulation of federal legal doctrine. And this implies that a court of appeals is right to treat the decisions of other circuits as persuasive rather than authoritative; otherwise the first panel that happened to decide a particular kind of case would have a monopoly over the formulation of doctrine to govern that kind of case. Still, courts of appeals give less weight to the decisions of other circuits than they ought to. If a question is a close one in the mind of the second circuit to consider it, this circuit ought to defer to its sister circuit in the interest of promoting legal certainty, even if as an original matter it would have gone the other way.

Moreover, the proposition that a court of appeals should give somewhat less weight to the decisions of other circuits than to its own decisions, in order to generate the competitive process that is a worthwhile feature of the circuit system, does not have any merit if there already is a conflict between circuits. Suppose that in case 1 the Third Circuit holds X; in case 2 the Fourth Circuit holds not X; and case 3 now comes to the Third Circuit, and raises the same issue again. I do not think the Third Circuit should take the position that *stare decisis* requires it to adhere to X notwithstanding the intervening decision of the Fourth Circuit, or even to presume the correctness of X. On what basis could the Third Circuit think its earlier decision more authoritative than the Fourth Circuit's contrary decision? It ought to reexamine its previous decision conscientiously and without preconceptions. This practice would not add too much uncertainty to the law of the circuit, since, whenever there is a conflict between two circuits, the law of both circuits is unstable because the Supreme Court is likely sooner or later to intervene.

The adoption of the approach I have suggested might go some way toward alleviating the problem of long-persisting conflicts between circuits. If the first circuit to decide an issue treats its decision as a binding precedent despite what other circuits later do, then only the Supreme Court can eliminate conflicts between circuits. But the Supreme Court may not have the time to settle every intercircuit conflict, and the first-deciding circuit should therefore recognize its responsibility, coequal with that of the circuit that created the conflict and other circuits that choose sides later, to eliminate conflicts where possible. I do not, however, agree with the suggestion that a circuit should not be permitted to go into conflict with another circuit except in an en banc proceeding.

Because of the burdens of en banc hearings on the circuit judges, this would often give a practical monopoly of law creation to whatever circuit happened to be presented with a particular issue first. I repeat here my alternative suggestion for dealing with the problem of conflicts between circuits: adopting, as a special rule of *stare decisis*, the practice that when the first three circuits to decide an issue have decided it the same way, the remaining circuits defer to that decision.

Having spent so much time discussing the role of the subsequent-deciding court in a system of precedent, I want to return briefly to the role of the first court to decide a question in crafting its decision as a precedent to guide future decisions. By abstracting from most of the facts before it, it can try to create a very broad precedent. Suppose, for example, that in the first case raising the question of whether an indigent litigant has a constitutional right to appointment of counsel, which happens to be a capital case, the court holds that any indigent litigant, civil or criminal, has such a right. The court would be abstracting from the fact that the litigant before it is a criminal defendant, and not merely a criminal defendant but a felony defendant, and not merely a felony defendant but a defendant in a case in which the punishment upon conviction is death. By throwing out many of the actual facts before it, the court would be resolving future cases that would present different facts and that would therefore also present a different weighting, perhaps, of the considerations pro and con giving an indigent defendant a right to counsel. Unless the court has a well-founded confidence in its ability to decide all these other cases without the benefit of a factual record or an adversary proceeding in them, it should not formulate such a broad holding.

Although broad holdings are troubling, I am not particularly troubled either by dicta or by alternative holdings.[47] Dicta clearly so identified do not bind the future; they need be given no more weight than they intrinsically deserve; and they have the value of showing the direction of the judges' thinking. The only question about them, therefore, should be whether they are intelligent. Alternative holdings are illustrated by the following example: "We think the defendant's right to confront the witnesses against him was not infringed, but if this is wrong, and it was infringed, it was a harmless error; it could not have changed the outcome, and should therefore be ignored." Either the holding that the defendant's right was not violated or the holding that any error was harmless is sufficient to support the result, so one of the

47. But see the cautionary note sounded in Professor (now Judge) Scalia's article, "Vermont Yankee: The APA, the D.C. Circuit, and the Supreme Court," 1978 *S. Ct. Rev.* 345, 372–373.

two could be discarded. But unless the court lacks confidence in one, or one raises some explosive issue better deferred until it is inescapably presented, I see no reason why the court should not set out both holdings for the greater guidance of the bar and lower courts. Each is fully grounded in the facts, which is some guarantee of reliability. True, if the court is an intermediate rather than a final court, a federal court of appeals rather than the Supreme Court, there is the objection that by casting its decision in the form of alternative holdings it reduces the probability of further judicial review. The Supreme Court might disagree with one of the holdings, but if it agreed with the other it would have no reason (or less reason) to take the case. But all this does is to reduce—very slightly in most cases, since the Supreme Court reviews so few court of appeals decisions anyway—the authority of one of the alternative holdings.

As this example suggests, however, an alternative holding is not entitled to be given quite the same weight in subsequent decisions as a sole holding. There are other reasons for this conclusion. In some cases a decision will rest quite firmly on a holding of unimpeachable soundness, and then an alternative holding will be tossed in rather casually, as a kind of trial balloon, the court realizing that it is not really criticial whether the alternative holding is correct or not. In some other cases the fact that the judge thought it necessary to support the decision by alternative holdings may bespeak a lack of complete confidence in the soundness of any of them. Alternative holdings thus imply a certain tentativeness.

The system of *stare decisis*, it should be clear by now, reveals another facet of the collegial nature of the judicial process. The appellate judge not only operates in a collegial body, but every judge, trial and appellate, is a member of a community of judges—the predecessors and successors of the current judges, as well as the current judges themselves. Judicial decision making is collective in a profound sense, and the importance of institutional values in such a setting should be self-evident.

IV

IMPROVING FEDERAL
JUDICIAL PERFORMANCE

9

Interpreting Statutes

and the Constitution

IF THE PROPOSALS advanced in Chapters 5 through 8 were adopted, we would be some way toward solving the federal court's caseload crisis; it would then be possible to move on to those problems that would exist even if the caseload pressures were no greater today than they were 25 years ago. The federal courts would still be busy and important courts, and they would still face formidable challenges, although the challenges would be substantive rather than administrative. Indeed, the federal courts would in all likelihood still be in a critical state, but the crisis would be one of quality alone, rather than a crisis of quantity and a quantity-induced crisis of quality. The biggest challenge that the federal courts (especially at the appellate level) confront and will always confront is how to interpret statutes and the Constitution, and, in areas to which statutes or the Constitution do not speak, how to create and elaborate sound legal doctrines in common law fashion. This chapter and the next consider how the federal courts might meet this double challenge more effectively than they are doing today, or than they did even when they were not burdened with an excessive caseload.

Because the federal courts do not have a general common law jurisdiction, as state courts do, it is natural to think that the main thing federal courts do is interpret statutes, including the special statute known as the U.S. Constitution. But this is wrong. If "common law" is given a functional meaning, the federal courts (at least below the Supreme Court) are today, as they have always been primarily, common law courts, as we shall see in the next chapter. It is nevertheless true that the interpretation of statutes is an extremely important function of the federal courts and one that, except in the case of the Constitution, does not receive the systematic scholarly attention it deserves. This chapter will summarize what is known about the legislative process (particularly at the federal level); consider the implications of this knowledge for various issues of statutory and constitutional interpretation, with particular reference to the utility of the "canons of construction"; and suggest an alternative method of statutory interpretation to the canons.

THE THEORY OF LEGISLATION

To speak of "the" theory of legislation may strike those steeped in the diverse writings on legislation of lawyers, economists, political scientists, and historians as implying a unity that the study of legislation sadly lacks. But actually the seemingly divergent conceptions of legislation that have come from the various points of the academic compass can be fitted together rather nicely to form a single theory, which could help judges in dealing with problems of statutory interpretation.

The oldest strand in the theory is the "public interest" conception of legislation. Well represented in the writings of such economists as Baumol and Pigou,[1] and approximated by the traditional lawyer's view that legislation is designed to protect the public interest, implicitly defined in utilitarian terms,[2] this conception asserts that both the ideal and for the most part the actual function of legislation is to increase economic welfare by correcting "market failures" such as crime and pollution. Some though not all laws designed to transfer wealth from rich to poor can also be assimilated to this conception—that is, can be conceived as enhancing general welfare rather than as merely redistributing wealth. Free-rider problems might thwart private efforts to bring about the level of transfers from rich to poor that the rich would prefer (the money I give to the poor benefits you if you are distressed by poverty, but you do not compensate me for the benefit); to that extent,

---

1. See William J. Baumol, *Welfare Economics and the Theory of the State* (2d ed. 1965); A. C. Pigou, *The Economics of Welfare* (4th ed. 1962).

2. See, for example, 2 Henry M. Hart, Jr., and Albert Sacks, *The Legal Process: Basic Problems in the Making and Application of Law* 1410–17 (tent. ed. 1958). Four hundred years ago, in Heydon's Case, 76 Eng. Rep. 637, 638 (Ex. 1584), the court said that the essential steps in interpreting a statute are to ascertain "what was the mischief and defect for which the common law did not provide," "what remedy the Parliament hath resolved and appointed to cure the disease of the Commonwealth," and "the true reason of the remedy; and then the office of all the Judges is always to make such construction as shall suppress the mischief, and advance the remedy."

public charity is an appropriate public good no less than protection against crime or pollution.

The "interest group" conception, whose lineage can be traced back to the discussions of the corn laws in *The Wealth of Nations* and of factions in *Federalist* No. 10 (Madison), asserts that legislation is a commodity demanded and supplied much as are other commodities, so that legislative protection flows to those groups that derive the greatest value from it regardless of overall social welfare, whether the latter is defined as wealth, utility, or some other version of equity or justice.[3] An important determinant of the net benefits of legislative protection to a group is the costs of organizing effective political action. As the group becomes larger and more diverse, these costs rise; at the same time, the benefits to each member of the group become smaller. The individual's incentive to contribute to the group's endeavor will therefore weaken as the group expands unless the group can get a larger redistribution. But this will mean higher costs to those outside the group who have to be taxed to defray the redistribution, and hence will lead to more resistance to the group's objective. Thus effective interest groups will usually be small and directed toward a single issue. This will enable the benefits of redistributing wealth to them to be concentrated, the costs of organizing the group to be minimized, and the costs of the redistribution to be spread so widely that no one has much incentive to oppose it.

The interest-group approach to legislation has had some distinguished legal adherents. Holmes wrote in an early essay:

> In the last resort a man rightly prefers his own interest to that of his neighbors. And this is as true in legislation as in any other form of corporate action. All that can be expected from modern improvements is that legislation should easily and quickly, yet not too quickly, modify itself in accordance with the will of the *de facto* supreme power in the community, and that the spread of an educated

3. An older political-science literature on interest groups, represented by Arthur F. Bentley, *The Process of Government: A Study of Social Pressures* (1908), and David B. Truman, *The Governmental Process: Political Interests and Public Opinion* (1951), has given way to a largely economic modern literature whose seminal figure is George J. Stigler. See his article "The Theory of Economic Regulation," 2 *Bell J. Econ. & Mgmt. Sci.* 3 (1971), and his book *The Citizen and the State: Essays on Regulation* (1975). Other examples of this literature are William A. Jordan, "Producer Protection, Prior Market Structure and the Effects of Government Regulation," 15 *J. Law & Econ.* 151 (1972); Sam Peltzman, "Toward a More General Theory of Regulation," 19 *J. Law & Econ.* 211 (1976); Gary S. Becker, "A Theory of Competition among Pressure Groups for Political Influence," 98 *Q.J. Econ.* 371 (1983). Some modern treatments by political scientists are Jeffry Berry, *The Interest Group Society* (1984); Terry Moe, *The Organization of Interests: Incentives and Internal Dynamics of Political Interest Groups* (1980).

sympathy should reduce the sacrifice of minorities to a minimum. But whatever body may possess the supreme power for the moment is certain to have interests inconsistent with others which have competed unsuccessfully. The more powerful interests must be more or less reflected in legislation; which, like every other device of man or beast, must tend in the long run to aid the survival of the fittest . . . It is no sufficient condemnation of legislation that it favors one class at the expense of another; for much or all legislation does that . . . The fact is that legislation . . . is necessarily made a means by which a body, having the power, put burdens which are disagreeable to them on the shoulders of somebody else.[4]

Justice Black's opinion for the Supreme Court in *Eastern Railroad Presidents Conference v. Noerr Motor Freight, Inc.*,[5] which interpreted the Sherman Act as not forbidding collective action to obtain legislation intended to hurt competitors, is another noteworthy example of judicial realism about statutes. Black, a former United States senator, stated for the Court: "The right of the people to inform their representatives in government of their desires with respect to the passage or enforcement of laws cannot properly be made to depend upon their intent in doing so. It is neither unusual nor illegal for people to seek action on laws in the hope that they may bring about an advantage to themselves and a disadvantage to their competitors."[6] He went on to say that the Court's holding "restored what appears to be the true nature of the case—a 'no-holds-barred fight' between two industries both of which are seeking control of a profitable source of income."[7] In another case,[8] Black rejected the concept of "rationality review"—a rejection clearly implied, as we shall see later in this chapter, by the interest-group approach.

The properties that make legislative redistributions feasible have nothing to do with the public interest, whether defined in efficiency or in equity terms. If anything, they tend to make legislation systematically perverse from a public-interest standpoint by facilitating the redistribution of wealth from large groups to small ones. And yet despite this point there is no necessary incompatibility between the public-interest and interest-group conceptions of legislation. The former is

4. Oliver Wendell Holmes, Jr., "Herbert Spencer: Legislation and Empiricism," in *Justice Oliver Wendell Holmes: His Book Notices and Uncollected Letters and Papers* 104, 107–109 (Shriver ed. 1936).
5. 365 U.S. 127 (1961).
6. *Id.* at 139.
7. *Id.* at 144 (footnote omitted).
8. Ferguson v. Skrupa, 372 U.S. 726, 731–732 (1963).

mainly concerned with identifying market failures that could, at least in principle, be corrected by legislation, and its proponents would hardly be willing to shoulder the burden of establishing what proportion of the legislation that is actually enacted has this character. The latter does not deny the possibility that a large group—perhaps the whole society—occasionally might procure legislation in its behalf. If the benefits to the individual members of a large group are great enough and the costs to nonmembers small enough (there may be few or even no nonmembers), such legislation will be enacted. There will be free-rider problems, but they will not be insurmountable under the postulated conditions; the laws against murder are an illustration.

It should be possible, therefore, to classify statutes according to whether they advance the public interest or advance instead the interest of some (narrow) interest group. A number of statutes seem pretty clearly to belong in one group or another—examples are the basic criminal laws, the original antitrust law, and the provision of a court system in the public-interest category; and the Interstate Commerce Act and the regulation of taxicabs in the interest-group category.[9] But there are many intermediate cases, and to fit them into the eclectic theory we shall need a richer categorization, as shown in the following paragraphs.

Public Interest, Economically Defined. This category is limited to legislation that corrects market failures such as crime and pollution, though certain redistributions could be included because they correct failures in the market for charitable giving. Important examples of laws that serve the public interest, economically defined, are the provisions of the Constitution that establish the separation of powers and guarantee freedom of political speech, both devices for warding off a particularly costly form of monopoly—a monopoly of political power.

Public Interest in Other Senses. Whatever a judge's own conception of the public interest, he must not dismiss *a priori* other conceptions that are widely shared. For example, if the progressive income tax can be justified in terms of benefits received, it is in the previous category, but even if it cannot be justified in those terms it would still be public-interest legislation if justifiable in terms of some widely-held conception of the just distribution of wealth. This example also illustrates the equivocal nature of my classification. Many economists regard the progressive income tax either as a means of maximizing utility—which,

---

9. See George W. Hilton, "The Consistency of the Interstate Commerce Act," 9 *J. Law & Econ.* 87 (1966); Edmund W. Kitch, Marc Isaacson, and Daniel Kasper, "The Regulation of Taxicabs in Chicago," 14 *J. Law & Econ.* 285 (1971). The literature on particular statutes is now voluminous; much of it has been published in the *Journal of Law and Economics*.

depending on one's precise view of the meaning of "economic efficiency," could be part of either the previous category or this category—or alternatively as a means of soaking the rich, which would put it in the category of narrow-interest-group legislation below.

Public Sentiment. Much legislation cannot be justified on economic or conventional equity grounds, but perhaps only because not enough is known about its consequences. Legislation forbidding the sale of pornography is an example. It seems at first glance an interference with freedom of contract that must reduce efficiency just as a usury law does. But despite loose use of the term "special interests" in recent political discussion to describe people who feel strongly about an issue, the supporters of laws against pornography do not have the characteristics that make for an effective interest group. And the possible external effects of pornography (on the crime rate and on the family), though they have never been measured, conceivably may justify the laws or at least explain the intense hostility that many people feel toward pornography.

Laws based on public sentiment rather than on an objective weighing of demonstrable pros and cons or on cartel-like pressures for redistributing wealth resemble public-interest legislation in that their support seems both widespread and not motivated by economic self-interest. But they cannot easily be defended on the usual economic or utilitarian grounds, given our deficient knowledge of their effects.

Narrow-Interest-Group Legislation. Most analyses of legislation in the social science literature have focused on statutes such as the Interstate Commerce Act and the Civil Aeronautics Act of 1938 that appear in light of modern economic theory to promote the narrow self-interest of a particular industry, or of a group of firms within an industry—though these statutes in their heyday were considered appropriate responses to deficiencies or excesses of competition. Occupational-licensure laws and industry-specific tax and subsidy schemes furnish other examples. Interest-group theorists have been less successful in explaining economy-wide legislation, notably health and safety laws. Some of these may serve the public interest; others may not—and may not promote the interests of a politically effective group either. The effectiveness of a variety of consumer protection, health, and safety laws in achieving their stated purposes has been questioned in empirical studies, which fail, however, to explain why the legislation was enacted.[10]

Another part of the modern literature on legislation focuses on the

10. See, for example, Sam Peltzman, "An Evaluation of Consumer Protection Legislation: The 1962 Drug Amendments," 81 *J. Pol Econ.* 1049 (1973); Paul E. Sands, "How Effective Is Safety Legislation?" 11 *J. Law & Econ.* 165 (1968).

operation, rather than the legislative output, of legislatures,[11] illuminating phenomena such as "log rolling." Some of the literature tries simply to describe the legislative process realistically, by identifying the respective roles of legislators, staff, lobbyists, and executive branch officials in various stages of the process, notably legislative drafting.[12] Although much that is described comes as no surprise, for example that Congress participates fully in the usages of the ghostwriting society, this is an area where education in the obvious, in Holmes's characteristically felicitous phrase, can be a useful antidote to the fictionalizing tendencies in judicial discussions of the legislative process.

IMPLICATIONS FOR STATUTORY INTERPRETATION

The theory of legislation sketched in the preceding section can illuminate a number of issues involved in the interpretation of statutes, although one of these—the appropriate role of the canons of construction—I defer to a later section.

Motive versus Intent. The familiar principle that in analyzing a statute courts are to look to the intent but not the motive of the enacting legislature is usually invoked in constitutional cases,[13] where the issue is whether a statute should be invalidated because of the motive behind its enactment. But this principle also defines the scope of appropriate judicial inquiry into the meaning of a statute in cases where the statute is assumed to be valid and only its application is in dispute. Courts look to the language of the statute, to the legislative history, and to other evidence of legislative intent, but they do not speculate on the legislators' motives; they do not, in short, conduct a social-scientific inquiry into the pattern of interest-group pressures behind the statute.

Although this limitation may seem hopelessly inconsistent with a realistic view of the political process, it is merely inevitable. Courts do not have the research tools needed to uncover the motives behind legislation. Nor can they just presume the presence of an interest group somewhere behind the scenes. Many statutes really are enacted in the public

11. Notable works in this genre are James M. Buchanan and Gordon Tullock, *The Calculus of Consent: Logical Foundations of Constitutional Democracy* (1962), and Anthony Downs, *An Economic Theory of Democracy* (1957).

12. See, for example, Stephen K. Bailey, *Congress Makes a Law: The Story behind the Employment Act of 1946* (1950); Kenneth Kofmehl, *Professional Staffs of Congress* 117–126, 189–193 (3d ed. 1977); Michael J. Malbin, *Unelected Representatives: Congressional Staff and the Future of Representative Government* (1980); Norman J. Ornstein and Shirley Elder, *Interest Groups, Lobbying and Policymaking* 155–185 (1978); David E. Price, *Who Makes the Laws? Creativity and Power in Senate Committees* (1972).

13. See, for example, Palmer v. Thompson, 403 U.S. 217, 224–225 (1971).

interest; in these statutes, the actual and the ostensible purposes coincide. Moreover, even when it is obvious that a particular statute was procured by an interest group—the Wagner Act by the labor movement, for example—it will often be unclear, without an inquiry that is beyond judicial capacity to undertake, how completely the group prevailed upon Congress to do its will; the statute as ultimately enacted may well represent, to some unknown degree, a compromise with competing interest groups. If, therefore, the legislature wants to indicate the lines of political pressure along which the law should be interpreted, it had better say so explicitly, either in the statute or in the legislative-history materials to which courts have ready access. If legislators use Aesopian language to deceive potential opponents of the interest groups behind the legislation, they may fool the courts as well and thereby—paradoxically—curtail the political powers of those interest groups. Thus, although interest groups can take advantage of voters' limited incentives for informing themselves about public issues to procure legislation that the voters would not want if they knew what was going on, the interposition of a judiciary that is limited to public materials in interpreting legislation offsets to some extent the distortions introduced by voter ignorance. At least this is the tendency of judicial interpretation; in some cases the courts will miss the intended compromise and, by interpreting the statute broadly, give the interest group behind it more than it actually gained in the legislative bargaining process.

Reasoning from One Statute to Another. In piecing out the meaning of a statute courts are reluctant to use the purpose behind one statute to elucidate the purpose behind another. That is, generally they do not treat statutes in the same way that a common law court treats prior cases—as precedents whose reasoning may illuminate the issues in a novel case.[14] Although this seeming myopia has been criticized,[15] it makes sense if a realistic view of the legislative process is taken. If some statutes—and the courts will have trouble knowing which ones—reflect the pressure of narrow interest groups rather than any coherent view of the public interest, it is perilous to use one statute to illuminate the meaning of another. There is no assurance that the particular constellation of political forces that produced the first statute was also in play

14. There is an exception for very closely related statutes (*in pari materia*). See for example, Erlenbaugh v. United States, 409 U.S. 239, 243–244 (1972); Miller v. United States, 597 F.2d 614, 616 (7th Cir. 1979). Most of these cases raise the issue of implied statutory repeals, discussed later in this chapter.

15. See James M. Landis, "Statutes and the Sources of Law," in *Harvard Legal Essays* 213 (Roscoe Pound ed. 1934).

when the second was adopted. And because the first statute may have been purely the product of pressure from a narrow interest group and not of a search for the general public good, it cannot serve as a dependable *reason* for interpreting the second in a particular way.

Legislative History. There is a long-standing debate on whether it is ever proper for judges to use committee reports, hearings, floor debates, and other legislative history in interpreting statutes; and though now academic, the debate is relevant to a more practical question: what parts of the legislative history of a statute actually cast light on its meaning?[16]

It is tempting to argue that because legislators vote on the statutory language rather than on the legislative history, they cannot be presumed to have assented to all that has been said, either in the committee reports or on the floor, about a bill that becomes law. But if legislators know that courts look to legislative history in interpreting statutes—and they do know this—then when they vote for a bill they are assenting, in a sense, to at least some of what is in that history. Moreover, the emphasis that the argument places on assent may be misplaced. It assumes that every bill that is enacted reflects the convictions of a majority of legislators voting on it. But since an unknown fraction of all bills represent "deals" struck with or between interest groups, it is not necessarily true that each member of the legislative majority behind a particular bill will have bothered to study the details of the bill he voted for; he may simply have assented to the deal struck by the sponsors of the bill. And unless the terms of the deal are stated accurately in the committee reports and in the floor comments of the sponsors, the sponsors will have difficulty striking deals in the future.

This picture is especially persuasive if we assume, as we should, that there is "log-rolling"—that is, vote trading—in the legislative process. Log rolling implies that legislators often vote against their personal convictions. This makes it unrealistic to deem that each legislator assents only to those aspects of statutory meaning that are fixed unambiguously in the language of the bill, interpreted without reference to the sponsors' intentions as reflected in their statements in the committee reports and on the floor.

---

16. On legislative history see the excellent treatment, both analytic and bibliographic, in Gwendolyn B. Folsom, *Legislative History: Research for the Interpretation of Laws* (1979); and the useful and very up-to-date discussion, with many references, in Reed Dickerson, "Statutory Interpretation: Dipping into Legislative History," 11 *Hofstra L. Rev.* 1125 (1983). There is a nice discussion in SEC v. Robert Collier & Co., 76 F.2d 939, 941 (2d Cir. 1935) (L. Hand, J.), rev'd, 298 U.S. 1 (1936).

But it is one thing to assume that legislators who vote for a bill defer to the understanding of the bill expressed by its sponsors and another to assume that they adopt the statements of witnesses, or nonsponsoring legislators (perhaps opponents of the legislation), who want to impart some twist to the statute when it is applied by the courts. Floor debates in Congress often are poorly attended, and Congressmen do not plow through transcripts of hearings before committees of which they are not members (many committee hearings are poorly attended even by committee members). Building up statutory meaning out of isolated and self-serving statements in hearings or on the floor is one of the less edifying forms of judicial formalism.

Postenactment statements, whether by sponsoring legislators or by other members of Congress, as to what the legislation meant should also be given little or no weight in general.[17] The deal is struck when the statute is enacted. Judges who pay attention to subsequent expressions of legislative intent not embodied in any statute may break rather than enforce the legislative contract. Nor, if one takes seriously the interest-group theory of politics, can subsequent expressions of legislative understanding be treated simply as impartial interpretations of the law.

Implied Rights of Action. A statute will often provide for criminal or other public remedies for its violation but will not say whether private individuals may sue to enforce it. The theory of legislation presented earlier may shed some light on the question of when a private right of action can properly be "implied" in a statute that is silent on private remedies.

The question has an antecedent in the interplay between criminal safety statutes and the standard of care in negligence cases. Suppose a legislature passes a statute forbidding people to drive automobiles faster than 55 miles per hour, and someone violates the statute, injuring another as a result. If the victim sues, may the violation of the statute be used as evidence, perhaps conclusive, of the injurer's negligence? The public-interest conception implies that a legislative pronouncement on safety should be given great weight: the legislature was trying to set an optimal safety standard, and it has tools not available to courts for doing so.[18] The interest-group approach implies, to the contrary, that there is no presumption that a legislative safety standard represents a sincere effort to bring about an optimal level of safety, so courts should give it no more weight in tort cases than the legislature prescribed.

17. This is the usual view. See, for example, Oscar Mayer & Co. v. Evans, 441 U.S. 750, 758 (1979).
18. For an influential statement of this point of view, see Ezra Ripley Thayer, "Public Wrong and Private Action," 27 *Harv. L. Rev.* 317, 321–323 (1914).

The use of safety statutes in tort cases is of relatively esoteric interest to the federal courts, but implied rights of action are of great interest because of the many federal regulatory statutes. Until 1975 a private damage right of action would be implied routinely in favor of the apparent beneficiaries of a regulatory statute. In the words of the leading case, *Texas & Pacific Railway v. Rigsby*,[19] "A disregard of the command of the statute is a wrongful act, and where it results in damage to one of the class for whose especial benefit the statute was enacted, the right to recover the damages from the party in default is implied." However, beginning with *Cort v. Ash*[20] and culminating a few years later in *Touche Ross & Co. v. Redington*,[21] the Supreme Court moved away from the traditional approach toward one in which affirmative evidence of congressional intent to allow private suits under the statute is required to imply a private right. (Lately the pendulum may have swung back some, however.)[22] What is interesting about the movement from *Rigsby* to *Redington* is that it parallels the shift in scholarly thinking about legislation from a rather naive faith in the public-interest character of most legislation to a more realistic understanding of the importance of interest groups in the legislative process. If a statute is in the public interest, it is natural to assume that the omission to provide explicitly for private remedies was an oversight; such remedies increase the likelihood that the statute will be enforced by freeing enforcement from the budget constraints on government enforcement agencies. But if the statute is just the result of a clash of interest groups, adding remedies to those expressly provided in the statute may upset the compromise. This is possible even if the statutory remedies are patently inadequate. The absence of effective remedies implies to the interest-group theorist merely that the group that procured the legislation lacked the political muscle to get an effective statute passed; and it is not the courts' business to give an interest group a benefit denied to it by the legislature.

It seems, therefore, that for a court to decide whether to imply a private right of action requires an anterior choice between characterizing a particular statute as public-interest or as interest-group legislation. The choice is normally slanted in favor of the public-interest characterization: all statutes have an ostensible public-interest justification, and even where the fig leaf is thin it is difficult for the courts to see through it. This makes the swing in the 1970s away from *Rigsby* surprising. It may reflect skepticism about the public-interest theory of legislation, a

19. 241 U.S. 33, 39 (1916).
20. 422 U.S. 66 (1975).
21. 442 U.S. 560, 575 (1979).
22. See Merrill Lynch, Pierce, Fenner & Smith v. Curran, 456 U.S. 353 (1982); Herman & MacLean v. Huddleston, 103 S. Ct. 683 (1983).

dislike for the substantive objectives of the statutes in question, or a concern with the inundation of the federal courts by federal question cases. It may even reflect—though more likely is the cause of—the revival of the canons of construction in Supreme Court jurisprudence; for one of them, *expressio unius est exclusio alterius*, provides, as we shall see, an alluring rationalization for refusing to correct legislative omissions, remedial or otherwise.

IMPLICATIONS FOR CONSTITUTIONAL INTERPRETATION

Strict or Loose? The term "strict construction" makes temperatures rise in debates over constitutional interpretation, but what exactly does it mean? To me it means sticking close to dictionary meanings—refusing to take liberties with them even in situations where changed circumstances since enactment make it impossible to achieve the apparent purposes of a provision if the words are taken literally. "Strict" and "literal" are therefore approximate synonyms, and so are "flexible" and "purposive."

Although the framers made it difficult to amend the Constitution, in order to avoid instability in the nation's fundamental institutions, it does not follow that they would have rejected flexible interpretation of constitutional provisions if the question had been put to them. Flexible interpretation is at once necessary to prevent the rapid obsolescence of a constitution and unlikely to change the nature of the instrument as radically as amendment. Text and history place limits on interpretation (though in some eras precious few) but virtually none on amendment. Flexible interpretation of the Constitution is to some extent merely inevitable. It is extraordinarily difficult to ascertain the meaning of a centuries-old document. Its cultural, political, even linguistic setting is so remote that reconstructing its meaning becomes a task for the historian rather than for a lawyer. Judges do not have the time or the training, nor in most cases the temperament or the taste, for historical research— which even when done by competent legal historians is often inconclusive. If the intended meaning of a provision is difficult to recover because of the passage of time, any interpretation of the provision (except one that denies it any contemporary application at all) will seem "loose" to opponents of that interpretation.

If historical research *does* yield an unambiguous answer regarding the meaning of some constitutional provision in a particular case, should a court feel bound by that meaning? If a contrary meaning is well established in the case law, my answer is no. Legal principles that have been settled for a century or more should not exist at the sufferance of historians, so that a piece of brilliant historiography could change the nation's public policy at a stroke. This conclusion, related as it is to the policies that underlie *stare decisis* and statutes of limitations, does not necessarily flout the intent of the framers of the Constitution. Practical men, they would not have wanted the country to pay a big price for correcting mistakes in interpretation many years after such mistakes had been made and the country had adapted to them.

The disruption of established institutions is a less acute problem in the case of old statutes, though otherwise the problem of unrecoverable meaning is the same. If legislative history of the Sherman Act (1890) turned up that conclusively proved that the act had been intended to protect competitors rather than consumers, so that almost a century of judicial construction would be rendered unsound, Congress could restore the judicial interpretation with the stroke of a pen. It could not do the same thing if the American Historical Society certified that the due process clause of the Fourteenth Amendment had not been intended to place any substantive limitations on state action.

Since most constitutional provisions are older than most statutes still in force, and therefore difficult to interpret, constitutional adjudication is inescapably more difficult than statutory construction (and is becoming more so with every passing year). The incidence of error is therefore likely to be higher in constitutional than in statutory adjudication. So we must decide which kind of error is more costly—the erroneous denial of the legislative will expressed in a statute (or in administrative or executive action thereunder) invalidated on constitutional grounds, or the erroneous denial of a constitutional right. I suggest the former—especially if interest-group legislation is only a fraction of all legislation. It must be better in general to thwart the desires of a small group seeking to get from the courts what, by definition, it was unable to get from the political branches than to thwart the will of the majority, even if not every statute embodies the will of the majority.

I am speaking only of cases in which the meaning of the Constitution is unclear. I do not mean to place the minority at the mercy of the majority; that would deny the very concept of a constitutional right. If someone has a clear constitutional right it must be enforced. But if a court cannot honestly determine whether such a right exists then it should be denied; doubts should be resolved against the claimant.[23] This conclusion may hold, though with less certainty, even if most statutes are assumed to be the product of interest-group pressures. Such legislation reflects and expresses the dominant power in the community, and it is the counsel of prudence for courts to yield to the domi-

23. As urged in James Bradley Thayer's classic essay, "The Origin and Scope of the American Doctrine of Constitutional Law," 7 *Harv. L. Rev.* 129, 144 (1893).

nant power when to do so does not deny a clear constitutional right. When in doubt, the democratic principle, reinforced by concern for maintaining the courts' political capital, should lead the courts to interpret governmental powers broadly, and rights against government narrowly. This, rather than strict construction, is the method of constitutional interpretation that furthers judicial restraint.

Rationality Review. Since it is inevitable that interest groups will influence the legislative process, it cannot be right to invalidate legislation just because it was procured by an interest group. Yet that would be the effect of requiring in the name of the Constitution (due process or equal protection) that legislation be rationally related to a "proper"—a public-interested—purpose ("rationality review"), if the requirement were taken seriously and applied neutrally. Legislation passed on behalf of an interest group typically will flunk any test of rationality other than self-interest. It is different if such legislation infringes on someone's express constitutional rights, but that is not the issue where legislation is invalidated merely because it is irrational; there is no express constitutional right not to be disadvantaged by the characteristic operation of the political process.

Responding to the problem of interest groups that exploit voters' ignorance to subvert the ideal operation of the democratic system, Professor Gerald Gunther has proposed that legislation not reasonably related to the legislators' stated end be held to violate the equal protection clause of the Fourteenth Amendment.[24] This would force the legislature to state its actual purpose clearly and by doing so give the electorate more information about what its representatives are really up to. Gunther's proposal seems radical, but actually may be redundant. To repeat an earlier point, if the judiciary is constrained to interpret statutes in accordance with their stated rather than true ends, the ability of interest groups to manipulate an ignorant electorate is automatically limited. Only in cases where the stated objective is completely out of line with the actual statutory directive (for example, requiring the licensing of shoe salesmen in order to limit the spread of athlete's foot) would Gunther's principle require invalidating the legislation whereas interpretation would allow attainment of the interest group's desires. But any case so transparent to a court will also be transparent to the electorate or its representatives, while if the lack of reasonable connection between means and stated end is not so blatant, the judges are apt to be fooled along with the voters.

24. Gerald Gunther, "In Search of Evolving Doctrine on a Changing Court: A Model for a Newer Equal Protection," 86 *Harv. L. Rev.* 1, 20–21, 23 (1972).

Strict Scrutiny. The Supreme Court has taken to declaring that statutes infringing "fundamental rights" are valid only if they survive "strict scrutiny" of the justifications offered for them. There can be no objection to this standard—except perhaps that it is too lax—if the fundamental right in question has firm constitutional roots, as does, for example, the right not to be discriminated against on racial grounds. But when the concept of fundamental rights is expanded to take in a host of interests with no specific constitutional provenance, and when, moreover, most of these interests involve sexual activity or its consequences,[25] the practical effect of the strict-scrutiny standard is to prevent serious consideration of any possible justifications for the challenged statute.

Laws regulating sex fall into the class of statutes that I call "public-sentiment" statutes; they rest on public feeling rather than on a utilitarian or economic calculus. A strict-scrutiny standard asks the state to furnish clear and convincing reasons for its regulation; and whatever may be the status of utilitarianism among contemporary philosophers, the reasons that strike judges as clear and convincing are usually utilitarian ones.[26] To show that a statute confers sufficient benefit to justify infringing a "fundamental" right requires showing that the statute promotes a "compelling state interest," which in practice means the greatest good of the greatest number. But it is the nature of public-sentiment statutes that they are not susceptible of utilitarian justification; the utilitarian considerations are all on the other side. Courts perceive the claims of the woman seeking an abortion or of the teenage girl seeking to enjoy sex without the threat of pregnancy as claims to happiness not offset by any happiness claim on the other side, with the result that statutes forbidding abortions or denying teenagers access to contraceptives flunk an elementary Benthamite test. So strong is the utilitarian hold over the judicial imagination that even in an area not (yet) governed by a strict-scrutiny standard—sex discrimination—the Court prefers a specious utilitarian justification to a frank acknowledgment that a challenged statute rests on public sentiment. For example, in *Michael M. v. Superior Court,*[27] where a young man challenged the constitutionality of his conviction for statutory rape on the ground that the statute did not punish females, the Court upheld the conviction on an unconvincing

---

25. Among the landmarks are Stanley v. Illinois, 405 U.S. 645 (1972); Weber v. Aetna Casualty & Surety Co., 406 U.S. 164 (1972); Roe v. Wade, 410 U.S. 113 (1973); Zablocki v. Redhail, 434 U.S. 374 (1978). I have discussed some of the Supreme Court's sexual privacy cases in my book *The Economics of Justice* 323–331 (1981).

26. See, for example, Benjamin Kaplan, Book Review, 95 *Harv. L. Rev.* 528, 533 (1981).

27. 450 U.S. 464 (1981).

deterrent ground (that excusing females from liability would, by encouraging them to report rapes, have a greater deterrent effect than would making them liable as well as males), although the statutory distinction obviously rested on conventional views regarding the male and female roles in sexual activity.

THE CANONS OF CONSTRUCTION

A realistic understanding of legislation is devastating to the canons of construction, a list of ancient interpretive maxims catalogued in such works as *Sutherland on Statutory Construction*[28] and invoked with great frequency by federal as by state judges in dealing with questions of statutory interpretation.[29] Among the principal canons are the following: one starts with the language of the statute; if the language is plain, construction is unnecessary; repeals by implication are disfavored; penal statutes are to be construed narrowly but remedial statutes broadly; *expressio unius est exclusio alterius.*[30]

A frequent criticism of the canons, made forcefully by Professor Llewellyn many years ago,[31] is that for every canon one might bring to bear on a point there is an equal and opposite canon. This is an exaggeration; but what is true is that there is a canon to support every possible result. If a judge wants to interpret a statute broadly, he does not mention the plain-meaning rule; he intones the rule that remedial statutes are to be construed broadly, or some other canon that leans toward the broad rather than the narrow. If he wants to interpret the statute narrowly, he will invoke some other canon. This point answers the suggestion (for which, incidentally, there is no supporting evidence) that whether good or bad as an original matter, the canons constitute a code that Congress expects the courts to use in interpreting statutes. That might make some sense if most questions of statutory interpretation fell within only one canon's domain. For example, suppose Congress decided that if the meaning of a statute as applied to some problem was plain as a linguistic matter, the statute should be interpreted in accordance with that meaning even if it was contrary to Congress's actual purpose in enacting the statute. So if Congress grants a tax exemption to "minister[s] of the gospel,"[32] rabbis should not be held eligible,[33] and

28. See J. G. Sutherland, *Statutes and Statutory Construction* (4th ed., Sands, 1972).

29. For an amusingly dense collocation of canons, with many citations, see United States v. Scrimgeour, 636 F.2d 1019, 1022–24 (5th Cir. 1981).

30. The expression of one thing is the exclusion of another.

31. See Karl N. Llewellyn, *The Common Law Tradition: Deciding Appeals* 521–535 (1960).

32. 26 U.S.C. § 107.

33. But see Salkov v. Commissioner, 46 T.C. 190, 193–199 (1966).

if this makes the exemption unconstitutional under the First Amendment because it discriminates against a religion, too bad. The problem with this and virtually any other example one could give is that the plain-meaning canon is not the only canon; and in the example just given, it runs up against the canon that statutes should be construed if possible to avoid being held unconstitutional. Thus the court has to choose between canons, and there is no canon for ranking or choosing between canons; the code lacks a key.

The canons are sometimes defended as limiting the delegation of legislative power to the courts. The plain-meaning rule forces a legislature to draft statutes carefully; the rule that repeals by implication are not favored limits the scope of newly enacted statutes; the rule that statutes in derogation of the common law are to be construed strictly[34] narrows the scope of all statutes applied in areas where common law principles would otherwise govern. But other canons look in the opposite direction, such as the important canon that remedial statutes are to be construed broadly. The canons, considered as a whole, do not express a general principle of limited government or separation of powers.

Another line of defense is that the canons are fine as commonsense guides to interpretation; they just should not be applied rigidly. But I shall argue that, with a few exceptions, they have no value even as flexible guideposts or rebuttable presumptions, even when taken one by one, because they rest on wholly unrealistic conceptions of the legislative process. I begin this demonstration with a canon that has an apparent reasonableness that many others lack. A milder version of the older, and still frequently invoked, plain-meaning rule,[35] it holds that in interpreting a statute one should begin, though perhaps not end, with the words of the statute.[36] Offered as a description of what judges do, the proposition is false. The judge rarely starts his inquiry with the words of the statute and often, if the truth be told, he does not look at the words at all. This is notoriously true with regard to the Constitution. More often than not briefs and judicial opinions dealing with free speech, due process, the right to assistance of counsel, and other constitutional rights do not quote the language of the applicable provi-

34. A canon one might have thought thoroughly discredited—yet recently described by the Supreme Court as "well-established." Norfolk Redevelopment & Housing Authority v. Chesapeake & Potomac Tel. Co., 104 S. Ct. 304, 307 (1983).

35. See, for example, American Bank & Trust Co. v. Dallas County, 103 S. Ct. 3369, 3374 (1983); Griffin v. Oceanic Contractors, Inc., 458 U.S. 564, 571 (1982); Western Union Tel. Co. v. FCC, 665 F.2d 1126, 1137 and n.21 (D.C. Cir. 1981).

36. See, for example, International Brotherhood of Teamsters v. Daniel, 439 U.S. 551, 558 (1979); Massachusetts Bonding & Insurance Co. v. United States, 352 U.S. 128, 138 (1956) (Frankfurter, J., dissenting).

sion—and not because all concerned know these provisions by heart. The constitutional provisions are in reality the foundations, or perhaps in some cases the pretexts, for the evolution of bodies of case law that are the starting point and usually the ending point of analysis of new cases.

There are many statutes of which this is also true, such as the Sherman Act.[37] Lawyers and judges do not begin their analyses of a challenged competitive practice by comparing the practice with the language of the act and then, only if they have satisfied themselves that there is some relationship, proceed to analyze the case law. They start with the case law and may never return to the statutory language—to "restrain trade or commerce" or to "attempt or conspire to monopolize." Even in dealing with statutes that have not generated a body of case law, a judge usually begins not with the language of the statute but with some conception of its subject matter and the likely purpose—if only one derived from the name of the statute or the title of the U.S. Code in which it appears. He is right to do so, because it is impossible to read statutory (or other) language in a vacuum.

I am assuming that the "start with the words" canon has reference to temporal rather than to logical priority. I think that is how it is usually meant, but perhaps I am being too literal and what really is intended is that the language of a statute is the most important evidence of its meaning—which normally is true—or at least indispensable evidence —which always is true. It is ironic that a principle designed to clarify should be so ambiguous.

The "start with the words" canon (taken in its temporal sense), like the plain-meaning canon itself, goes wrong by being unrealistic about how language is actually read. Another very popular canon, "remedial statutes are to be construed broadly," goes wrong by being unrealistic about legislative objectives. The idea behind this canon is that since the legislature is trying to remedy some ill, it would want the courts to construe the legislation in such a way as to make it a more rather than a less effective cure for that ill. This would be a sound working rule if every statute—at least every statute that could fairly be characterized as "remedial" (nowadays, almost every statute that does not prescribe penal sanctions[38] and so comes under another canon)—were passed because a majority of the legislators wanted to stamp out some practice they considered to be an evil. But if, as is often true, the statute is a compromise between one group of legislators that has a simple reme-

---

37. 15 U.S.C. §§ 1 *et seq.*
38. See 13 Sutherland, supra note 28, at 31–34.

dial objective but lacks a majority and another group that has reservations about the objective, a court that construed the statute broadly would upset the compromise that the statute was intended to embody.

The use of postenactment legislative materials to interpret a statute invites (as I have already suggested) a similar objection. Postenactment statements are likely to reflect the current preferences of legislators, and of the interest groups that determine or at least influence those preferences, but the current preferences bear no necessary relationship to those of the enacting legislators, who may have been reacting to a different constellation of interest-group pressures. To give effect to the current legislator's preferences is to risk spoiling the deal cut by the earlier legislators—to risk repealing legislation, in whole or in part, without going through the constitutionally prescribed processes for repeal. Therefore, a court should adhere to the enacting legislature's purposes (as far as those purposes can be discerned) even if the court is certain that the current legislature has contrary purposes and will respond by amending the relevant legislation to reverse the court's interpretation. Adherence to the initial compromise will not be futile. The amending legislation will probably be prospective (that is, applicable only to conduct taking place after the date of amendment), while judicial interpretations of legislation normally are retrospective (that is, applicable to past conduct at issue in a pending case). If the court were to carry out the preferences of the current legislature it would in effect be repealing the statute earlier than the legislature itself could have repealed it.

All of this assumes that the court can predict the preferences of the current legislature, but of course it cannot. It is one thing to use a committee report to explain the meaning of a statute passed on the basis of the report, and another to use a committee report that did not result in legislation to predict how the entire legislature will act if the court does not interpret the existing statute in a particular way. Judges cannot make such predictions with any confidence.

I do not want to anathematize completely the use of postenactment materials to interpret a statute, because such materials may in some cases reflect a disinterested and informed view by a committee that is monitoring the administration of a statute; the problem is to identify those cases. I also want to distinguish between postenactment materials and a subsequently enacted statute. Obviously a statute can change the meaning of an earlier statute even if the later one does not expressly amend the earlier one; I shall have something to say shortly about the canon against implied repeals.

Another canon that reflects an unrealistic view of the political process is that courts should give great weight to the interpretation of a statute by the administrative agency that enforces it.[39] There is no reason to expect administrative agency members, appointed long after the legislation they enforce was enacted, to display a special fidelity to the original intent of the legislation rather than to the current policies of the Administration and the Congress. They may, of course, know more about the legislation than the courts do, particularly if interpretation requires technical knowledge, and to the extent that they support their interpretation with reasons attributable to superior knowledge, the courts should give that interpretation weight. But the mere fact that it is the interpretation of the current agency does not entitle it to weight, unless the interpretation has persisted through several changes of Administration, thus rebutting any inference that it reflects a Johnny-come-lately view of the statute.

Many canons of statutory construction go wrong because they impute omniscience to Congress. Omniscience is always an unrealistic assumption, and particularly so when one is dealing with the legislative process. The most important reason why statutes are so frequently ambiguous in application is not that they are poorly drafted—though many are—and not that the legislators failed to agree on just what they wanted to accomplish in the statute—though often they do fail—but that a statute necessarily is drafted in advance of, and therefore with imperfect appreciation for, the problems that will be encountered in its application. As explained by Edward Levi,

> For a legislature perhaps the pressures are such that a bill has to be passed dealing with a certain subject. But the precise effect of the bill is not something upon which the members have to reach agreement. If the legislature were a court, it would not decide the precise effect until a specific fact situation arose demanding an answer. Its first pronouncement would not be expected to fill in the gaps. But since it is not a court, this is even more true. It will not be required to make the determination in any event, but can wait for the court to do so. There is a related and an additional reason for ambiguity. As to what type of situation is the legislature to make a decision? Despite much gospel to the contrary, a legislature is not a fact-finding body. There is no mechanism, as there is with a court, to require the legislature to sift facts and to make a decision about specific situations. There need be no agreement about what the sit-

---

39. See, for example, NLRB v. Hendricks County Rural Electrical Membership Coop., 454 U.S. 170, 177, 178–179 (1981).

uation is. The members of the legislative body will be talking about different things; they cannot force each other to accept even a hypothetical set of facts. The result is that even in a non-controversial atmosphere just exactly what has been decided will not be clear.[40]

An example of a canon founded on the assumption of legislative omniscience is that every word of a statute must be given significance; nothing can be treated as surplusage.[41] So if there is language that could be used to resolve a question under the statute, it is used, even if the result is an answer that the legislators would not have given if the question had been asked of them. Applied to the words "of the gospel" in the statute I discussed earlier, this canon would do great violence to the actual purposes of the legislators. The words almost certainly were tossed in with no consideration of their sectarian significance. The conditions under which legislators work are not conducive to careful, farsighted, and parsimonious drafting. Nor does great care guarantee economy of language; a statute that is the product of compromise may contain redundant language as a by-product of the strains of the negotiating process. Moreover, redundant language is sometimes used merely for purposes of emphasis, to reassure supporters or opponents about a point particularly important to them. Thus courts that follow the "no surplusage" canon will sometimes strain to find an independent meaning in words intended to bear none.

Consider now the popular canon that repeals by implication are disfavored,[42] and try to imagine what the idea behind it might be. Perhaps it is that whenever Congress enacts a new statute it combs the United States Code for possible inconsistencies with the new statute, and when it spots one repeals it explicitly. This would imply legislative omniscience in a particularly uncompromising form; if Congress could foresee and make provision for every possible application of a new statute, there would be no occasion for judicial interpretation. An alternative basis for this canon is the idea that if the choice is between giving less scope to the new statute and cutting down the intended scope of the old (because both cannot be enforced to the hilt without conflict), Congress must desire the courts to do the first. But the oppo-

40. Edward H. Levi, *An Introduction to Legal Reasoning* 30–31 (1949) (footnote omitted). See also H.L.A. Hart, *The Concept of Law* 125–127 (1961).

41. See, for example, Co-Petro Marketing Group, Inc. v. Commodity Futures Trading Comm'n, 680 F.2d 566, 569–570 (9th Cir. 1982).

42. See, for example, Kremer v. Chemical Construction Corp., 456 U.S. 461, 468 (1982); American Bank & Trust Co. v. Dallas County, 103 S. Ct. 3369, 3377 (1983).

site inference is, if anything, more plausible—that the enacting Congress cares more about its own statutes than those of previous Congresses.

The canon *expressio unius est exclusio alterius* is also based on the assumption of legislative omniscience, because it would make sense only if all omissions in legislative drafting were deliberate. Although this canon seemed dead for a while, it has been resurrected by the Supreme Court to provide a basis for refusing to create private remedies for certain statutory violations.[43] Its recent disparagement by a unanimous Court[44] puts its future in some doubt but more likely just confirms that judicial use of canons of construction is opportunistic. Whether the result in the private-action cases is right or wrong, the use of *expressio unius* was not helpful. If a statute lacks effective remedies because the opponents were strong enough to prevent their inclusion, the courts should, as I have emphasized, honor the legislative compromise. But if the omission was an oversight, or if Congress thought the courts would provide appropriate remedies for statutory violations as a matter of course, the judges should create the remedies necessary to carry out the legislature's objectives: "The major premise of the conclusion expressed in a statute, the change of policy that induces the enactment, may not be set out in terms, but it is not an adequate discharge of duty for courts to say: We see what you are driving at, but you have not said it, and therefore we shall go on as before."[45]

My last example of a canon apparently premised on an assumption of legislative omniscience is one that even Judge Friendly, our most trenchant living critic of the canons of construction,[46] has occasionally, though cautiously, invoked: that the reenactment without change of a statute that the courts have interpreted in a particular way is evidence that Congress has adopted that construction. Consider Judge Friendly's example of the domestic-relations exception to the diversity jurisdiction of the federal courts.[47] This entirely judge-made exception is very old,[48] and the grant of diversity jurisdiction to the federal courts has

43. A development described in a justly celebrated student Note, "Intent, Clear Statements and The Common Law: Statutory Interpretation in the Supreme Court," 95 *Harv. L. Rev.* 892–896 (1982), and deplored in an unfortunately unpublished, but very worthwhile, paper by Judge Henry J. Friendly, "Statutorification of Federal Law" 10–16 (July 1981).

44. See Herman & MacLean v. Huddleston, 103 S. Ct. 683, 690 (1983).

45. Johnson v. United States, 163 Fed. 30, 32 (1st Cir. 1908) (Holmes, J.).

46. See Friendly, supra note 43; Henry J. Friendly, "Mr. Justice Frankfurter and the Reading of Statutes," in Friendly, *Benchmarks* 196 (1967).

47. See Phillips, Nizer, Benjamin, Krim & Ballon v. Rosenstiel, 490 F.2d 509, 514 (2d Cir. 1973).

48. See Barber v. Barber, 62 U.S. (21 How.) 582, 584 (1859) (dictum).

been reenacted several times since the exception was first recognized; yet neither the texts nor legislative histories of the successive reenactments have ever referred to it. Can we nevertheless take these reenactments to signify legislative adoption of the judicially created exception? It is just as likely that a majority of the legislators who voted on each reenactment never heard of the exception, which after all is unknown to all but a small number of specialists in federal jurisdiction and domestic relations, or that they heard of it but had no desire to freeze the existing judicial construction into statute law, being indifferent to whether the courts continued to recognize the exception or whether they modified or abolished it.[49]

I want to turn now to three canons that have arguable merit. The first is that penal statutes should be construed narrowly.[50] Every statute overdeters to a certain extent, because its bounds are uncertain and fear of inadvertent liability causes some people to steer well clear of those bounds; the harsher the sanctions for violation, the greater is the over-deterrence. Overdeterrence can be reduced by careful specification of the statutory limits. If for this reason a statute is intended to be specific, courts should not construe it broadly. Probably most criminal statutes are of this character; therefore courts should assume that legislatures want criminal statutes interpreted narrowly unless the legislators specify otherwise.

True, a statute can underdeter rather than overdeter; if overdeterrence is the characteristic vice of broad construction, underdeterrence is the characteristic vice of narrow construction. But it is not always necessary to make this Hobson's choice. The harsher the sanction for a violation of a statute, the higher is the appropriate level of care in drafting. Careful drafting avoids both underdeterrence and overdeterrence. If the legislature can be assumed to draft criminal statutes more carefully than civil statutes, then courts that construe criminal statutes more narrowly than they construe civil statutes (as they do)[51] do not run a serious risk of disserving the legislative will through underdeterrence.

49. A similar point is made by Judge Friendly himself in *Benchmarks*, supra note 46, at 232–233.

50. See, for example, United States v. Campos-Serrano, 404 U.S. 293, 297 (1971).

51. Of course, not all criminal sanctions are more severe than civil sanctions. For example, the maximum criminal fine that can be imposed on a corporation for violating the Sherman Act is $1 million, but the automatic tripling of civil damages for Sherman Act violations makes two-thirds of every private damages judgment penal. Thus, the sky is the limit to the amount a corporation might be forced to pay in a civil suit. However, the question of when civil penalties should be equated with criminal sanctions and therefore be hedged about by the same procedural safeguards is beyond the scope of this book.

The canon against broad construction of penal statutes is related to the constitutional requirement of reasonable notice of potential criminal liability.[52] If a legislature stated in the preamble to a criminal statute that it had made the statute vague in order to enhance its deterrent effect, the canon against broad construction of penal statutes could not be applied by reference to legislative intent. Yet it might be applied as an instance of the canon that enjoins the courts to interpret statutes, wherever possible, to avoid making them unconstitutional.[53] Perhaps the "rule of lenity" (as the canon that penal statutes are to be construed narrowly is sometimes called) is therefore best viewed simply as a special instance of the construe-to-make-constitutional canon. And this canon is sensible, provided it is not pressed too hard; it rests on the commonsense assumption that the legislators would rather not have the courts nullify their effort entirely unless the interpretation necessary to save it would pervert their goal in enacting it.[54]

A closely related canon is that statutes should be construed not only to save them from being held unconstitutional but to avoid even raising serious constitutional questions.[55] Judge Friendly has criticized this canon with his customary power;[56] he asks why the legislature should care that its statute raises a constitutional question, as long as the court concludes that it is constitutional. (If the court is inclined to hold the statute unconstitutional, the canon on construing to avoid unconstitutionality, which Judge Friendly accepts, comes into play.) This criticism is convincing as far as it goes but, as Judge Friendly himself recognizes, is incomplete. It leaves out of account the policy of judicial self-restraint, a corollary of which is the desirability of avoiding unnecessary constitutional decision. The canon leaves everything pleasantly vague. Congress can amend the statute if it feels strongly, and so precipitate a constitutional controversy that it may lose—not that it must lose, as would be the case if it amended a statute to nullify an interpretation that was necessary to make the statute constitutional. But if it does not amend the statute, a collision with the courts has been averted. And even if the courts were to uphold the statute's constitutionality if forced to grasp the nettle, in the course of doing so they might say something that would put a constitutional cloud over some other legis-

---

52. See, for example, Lanzetta v. New Jersey, 306 U.S. 451, 453 (1939); Kolender v. Lawson, 103 S. Ct. 1855 (1983).

53. See, for example, Textile Workers Union v. Lincoln Mills, 353 U.S. 448, 477 (1957) (Frankfurter, J., dissenting).

54. Trust lawyers will see an analogy to the *cy pres* doctrine of charitable trusts.

55. See, for example, United States v. Rumely, 345 U.S. 41, 45 (1953).

56. See Friendly, *Benchmarks,* supra note 46, at 210–212.

lation. Construing legislation to avoid constitutional questions, as well as to avoid actual nullification, is thus one of those buffering devices by which the frictions created by the institution of judicial review are minimized.[57]

But this does not make the canon a good one. It just shifts the plane of analysis from that of interpreting legislative intent to that of smoothing the relations between Congress and the courts; and on this other plane it fails too. The Constitution as interpreted in modern cases is extraordinarily far-reaching—a written Constitution in name only—yet Congress's practical ability to overrule a judicial decision misconstruing one of its statutes, given all the other matters pressing for its attention, is less today than ever before, and probably was never very great.[58] The practical effect of interpreting statutes to avoid raising constitutional questions is therefore to enlarge the already vast reach of constitutional prohibition beyond even the most extravagant modern interpretations of the Constitution—to create a judge-made "penumbra" that has much the same prohibitory effect as the judge-made (or at least judge-amplified) Constitution itself—and in doing so to sharpen the tensions between the legislative and judicial branches.

If the canon against broad construction of penal statutes can be thought of as derivative from the canon that statutes should be construed if possible to avoid being held unconstitutional, then the latter canon is the only one I have discussed that should be retained. But where does that leave us? Might it not be better for the judges to be under the discipline of the canons, even if the canons are in some ultimate sense wrong, than to have them approach the task of statutory construction without any standards at all to guide them? But far from imposing a discipline of any sort on judges, the canons promote judicial activism. Nondirective as they are when considered in gross, the canons do not constrain judicial decision making; they merely enable a judge to create the appearance that his statutory decisions are constrained. Recall that a standard defense of judicial activism is that it "is, in most instances, not activism at all. Courts do not relish making such hard decisions and certainly do not encourage litigation on social or political problems. But . . . the federal judiciary . . . has the paramount and the continuing duty to uphold the law."[59] By making statutory interpreta-

---

57. See Alexander M. Bickel, *The Least Dangerous Branch: The Supreme Court at the Bar of Politics* 181 (1962).

58. Cf. Beth Henschen, "Statutory Interpretations of the Supreme Court: Congressional Response," 11 *Am. Politics Q.* 441, 453 (1983).

59. Frank M. Johnson, Jr., "The Role of the Judiciary with Respect to the Other Branches of Government," 11 *Ga. L. Rev.* 455, 474 (1977).

tion seem mechanical rather than creative, the canons conceal the extent to which the judge is making new law in the guise of interpreting a statute. The judge who recognizes the degree to which he is free rather than constrained in the interpretation of statutes, and refuses to make a pretense of constraint by parading the canons of construction in his opinions, is less likely to act willfully than the judge who either mistakes freedom for constraint or has no compunctions about misrepresenting his will as that of Congress.

The continued popularity of the canons is one of the most conspicuous modern examples of the tenacity of formalist style.[60] The canons enable the author of a statutory opinion to give his opinion the form of logical deduction; the reality is something else. As Judge Wald notes in her recent examination of the use of legislative history by the Supreme Court, "Frankly, the same Justices who rely on plain language and repudiate thirty years of contrary judicial interpretation in one case say in another that they must look to the broad purposes of the act and not to any cramped phraseology."[61] She immediately adds: "I certainly do not suggest disingenuousness or opportunism; rather, in the present state of the law, the various approaches to statutory construction are drawn out as needed, much as a golfer selects the proper club when he gauges the distance to the pin and the contours of the course."[62] This is properly deferential; but what she has described, not in golf but in law, indeed smacks of disingenuousness and opportunism. There is no contradiction in a golfer's using a wood when he is teeing off and a putter when he is on the green, but it is a contradiction for the same justice, in the same term of court, to use the plain-meaning rule in one case and to make fun of it in another.[63] (In fairness, however, it should be noted that some contradictions among a judge's opinions are the unavoidable consequence of necessary compromises with other judges.)

AN ALTERNATIVE APPROACH

As an alternative to viewing statutory interpretation as the application of the canons of construction, I suggest a two-part approach. First, the judge should try to put himself in the shoes of the enacting legislators

60. Those who doubt the continued popularity of the canons should read the battle of the canons in American Bank & Trust Co. v. Dallas County, 103 S. Ct. 3369 (1983), a fairly typical example of recent statutory opinions in the Supreme Court.

61. Patricia M. Wald, "Some Observations on the Use of Legislative History in the 1981 Supreme Court Term," 68 *Ia. L. Rev.* 195, 215 (1983).

62. *Id.* at 215–216.

63. Compare Griffin v. Oceanic Contractors, Inc., 102 S. Ct. 3245, 3250 (1982), with FBI v. Abramson, 456 U.S. 615, 625 n.7 (1982).

and figure out how they would have wanted the statute applied to the case before him. This is the method of imaginative reconstruction.[64] If it fails, as occasionally it will, either because the necessary information is lacking or because the legislators had failed to agree on essential premises, then the judge must decide what attribution of meaning to the statute will yield the most reasonable result in the case at hand—always bearing in mind that what seems reasonable to the judge may not have seemed reasonable to the legislators, and that it is their conception of reasonableness, to the extent known, rather than the judge's, that should guide decision.

The limitations of this approach, especially the first part, should be plain from my earlier discussion of the difficulties of reconstructing history. And it invites the criticism that judges do not have the requisite imagination and that what they will do in practice is to assume that the legislators were people just like themselves, with the result that statutory construction will consist of the judge's voting his own preferences and ascribing them to legislators. But the irresponsible judge will twist any approach to yield the outcomes that he desires, and the stupid judge will do the same thing unconsciously.

The judge who follows the suggested approach will not only consider the language, structure, and history of the statute, but also study the values and attitudes, as far as they can be known today, of the period when the legislation was enacted. It would be a mistake to ascribe to legislators of the 1930s or the 1960s and early 1970s the skepticism regarding the size of government and the efficiency of regulation that is widespread today, or to impute to the Congress of the 1920s current ideas of conflict of interest.[65] The judge's job is not to keep a statute up to date in the sense of making it reflect contemporary values, but to imagine as best he can how the legislators who enacted the statute would have wanted it applied to situations they did not foresee.

The judge will be particularly alert to any sign of legislative intent regarding the freedom with which he should exercise his interpretive

---

64. There is nothing new in this suggestion. In addition to Heydon's Case, supra note 2, see 1 William Blackstone, *Commentaries on the Laws of England* 59–61 (1765); 3 *id.* at 430–431 (1768); Ronald Dworkin, "How to Read the Civil Rights Act," *New York Rev. of Books,* Dec. 20, 1979, at 37; Lon L. Fuller, "Positivism and Fidelity to Law—A Reply to Professor Hart," 71 *Harv. L. Rev.* 630, 662–667 (1958); John Chipman Gray, *The Nature and Sources of the Law* 172–173 (2d ed. 1921); Lehigh Valley Coal Co. v. Yensavage, 218 Fed. 547, 553 (2d Cir. 1914) (L. Hand, J.); "How Far Is a Judge Free in Rendering a Decision?" in Learned Hand, *The Spirit of Liberty: Papers and Addresses* 103, 105–110 (Dilliard 3d ed. 1960); speech by Learned Hand, in Ruggero J. Aldisert, *The Judicial Process: Readings, Materials and Cases* 184–185 (1976).

65. See CBI Industries, Inc. v. Horton, 682 F.2d 643 (7th Cir. 1982).

function. Sometimes a statute will state whether it is to be broadly or narrowly construed;[66] more often the structure and language of the statute will supply a clue. If the legislature enacts into statute law a common law concept, as Congress did when in the Sherman Act it forbade agreements in restraint of trade, this is a clue that the courts are to interpret the statute with the freedom with which they would construe and apply a common law principle—in which event the legislators' values may not be controlling after all.

The opposite extreme is a statute that sets out its requirements with some specificity, especially against a background of dissatisfaction with judicial handling of the same subject under a previous statute or the common law (much federal labor and regulatory legislation is of this character). Probably the legislature does not want the courts to paint with a broad brush in adapting such a statute to the unforeseeable future. The Constitution contains several such provisions—for example, the provision that the President must be at least 35 years old. This provision does not invite interpretation; it does not invite a court to recast the provision so that it reads "the President must be mature." There is nothing the court could point to in or behind the Constitution that would justify such an interpretation. It is not that the words are plain, but rather that read in context, as words must always be read in order to yield meaning, they do not authorize any interpretation except the obvious one.

Although the approach I have sketched has obvious affinities with the "attribution of purpose" approach of Professors Hart and Sacks, I want to stress one difference. They say that in construing a statute a court "should assume, unless the contrary unmistakably appears, that the legislature was made up of reasonable persons pursuing reasonable purposes reasonably."[67] Coupled with an earlier statement that in trying to divine the legislative will the court should ignore "short-run currents of political expedience,"[68] Hart and Sacks appear to be suggesting that the judge should ignore interest groups, popular ignorance and prejudice, and anything else that deflects legislators from the single-minded pursuit of the public interest as the judge would conceive it. But this approach risks attributing to legislation not the purposes reasonably inferable from the legislation itself but the judge's own conception of the public interest. When Hart and Sacks were writing—in the wake of the New Deal—the legislative process was widely regarded

66. See, for example, section 904(a) of Racketeer Influenced and Corrupt Organizations (RICO), 18 U.S.C. § 1961 note.

67. 2 Hart and Sacks, supra note 2, at 1415.

68. 2 id. at 1414.

as progressive and public-spirited. Today there is less agreement that the motives behind most legislation are benign, and this should make the judge wary about too readily assuming a congruence between his conception of the public interest and the latent purposes of the statutes he is called on to interpret.

A related characteristic of the passages I have quoted from Hart and Sacks is a reluctance to recognize that statutes often are the product of compromise between opposing groups and that a compromise is unlikely to embody a single consistent purpose. Of course, as I pointed out earlier, it is hard for judges, limited as they are to the formal materials of the legislative process, to identify the existence of compromise. But where the lines of compromise are discernible, the judge's duty is to follow them,[69] to implement not the purposes of one group of legislators but the compromise itself.[70]

If the lines of compromise are not clear, if the judge's scrupulous search for the legislative will does not turn up anything, the second part of my approach ("reasonable result") comes into play—provided the case is at least within the statute's domain. If someone was short-changed on the purchase of a bag of oranges and brought suit against the seller under the federal securities laws, arguing that the court should read "security" to include an orange because fraud is a bad thing, he would receive short shrift. The securities laws do not authorize the courts to deal with a sale of oranges. But if the case involves something that is or may be a security, and the judge is simply very uncertain whether the statute was meant to apply, he cannot just dismiss the case out of hand; it is within the scope of the legislative delegation to him. He must decide the case, even though on the basis of considerations that cannot be laid at Congress's door. These might be considerations of judicial administrability—what interpretation of the statute will provide greater predictability, require less judicial fact-finding, and otherwise reduce the cost and frequency of litigation under the statute? Or they might be considerations drawn from some broadly based conception of the public interest. It is always possible, of course, to refer these considerations back to Congress—to say that Congress would have wanted the courts, in cases where they could not figure out what interpretation would advance the substantive objectives of the

69. For good examples of this see Morrison-Knudsen Construction Co. v. Director, Office of Workers' Compensation Programs, 103 S. Ct. 2045, 2052 (1983); NLRB v. Rockaway News Supply Co., 197 F.2d 111, 115–116 (2d Cir. 1952) (dissenting opinion), aff'd on other grounds, 345 U.S. 71 (1953).

70. As clearly recognized by the courts in interpreting consent decrees. See, for example, United States v. Armour & Co., 402 U.S. 673, 681–683 (1971).

statute, to adopt the "better" one; or to say in the manner of Hart and Sacks that legislators should be presumed reasonable until shown otherwise. But these methods of imputing congressional intent are artificial; and it is not healthy for a judge to conceal from himself that he is being creative.

The alternative to exercising creativity is for the judge to say to whichever party is relying on the statute, "You have not persuaded me that it applies, so you lose." This is fine if there are no benefits to be gained from resolving the statutory question in the proponent's favor. But what if there are, even if they cannot honestly be referred back to the intentions of the enacting Congress? What if, for example the statute would be much cheaper to administer if it were interpreted as embracing the claim made by this party? I consider this a proper reason for "interpreting" the legislation to cover the claim. By assumption the legislators' intent is not being thwarted; and there is a sense in which it is actually being served. Often when there are political pressures to do something about a problem but the legislature cannot agree exactly what to do about it, it will pass a statute the effect (as well as the undisclosed purpose) of which is to dump the problem in the lap of the courts, taking advantage of the fact that the courts are a kind of political lightning rod. But this implies that the courts are expected to try to solve the problem; they have a mandate, though no specific directions. So unless this mode of legislation is thought to be unconstitutional, the courts have a duty and not merely a power to solve the problem in a reasonable way. This is invention rather than discovery; it is "interpretation" only in a special sense; but it is not usurpative.

I want to end by comparing my suggested approach to two other positions in the current literature on interpretation. Although the debate is mostly over constitutional rather than statutory interpretation, Professor Calabresi's already celebrated book carries it into the statutory arena.[71] His basic thesis is that courts ought to have the same power in dealing with statutes that they do in dealing with their own precedents: the power to discard them because they are obsolete, without having to find them unconstitutional. I shall assume this power could be given to the courts by legislation (though there is some question, if the courts are federal, whether the power would really be "judicial" within the meaning of Article III); and this is Calabresi's preferred route. The main objections to it are that it greatly exaggerates the courts' ability to legislate intelligently—and the judgment whether a statute has outlived its

71. Guido Calabresi, *A Common Law for the Age of Statutes* (1982). See also a notable recent review essay by Professor Robert Weisberg, "The Calabresian Judicial Artist: Statutes and the New Legal Process," 35 *Stan. L. Rev.* 213 (1983).

usefulness is a legislative rather than a judicial judgment—and that it would greatly increase the work of the courts. But since in any event such a statute is not about to be passed—not by the United States Congress anyway—the question arises whether Calabresi's goal of empowering the courts to update statutes can be attained without legislative authorization. He seems to think it can be. He flirts with judicial "misreading" of statutes as a second-best route to his end, remarks that "the limits of honest interpretation are too constricting," and expresses at least qualified approval of judicial amendment of statutes where legislative amendment is blocked by interest-group pressures.[72] Although I am disturbed that Professor Calabresi should approve, even with reservations, such judicial shenanigans as deliberately misreading a statute to bring about a desired result, I must in fairness acknowledge his own preference for judicial candor. But I am not reassured. Although under current conventions of the judge's role, forcing judges to admit publicly when they were rewriting statutes would quickly end the practice, Calabresi wants to change these conventions—wants to encourage candor about what is now considered judicial usurpation by persuading the legal community that it should not be considered any longer usurpative for judges to treat old statutes with the freedom they treat old precedents.

But in the absence of express legislative authorization it *would* be usurpation. Calabresi's contrary view rests on too tight an embrace of the public-interest conception of legislation. (His book ignores the modern social science literature on legislation.) If all legislation were public-interest legislation, legislatures might be content to have courts repeal a statute when it became obsolete and the legislators were too occupied with other matters to repeal the statute themselves. (Even then they might have doubts about the ability of courts to decide when a statute has become obsolete, as would I; but I shall pass by that point.) But interest-group legislation is not obsolete until the interest-group pressures that led to its enactment have changed, and courts do not have the research capabilities for discovering when that has happened. Moreover, it is unclear what it means to say that an interest-group statute has become obsolete. Does it mean that the interest group that procured the passage of the statute no longer could get it through the legislature? If so, courts would often be striking down statutes within months of their enactment. If, alternatively, it means that some competing interest group is now strong enough to get the legislation repealed, there is no judicial role in determining when a statute is

72. Calabresi, supra note 71, at 34, 38.

obsolete; it is obsolete when it is repealed, and not before. Calabresi's view may be that interest-group legislation is illegitimate, and judicial "sunsetting" a way of getting rid of it without having to expand the constitutional limitations on legislation. But to set the courts against the interest-group state would be to embrace judicial activism in a most far-reaching form—unless, as I have said, legislatures can be persuaded to adopt Calabresi's proposal.

Although premised on a public-interest conception of legislation, Calabresi's proposal is not friendly to the legislative process; it contemplates a big shift of legislative power from the legislatures to the courts. In this respect it resembles the very different approach to statutes taken by Professor Easterbrook in a recent article.[73] Being highly skeptical of the possibility of reconstructing legislative intent in other than simple cases, Easterbrook proposes "declaring legislation inapplicable unless it either expressly addresses the matter or commits the matter to the common law."[74] Gap filling based on references to legislators' presumed goals is ruled out. If the legislature made a broad delegation of common-law rule-making authority to the courts, as in the antitrust laws, then the courts would have great freedom; but if the legislation set forth rules rather than a general standard, the courts would not be able to add to them to take care of problems not anticipated by the enacting legislature.

This position is unfriendly to the legislative process in that it denies the courts a *helpful* role in relation to legislation. In our system legislation often emerges from the legislative mill in a seriously incomplete form, and often this is due to political tensions rather than to the inherent limitations of foresight that prevent legislators from anticipating all of the problems that will arise in the administration of a statute. There is also the great problem of conflicting and overlapping statutes, passed at different times with incomplete appreciation of the statutory landscape. Judges have to play a constructive, helping role if legislation is to work.

Although it would oversimplify Easterbrook's position to describe it as "strict constructionism," it does resemble strict constructionism, a concept that I have already noted is unfriendly to legislation though sometimes promoted as the only philosophy that ensures fidelity to legislative intent. The concept is the lineal descendant of the canon that statutes in derogation of the common law are to be strictly construed, and like that canon was used in nineteenth-century England to emascu-

---

73. See Frank H. Easterbrook, "Statutes' Domains," 50 *U. Chi. L. Rev.* 533 (1983).
74. *Id.* at 552.

late social welfare legislation.[75] As I noted briefly in Chapter 7, to construe a statute strictly is to limit its scope and its life span—to make Congress work twice as hard to produce the same effect.[76] An anecdote told by Holmes is pertinent here: "There is a story of a Vermont justice of the peace before whom a suit was brought by one farmer against another for breaking a churn. The justice took time to consider, and then said that he had looked through the statutes and could find nothing about churns, and gave judgment to the defendant."[77]

It is not an accident that most "no constructionists" are political liberals and most "strict constructionists" are political conservatives. The former think that modern legislation does not go far enough and want the courts to pick up the ball that the legislators have dropped; the latter think it goes too far and want the courts to rein the legislators in. Each school has developed interpretive techniques appropriate to its political ends.

75. See Gareth Jones, "Should Judges Be Politicians? The English Experience," 57 *Ind. L.J.* 211, 213 (1982).

76. Easterbrook, supra note 73, at 548–549, defends his approach as a limitation on legislative power.

77. Oliver Wendell Holmes, "The Path of the Law," 10 *Harv. L. Rev.* 457, 474–475 (1897).

10

Common Law Adjudication

in the Courts of Appeals

I HAVE TWO distinct purposes in this chapter. I want to show that despite appearances, and despite any inference that might be drawn from the length of the last chapter, the federal courts are primarily common law courts (though I shall also raise briefly the question whether they will continue to be so); and I want to argue that they can improve their performance in common law adjudication by using some simple but powerful tools of economic analysis. I shall be using "common law" in the same functional sense as in Chapter 1: not as limited to the business of the royal courts of Westminster in the eighteenth century (the approximate sense in which "common law" is used in the Seventh Amendment and in the Judiciary Act of 1789), but as encompassing all fields that have been shaped mainly by judges rather than by legislators. Common law thus includes, among other fields, admiralty, equity, and modern federal civil procedure (the rules of which have been formulated under the direction of the Supreme Court justices), as well as torts, contracts, property, trusts, future interests, agency, remedies, and much of criminal law and procedure. We shall also see that many ostensibly statutory and constitutional fields really are common law fields.

Both in the traditional sense and in the broader functional sense in which I am using the term, the common law has seemed to some economic analysts of law to be heavily influenced by a concern, more often intuitive than explicit to be sure, with promoting economic efficiency.[1]

1. See, for example, Richard A. Posner, *Economic Analysis of Law*, pt. II (2d ed. 1977); William M. Landes and Richard A. Posner, "The Positive Economic Theory of Tort

The "efficiency theory" of the common law is controversial, but the controversy primarily concerns the extent to which efficiency has influenced and should influence the common law; only a few diehards argue that it has had or should have no place at all. Considering the strong attachment of most Americans, including most American judges, to utilitarianism, it would be surprising if economics—viewed not as a collection of arcane mathematical theorems relating to unemployment, inflation, the balance of payments, and other aggregate phenomena remote from the professional concerns of judges and lawyers, but as the theory of rational choice in a world of limited goods—did not have great relevance to common law adjudication. Not only do many fields of the common law, such as contracts, regulate explicitly economic relationships, but it takes only a little imagination to realize that even in ostensibly noneconomic fields, such as torts, many of the issues that the courts are concerned with (such as whether a potential injurer ought to take a particular precaution in light of the probability of an injury of a given severity, on pain of being deemed negligent and therefore liable if he does not and injury results) require an economic judgment. This was clear to Holmes a century ago;[2] his advice of a few years later that "every lawyer ought to seek an understanding of economics"[3] is, belatedly, being taken. But it remains highly controversial. I will not try to argue systematically for the relevance of economics to common law adjudication, but I shall offer illustrations that may have some persuasive force for those willing to suspend their disbelief temporarily.

This chapter and the previous one are continuous rather than dichotomous. I argued there that the modern social science literature on legislation, which is mainly an economic literature, is indispensable to the intelligent discharge by the federal courts of their responsibilities for statutory and constitutional interpretation. I argue here that another economic literature, the literature on the economic structure of the common law, is indispensable to the intelligent discharge of their almost equally important (and actually, I believe, more time-consuming) responsibilities for common law adjudication.

Law," 15 Ga. L. Rev. 851, 852–864 (1981). For a comprehensive review essay on the entire field of "law and economics," see C. J. Veljanovski, The New Law-and-Economics: A Research Review (1982).

2. See Oliver Wendell Holmes, Jr., The Common Law 94–96 (1881).

3. Oliver Wendell Holmes, "The Path of the Law," 10 Harv. L. Rev. 457, 474 (1897).

QUANTITATIVE ANALYSIS

The basic data for this chapter come from the same sample of court of appeals opinions in 1960 and 1983 that formed the basis of Tables 3.5 and 3.6 in Chapter 3. But here the opinions will be organized not by subject matter but by issue types that cut across conventional subject-matter classifications used by the Administrative Office of the U.S. Courts.

Table 10.1 displays this classification for the two years. Notice to begin with that since some cases raise issues of more than one type, there are more issues (254) than there are cases (200). (Two or more issues of one type are counted as just one issue.) I have classified issues in six major categories, some with subcategories. The major categories are "pure" common law and "quasi" common law, criminal procedure, evidence, statutory construction, and federal regulation. The difference between statutory construction and statutory application (which is what the "federal regulation" category is) is that construction, as I define it, is

Table 10.1. Classification of issues in 1960 and 1983 opinion sample

Issue	1960 (%) (N = 116)	1983 (%) (N = 138)
Pure common law	40.5	18.1
Diversity	15.5	5.1
Other state common law	8.6	4.3
Labor contracts	0.9	1.4
Other federal common law	15.5	7.2
Quasi common law	21.6	27.5
Antitrust	0.9	1.4
Intellectual property	3.4	2.2
Choice of law	0.0	1.4
Procedure and remedies	7.8	13.8
Jurisdiction	5.2	5.1
Constitution	2.6	3.6
Attorney fees	1.7	1.4
Criminal procedure	16.4	23.2
Evidence	3.4	4.3
Statutory construction	6.9	13.0
Federal regulation	10.3	12.3
Labor	6.0	0.0
Civil rights	0.0	1.4
Other	4.3	10.9

the search for the meaning of the statute, and application the fitting of a settled meaning to particular facts. A case involving issues of both construction and application is counted only once, under statutory construction, so that a case that involved the construction of one of the civil rights acts would appear not in the civil rights subcategory of federal regulation but under statutory construction. Of course this and other nomenclature used in Table 10.1 is not legally precise, but it is serviceable for my purposes.

"Pure" common law includes issues involving labor contracts (an area of federal common law), other cases involving federal common law, and state common law issues arising either in diversity or in other cases. "Quasi" common law includes areas where (I shall argue) the common law method is dominant: antitrust, intellectual property (patents, copyrights, and trademarks), choice of law, procedure and remedies, jurisdiction, the Constitution (apart from civil rights, which I classify separately; jurisdictional issues of constitutional stature, which are under jurisdiction; and issues of constitutional criminal procedure, which are under criminal procedure), and the allowance of attorneys' fees under any of the growing number of statutes (and, in rare cases, common law principles) that allow the winning party in a lawsuit to recover his legal expenses from the loser. The criminal procedure category includes issues raised in habeas corpus and other collateral attacks on conviction, state or federal, as well as direct appeals from federal criminal convictions. The federal regulation category comprises noncontract issues arising under the federal labor laws; civil rights enforcement, whether statutory or constitutional; and a large catch-all category that includes social security disability, trucking and railroad regulation, truth in lending, freedom of information, and many others.

I shall discuss these categories in some detail; but first I want to make some observations about the figures in Table 10.1. To begin with, they should be taken with a grain of salt: the sample is too small to be reliable with respect to the finer categories, and there are evident anomalies that must be due to sample size, such as the decline in the number of opinions dealing with attorneys' fees. But the trends in the larger categories seem pretty reliable, or at least consistent with one's casual impressions. The table shows a big drop since 1960 in the fraction of "pure" common law issues being decided by signed, published opinions in the courts of appeals; and although this drop has been offset to some extent by a growth in the fraction of issues in the "quasi" common law category, nevertheless the overall fraction of common law issues has fallen from 62.1 to 45.6 percent. The criminal procedure category has increased its share of issues markedly, as has statutory construction.

Since people often are more sensitive to changes than to absolute levels, Table 10.1 should help to explain why so many observers think the federal courts are dominated by statutory questions. It is not true. These courts are still—if one bears in mind that evidence is a field basically of common law (I shall explain in due course why I have nonetheless listed it separately) and criminal procedure largely so— predominantly common law courts. But they are less so than they were in 1960, and they are more concerned with statutory questions now than they were then—though many readers will be surprised at the degree to which the courts of appeals remain common law courts and at the relatively small (though vitally important) role that statutory construction plays in their work, as evidenced by their most important work product, the signed and published majority opinion.

QUALITATIVE ANALYSIS

I want now to defend my categorization of particular issue areas as common law. I expect relatively little quarrel with the subcategories in "pure" common law. Issues of state common law are quintessentially common law issues, and it makes no difference whether they arise under the diversity jurisdiction or under the many other sources of federal jurisdiction to decide issues of state law—such as pendent and ancillary jurisdiction, or jurisdiction over federal statutes that incorporate state law expressly or by implication, such as the Bankruptcy Act, the Federal Tort Claims Act, and the Internal Revenue Code. For example, since under the Social Security Act certain entitlements may depend on whether a child is "legitimate," enforcement of the act may require a federal court to decide an issue of state law—the meaning of legitimacy; and if under the law of the state in question this is an issue of common law rather than statutory law, it would be placed in the second common law subcategory. Under the regime of *Board of Regents v. Roth*,[4] even constitutional cases sometimes depend on an interpretation of state common law: for example, whether an interest is "property," in which case the state cannot (without violating the Fourteenth Amendment) deprive a person of it without giving him due process of law.

The only quarrel I expect with regard to my classifying state common

4. 408 U.S. 564 (1972).

law issues under federal judge-made law is over the significance of federal judicial decisions on these issues after the *Erie* decision. As I noted in Chapter 5, despite colorful talk about the federal judge's role in diversity cases (or any other case in which the critical issue is one of state law) as having been reduced by *Erie* to that of a ventriloquist's dummy, federal diversity decisions continue to have substantial precedential significance. Because of the great deference that the federal courts of appeals pay not only to district court fact-finding but also to district court decisions on matters of state law, a diversity case, if appealed at all on substantive grounds, is unlikely to be decided by a signed, published opinion unless it raises an issue of some novelty—that is, an issue that cannot be resolved by mechanical extrapolation from existing precedents. In such cases the judge must be as creative as an intermediate state appellate judge would be if called upon to decide the same issue.[5]

My next category, federal common law,[6] departs from conventional usage, which confines the term to the small number of fields in which the Supreme Court has used the term to describe the creation of federal law *ex nihilo*, as it were. The principal examples are admiralty cases, over which Congress has given the federal courts jurisdiction but no guidelines as to the substantive principles that the courts should apply, thus inviting the courts to continue applying and to develop further the judge-made law of admiralty; suits involving federal government contracts; and suits to enforce collective bargaining contracts—the grant of federal jurisdiction in section 301 of the Taft-Hartley Act[7] having been construed by the Supreme Court in the *Lincoln Mills* case[8] as a directive to the federal courts to create a common law of collective bargaining contracts. The federal labor contract cases that I have placed in a separate subcategory within the overall common law category are section 301 cases.

The conventional areas of federal common law do not begin to exhaust a functional definition of this category. For example, the federal courts have created a "duty of fair representation," the violation of

5. Or almost as creative: an intermediate appellate court is freer to disregard the view of another intermediate appellate court of the same state than a federal diversity court would be, unless there is disagreement among the state's intermediate appellate courts.

6. On which see the interesting recent treatment in Thomas W. Merrill, "The Common Law Powers of Federal Courts" (unpublished, n.d., Northwestern University Law School).

7. 29 U.S.C. § 185.

8. Textile Workers Union v. Lincoln Mills, 353 U.S. 448 (1957), discussed briefly in Chapter 6.

which is a tort for which a worker can get damages from a union in federal court.[9] The ultimate basis of the duty is statutory, but its contours and its damage remedy are judge-created. It illustrates the growing federal common law of torts, as do tort suits against federal officers and tort suits brought under 42 U.S.C. § 1983 against state officers. Suppose a policeman beats up a citizen, who sues under section 1983, citing *Monroe v. Pape*[10] as precedent. Such suits are extremely common. Most of the issues raised in them are conventional tort issues—causation, damages, immunity, self-defense, and so on. Or consider the SEC's Rule 10b-5, which has been held to create a private right of action for damages.[11] In most applications Rule 10b-5 is little more than the source of authority for bringing a fraud case in federal court; in deciding such questions as whether *scienter* (knowledge that the representation is false) is necessary in these suits, the federal courts are deciding common law questions with no guidance from any legislative or administrative authority.

Nor is the domain of federal common law exhausted by damage suits. Federal labor law distinguishes between employees and independent contractors for many purposes, and in deciding whether a particular individual is one or another, the federal courts apply common law principles. Consent decrees are interpreted much like contracts,[12] and the law applied is a special federal common law of contracts. And so forth.

Several of the cases in my federal common law category involve judge-made concepts of substantive criminal law, such as the meaning of and requirements for proving conspiracy. These cases are no less genuine examples of federal common law than admiralty cases. Conspiracy is one of many important doctrines of the English common law of crimes that have been incorporated into federal criminal law;[13] the insanity defense is another. If the issue in a criminal case, though substantive, is not a common law issue, it is classified elsewhere in Table 10.1: under either statutory construction or federal regulation.

I turn now to what I call "quasi" common law fields. Some of these are common law fields in the lawyer's sense and some are not, but all have in common that they are areas that are dominated by judge-made law *and* that appear, like my "pure" common law fields (but less clearly) to require the type of balancing of utilitarian values, of benefits

---

9. See, for example, Vaca v. Sipes, 386 U.S. 171 (1967).
10. 365 U.S. 167 (1961).
11. As reaffirmed recently in Herman & MacLean v. Huddleston, 103 S. Ct. 683 (1983).
12. See, for example, White v. Roughton, 689 F.2d 118 (7th Cir. 1982).
13. It is also a civil doctrine, for example in antitrust cases.

COMMON LAW ADJUDICATION 301

and costs, that makes a field of law economic at its core. It should thus be clear that I associate the term "common law" not merely with judge-created law but with law that is dominated by utilitarian, or in economic terms efficiency-maximizing, values.

To classify antitrust as a field of common law is, at one level, easily defended by pointing out that although there are a number of federal antitrust statutes, all but the Robinson-Patman Act, which is not much enforced these days, have an elusive generality. Their key terms, such as "restrain trade"[14] or "substantially to lessen competition,"[15] invite the courts to impose meaning on a statute realistically viewed as a grant of rule-making authority to the courts.[16] But at another level the inclusion of antitrust may seem simply to demonstrate the fatuity of my enterprise of associating federal common law with economic efficiency. For is it not the teaching of an extensive literature—to which I, among many others, have contributed[17]—that the courts, in interpreting the antitrust statutes, have misused economic principles to produce a body of doctrine fairly riddled with economic fallacies?

A complete answer to this question would carry me too far afield, and I will content myself with a brief sketch of the history and criticisms of antitrust law. As is well known, economists in the nineteenth century were largely oblivious to the problem of monopoly. But by the time of the enactment of the Sherman Act, the first federal antitrust statute, in 1890, the common law had taken two big steps toward a rational law of monopoly. First, it had made cartel agreements unenforceable,[18] thereby exposing cartels to the ravages of free-riding by members who realize they can increase their profits by covertly selling more than their quota at a shade below the cartel price. Even today there are economists who believe that simply denying cartel agreements enforceability would be enough to limit the cartel problem to manageable proportions.[19] Second, the common law refused to regard competition itself as a tort,[20] even though the act of setting up in competition with an existing seller—desiring to take sales away from him

14. Sherman Act, § 1, 15 U.S.C. § 1.

15. Clayton Act, §§ 2, 3, 7, 15 U.S.C. §§ 13, 14, 19.

16. This makes the Supreme Court's disclaimer, in Texas Industries, Inc. v. Radcliffe Materials, Inc., 451 U.S. 630 (1981), of a common law power to create antitrust remedies hard to understand.

17. See, for example, Richard A. Posner, *Antitrust Law: An Economic Perspective* (1976).

18. See, for example, Craft v. McConoughy, 79 Ill. 346 (1875).

19. See, for example, Dominick T. Armentano, *Antitrust and Monopoly: Anatomy of a Policy Failure*, chap. 5 (1982); Yale Brozen, *Concentration, Mergers, and Public Policy*, chap. 6 (1982); Donald Dewey, "Information, Entry, and Welfare: The Case for Collusion," 69 *Am. Econ. Rev.* 587 (1979).

20. See Keeble v. Hickeringill, 11 East. 574, 103 Eng. Rep. 1127 (K.B. 1706 or 1707).

and knowing that this would be the result of competing with him—could readily have been analogized to such intentional torts as interference with contract (indeed, could have been thought an instance of that tort). The common law was also skeptical about arguments that some forms of competition should be forbidden because they were "unfair," such as predatory pricing.[21] In this regard the common law judges showed an undeniable prescience.

Against this background the principal significance of the Sherman Act was to make cartel agreements, and mergers to monopoly designed to overcome the free-riding problem created by unenforceable cartel agreements, illegal (that is, not just not enforceable, but punishable) and thus strengthen the existing anti-cartel policy of the common law. Later statutes went beyond the limits of an economically justifiable monopoly policy, but one can view the most important of the later statutes, the Celler-Kefauver Antimerger Act of 1950,[22] as a supplement to the anti-cartel policy of the Sherman Act; for mergers between competing firms, short of monopoly, can facilitate cartel pricing in forms difficult to detect and punish directly under the Sherman Act.

A policy of limiting cartelization and mergers that facilitate cartel pricing can hardly be regarded as an affront to economic analysis; and despite all the criticisms that have been leveled against antitrust decisions over the years, this policy has always dominated antitrust enforcement, particularly public enforcement. Moreover, most of the decisions that are sharply criticized from an economic standpoint come from the Supreme Court during the chief justiceship of Earl Warren. Because district court decisions in government antitrust cases were appealable as of right directly to the Supreme Court by either party during this entire period,[23] and because most significant antitrust cases were government rather than private cases, antitrust policy at the appellate level (the level at which most common law is fashioned) was determined by a handful of judges, usually reversing one another and often disagreeing among themselves. Policy so determined is unlikely to be very stable.

Since the repeal (in 1974) of the automatic right of direct appeal to the Supreme Court in government antitrust cases, the Court has played a smaller role in the formulation of judicial antitrust policy. Power has become more diffused, and there has been a movement toward an antitrust policy influenced more than in the previous era by efficiency considerations. This movement has been accelerated by the Supreme

21. See Mogul v. McGregor, 23 Q.B.D. 598 (1889), aff'd, [1892] A.C. 25.
22. Amending section 7 of the Clayton Act, 15 U.S.C. § 18.
23. See 15 U.S.C. § 29.

Court's recent insistence, on the relatively infrequent occasions when it decides antitrust cases these days, that the policy of the antitrust laws is one of promoting economic welfare.[24] With this as their guiding principle, the lower federal courts are now steering antitrust policy by the lights of economic efficiency. Whatever may once have been true—and I have suggested that the history is less dismal than the antitrust specialists, including myself, are wont to make out—it is a fair statement today that antitrust law is a field in which federal judges not only exercise a broad common-law type of discretion but have been told by their judicial superiors to guide the exercise of that discretion by economic principles.[25]

Although the statutes in the intellectual property field are more detailed than the antitrust statutes, key concepts in the law of intellectual property such as originality, obviousness, fair use, and potential for confusion require considerable judicial discretion in formulation and application, and that discretion is generally guided by a more or less conscious concern with efficiency. The accepted goal of the patent, copyright, and trademark laws is to create property rights in intangibles—productive ideas, works of art and entertainment, identifying names—so that people will have the proper incentives to invest in creating those intangibles. This is an economic goal, elaborated in an extensive scholarly literature.[26] In fairness it should be noted that the performance of Congress in these areas has often been more impressive from an economic standpoint than that of the courts, particularly in regard to the problem of the copyright liability of cable television systems. The Supreme Court's decisions in *Fortnightly Corp. v. United Artists Television, Inc.*[27] and *Teleprompter Corp. v. CBS, Inc.*[28] interpreted the Copyright Act of 1909 as not protecting the owner of a copyrighted television program against a cable television system that retransmitted the program without his consent. Congress responded in the Copyright Act of 1976 by setting up an elaborate system of compulsory licensing designed to give the copyright owners some return from cable television carriage of their programs.[29] This system represents an effort to

24. See, for example, Reiter v. Sonotone Corp., 442 U.S. 330, 342–344 (1979).

25. This, of course, need not be true in deciding issues of antitrust immunity, which I classify under regulation rather than antitrust.

26. A good entry to this literature is through Professor Edmund Kitch's essays. See "Graham v. John Deere Co.: New Standards for Patents," 1966 *Sup. Ct. Rev.* 293; "The Nature and Function of the Patent System," 20 *J. Law & Econ.* 265 (1977); "The Law and Economics of Rights in Valuable Information," 9 *J. Legal Stud.* 683 (1980).

27. 392 U.S. 390 (1968).

28. 415 U.S. 394 (1974).

29. 17 U.S.C. § 111.

close a loophole in the scheme of property rights for television pro-
gramming created by the Supreme Court's interpretations of the 1909
act—interpretations that could easily have gone the other way, since
cable television was totally beyond the contemplation of the framers of
that act. This is a good example of legislative intervention to put the
courts back on the efficiency track.

Choice of law, which I interpret broadly to cover such issues as jurisdiction over nonresidents ("personal jurisdiction") and the choice between federal and state common law as the rule of decision, is a field
very largely of judge-made law, and thus a common law field in my terminology. I treat it separately because there has been so little economic
analysis of it that a simple assertion that it is a field in which we can
expect the judges to be guided by economic considerations, as seems
plausible in the "pure" common law fields, would lack much credibility. My first illustration is the branch of due process analysis of
personal jurisdiction that descends from *International Shoe Co. v. Washington*,[30] where the Supreme Court indicated that the main question in
deciding whether a state could, without violating the due process clause
of the Fourteenth Amendment, assert jurisdiction over a nonresident
was the reasonableness of allowing the litigation to proceed in that
state. The factors bearing on reasonableness under this analysis resemble those used in applying the doctrine of *forum non conveniens*, which
prescribes an explicit balancing of the costs and benefits of alternative
forums for the litigation. But as later cases make clear,[31] there is more to
the economic calculus of personal jurisdiction than the relative costs of
alternative forums; there is also the notion that a state should not be allowed to hail a nonresident before its courts unless the existence of the
state and the services it provides can be said to confer a significant benefit on the nonresident to balance the cost of exposure to suit in a state
other than his own. If the nonresident carries on business in the state,
this normally is enough. But suppose the nonresident, a dealer in state
X, sells an automobile to a resident of X, and the resident has an accident in state Y and tries to sue the dealer there on a theory of breach of
warranty. The dealer derives some benefit from the existence of state Y
and the fact that it has roads and road services and so forth, because the
demand for cars by residents of X will be greater the more places they
can drive their cars. But these benefits are too tenuous to allow the suit
to be maintained in Y, consistent with the requirements of due process
(*Woodson*).

30. 326 U.S. 310 (1945).
31. Notably World-Wide Volkswagen Corp. v. Woodson, 444 U.S. 286 (1980).

Consider now the more conventional choice-of-law issue that arises when, for example, two nonresidents are involved in an accident in a state and the question is whether the law applied should be the law of that state or the law of the state (or states) in which the parties are domiciled. William Baxter, the former head of the Antitrust Division of the Department of Justice, wrote a paper many years ago on choice of law that proposed an approach based on what he called the "comparative impairment" principle: "to subordinate, in the particular case, the external objective of the state whose internal objective will be least impaired in general scope and impact by subordination in cases like the one at hand."[32] An "internal" objective is an objective relating to the behavior of residents; an "external" objective is one relating to the behavior of nonresidents. Suppose a resident of state Y injures a resident of X while driving in X, and the question is whether liability should be determined by the law of X or of Y. Baxter points out that X has an interest in regulating the safety of driving on its highways for the benefit of its residents, and that both X and Y have interests in protecting their respective residents from the wealth loss caused either by the accident itself or by the judgment in a tort suit arising from the accident. But, Baxter argues, these "loss-distribution factors" cancel out, since X will benefit from one outcome and Y equally from the opposite outcome, leaving only the regulatory interest as a basis for differentiating the interests of the two states in the rule of decision; and the only regulatory interest is that of X, since the accident occurred in X and the victim is a resident of X.[33] The California courts have adopted Baxter's approach,[34] and there is support for it elsewhere.[35]

I am not fully persuaded by Baxter's analysis. It depends critically on the claim that only state X has a regulatory interest—the distributional interests of X and Y being, as Baxter says, a wash. But X's interest in protecting its residents from the danger of careless driving is balanced by Y's interest in its residents' not having to drive too slowly, in X or elsewhere, since lost time is a cost. However, whether the economic analysis in a 20-year-old article is correct is not the point. The point is that choice of law invites economic analysis, and I believe receives it from the courts in the usual implicit way, and from the courts' critics as well. In particular, information costs receive great attention; the criticism of the modern trend away from mechanical choice-of-law rules is that

32. William F. Baxter, "Choice of Law and the Federal System," 16 *Stan. L. Rev.* 1, 18 (1963).
33. See *id.* at 12–14.
34. See Offshore Rental Co. v. Continental Oil Co., 22 Cal. 2d 157, 583 P.2d 721 (1978).
35. See Johnson v. Johnson, 107 N.H. 30, 32, 216 A.2d 781, 783 (1966).

they make it difficult for people contemplating activity in another state to know what laws they have to comply with, and their ignorance reduces the deterrent effect of all states' laws. A competing consideration, however, is comparative regulatory advantage. In an accident case, the tort law of the state where the accident occurred is more likely than any other state's tort law to be tailored to the conditions of safety prevailing in that state. This is an argument for applying that state's tort law to most issues of liability, as continues to be done. On the other hand, if the issues involve capacity (for example, the age at which a person may make a binding contract), the state of domicile may have the comparative regulatory advantage. And if the issue is procedure the forum state may have the advantage. To illustrate, if the length of the pertinent statute of limitations of the forum state is based on a judgment about the capacity of judges and jurors in the state to deal competently with stale evidence, that statute should (other things being equal) be applied to the case. But if the state where the accident occurred has a shorter statute of limitations, intended to free people conducting business in the state from the uncertainties of liability based on acts that happened long ago, the forum state may decide, and properly so, to apply that statute instead of its own.

The tendency in the modern law is to make the selection of the state whose law is to be applied turn on an analysis of the relative concern or "interest" of the state in particular issues, as in my examples, but with some unknown increase in information costs, compared to the old rule whereby all issues of liability in a tort case were decided according to the law of the state where the tort took place. In addition, the uncertainties of "interest analysis" often lead the forum state almost by default to apply its own law regardless of comparative regulatory advantage. This tendency results in forum shopping and in turn increases information costs—a tendency held in check mainly by the limitations imposed by the due process clause on getting jurisdiction over nonresidents. All of this shows the (economic) wisdom of the Supreme Court's holding in *Klaxon v. Stentor Elec. Mfg. Co.*[36] that a federal court in a diversity case must apply the conflict-of-law rules of the forum state. If the federal courts had their own conflict rules for diversity cases, the incentive to engage in a type of forum shopping—electing to bring a diversity case in a federal court rather than in a state court in the same state—that could not be controlled by the due process limitations on suing in remote forums would be greatly increased, with a resulting rise in information costs.

36. 313 U.S. 487, 496–497 (1941).

Although the situation in modern conflicts law is not satisfactory, it seems that the concepts the courts are struggling with are at bottom economic, or—what amounts to the same thing—can be formulated in economic terms that are not vacuous. The basic trade-off, as I have suggested, is between the costs of information (of which the major cost in this context is a reduction in the deterrent effect of the law) that are created by uncertainty as to which state's law will govern a particular dispute, and the costs of applying to the dispute the law of a state that does not have the comparative advantage in resolving the dispute most efficiently.

This discussion is, of course, a most superficial and incomplete introduction to a field that has with one notable exception (Baxter's article) thus far escaped the attention of economic analysts of law. I have merely tried to suggest that choice of law is as natural a field of the common law to subject to economic analysis as torts, contracts, property, or any other fields that economic analysts have explored.

The next and largest subcategory of what I call "quasi" common law is procedure (including remedies) in civil cases—the overall field of which choice in law is one part. Unlike choice of law, a fairly pure common law field, federal jurisdiction is conferred by the Constitution and by statute; but most of the distinctive doctrines of federal jurisdiction—abstention in its several forms, the well-pleaded-complaint rule, the requirement of "complete" diversity, pendent and ancillary jurisdiction, and so forth—are judge-made.[37] Federal procedure is largely prescribed by rules—but rules drafted under the supervision of, and adopted by, judges (the Supreme Court justices); and important areas of federal procedural law, notably res judicata and related doctrines, are judge-made in the usual common law fashion.[38] There is scholarly support for regarding issues of procedure as being economic in character and being treated as such by federal judges, whether they are interpreting the Federal Rules of Civil Procedure or applying explicitly common law procedure doctrines;[39] and we had a taste of the economic approach to federal jurisdiction in Chapter 6. I believe that a large proportion of decisions in matters of jurisdiction and procedure are (or can be explained as) attempts to minimize the sum of two types of cost: the cost of an erroneous decision and the administrative cost (to the parties,

37. All discussed very lucidly and competently in Charles Alan Wright, *Handbook of the Law of Federal Courts* (4th ed. 1983).

38. Except that 28 U.S.C. § 1738 requires federal courts to give state court judgments at least as much res judicata and collateral estoppel effect as the state itself would in its own courts.

39. See, for example, Posner, supra note 1, chap. 21.

and to the judicial system) of decision. The two types of cost actually overlap to a considerable degree, though it is analytically convenient to treat them separately. The principal administrative cost that concerns federal courts dealing with jurisdictional and procedural issues is the degradation in their own performance—the first cost writ large—from having to entertain too many cases. This is the concern underlying the frequent references in judicial opinions to considerations of "judicial economy." It would not be a serious concern if the productive capacity of the federal courts could easily be expanded—if in other words the supply of judicial resources were highly elastic. But as stressed throughout this book, the opposite is surely true today.

Consider the question whether a finding of fact should have collateral estoppel effect when the party sought to be estopped could not get appellate review of the finding. (Maybe the decision in which the finding was made had an alternative ground to which the finding was unrelated and on which the appellate court affirmed—or might have affirmed, had the decision been appealed, which it may not have been precisely because the alternative ground was unassailable.)[40] The issue can easily be cast in an economic mold. The cost of giving a finding collateral estoppel effect is that the finding may have been erroneous. This is always a possibility, but it is greater when there has been no opportunity for appellate review. But given the limited scope of appellate review of findings of fact, perhaps the additional probability and hence cost of error that nonappealability creates is slight. The benefit of giving the finding collateral estoppel effect is clear enough: it saves the judicial system and the parties the time and other costs of having to establish the fact anew. But there is an offset that must be considered: giving the finding collateral estoppel effect will increase the incentive to appeal the decision in which the finding was made and will thus create a judicial diseconomy, though at the appellate rather than the trial level. I do not want to add up the costs and benefits; I just want to suggest that the issue is economic whatever the judicial vocabulary in which it is discussed.

Consider now an example from the law of federal jurisdiction. A brings a suit in state court against B. B then brings a suit in federal court against A arising out of the same events (maybe A sued B for unfair competition, and B sues A for theft of trade secrets), basing federal jurisdiction on diversity of citizenship. A moves the federal court to stay B's action until A's suit against B runs its course in state court.

---

40. See Jo Desha Lucas, "The Direct and Collateral Estoppel Effects of Alternative Holdings," 50 U. Chi. L. Rev. 701 (1983).

What should the district court do?[41] Again I contend that the question can fruitfully be formulated in economic terms. Staying the federal suit will promote judicial economy by avoiding a second suit, since principles of res judicata and collateral estoppel will prevent the federal court from relitigating issues decided in the state suit if that suit goes to final judgment before the stay is lifted and the federal suit resumes. But the stay may increase the risk of legal error. The diversity jurisdiction is premised (however dubiously) on a fear that state courts will be prejudiced against nonresident litigants. Although this fear may today be largely groundless and the diversity jurisdiction a costly anachronism, a federal judge is not free to question the premise of a constitutionally valid statute; he must decide diversity cases as if consigning a nonresident to suit in a state court involved a risk of prejudice and therefore a higher expected error cost than if the suit were tried in federal court. The federal judge in my example is therefore forced to trade off a judicial diseconomy against an expected error cost. This is usually very difficult to do, although in some cases it will be easy. Suppose B could have removed A's state court suit to federal court. If he had done this, he would have been completely protected, at no inconvenience, against the assumed higher probability of error in state court yet have avoided a duplication of lawsuits. In such a case A should get his stay.

A recurrent issue of federal jurisdiction is whether judicial review of an administrative agency's decision may be sought in a federal district court in the first instance or must be sought directly in a federal court of appeals.[42] The former route involves the judicial diseconomy of having two courts—the district court and then the court of appeals, to which the losing party can always appeal the district court's determination—decide the same issue. Although the probability of error is reduced by having an additional layer of judicial review, this gain must be compared with the loss from increasing the number of judicial proceedings. One could imagine using the following formula to guide decision: the higher the rate of appeal from the district court to the court of appeals, the longer the time that the court of appeals takes to dispose of cases, the more layers of review provided within the administrative agency itself, and the more complete the administrative record, the weaker is the case for channeling judicial review into the district court in the first in-

41. See, for example, Evans Transport. Co. v. Scullin Steel Co., 693 F.2d 715 (7th Cir. 1982); Microsoftware Computer Systems, Inc. v. Ontel Corp., 686 F.2d 531 (7th Cir. 1982).

42. This was touched on in Chapter 8. See the thorough analysis in David P. Currie and Frank I. Goodman, "Judicial Review of Federal Administrative Action: Quest for the Optimum Forum," 75 *Colum. L. Rev.* 1 (1975).

stance. These factors either increase the judicial diseconomy of the two-court route or lessen the benefit of the route in reducing the risk of error. The obverse of each factor increases the attractiveness of the route: for example, if the administrative record is incomplete, this suggests that the district court's fact-finding competence, which is superior to that of the court of appeals, could usefully be employed in the judicial review process. Or if very few cases decided by the district court on review of the particular agency's action are appealed to the court of appeals, the costs of duplicative judicial effort from having two layers of judicial review will be small.

Jurisdictional concepts such as standing and ripeness also lend themselves to economic analysis. Since the literature already contains an economic analysis of standing,[43] I shall confine my remarks to ripeness. The decision as to whether some action—say the decision of an administrative agency—is ripe for judicial review can again be broken down into a comparison of error costs and administrative costs. If an issue is unripe in the sense of unfocused, this implies that an immediate adjudication will have a higher than normal probability of error. If it is unripe in the further sense that its consequences are as yet uncertain, immediate review will also involve a judicial diseconomy (administrative cost), for if the party who was seeking judicial review had waited for the administrative agency to clarify or reconsider its action he might have discovered that the harm he anticipated was not going to materialize after all, and the costs of judicial review would be avoided entirely. Against the costs of immediate review must be weighed the costs to the party seeking that review of whatever irrevocable harm he will suffer by waiting, discounted by the probability that the action of which he is complaining really is erroneous. Although the courts do not put these considerations into an explicitly economic formula, I think my analysis captures the essence of what they are doing.

Also in my "quasi" common law category are cases under the Constitution, other than those dealing with civil rights, criminal procedure, or jurisdiction, which are classified elsewhere. With these exceptions modern constitutional law is, strange to say, dominated by economic issues. This is plain enough when the case involves the just-compensation clause of the Fifth Amendment or the impairment-of-contracts clause, the commerce clause, or equal-protection "rationality review"; but it is scarcely less obvious when it involves "procedural" due process or freedom of speech. The first category is controlled by the Su-

---

43. See Kenneth E. Scott, "Standing in the Supreme Court—A Functional Analysis," 86 *Harv. L. Rev.* 645, 670–683 (1973).

preme Court's decision in *Mathews v. Eldridge*,[44] which adopted virtually an explicit economic test to determine how many procedural safeguards, and when, must be provided to someone whom the government wants to deprive or has deprived of a property right. The second category involves the interpretation of a constitutional provision that, as interpreted by the courts, is designed to protect a free market in a particular commodity—ideas—and that can be analyzed by the same tools that economists use to analyze conventional markets.[45] All but one of the eight constitutional cases in my sample involved one of the issue types I have mentioned.

The final subcategory in what I call "quasi" common law comprises the growing number of cases (though the growth is not revealed in my sample) in which courts are called upon to admeasure attorney fees under a statute or (rarely) common law principle allowing the prevailing party to get reimbursement of his attorney fees from the losing party.[46] The courts in these cases are engaged in a valuation process similar to the computation of damages in tort cases, or of rewards to salvors in admiralty cases,[47] that can reasonably be described as trying to put a value on a hypothetical market transaction. For the court is asked to determine not the actual, but the reasonable, attorney fee—that is, the hypothetical free-market price of the services in question.

The next major category in Table 10.1 is criminal procedure. Most issues litigated at the appellate level in criminal matters (broadly defined as in previous chapters to include both prisoners' collateral attacks on conviction and prisoner civil rights suits complaining that the conditions of their confinement constitute cruel and unusual punishment) are procedural (or evidentiary, a separate category in my table); substantive issues, such as the meaning of conspiracy, crop up sometimes but are classified elsewhere in the table.

I have not classified criminal procedure as a common law category—though not because the Bill of Rights contains some rather specific provisions on criminal procedure and thus reduces the scope for judge-made law. Most of the modern law on federal criminal procedure (including in the term the federal constitutional limitations on state criminal procedure) can be referred back to the Bill of Rights only indirectly, being in fact a product of free interpretation. This is especially

44. 424 U.S. 319 (1976).

45. See, for example, Posner, supra note 1, chap. 28.

46. See, for example, Ruckelshaus v. Sierra Club, 103 S. Ct. 3274 (1983).

47. On which see William M. Landes and Richard A. Posner, "Salvors, Finders, Good Samaritans, and Other Rescuers: An Economic Study of Law and Altruism," 7 *J. Legal Stud.* 83, 100–105 (1978).

clear with respect to the application of provisions of the Bill of Rights to the states—a matter of free interpretation of the due process clause of the Fourteenth Amendment. Moreover, the criminal procedure provisions of the Bill of Rights were originally intended to codify what the framers understood to be common law principles—and perhaps to authorize the courts to continue to develop them in common law fashion.

The problem rather is that many of the procedural safeguards that have been accorded to criminal defendants in the name of the Bill of Rights, including such fundamental safeguards as the right not to be forced to incriminate oneself and the right not to be subjected to cruel and unusual punishment, do not have any apparent economic rationale, or to put it another way do not lend themselves to the type of utilitarian balancing that I have described as the hallmark of common law. I do not on that account question their legitimacy or importance; but their existence prevents me from placing the criminal procedure category in my common law domain. And yet many of the judge-made procedural issues that arise in criminal cases do have an implicit economic or utilitarian character. For example, although the exclusionary rule in search and seizure cases is vulnerable to serious economic criticisms, the basic principle that the Fourth Amendment vindicates—call it privacy[48]—can be given an economic interpretation; and the whole area of search and seizure is, I believe, a very fruitful and promising one for economic analysis.[49] The requirement of proof beyond a reasonable doubt, which plays so important a role in the criminal process, and the provision of counsel to indigent defendants, a frequent issue in the cases in my sample (was counsel "effective"?), also have implicit economic rationales.[50] Double jeopardy is the criminal counterpart to res judicata, which as I have already suggested can be analyzed in economic terms—as can harmless error,[51] plea bargaining,[52] and even entrapment. To explain, if police efforts to entrap induce the commission of a crime that would otherwise not occur, those efforts are wasted from a social standpoint. But if the criminal would have committed the crime

---

48. See Richard A. Posner, *The Economics of Justice*, pt. III (1981).

49. See Richard A. Posner, "Rethinking the Fourth Amendment," 1981 *Sup. Ct. Rev.* 49; Richard A. Posner, "Excessive Sanctions for Governmental Misconduct in Criminal Cases," 57 *Wash. L. Rev.* 635 (1982).

50. See Posner, supra note 1, at 433–434, 477.

51. See Posner, "Excessive Sanctions for Governmental Misconduct in Criminal Cases," supra note 49, at 643–645.

52. See Frank H. Easterbrook, "Criminal Procedure as a Market System," 12 *J. Legal Stud.* 289 (1983), arguing that not only plea bargaining but also prosecutorial and sentencing discretion can be fruitfully analyzed in economic terms.

anyway, and all the police did was to arrange that it be committed in circumstances where the criminal could be apprehended and prosecuted with minimum effort, then the entrapment is efficient. And this is the line that the law seems to draw between the permitted and the forbidden entrapment, though it does so in terms of "criminal disposition"[53] rather than the economic terms that I have used. "Criminal disposition" means in this context that the criminal would have committed the crime anyway, but in circumstances where it would have been more difficult to catch and convict him.

The categories in my sample that are dominated by noneconomic considerations are evidence, a largely common law field but one dominated by considerations that belong to psychology and epistemology rather than to economics (though economics occasionally enters in the form of concern with judicial economy), and the interpretation and application of statutes (other than statutes dealing with antitrust and intellectual property). I do not wish to disparage these areas of federal law but merely to put them beyond the pale of economic analysis—and yet not entirely. For while the program of disability benefits for social security recipients is not easily deducible from an economic model of law, when the issue in a social security disability case is whether the applicant should be disqualified because of fault, and fault can be given its usual economic meaning of failing to use resources economically, the case has an economic character. A more refined analysis than I have attempted would divide up the rather gross categories of federal statutory interpretation and application into finer categories of economically influenced and noneconomically influenced interpretations and applications.

Furthermore, there are areas of law that are fundamentally economic even though the goal of the law is not to promote economic efficiency. A good example is the National Labor Relations Act, administered by the National Labor Relations Board. The object of the law, an object that was blunted but not deflected by the Taft-Hartley amendments, is to foster unionization; and the object of unionization is to enable workers to raise their wages and improve their working conditions by bargaining collectively, with the threat of strike in the background to help drive a hard bargain. In economic terms, what is involved is an effort to cartelize the supply of labor so that the workers can obtain supracompetitive wages. Many of the rules of labor law, such as the unit-determination rules and the use of majority vote to bind all members of the

53. See, for example, United States v. Kaminski, 703 F.2d 1004 (7th Cir. 1983).

unit, can be fully understood only by recognizing the function of the rules in making it easier to cartelize labor.[54] A judge who understands the basic economics of cartels is therefore in a better position to apply the rules of labor law in accordance with their basic spirit than one who does not. Lest I be misunderstood, I add that I am not using "cartel" in any pejorative sense, but merely as a description in economic language of the means by which unions seek to better the lot of their members.

Another example is the regulation of transportation by the Interstate Commerce Commission under a statute (the Interstate Commerce Act) originally designed, it now appears, to shore up transportation cartels.[55] Recent "deregulatory" amendments have considerably altered the thrust of the act but have not made it less important for judges to understand some transportation economics if they want to do a first-rate job of judicial review of the ICC's decisions. And as for the very important functions that the federal courts perform in adjudicating securities and commodities questions, the growing economic literature on corporate finance and governance has become an aid to understanding that bench and bar can ignore only at their peril.[56]

THE FUTURE OF COMMON LAW IN FEDERAL COURTS

To recapitulate, although it is often said that we live in an age of statutes, that the federal courts are not common law courts, and that the dominant ideology today, especially among "elite" strata in the society, is collectivist and anti-economic, it seems that at least half the issues that the federal courts of appeals are being called upon to decide today are issues that—the literature on economic analysis of law suggests—are most often decided by judges as if their goal were to promote economic efficiency. Though perhaps startling at first glance, this conclusion becomes more plausible when one reflects on the lack of discipline of our legislative processes, which characteristically deliver to our judges radically unfinished statutes, and the continued if not unchal-

---

54. As I have argued in "Some Economics of Labor Law," forthcoming in *University of Chicago Law Review.*

55. See, for example, George W. Hilton, "The Consistency of the Interstate Commerce Act," 9 *J. Law & Econ.* 87 (1966); Gabriel Kolko, *Railroads and Regulation 1877–1916* (1965); Paul W. MacAvoy, *The Economic Effect of Regulation: The Trunk-Line Railroad Cartels and the Interstate Commerce Commission before 1900* (1965). This view is questioned in Thomas S. Ulen, "The Market for Regulation: The ICC from 1887 to 1920," 70 *Am. Econ. Rev. Papers and Proceedings* 306 (1980); Thomas S. Ulen, "Railroad Cartels before 1887: The Effectiveness of Private Enforcement of Collusion," 8 *Research in Econ. Hist.* 125 (1983).

56. See papers collected in Richard A. Posner and Kenneth E. Scott, *Economics of Corporation Law and Securities Regulation* (1980), for a glimpse of the literature.

lenged dominance of American law by utilitarian, pragmatic, "free enterprise," and "balancing" thinking, all of which fits comfortably with—indeed is a lay version of—economics viewed broadly as the science of rational choice.

How long all this will continue is problematic. On the one hand, there is very little indication that the Congress is about to become a disciplined legislature in the sense in which the English Parliament is disciplined—that is, a legislature under the thumb of the executive (the Cabinet). It is therefore unlikely that Congress will, in the foreseeable future, become any more capable than it is today of enacting statutes in a form in which little is left to the judicial imagination. And as the economics of law continues to develop and becomes better known to bar and bench, I expect judges increasingly to identify and exploit opportunities to use economics to guide decision making within their broad common law domain (and elsewhere, as I suggested in my brief discussion of labor and regulatory law). On the other hand, certain technological developments are making it more difficult to regulate by common law. The growth of intangible property, and our growing knowledge of subtle and long-delayed causal effects difficult to deal with by liability rules, may augur a continued shift of regulatory responsibilities from common law courts (state or federal) to specialized regulatory agencies. But on balance it seems likely that the common law, broadly defined, will continue to be an important and possibly dominant element of federal judicial decision making, at least at the court of appeals level. Whether a generalist judiciary, with our current methods of selecting and compensating federal judges, can realize the promise of economic analysis of law is a separate question.

11

Conclusions: Implications for

Legal Education and Scholarship

SOME EFFORT at summarizing the book to this point seems in order and will set the stage for a concluding discussion of the role of the law schools in improving the federal court system. Much of the book has been concerned with what I have called the caseload "crisis" of the federal courts. The word is used advisedly, and is not, I hope, exaggerated. The fact that judges and commentators were complaining about federal judicial caseloads 25 years ago, when those caseloads were but a fraction of what they have become, yet the system still has not collapsed, will make some readers think that I, too, am crying wolf. But the wolf really does seem to be at the door. It is not the number of cases alone that makes a caseload crisis; it is, as I have argued, the difficulty of expanding a unitary judicial system to absorb an ever-growing number of cases that eventually brings about a critical situation. The federal judicial system is a pyramid the apex of which—the Supreme Court—is fixed in size. The midsection of the pyramid, consisting of the federal courts of appeals, is not fixed, but it cannot be expanded, beyond a point that seems to have been reached, without either creating extremely poor working conditions at the court of appeals level (by making each such court too large to function effectively) or placing unreasonable demands on the Supreme Court. In these circumstances, the fact that district judges can be added with relatively little threat to the effective operation of the district courts (the base of the pyramid) is only a small comfort.

With the pyramid so difficult to expand, two responses might have been expected to the growing number of cases. The first would be to limit demand, both by raising filing fees and by limiting jurisdiction, the latter by, for example, increasing the minimum amount in controversy that is required to bring a diversity of citizenship suit in federal court. For reasons discussed in Chapter 4, a demand-limiting response has not been forthcoming. On the contrary, filing fees and minimum-amount-in-controversy requirements have been allowed to fall in real terms (an unsuspected consequence of the rampant inflation of the 1970s), and subsidies have been provided for some classes of federal litigants, such as federal criminal defendants. These developments have accelerated the rise in the demand for access to the federal courts that would have occurred anyway as a result of the creation of new statutory and (through interpretation) constitutional rights. The second response—what one might call the supply-side response—is, while recognizing the difficulty of expanding the pyramid directly by adding many more appellate judges (and justices), to expand the productivity of each judge by adding to the ranks of the judicial adjuncts to whom the judges can delegate a portion of their judicial responsibilities. This has been the dominant response to the caseload explosion and has resulted in a vast augmentation in the ranks of the law clerks, as well as the creation of new classes of judicial adjuncts—magistrates, staff attorneys, and externs. At the same time, there has been a modest increase in the number of judges. The combination of more judges and many more adjuncts has created (or perhaps merely aggravated) a bureaucratic style of judicial opinion writing and has contributed to a decline in the sense of institutional responsibility in our federal appellate courts. A related and also ominous supply-side response has been the great increase in the fraction of cases disposed of by unpublished opinion, and concomitantly the great reduction in the frequency and length of oral argument of appeals. This response would not have been feasible without the increase in the number of adjuncts, which has allowed a larger stream of cases per judge to be processed.

The crisis in quantity has endangered the quality of federal justice. The adaptations to the caseload crisis just discussed are threats to that quality. In addition, the same inflation that accelerated the increase in federal caseloads (by reducing, in real terms, the pecuniary barriers to the federal courts) has caused a dramatic decline in the real compensation of federal judges, even though their work has become harder and their nonjudicial activities have been restricted. The result has been increased turnover of federal judges and increased difficulty in recruiting successful lawyers into the federal judiciary—dangerous trends when it is considered that federal judicial selection is not predominantly meritocratic to begin with and that selection and retention of the best are most threatened by these trends. Moreover, even in the best of times the job of a federal judge is extremely difficult to do well, and it is becoming more difficult, quite apart from the caseload crisis, because of the advance of knowledge in technical directions that many people trained in the law find hard to follow. Another difficulty is that the jurisdiction of the federal courts is enormously varied, and it places on the judges a great burden of original thinking because the Constitution, statutes, and judicial precedents are so often nondirective (at least if one takes a "realistic" as distinct from "formalistic" view of law). The intellectual burden is perhaps greatest at the appellate level, especially in civil cases, most of which are not appealed unless there is at least some uncertainty about the correctness of the district court's or administrative agency's interpretation of the law.

Although the crisis is upon us, and although I have no single proposal for resolving it, despair would be premature. This book has put forth a number of proposals, none radical in the sense of requiring a complete rethinking of our legal and judicial systems, that together would bring the crisis under control at least for the number of years required to consider fully and adopt more radical measures. These moderate proposals—some legislative, others within the power of the courts themselves (particularly the Supreme Court) to adopt—include raising the filing fees in all federal courts, moving toward the English and Continental system whereby the winning party to a lawsuit is entitled to recover a reasonable attorney's fee from the loser, and increasing the minimum amount in controversy required in diversity cases from the present $10,000 (set back in 1958) to $35,000 or $50,000; the expansion of appellate capacity within federal administrative agencies such as the National Labor Relations Board and the Social Security Administration, and the creation of a new federal court with exclusive jurisdiction of all tax appeals from the Tax Court and from the federal district courts; a rededication by federal judges to the principles of judicial self-restraint and institutional responsibility, the latter implying such specific reforms as greater brevity in opinions, a greater willingness to impose sanctions on parties (and their lawyers) who abuse federal judicial processes, a modest shift from loose, multifactored standards to precise rules, a reduction in the number of concurring opinions, and rules of intercircuit deference by which a circuit will not reexamine a question that has been decided the same way by all the other circuits (at least three) to have considered it and will freely reexamine its own precedent after that precedent has been rejected by another circuit; a reallocation of judicial responsibilities from the federal courts to the state courts, including repeal of the federal admiralty jurisdiction over purely domestic admiralty matters, repeal of federal jurisdiction over FELA cases, renunciation of habeas corpus jurisdiction to determine the innocence of a state criminal defendant, limiting federal civil rights jurisdiction to "real" civil rights cases (as distinct from disputes over the tenure rights of public employees or the property rights of businessmen), and repealing exclusive federal jurisdiction of cases based on federal statutes such as the patent and copyright laws; and finally a greater realism about the interpretation of statutes and the Constitution and about the economic foundations of many of the common law principles that the federal courts elaborate and enforce.

Speaking of realism, I want to stress that much of what I have said in this book in both a descriptive and a hortatory vein rests on my rejection of legal formalism as a feasible philosophy for federal judges, and my concern that the persistence of formalist illusions—for example, that politics can be banished from judicial selection, that principles such as judicial activism and restraint are not political principles, that the canons of construction can be used to banish value choices from statutory interpretation, and that specialization can transform the quality and character of federal judging—is responsible for a great deal of confused thinking about the federal courts and a great many misconceived proposals for improving them. All this is not to say that logic is not important to law or that judges should not pay great attention to rules and precedents. I reject the extreme form of legal realism that reduces law to personal whim, or class bias, or political preference, or some combination of these. Most decisions are reasoned and principled. But they are not logical deductions from unquestioned premises; law is not, not often anyway, an axiomatic science.

In any evaluation of proposals to reduce the workload of the federal courts, it is necessary to consider the impact on the state courts; for most cases diverted from the federal judicial system will show up on the dockets of the state courts. Although the shift of considerable judicial business from federal to state courts would not be without cost to the latter, the shift seems on balance highly worthwhile to all. The growth of federal law in recent decades has brought about an unnecessary and unhealthy concentration of judicial (and political) power in the federal courts. We need some judicial decentralization, and because there are so many states it should be possible for each to absorb an increase in business without incurring heavy judicial diseconomies of scale.

As should be wholly obvious, none of my specific suggestions for reform is a panacea; and it is unrealistic to hope that most will be adopted within the foreseeable future. But if some of them were adopted, this would at least buy some time while more radical reforms were considered. High on the list of such reforms is abolishing or at least curtailing the jury in civil litigation. Although an argument can be made for retaining the jury in federal tort (including civil rights) cases, I can see no good argument at all for retaining it in commercial litigation—though I do not expect to convince many readers of a position merely announced, and not developed, in this book.

Finally, there are modest and achievable reforms that I have not even discussed—not because I do not advocate them but because I have little or nothing to add to what others have said about them. One of the most important of these is the use of compulsory arbitration as an adjunct to district court proceedings, to promote settlement. This device, which has been used on an experimental basis in several districts,[1] operates as follows. After a case is filed but well before trial begins, the parties are required to make brief presentations (much as they would do if they were making submissions pro and con the grant of a preliminary injunction) to a panel of experienced private practitioners, who then render a "decision" as if they were the judge (or the judge and jury, if it is a jury case) at trial. Their decision is not binding, but it gives the parties information about the likely outcome of the case if it is tried. This information is not complete, of course. But anything that makes it easier for the parties to predict the outcome of the trial will, according to the model developed in Chapter 1, make a settlement of the case more likely; and the arbitrators' decision should do so. And with settlement there will not only be no trial, but no appeal. One might ask why, if this type of arbitral process would facilitate settlement, the parties themselves would not conduct it voluntarily, without having to be forced to do so by the court. Sometimes they would; but since the benefits of settlement would accrue not only to them but also to other users of the court system, while the costs would be borne entirely by them, they will not do so to the full extent that is socially desirable. A similar argument has been used to advocate the subsidy of litigation through paying the costs of the judges, courtrooms, and so forth. But with the federal courts as choked by litigation as they are now, the time has come to subsidize settlement rather than litigation; and this can be done by forcing the litigants to attempt a resolution of their dispute through arbitration. An intermediate step would be for the government to pay for the arbitral process but not compel the use of it; and perhaps that should be attempted before we move to a compulsory system.

The caseload crisis gives this book its topicality. But I hope the reader

1. See E. Allan Lind and John E. Shepard, *Evaluation of Court-Annexed Arbitration in Three Federal District Courts* (Fed. Judic. Center, March 1981); Paul Nejelski and Andrew S. Zeldin, "Court-Annexed Arbitration in the Federal Courts: The Philadelphia Story," 42 *Md. L. Rev.* 787 (1983).

will not overlook its less topical, but possibly more interesting, aspects. The book is a venture into a rather neglected, rather unfashionable genre of legal studies, the institutional analysis. Most writing about law is writing about the rules of law as they are expressed in constitutional and statutory provisions and in judicial opinions, mostly appellate, rather than about legal institutions such as a court system. To seek to explain institutional characteristics such as the selection and compensation of judges, the pyramidal structure of a court system, the distribution of cases across subject areas and through time, the rise of judicial bureaucracy, the length of and number of citations in judicial opinions, the division of responsibilities between different courts and court systems, and the effect of the number of judges on judicial performance requires skills and methods besides those needed for the analysis of legal doctrine. Even to discuss such quintessentially legal institutional characteristics as the role of judges in interpreting statutes and precedents or the proper balance between restraint and activism in judicial decision making, characteristics to which doctrinal labels are often attached (the "canons of construction," the doctrine of "political questions," "separation of powers," and so forth), some broader perspective—informed by philosophical, economic, political-science, and perhaps other nonlegal knowledge—seems required than is the case with analyzing most substantive or procedural rules of law. From the standpoint of institutional analysis, this book has, I hope, a value that is independent of my specific suggestions for meeting the federal courts' caseload crisis. Indeed, the diagnosis may be more important than the proposed treatments, the principal elements of the diagnosis being the economic model of adjudication developed in Chapter 1 and the statistical descriptions of the federal judicial system—its structure, personnel, outputs, problems, and relations to other systems.

If I am right that the understanding and improvement of the federal courts require skills and methods that are not required for the analysis of legal doctrine, the question arises whether the law schools, as they are constituted at present, can do much to advance that understanding. This may seem a heretical question. Particularly those law schools that consider themselves national rather than regional or local schools—that is, that draw and place their students nationwide—have long placed predominant emphasis both on federal substantive law and the federal court system. The University of Chicago Law School, for example, which is typical of the national schools in this respect, offers a course on federal courts but not a course on state courts or on the courts of any particular state, such as Illinois; the school's civil-procedure courses are courses mainly in the Federal Rules of Civil Procedure; the criminal procedure taught is mainly federal criminal procedure; the constitutional law taught is federal constitutional law. In fact, after the first year of law school, which is still given over in the main to the traditional common law subjects (except that federal civil procedure is also taught), most courses offered at the school are courses in federal law.

One might expect therefore that the curriculum, and the professors' scholarly writings, which usually are related to the courses they teach, would place the subject matter of this book at the center of legal teaching and research. But one would be mistaken. The overwhelming concern of law teachers and law students at national (indeed at all) law schools is with the study of doctrines rather than institutions. A course in civil procedure is at most law schools a course about procedural law; a course in federal courts is a course about the doctrines of federal jurisdiction. Courses in particular statutes are taught—courses, that is, that explicate the law created by or under the aegis of the statute—but courses in legislation are rare. Even federal common law is not a subject taught or (with rare exceptions) written about as such, though of course particular fields of federal common law, such as admiralty and section 301 of the Taft-Hartley Act, are. Courses in judicial administration are extremely rare, which means that the causes and consequences of court delay are not taught and that judicial statistics are ignored; as for questions of judicial selection, promotion, ethics, and compensation, they would fetch a big yawn at most law schools. I know that most law students are not even aware of the enormous growth in the caseload of the federal courts over the past 25 years. Among the principal topics in this book, only the history and scope of federal jurisdiction and the meaning and merits of judicial self-restraint engage the close and fruitful attention of the law academy.

I do not doubt that legal doctrine should be the primary focus of legal education and scholarship, at national as at other law schools. And my view is still, as it has long been, that the second most important thing that law schools can do is to give the students (and, through academic scholarship, the profession and the judiciary) a better sense of the use of economics to illuminate legal doctrine; the preceding chapter provides additional support for this view. But the institutional issues that have primarily concerned me in this book, even if they do not deserve first or even second place in a law school's priorities, deserve a higher place than they occupy. The federal court system over the past 25 years has been undergoing fundamental, far-reaching, and ominous changes to which the law schools have been little better than indifferent spectators. The growing infiltration of the judicial process by the habits of the ghostwriting society, the incessant expansion in litigation (despite its rising cost), the widening gap between what juries are asked to do and what they are capable of doing, the nascent movement toward specialized federal courts, the increasingly anachronistic character of the diversity jurisdiction, the engulfment of the federal courts by prisoner petitions, the proliferation of collateral litigation over lawyers' fees, the increasing turnover of federal judges—none of these developments is receiving any systematic attention from our leading law schools.

Part of this neglect is due to the institutional barriers that confront any effort to displace doctrinal analysis by another form of teaching or scholarship within the law school. Our law schools are set up to do one thing very well, and that is the teaching and researching of legal doctrines. Doctrinal analysis is carried on in classroom instruction, in articles published in the traditional, student-edited law reviews, and in casebooks, hornbooks, and treatises. It involves the careful reading and comparison of appellate opinions with a view to identifying ambiguities, exposing inconsistencies between cases, reconciling holdings, and otherwise exercising the characteristic skills of legal analysis. It is the scholarly tradition most closely associated with the Harvard Law School, though it is on the wane there. It is embodied in such works as Austin Scott's treatise on trust law,[2] Warren Seavey's essays on tort law,[3] Thomas Reed Powell's essays on the commerce clause,[4] and the Hart and Wechsler casebook on federal jurisdiction.[5] A contemporary example is Phillip Areeda's antitrust casebook.[6] Of course, many more examples, recent and remote, could be cited.

This branch of legal education and scholarship is largely autonomous; that is, its practitioners do not have to know any other field of learning in order to contribute to it. This is not surprising when one reflects on the origins of the "case method" in the nineteenth-century formalist thinking of Dean Langdell, touched on in Chapter 7. Lang-

2. Austin W. Scott, *The Law of Trusts* (3d ed. 1967). The traditional legal treatise, of which *Scott on Trusts* is one of the classic exemplars, is on the decline. See the interesting speculations, which are quite congruent with my own thoughts on the apparent decline of doctrinal analysis, in A. W. B. Simpson, "The Rise and Fall of the Legal Treatise: Legal Principles and the Forms of Legal Literature," 48 *U. Chi. L. Rev.* 632, 676–679 (1981).

3. Warren A. Seavey, *Cogitations on Torts* (1954).

4. Examples are "Commerce, Pensions, and Codes (pts. 1–2)," 49 *Harv. L. Rev.* 1, 193 (1935); "Contemporary Commerce Clause Controversies over State Taxation (pts. 1–2)," 76 *U. Pa. L. Rev.* 773, 958 (1928); "Current Conflicts between the Commerce Clause and State Police Power, 1922–1927," 12 *Minn. L. Rev.* 321 (1928).

5. Paul M. Bator, Paul J. Mishkin, David L. Shapiro, and Herbert Wechsler, *Hart and Weschsler's The Federal Courts and the Federal System* (2d ed. 1973); Henry M. Hart, Jr., and Herbert Wechsler, *The Federal Courts and the Federal System* (1953).

6. Phillip Areeda, *Antitrust Analysis: Problems, Text, Cases* (3d ed. 1981).

dell's idea was that all the principles that a judge needed in order to decide a novel case could be found in appellate opinions (plus constitutional and statutory texts, where applicable, but these were not very important sources of law in his day), and therefore the way to learn law was to read cases and to deduce principles from them that could be used to decide new cases. This remains a valid, indeed essential, pedagogic method even though few thinking people any more are thoroughgoing formalists. But in the age of realism, doctrinal analysis can no longer be purely formal. And in fact the doctrinal analyst, in evaluating a judicial opinion, has long considered not only whether the opinion is clear, well reasoned, and consistent with the precedents, the statutes, and the Constitution, but also whether it is right in the sense of being consistent with certain premises about justice and administrative practicality. In making judgments on these points, doctrinal analysts necessarily go outside the logic of the opinion or the series of opinions that they are examining—but they do not go far. They use their study of cases, their experience as lawyers, their common sense, and their moral and political values to evaluate the practicality and justice, as well as the clarity and consistency, of existing or proposed legal rules. But they do not use the theories or methods of the social sciences or of philosophy. When Ames, in advocating tort liability in certain cases of failure to warn or rescue a stranger in distress, stated that "the law is utilitarian,"[7] he was stating what was then a commonplace of educated opinion about the relationship between law and morality; he was not expounding a philosophical concept. The same is true of Dean Prosser's statement that it is "unjust" that the rule of no contribution among joint tortfeasors lets a wrongdoer get off scot-free just because his victim chooses to levy the entire judgment against another tortfeasor.[8]

Doctrinal analysts have opinions about institutional problems, whether these involve judicial selection or compensation, the causes of caseload growth, or the relative merits of general and specialized courts; and these opinions are entitled to respectful consideration. But the training and experience of doctrinal analysts limit the contribution they can make to the solution of what are, after all, largely economic, political, and managerial problems. The problem is informational as well as methodological; judicial opinions, fascinating as they are, simply do not convey the quantitative data and institutional facts that are necessary for the analysis of legal institutions as distinct from legal rules. Indeed, the appellate process "bleaches out" many of the true

7. James Barr Ames, "Law and Morals," 22 *Harv. L. Rev.* 97, 110 (1908).
8. William L. Prosser, *Handbook of the Law of Torts* 307 (4th ed. 1971).

facts of a case, making appellate opinions a rather unreliable, and certainly an incomplete, source of factual information, as distinct from doctrine.

Even with regard to the jurisprudential aspects of the judicial process, such as the question of judicial self-restraint discussed in Chapter 7 or the questions of appellate technique discussed in Chapter 8, doctrinal analysts are handicapped by limitations of their methods. Traditional legal discourse, including that of judicial opinions, is highly rhetorical. Terms that must be defined precisely if there is to be progress in understanding the basic problems of federal adjudication—terms such as "restraint" and "activism," "holding," and "dictum"—are characteristically used as weapons of rhetorical aggression by legal scholars and judges alike. Dealing effectively with these problems of judicial process will require supplementing doctrinal analysis by a more philosophical attention to the ambiguities of normative language.

Because doctrinal analysis is, for good or ill, still largely an autonomous sphere of legal teaching and research, its pursuit within the existing framework of legal education—a framework unchanged in essentials in the century since Langdell presided over the Harvard Law School—is unproblematic; it is, as it were, the path of least resistance. Legal education aims to develop precisely those skills of legal analysis that are deployed by doctrinal analysts. And since students who get excellent grades in law school thereby demonstrate their mastery of those skills, the possession of which is the main qualification for doing doctrinal analysis (though it is only one of several qualifications for being an outstanding judge or practitioner), law school grades can be used to screen applicants for law teaching jobs. Finally, when the students who staff law reviews are those who have demonstrated by their excellent grades that they possess good skills of doctrinal analysis, they are likely to prove skillful editors of doctrinal-analytic scholarship. Thus the classroom technique, the method of recruiting teacher-scholars, and the mode of publishing the fruits of scholarship fit snugly together when the scholarly pursuit is the clarification of legal doctrine.

Doctrinal analysis can do much to improve federal judicial performance, but it cannot resolve a caseload crisis whose roots go far deeper than the inevitable, if frequent, analytical errors that judges make. For that the tools, both theoretical and empirical, of social science are indispensable. And with the maturing of the social sciences—dramatically illustrated by the growth in recent decades in the scope and sophistication of economics—the scientific study of the legal system in general and judicial institutions in particular is now feasible. But the institutional structure of legal education, geared as it is to doctrinal analysis, is an impediment. And there are other problems:

1. Law professors are not trained to do research in the social sciences; they are trained to do doctrinal analysis.

2. Law students have little interest in the scientific study of the legal system. Few aspire to be academics, and of those who do, most expect to be doctrinal analysts. The vast majority of law students are interested only in studies that will contribute directly to success as a practicing lawyer. Because a knowledge of economics is a recognized asset today in certain fields of legal practice, including many fields to which the graduates of the national law schools gravitate—such as antitrust, regulated industries, corporations, securities regulation, international trade, and banking—there is a substantial market for instruction in economics. But there is little interest in applying economics to judicial administration; and there is virtually no market for acquiring the research skills necessary to do positive (that is, descriptive and empirical) social scientific studies of the legal system. As a result, those members of a law school's faculty who want to do positive analysis of law do not receive feedback from students, find it difficult to integrate their teaching and research activities, and do not have at their disposal a corps of apprentices, corresponding to doctoral candidates in other fields, to extend their research.

3. Doctrinal analysts, who still dominate most law schools, are not in a good position to evaluate the work of social scientists or of lawyers using social science methods. This introduces a random element into the academic appointment and promotion process: some individuals who may not be good social scientists are appointed and promoted because they impress the doctrinal analysts, and others who may be good social scientists are not appointed or promoted because they do not impress the doctrinal analysts.

4. The difficulty that doctrinal analysts face in evaluating the work of social scientists comes not only from a lack of understanding of the theories and empirical tools of the social scientist, but also from a difference in outlook or culture. Despite the claims of Langdell and his disciples, doctrinal analysis is a humanistic rather than a scientific discipline. As in some of the other humanities, great emphasis is placed on writing well (sometimes on writing impressively—which is not the same thing), footnoting copiously, treating every topic exhaustively, and staying within the linguistic and conceptual parameters of the doctrines being analyzed. Soundness is valued above originality, thorough-

ness above brevity. Originality, where present, tends to be concealed. In these respects doctrinal analysis also resembles appellate legal practice; the heavy emphasis on precedent and other sources of authority in judicial decision making leads judges and advocates to stress continuity, rather than originality, in advancing novel legal theories. The writing style, the research interests, the overall approach of the doctrinal analyst are close to those of judges and brief writers, and doctrinal analysts move smoothly between academic positions and positions in private practice, in the judiciary, and in governmental legal service, as well as legislative or quasi-legislative drafting posts such as being a reporter for one of the uniform codes or for one of the American Law Institute's "Restatements" of the law. The doctrinal analyst, in short, identifies more with the community of lawyers than with the community of scholars.

The style, broadly conceived, of the social-scientific legal scholar is different. Emphasis on fine writing and copious documentation gives way to emphasis on originality of ideas and economy of expression. An article in the social sciences usually begins with an explicit statement of the article's place in the literature and of its incremental contribution to knowledge. One rarely finds such a preface in the work of legal-doctrinal analysts, originality being valued less. The social scientist is not concerned with being thought sound by judges and practicing lawyers; nor is he concerned with writing in a language they will understand or with using concepts familiar to them. He is not one of them; he is part of the scholarly rather than the legal community.

These differences in values create barriers to communication and make it difficult for the doctrinal analyst to evaluate the work of the social scientist. They also make it difficult for the social scientist to evaluate the work of the doctrinal analyst, but this is less important insofar as doctrinal analysts continue to dominate the faculties of the law schools.

5. The doctrinal analyst and the social scientist differ in the emphasis each places on scholarship relative to teaching. The greatest thrill of scholarship is the sense of having discovered something new, but it is a thrill only rarely experienced by the doctrinal analyst. He is not engaged in a search for something new but in tidying the doctrinal product of judges. His *métier* is not the discovery of new knowledge; it is the cut and parry of the classroom. Most doctrinal analysts are not highly productive as scholars by the usual standards of the social sciences, and much of their scholarly production takes the form of teaching materials. (The treatise writers are a major exception to this generalization, but treatise writing as a genre of legal scholarship seems to be in decline.) Social scientists tend to view teaching either as an adjunct to

their research or as the price they pay for being given time to do research. They are rarely heard to discuss their teaching, whereas teaching is a staple of conversation among doctrinal analysts.

The conflict between doctrinal analysts and social scientists over the relative emphasis to be placed on scholarship and teaching is a barrier to the positive analysis of law by the methods of the social sciences. The doctrinal analyst may be little impressed by, and little interested in encouraging or rewarding, the scholarly productivity of social scientists. He may instead want them to place an emphasis on teaching that they may consider destructive to their scholarly careers. But I do not want to exaggerate this conflict: because the demand by law students for instruction in the social sciences is limited, the law school may be quite willing to offer social scientists a reduced teaching load. The social scientist also escapes the burden of supervising doctoral dissertations, though, as I have suggested, this involves a loss as well as a gain. But if the social scientist appointed to a law faculty comes to share the law professors' preoccupation with teaching, his scholarly career may be seriously compromised.

6. The mode of publication of legal scholarship is unusual by the standards of most other fields of academic inquiry, and makes it difficult for social-scientific research on the legal system to flourish in law schools. When the doctrinal analyst writes an article he may circulate drafts to some colleagues, but he is unlikely to present it at workshops or seminars at his own or other universities, and he will submit the article for publication to a student-edited law review that rarely uses referees to assist it in making publication decisions or in providing authors with suggestions for improvement. Since there are literally hundreds of such journals, rejection by one—or many—is no impediment to publication. Thus there is no effective publication filter.

The pattern in other academic fields is dramatically different. Most papers are not submitted for publication until they have been presented at one or more workshops at which the author is exposed to the criticism of both peers and graduate students. The paper is then submitted to a journal that is edited by the author's peers, not by his students, and normally the editors do not make a publication decision without submitting the paper to one or more referees, who are scholars familiar with the particular subject on which the author is writing. Whether or not the paper is accepted by the journal, the referee's anonymous comments are sent to the author to help him improve it. And since there are a limited number of journals in each field, the junk is filtered out and national quality standards are imposed that facilitate the absorption and evaluation of scholarship.

The publication system in the social sciences may be superior to that in legal scholarship even for doctrinal analysis. But it is clearly suboptimal to process social-scientific studies of the legal system in the manner of conventional legal scholarship—that is, not presented at workshops, not submitted to peer-edited journals, and not refereed. The lack of competent evaluation and criticism results in the publication of social-scientific papers on law that should not be published at all, or at least that would have been improved greatly by the publication process used in academic fields other than law.

These barriers to integrating social science into the law schools would be of little importance to the subject matter of this book if the research necessary to solve the institutional problems of the federal courts could be pursued elsewhere. But it cannot be, not enough of it anyway. Although much good work is done by the Federal Judicial Center and other nonuniversity centers for research in judicial administration, experience teaches that a university environment is necessary for sustained, effective, high-quality, credible, and influential social science scholarship, with exceptions too few to encourage hope that judicial administration might be one. And if it is not done in a law school, research on the problems of the courts will not be done, in any quantity anyway, elsewhere in the university.

Despite all I have said about the barrier between law and the social sciences, economists in increasing numbers are hurdling the barrier and finding positions on law school faculties. True, some of them are treated as distinctly marginal to the enterprise of the law school, but many are influential members of the faculty. This is a welcome development, and before I began work on this book I would not have been greatly upset if no other social scientists could make it across the barrier. I now realize that political scientists have made a great contribution to the study of judicial administration in general and the organization and staffing of the federal courts in particular, and yet I know of no law school that has a political scientist as a full-time member of its faculty. This seems to me a regrettable deficiency.

Although I think that the law schools must become more hospitable to the social sciences, I also think they need better doctrinal analysis. Not only is disinterested criticism of judicial decisions an essential if incomplete check on judicial irresponsibility, and not only are important issues bearing on the caseload crisis of the federal courts doctrinal in nature, but doctrinal analysts are in a good position to spot some of the growing deficiencies of federal judicial performance as a result of caseload pressures—for example, the increasing delegation of opinion writing to law clerks. Legal scholars have done some useful work in this area, as we saw in Chapter 4, but not enough to arrest what is an evident decline in disinterested doctrinal analysis. Apart from those exotic variants of traditional legal scholarship, most notably "critical legal studies," that occupy more and more of the attention of legal scholars with little payoff in solving any of the practical problems of the legal system, doctrinal analysts seem increasingly preoccupied with advocacy of new concepts of constitutional law, to the growing exclusion of attention to the more workaday performance of the courts. Table 11.1 gives a sense of this phenomenon; the table indicates that almost 60 percent of all law review comments on federal cases are comments on Supreme Court cases. (These are student-written comments; but the students are reflecting the interests of their professors.) Now the average Supreme Court decision is indeed far more important than the average federal court of appeals decision. But is importance the only criterion of whether a decision should be analyzed in a law review? In the period in which the Supreme Court decided 281 cases, the courts of appeals must have decided about 10,000 (in signed, published opinions). Is it credible that only 3 percent of these decisions (328 out of 10,-000) were worthy of comment by law reviews? Many court of appeals cases are just as interesting analytically as the average Supreme Court case, and it is certain that court of appeals judges pay more attention to academic feedback than the lofty justices of the Supreme Court. Is not a misallocation of academic resources implied by the figures in this table?

Although the growing variety and complexity of our law ought to provide an ever-richer menu of challenges and opportunities for doctrinal analysts, a malaise afflicts this most vital branch of legal teaching and research: it fails to generate the excitement of the newer branches of legal scholarship, and many of its practitioners seem dispirited and defensive. One reason for the malaise is highly practical: it is the growing disparity in income between the teaching and the practice of the law, teaching salaries having lagged in the 1970s and 1980s just as judicial salaries have. This disparity has had its greatest impact on the doc-

Table 11.1. Law review comments on federal cases

Type of court	No. of cases	No. of law review comments
Supreme Court	281	805
Courts of appeals	328	454
District courts	89	95

Source: *Index to Legal Periodicals,* Sept. 1981–Aug. 1982.

trinal analysts because the practice of law is so close a substitute for what they do as teachers and, especially, as scholars. I do not have statistics, but it is reasonably clear that since the late 1960s, when inflation began to surge, the income of law teachers (apart from the minority who are heavily involved in consulting or part-time practice) has barely kept pace with inflation, while the growth in income of practitioners in the best law firms, which compete with the best law schools in recruiting, has exceeded the rate of inflation, although there has been a recent softening.

The divergence in the trends of overall job satisfaction has been even greater than in the trends of income. The "tenure" period at law firms has been shortening in recent decades (though very recently it has begun to lengthen); and the practice of law at the leading law firms has become more interesting, both because firms now use paralegals to do more of the drudge work and because the legal departments of corporations do an increasing amount of the routine corporate law work. Furthermore, in a number of fields the courts have been impatiently sweeping away the nice distinctions that challenge the doctrinal analyst. In tort law, for example, the state courts have been busily abolishing the doctrines of assumption of risk and last clear chance and the distinctions between a landowner's duty of care to licensees and invitees, between indemnity and contribution, and between the proprietary and governmental functions of municipalities. That most lawless body of law, federal constitutional law, has displaced large areas of tort and family law, further constricting the field for the traditional doctrinal analyst. Conflict of laws has become a field largely without rules. There seems to be a general tendency for our law to become more a matter of discretion, explicit policy, and politics and less a matter of rules and distinctively legal principles, and this tendency has made academic law less congenial to the doctrinal analyst.

Another reason for the malaise of doctrinal analysis is that some of the practitioners of the newer fields of legal scholarship do not respect doctrinal analysis. I will give two examples of this attitude. The first is from Packer and Ehrlich's 1972 report on legal education, prepared for the Carnegie Commission on Higher Education:

> We must admit, however, that [law teachers'] research output is rather slight. Legal writing has tended, until very recently, to be primarily doctrinal and to be based mainly on research in the law library. To the extent that law teachers have written, their books have tended to be treatises (often multivolume) on doctrinal subjects. Their articles, published in the 80-odd law reviews, have

been treatments of less general legal problems, again purely from a doctrinal, analytic standpoint. The reasons for this heavily focused unproductivity are manifold.[9]

The tone of disparagement is unmistakable. Law professors' research output is "rather slight" and is not redeemed by their penchant for multivolume treatises. Their writing is "purely doctrinal," and adds up to "heavily focused unproductivity."

The next example is from a talk by the dean of the Yale Law School, Harry Wellington:

> There are a dozen or so university law schools in the country that can properly claim to be more than trade schools. A trade school is an institution that views its purpose as graduating students who will pass a bar examination. Schools that are more than trade schools share this purpose, but they are centrally concerned with the advance of knowledge through teaching and research. Among the twelve or so law schools with these larger aspirations, Yale rightly is regarded as the most ambitious.
>
> This is an exciting time for academic law, perhaps the most exciting time since the end of the second World War. In the 1920s and early '30s, academic law in America was, as you know, transformed by legal realism. The realist movement established itself at Yale and Columbia and was a reaction to the excessive formalism that had beset legal thinking and that was practiced most successfully at Harvard . . .
>
> Academic lawyers today are concerned with the appropriate limits of law and with the interrelationship between procedural matters—in the large sense of that term—and substantive and distributive justice. Relative to his predecessor, today's young academic is enormously sophisticated in humanistic and social science studies. To get a grip on the limits of law, an academic must work in political philosophy; so, too, if he is interested in distributive justice. Nor can he fail to know economics, and he is delinquent if he ignores history. The demands, then, on the academic lawyer are truly prodigious. But the challenge is being met and Yale has assumed a leadership role. No one who knows can doubt this.[10]

In this passage Dean Wellington describes the advance of legal scholarship as having occurred in two stages: a first, essentially negative

9. Herbert L. Packer and Thomas Ehrlich, *New Directions in Legal Education* 32 (1972).
10. *Yale Law Report*, Winter 1978–1979, at 7–8.

stage—legal realism—when the "excessive formalism" of the Harvard Law School was discredited; and a second, constructive stage, the stage we are now in, when the academic lawyer must master every relevant branch of learning in order to meet the prodigious challenge that has been laid at his feet of understanding the limits of law and the nature of justice. The academic lawyer, or at least the academic lawyer who aspires to a status loftier than that of a teacher at a trade school, studies not procedure but "procedural matters—in the large sense of that term." The academic lawyer who makes it his business to be learned in the law and expert in parsing cases and statutes is made by Dean Wellington to seem a paltry fellow—a philistine who has shirked the more ambitious and challenging task of mastering political and moral philosophy, economics, history, and other social sciences and humanities so that he can discourse on large questions of policy and justice.

I agree that doctrinal analysis cannot provide the complete fare of a law school education or a law faculty's research output. But apart from modest advances in integrating economics into the law school curriculum and into legal scholarship, our leading law schools appear to be moving away from disinterested doctrinal analysis without being able to find anything worthwhile to put in its place. The ambitious intellectualism celebrated by Dean Wellington has had little payoff in useful scholarship.

Another factor contributing to the malaise of doctrinal analysis is the growing politicization of legal scholarship. Twenty years ago the vast majority of law professors occupied a very narrow band of the political spectrum—and a band right in the middle of it. Broad agreement on fundamental premises made many questions of legal analysis seem technical and therefore a proper subject to interest highly skilled professionals. Today a number of respectable law professors are extremely left-wing and a growing band of equally respectable law professors are extremely right-wing. Both groups disparage traditional doctrinal analysis; they want to debate fundamental premises. The doctrinal analysts find themselves increasingly trapped in a methodological and political cross-fire. It is no wonder that disinterested doctrinal analysis seems to be on the decline, but it is bad news for the federal courts and for society.

I want to close on a more constructive note by making three specific suggestions for new courses, related to the subject matter of this book, to law schools seeking to enrich their curricula. These would be courses on opinion writing, judicial administration, and legislation. At national law schools a significant fraction of the graduating students become law clerks to state and (mainly) federal judges: the current figure at the University of Chicago Law School is between 15 and 20 percent. Since most judicial opinions today are drafted in the first instance by law clerks rather than by judges (and will continue so, despite the reservations suggested in Chapter 4), it is time that some of the national law schools bowed to reality and offered a course or seminar in judicial opinion writing. Such a course would consider the audience for a judicial opinion, examine closely some models of good and bad opinions from the past, consider problems of organization and style, study the role of citations, and give the students practice in writing opinions under faculty supervision. It would be a labor-intensive course for faculty to teach, and it would rarely touch the higher peaks of intellectual excitement, but it would perform an important service for the federal and state courts and would, I am sure, be warmly welcomed by the prospective law clerks (who know who they are by the beginning of the third year of law school). It is not open to the standard objection to how-to courses in the law school curriculum: that the skill is better learned by apprenticeship. Law clerks do not have time to learn by doing; most of them are clerks only for a year, and almost none for more than two. Their on-the-job training can be very costly for society, given the prominent role that they play as writers of judicial opinions.

The course in judicial administration would deal with the sorts of issues examined in Parts I and II of this book—issues such as the demand for and supply of litigation; the sources, significance, and limitations of judicial statistics; the recruitment, compensation, and evaluation of judges; the organization of court systems, state and federal, U.S. and foreign; the causes of litigation; court delay; the history and contemporary role of the jury; arbitration and other judicial substitutes and supplements; the pricing of judicial services; delay in court; the role of specialized courts; the delegation of judicial functions to magistrates, law clerks, masters, and other judicial adjuncts; and methods of caseload forecasting. Such a course could not, of course, be taught from the conventional law school course materials, that is, from judicial opinions; nor could it be taught by a lawyer unwilling to apply the methods and concepts of social science (especially, I think, economics and statistics, but also political science, anthropology, history, and psychology) to legal institutions. But taught with imagination, it could be a worthwhile and interesting course—and not only to the handful of students who might actually be thinking of a career in judicial administration.

I do not think I will meet with much resistance either to my suggestion that a course in judicial administration would be a valuable addition to a law school's curriculum or to the general scope of such a course as just discussed. This is not to say that such a course is about to be instituted at a major law school; it is not, because the subject lacks glamor, is nondoctrinal, and requires immersion in not only unconventional but rather forbidding materials ("math block" is a real problem for many lawyers, including law professors), and because course materials, at least for the type of course I envisage, do not exist. But I do think I will meet resistance (as distinct from indifference) to my third suggestion, which is for a course in legislation. This suggestion will be thought otiose; for how can it be argued that law schools neglect to impart an understanding of legislation to their students, when so many courses—indeed a majority of courses after the first year—are courses in statutory fields?

Although many academic lawyers are experts on particular statutes—which largely means experts on what the courts have said about the particular statutes they teach—few are experts on legislation. Few study legislation as an object of systematic inquiry comparable to the common law. It has been almost fifty years since James Landis complained that academic lawyers did not study legislation in a scientific (that is, rigorous, systematic) spirit,[11] and yet we know from Chapter 9 that the situation is largely unchanged. There are countless studies, many of high distinction, of particular statutes, but they are not guided by any overall theory of legislation. No one has ever done for legislation what Holmes did for the common law.[12] Not only the economists' study of interest groups, alluded to in Chapter 9, but the enormous political-science literature on Congress and the state legislatures,[13] is unknown at the practical level of the legal profession; so is the older political-science literature on the role of interest groups in legislation.[14]

11. James M. Landis, "Statutes and the Sources of Law," in *Harvard Legal Essays* 213, 234 (Roscoe Pound ed. 1934).

12. See Oliver Wendell Holmes, Jr., *The Common Law* (1881).

13. See, for example, Stephen K. Bailey, *Congress Makes a Law: The Story behind the Employment Act of 1946* (1950); Roger H. Davidson and Walter J. Oleszek, *Congress and Its Members* (1981); Malcolm E. Jewell and Samuel C. Patterson, *The Legislative Process in the United States* (3d ed. 1977); William J. Keefe and Morris S. Ogul, *The American Legislative Process: Congress and the States* (5th ed. 1981); Kenneth Kofmehl, *Professional Staffs of Congress* (3d ed. 1977); Michael J. Malbin, *Unelected Representatives: Congressional Staff and the Future of Representative Government* (1980); Walter J. Oleszek, *Congressional Procedures and the Policy Process* (1978); Norman J. Ornstein and Shirley Elder, *Interest Groups, Lobbying and Policymaking* 155–185 (1978); Robert L. Peabody, Jeffrey M. Berry, William G. Frasure, and Jerry Goldman, *To Enact a Law: Congress and Campaign Financing* (1972); David E. Price, *Who Makes the Law? Creativity and Power of Senate Committees* (1972); Randall B. Ripley, *Congress: Process and Policy* (2d ed. 1978).

14. See, for example, Arthur F. Bentley, *The Process of Government: A Study of Social Pressure* 360–381 (1908); David B. Truman, *The Governmental Process: Political Interests and Public Opinion* 321–394 (1951).

One can get a feeling for the situation by perusing the few published law-school textbooks devoted entirely to legislation.[15] Although all of these texts have their virtues, some considerable (Professor Hetzel's book in particular has a wealth of interesting descriptive material on the operation of the legislative process), none recognizes the fundamental role of interest groups in procuring legislation, although some mention it in passing, particularly in discussion of legal regulations of lobbying;[16] one text omits statutory construction as a topic;[17] and there is little reference to the economic or political science literature on legislation.[18] Most of the books give disproportionate attention to such specialized topics as reapportionment and the regulation of campaign financing, presumably because these are areas in which cases can be found for a casebook treatment of legislation. This shows that the editors do not really conceive of legislation as a distinct subject. A casebook on commercial law makes good sense; a casebook on legislation does not.[19]

Nor is it an adequate reply that every good course in a statutory field such as commercial law, taxation, labor law, or copyright law will impart to the students, in proper law school inductive fashion, a feel for the recurrent issues and problem involving legislation in general. Most teachers of statutory fields believe they have only enough time to give the students a sense of the field's scope and texture by working through the major statutory provisions and the principal cases construing them; they do not feel they have enough time to explore with the class the process by which the legislation is enacted, the political forces that shaped it, or even the methods the courts use to interpret it, as distinct from the particular interpretations that the courts have made. Moreover, such issues are rarely dealt with in casebooks, and what is not in the casebook is unlikely to get into the course in any systematic fashion.

I shall indicate briefly what I think a course in legislation should

15. See Otto J. Hetzel, *Legislative Law and Process: Cases and Materials* (1980); Hans A. Linde, George Bunn, Fredericka Paff, and W. Lawrence Church, *Legislative and Administrative Processes* (2d ed. 1981); Frank C. Newman and Stanley S. Surrey, *Legislation: Cases and Materials* (1955); Charles B. Nutting and Reed Dickerson, *Cases and Materials on Legislation* (5th ed. 1978); Horace E. Read, John W. MacDonald, Jefferson B. Fordham, and William J. Pierce, *Materials on Legislation* (4th ed. 1981).

16. See Linde, Bunn, Paff, and Church, supra note 15, at 161–220; Read, MacDonald, Fordham, and Pierce, supra note 15, at 407–432.

17. Linde, Bunn, Paff, and Church, supra note 15.

18. Except for scattered footnote references to miscellaneous works in *id.* at 123–141 and a brief excerpt in Nutting and Dickerson, supra note 15, at 110–113, from Arthur Bentley's classic, *The Process of Government* (note 14, supra).

19. Professor L. H. LaRue of William and Mary Law School has been kind enough to let me read his very imaginative course materials, entitled Problems of Legislation, which I highly recommend to teachers of the subject.

contain, in the hope that those who have more time than I to devote to curricular innovation will carry these ideas to fruition.[20]

The Process of Legislation. Many law students are ignorant of the process by which bills in Congress become law (most do not know even the first thing about the legislative process at the state level). Many law students also do not know who writes a bill, who testifies at hearings, what a conference report is, or the difference between adding an amendment to a bill on the floor and processing a bill in the usual way through committees. It is as if, in reading judicial opinions, they did not know how a case got into an appellate court. Reluctant as law professors are to impart mere information in the classroom, I can see no escape from their doing so (not necessarily orally) in this instance.

The Empirical Study of Legislation. It is not enough simply to give students an outline of how the legislative process operates and a synoptic view of the scholarly controversy over the nature of what it produces. They should also be exposed to the results of empirical studies. Law students ought to learn what political scientists have discovered about the respective roles of congressmen and staff in drafting legislation,[21] the contribution of lobbyists and administration officials, and the time and care devoted to actual drafting, so that they can form their own judgment on whether it is realistic to suppose that legislators are aware of the methods that courts will use to interpret their work.[22] They should also learn about the frequency and feasibility of legislative overruling of judicial decisions that interpret statutes contrary to the purpose of the legislation as conceived by either the enacting Congress or a subsequent one.[23] Such knowledge is essential to understanding and evaluating the judicial rule in statutory interpretation.

Techniques of Judicial Interpretation of Statutes. The student should be introduced to the debunking literature on the canons of construction, to

---

20. This may be a forlorn hope; a recent symposium entitled "The Law Curriculum in the 1980's," 32 *J. Legal Educ.* 315 (1982), does not include legislation among areas for curricular reform. However, an even more recent symposium, "Traditional Legal Education," in the Spring 1984 issue of the *Mercer Law Review,* contains three articles on the teaching of legislation. The lead article, Robert F. Williams, "Statutory Law in Legal Education: Still Second Class after All These Years," 35 *Mercer L. Rev.* 803 (1984), contains a wealth of references on the history of the teaching of legislation in American law schools.

21. On which see Malbin, supra note 13.

22. For an informative discussion of the legislative drafting process in Congress, see Kofmehl, supra note 13, at 117–126, 189–193; Price, supra note 13. And for interesting case studies see Bailey, supra note 13; Ornstein and Elder, supra note 13, at 155–185.

23. A notable recent contribution of this rather neglected genre, referencing the earlier literature, is Beth Henschen, "Statutory Interpretations of the Supreme Court: Congressional Response," 11 *Am. Politics Q.* 441 (1983).

the positive literature on statutory construction that is worth reading, and to those masterpieces of statutory interpretation, such as Judge Learned Hand's opinion in the *Fishgold* case,[24] that the student will not encounter in the regular curriculum because they deal with statutes (such as the veterans' reemployment provision[25] construed in *Fishgold*) that are not the subject of any regular course.[26]

Researching Legislative History. Almost three years of reading briefs in cases involving statutory interpretation have convinced me that many lawyers do not research legislative history as carefully as they research case law. It may be that they do not know how. It is more difficult to research legislative history than case law, yet instruction in the former is at most law schools rudimentary. Often it is crammed into the whirlwind tour of the library that law librarians offer to beginning students, who cannot comprehend the significance of what they are being told and shown. The many sources of compiled legislative histories[27] remain largely unknown to the profession. Research into U.S. government documents in general and legislative documents in particular is a formidable subspecialty of library science,[28] and I would guess that not one lawyer in a thousand has a real proficiency in it. He will not pick it up in his law firm, and he will not learn—not well anyway—by doing. The mastery of research techniques is not as intellectually stimulating as other elements of a law school education, but library science is a recognized field of learning at first-class universities; it would not demean our law schools to adapt some of these materials for a law school course.

Of course I do not suggest that courses in opinion writing, judicial administration, and legislation will solve all the problems of the federal courts, any more than the other proposals in this book. They are limited, modest, but practical suggestions for bringing the considerable intellectual resources of the nation's law schools to bear on the problems

24. Fishgold v. Sullivan Drydock & Repair Corp., 154 F.2d 785 (2d Cir.), aff'd, 328 U.S. 275 (1946).

25. The provisions construed in *Fishgold* were part of the Selective Training and Service Act of 1940, ch. 720, § 8(b), 54 Stat. 885, 890 (expired 1947). These provisions were replaced by the Veteran's Re-employment Act, ch. 625, § 9, 62 Stat. 614 (1948) (current version at 50 U.S.C. app. § 459).

26. Another fine example of statutory interpretation that is not likely to find its way into a casebook on the statute is J. C. Penney Co. v. Commissioner, 312 F.2d 65 (2d Cir. 1962) (Friendly, J.).

27. Catalogued in Nancy P. Johnson, *Sources of Compiled Legislative Histories: A Bibliography of Government Documents, Periodical Articles, and Books, 1st Congress–94th Congress* (Am. Ass'n of Law Libraries, AALL Publ. Ser. No. 14, 1979 with 1981 inserts).

28. For a sense of this, see Joe Morehead, *Introduction to United States Public Documents* (2d ed. 1978).

of the federal courts. If I have done no more in this book, I hope I have at least convinced the reader of the gravity and urgency of these problems. I also hope that I have made some contribution to our understanding of them; but obviously much more needs to be done to put the problems of the federal courts on the path to solution. It will be sad indeed if the law schools forgo a leading role in this intellectually and practically formidable task.

Appendixes

Index

Selected Provisions of the Constitution

of the United States

Article I, section 8, provides in part that "The Congress shall have Power . . . to constitute Tribunals inferior to the supreme Court."

Article II, section 2, provides in part that "The President . . . shall nominate, and by and with the Advice and Consent of the Senate, shall appoint . . . Judges of the supreme Court, and all other officers of the United States, whose appointments are not herein otherwise provided for, and which shall be established by Law."

Article III provides in part:

Section 1. The judicial Power of the United States, shall be vested in one supreme Court, and in such inferior Courts as the Congress may from time to time ordain and establish. The Judges, both of the supreme and inferior Courts, shall hold their Offices during good Behaviour, and shall, at stated Times, receive for their Services, a Compensation, which shall not be diminished during their Continuance in Office.

Section 2. The judicial Power shall extend to all Cases, in Law and Equity, arising under this Constitution, the Laws of the United States, and Treaties made, or which shall be made, under their Authority; —to all Cases affecting Ambassadors, other public Ministers and Consuls; —to all Cases of admiralty and maritime Jurisdiction; —to Controversies between two or more States; —between a State and Citizens of another State; —between Citizens of different States, —between Citizens of the same State claiming Lands under Grants of different States, and between a State, or the Citizens thereof, and foreign States, Citizens or Subjects.

In all Cases affecting Ambassadors, other public Ministers and Consuls, and those in which a State shall be Party, the supreme Court shall have original Jurisdiction. In all the other Cases before mentioned, the supreme Court shall have appellate Jurisdiction, both as to Law and Fact, with such Exceptions, and under such Regulations as the Congress shall make.

Article VI provides in part:

This Constitution, and·the Laws of the United States which shall be made in Pursuance thereof; and all Treaties made, or which shall be made, under the Authority of the United States, shall be the supreme Law of the Land; and the Judges in every State shall be bound thereby, any Thing in the Constitution or Laws of any State to the Contrary notwithstanding.

The Senators and Representatives before mentioned, and the Members of the several State Legislatures, and all executive and judicial Officers, both of the United States and of the several States, shall be bound by Oath or Affirmation, to support this Constitution; but no religious Test shall ever be required as a Qualification to any Office or public Trust under the United States.

The Eleventh Amendment provides:

The Judicial power of the United States shall not be construed to extend to any suit in law or equity, commenced or prosecuted against one of the United States by Citizens of another State, or by Citizens or Subjects of any Foreign State.

The Fourteenth Amendment provides in part:

Section 1. All persons born or naturalized in the United States, and subject to the jurisdiction thereof, are citizens of the United States and of the State wherein they reside. No State shall make or enforce any law which shall abridge the privileges or immunities of citizens of the United States; nor shall any State deprive any person of life, liberty, or property, without due process of law; nor deny to any person within its jurisdiction the equal protection of the laws.

Supplementary Tables

Table B.1. Salaries of federal judges, current and constant (1983) dollars, 1800–1983

Year	Associate justices of the Supreme Court		Circuit judges		District judges	
	Current dollars	1983 dollars	Current dollars	1983 dollars	Current dollars	1983 dollars
1800	3,500	20,828	—	—	800–1,800	4,761–10,712
1801	3,500	21,245	—	—	—	—
1802	3,500	24,703	—	—	—	—
1803	3,500	23,606	—	—	—	—
1804	3,500	23,606	—	—	—	—
1805	3,500	23,606	—	—	—	—
1806	3,500	22,601	—	—	—	—
1807	3,500	24,142	—	—	—	—
1808	3,500	22,130	—	—	—	—
1809	3,500	22,601	—	—	—	—
1810	3,500	22,601	—	—	—	—
1811	3,500	21,245	—	—	—	—
1812	3,500	20,828	—	—	—	—
1813	3,500	18,315	—	—	—	—
1814	3,500	16,861	—	—	—	—
1815	3,500	19,314	—	—	—	—
1816	3,500	20,828	—	—	—	—
1817	3,500	22,130	—	—	—	—
1818	3,500	23,092	—	—	—	—
1819	4,500	29,690	—	—	—	—
1820	4,500	32,518	—	—	1,000–3,000	7,226–21,679

	Associate justices of the Supreme Court		Circuit judges		District judges	
Year	Current dollars	1983 dollars	Current dollars	1983 dollars	Current dollars	1983 dollars
1821	4,500	34,144	—	—	—	—
1822	4,500	34,144	—	—	—	—
1823	4,500	37,934	—	—	—	—
1824	4,500	41,386	—	—	—	—
1825	4,500	40,169	—	—	—	—
1826	4,500	40,169	—	—	—	—
1827	4,500	40,169	—	—	—	—
1828	4,500	41,386	—	—	—	—
1829	4,500	42,680	—	—	—	—
1830	4,500	42,680	—	—	—	—
1831	4,500	42,680	—	—	—	—
1832	4,500	45,525	—	—	—	—
1833	4,500	47,095	—	—	—	—
1834	4,500	45,525	—	—	—	—
1835	4,500	44,056	—	—	—	—
1836	4,500	41,386	—	—	—	—
1837	4,500	40,169	—	—	—	—
1838	4,500	42,680	—	—	—	—
1839	4,500	42,680	—	—	—	—
1840	4,500	45,525	—	—	—	—
1841	4,500	44,056	—	—	—	—
1842	4,500	47,095	—	—	—	—
1843	4,500	48,777	—	—	—	—
1844	4,500	48,777	—	—	1,000–3,500	10,839–37,938
1845	4,500	48,777	—	—	—	—
1846	4,500	50,583	—	—	—	—
1847	4,500	48,777	—	—	—	—
1848	4,500	52,529	—	—	—	—
1849	4,500	54,630	—	—	—	—
1850	4,500	54,630	—	—	—	—
1851	4,500	54,630	—	—	—	—
1852	4,500	54,630	—	—	—	—
1853	4,500	54,630	—	—	—	—
1854	4,500	50,583	—	—	—	—
1855	6,000	65,036	4,500	48,777	2,000–5,000	21,679–54,196
1856	6,000	67,444	—	—	—	—
1857	6,000	65,036	—	—	—	—
1858	6,000	70,038	—	—	—	—
1859	6,000	67,444	—	—	—	—
1860	6,000	67,444	—	—	—	—

Year	Associate justices of the Supreme Court		Circuit judges		District judges	
	Current dollars	1983 dollars	Current dollars	1983 dollars	Current dollars	1983 dollars
1861	6,000	67,444	—	—	—	—
1862	6,000	60,700	—	—	—	—
1863	6,000	49,216	—	—	—	—
1864	6,000	38,745	—	—	—	—
1865	6,000	39,587	—	—	—	—
1866	6,000	41,386	—	—	—	—
1867	6,000	43,357	—	—	—	—
1868	6,000	45,525	—	—	—	—
1869	6,000	45,525	5,000	37,938	3,500–5,000	26,556–37,938
1870	6,000	47,921	5,000	39,934	—	—
1871	8,000	67,444	6,000	50,583	—	—
1872	8,000	67,444	6,000	50,583	—	—
1873	10,000	84,306	6,000	50,583	—	—
1874	10,000	89,265	6,000	53,559	—	—
1875	10,000	91,970	6,000	55,182	3,500–5,000	32,189–45,985
1876	10,000	94,844	6,000	56,906	—	—
1877	10,000	94,844	6,000	56,906	—	—
1878	10,000	104,655	6,000	62,793	—	—
1879	10,000	108,393	6,000	65,036	—	—
1880	10,000	104,655	6,000	62,793	—	—
1881	10,000	104,655	6,000	62,793	—	—
1882	10,000	104,655	6,000	62,793	—	—
1883	10,000	108,393	6,000	65,036	—	—
1884	10,000	112,407	6,000	67,444	—	—
1885	10,000	112,407	6,000	67,444	—	—
1886	10,000	112,407	6,000	67,444	—	—
1887	10,000	112,407	6,000	67,444	—	—
1888	10,000	112,407	6,000	67,444	—	—
1889	10,000	112,407	6,000	67,444	—	—
1890	10,000	112,407	6,000	67,444	—	—
1891	10,000	112,407	6,000	67,444	5,000	56,204
1892	10,000	112,407	6,000	67,444	5,000	56,204
1893	10,000	112,407	6,000	67,444	5,000	56,204
1894	10,000	116,731	6,000	70,038	5,000	58,365
1895	10,000	121,400	6,000	72,840	5,000	60,700
1896	10,000	121,400	6,000	72,840	5,000	60,700
1897	10,000	121,400	6,000	72,840	5,000	60,700
1898	10,000	121,400	6,000	72,840	5,000	60,700
1899	10,000	121,400	6,000	72,840	5,000	60,700
1900	10,000	121,400	6,000	72,840	5,000	60,700

	Associate justices of the Supreme Court		Circuit judges		District judges	
Year	Current dollars	1983 dollars	Current dollars	1983 dollars	Current dollars	1983 dollars
1901	10,000	121,400	6,000	72,840	5,000	60,700
1902	10,000	116,731	6,000	70,038	5,000	58,365
1903	12,500	140,509	6,000	67,444	5,000	56,204
1904	12,500	140,509	6,000	67,444	5,000	56,204
1905	12,500	140,509	6,000	67,444	5,000	56,204
1906	12,500	140,509	6,000	67,444	5,000	56,204
1907	12,500	135,491	6,000	65,036	5,000	54,196
1908	12,500	140,509	6,000	67,444	5,000	56,204
1909	12,500	140,509	6,000	67,444	5,000	56,204
1910	12,500	135,491	6,000	65,036	5,000	54,196
1911	14,500	157,170	7,000	75,875	6,000	65,036
1912	14,500	151,750	7,000	73,259	6,000	62,793
1913	14,500	148,173	7,000	71,532	6,000	61,313
1914	14,500	146,204	7,000	70,581	6,000	60,498
1915	14,500	144,762	7,000	69,885	6,000	59,901
1916	14,500	134,580	7,000	64,969	6,000	55,688
1917	14,500	114,603	7,000	55,326	6,000	47,422
1918	14,500	97,578	7,000	47,106	6,000	40,377
1919	14,500	84,957	8,500	49,802	7,500	43,943
1920	14,500	73,346	8,500	42,996	7,500	37,938
1921	14,500	82,104	8,500	48,130	7,500	42,467
1922	14,500	87,664	8,500	51,389	7,500	45,344
1923	14,500	86,120	8,500	50,484	7,500	44,545
1924	14,500	85,952	8,500	50,386	7,500	44,458
1925	14,500	83,824	8,500	49,138	7,500	43,357
1926	20,000	114,528	12,500	71,580	10,000	57,264
1927	20,000	116,731	12,500	72,957	10,000	58,365
1928	20,000	118,324	12,500	73,952	10,000	59,162
1929	20,000	118,324	12,500	73,952	10,000	59,162
1930	20,000	121,400	12,500	75,875	10,000	60,700
1931	20,000	133,114	12,500	83,196	10,000	66,557
1932	20,000	148,411	12,500	92,757	10,000	74,205
1933	20,000	156,443	12,500	97,777	10,000	78,222
1934	20,000	151,372	12,500	94,607	10,000	75,686
1935	20,000	147,689	12,500	92,305	10,000	73,844
1936	20,000	146,265	12,500	91,416	10,000	73,133
1937	20,000	141,163	12,500	88,227	10,000	70,581
1938	20,000	143,839	12,500	89,899	10,000	71,919
1939	20,000	145,913	12,500	91,196	10,000	72,957
1940	20,000	144,524	12,500	90,327	10,000	72,262

	Associate justices of the Supreme Court		Circuit judges		District judges	
Year	Current dollars	1983 dollars	Current dollars	1983 dollars	Current dollars	1983 dollars
1941	20,000	137,642	12,500	86,026	10,000	68,821
1942	20,000	124,385	12,500	77,741	10,000	62,193
1943	20,000	117,181	12,500	73,238	10,000	58,591
1944	20,000	115,180	12,500	71,988	10,000	57,590
1945	20,000	112,616	12,500	70,385	10,000	56,308
1946	25,000	129,701	17,500	90,791	15,000	77,821
1947	25,000	113,416	17,500	79,391	15,000	68,049
1948	25,000	105,236	17,500	73,665	15,000	63,141
1949	25,000	106,268	17,500	74,387	15,000	63,761
1950	25,000	105,236	17,500	73,665	15,000	63,141
1951	25,000	97,526	17,500	68,268	15,000	58,515
1952	25,000	95,440	17,500	66,808	15,000	57,264
1953	25,000	94,725	17,500	66,308	15,000	56,835
1954	25,000	94,255	17,500	65,978	15,000	56,553
1955	35,000	132,450	25,500	96,499	22,500	85,147
1956	35,000	130,498	25,500	95,077	22,500	83,891
1957	35,000	126,008	25,500	91,806	22,500	81,005
1958	35,000	122,662	25,500	89,368	22,500	78,854
1959	35,000	121,678	25,500	88,651	22,500	78,222
1960	35,000	119,758	25,500	87,252	22,500	76,987
1961	35,000	118,555	25,500	86,376	22,500	76,214
1962	35,000	117,246	25,500	85,422	22,500	75,373
1963	35,000	115,840	25,500	84,397	22,500	74,468
1964	39,500	129,045	33,000	107,809	30,000	98,009
1965	39,500	126,860	33,000	105,984	30,000	96,349
1966	39,500	123,336	33,000	103,040	30,000	93,673
1967	39,500	119,883	33,000	100,155	30,000	91,050
1968	39,500	115,050	33,000	96,118	30,000	87,380
1969	60,000	165,847	42,500	117,475	40,000	110,565
1970	60,000	156,578	42,500	110,909	40,000	104,385
1971	60,000	150,124	42,500	106,338	40,000	100,082
1972	60,000	145,331	42,500	102,943	40,000	96,887
1973	60,000	136,814	42,500	96,910	40,000	91,210
1974	60,000	123,290	42,500	87,331	40,000	82,194
1975	63,000	118,614	44,600	83,971	42,000	79,076
1976	63,000	112,144	44,600	79,391	42,000	74,762
1977	72,000	120,397	57,500	96,150	54,000	90,298
1978	72,000	111,832	57,500	89,310	54,000	83,874
1979	72,000	100,515	65,000	90,743	61,500	85,857
1980	88,700	109,078	70,900	87,189	67,100	82,516

Year	Associate justices of the Supreme Court		Circuit judges		District judges	
	Current dollars	1983 dollars	Current dollars	1983 dollars	Current dollars	1983 dollars
1981	93,000	103,618	74,300	82,783	70,300	78,326
1982	96,700	99,961	77,300	79,907	73,100	75,565
1983	96,700	96,700	77,300	77,300	73,100	73,100

Sources: For the salary figures, my sources are the Judiciary Act of 1789, which established the first federal judicial salaries, and the subsequent judiciary acts that changed those salaries from time to time. A complete list of those acts is available from the author. The Consumer Price Index was used to translate the salary figures into constant (December 1983) dollars. For 1983 my source for the CPI was U.S. Department of Labor, Bureau of Labor Statistics, CPI Detailed Report, December 1983, at 7 (table 1). For 1982 it was the Bureau's February 1983 Monthly Labor Review (table 20). For 1950 to 1981 it was U.S. Department of Commerce, Bureau of the Census, Statistical Abstract of the United States, 1982–1983, at 461 (table 757). And for 1800 to 1949 it was the Census Bureau's Historical Statistics of the United States, Bicentennial Edition 210–211 (ser. E 135–166). However, the figures for the years prior to 1913 are estimates and should not be taken to be exact. See *id.* at 191.

Note: District judges' salaries were not uniform until 1892, but varied among districts. The ranges are given for various years. Before 1869 there was only one circuit judge, for California. His salary is given for 1855, the first year of the position.

Table B.2. Federal court case filings, 1892–1983

Year	Total cases, courts of appeals	Civil cases, district courts	Criminal cases, district courts	Total cases, district courts
1892	841	18,388	—	—
1893	704	17,769	—	—
1894	902	19,681	—	—
1895	1,019	19,056	—	—
1896	929	16,111	—	—
1897	917	13,711	—	—
1898	948	13,764	—	—
1899	1,026	13,313	—	—
1900	1,093	13,605	—	—
1901	1,030	14,647	—	—
1902	1,157	14,854	—	—
1903	1,099	15,882	—	—
1904	1,160	14,888	18,488	33,376
1905	1,293	16,002	18,900	34,902
1906	1,418	15,986	17,435	33,421
1907	1,371	18,434	18,332	36,766
1908	1,482	14,905	13,345	28,250
1909	1,467	13,127	14,505	27,632

Year	Total cases, courts of appeals	Civil cases, district courts	Criminal cases, district courts	Total cases, district courts
1910	1,672	13,788	14,864	28,652
1911	1,442	14,001	15,057	29,058
1912	1,438	14,993	15,953	30,946
1913	1,465	14,935	16,753	31,688
1914	1,586	16,288	18,399	34,687
1915	1,629	15,268	19,868	35,136
1916	1,740	17,352	20,243	37,595
1917	1,447	17,551	19,628	37,179
1918	1,510	16,756	35,096	51,852
1919	1,506	18,800	47,443	66,243
1920	1,523	22,109	55,587	77,696
1921	1,838	32,175	54,487	86,662
1922	1,826	31,745	60,722	92,467
1923	1,956	30,716	71,077	101,793
1924	2,471	34,211	70,168	104,379
1925	2,525	38,035	76,136	114,171
1926	2,588	38,721	68,582	107,303
1927	2,525	40,856	64,614	105,470
1928	2,610	44,445	83,372	127,817
1929	2,926	45,287	86,348	131,635
1930	2,874	48,325	87,305	135,630
1931	2,893	49,332	83,747	133,079
1932	3,305	60,515	92,174	152,689
1933	3,105	52,453	82,675	135,128
1934	3,406	35,959	34,152	70,111
1935	3,514	36,082	35,365	71,447
1936	3,521	39,391	35,920	75,311
1937	3,231	32,899	35,475	68,374
1938	3,218	33,591	34,202	67,793
1939	3,318	33,810	34,808	68,618
1940	3,446	34,734	33,401	68,135
1941	3,213	38,477	31,823	70,300
1942	3,228	38,140	30,577	68,717
1943	3,093	36,789	36,588	73,377
1944	3,072	30,896	39,621	70,517
1945	2,730	53,236	39,429	92,665
1946	2,627	58,454	33,203	91,657
1947	2,518	49,606	34,563	84,169
1948	2,625	37,420	33,300	70,720
1949	2,834	44,037	35,686	79,723
1950	2,678	45,085	37,720	82,805
1951	2,815	41,938	39,830	81,768

Year	Total cases, courts of appeals	Civil cases, district courts	Criminal cases, district courts	Total cases, district courts
1952	2,931	48,442	39,022	87,464
1953	3,123	53,469	38,504	91,973
1954	3,343	49,058	43,196	92,254
1955	3,544	49,056	37,123	86,179
1956	3,438	52,174	30,653	82,827
1957	3,546	54,143	30,078	84,221
1958	3,552	59,308	30,737	90,045
1959	3,597	49,586	30,653	80,239
1960	3,765	51,063	29,828	80,891
1961	4,204	51,225	30,268	81,493
1962	4,823	54,615	31,017	85,632
1963	5,437	57,028	31,746	88,774
1964	6,023	61,093	31,733	92,826
1965	6,597	62,670	33,334	96,004
1966	6,979	66,144	31,494	97,638
1967	7,710	66,197	32,307	98,404
1968	8,916	66,740	32,571	99,311
1969	10,016	72,504	35,413	107,917
1970	11,440	82,665	39,959	122,624
1971	12,537	89,318	43,157	132,475
1972	14,292	92,385	49,054	141,439
1973	15,408	96,056	42,434	138,490
1974	16,327	101,345	39,754	141,098
1975	16,571	115,098	43,282	158,380
1976	18,312	128,362	41,020	169,382
1977	19,062	128,899	41,464	170,363
1978	18,863	137,707	35,983	173,690
1979	20,181	153,552	32,688	186,240
1980	23,155	167,871	28,921	196,792
1981	26,323	179,803	31,287	211,090
1982	27,890	205,505	31,301	236,806
1983	29,580	241,159	35,872	277,031

Sources: See Chapter 3, note 1.

Table B.3. Number of federal judges, 1789–1983

Year	Supreme Court	Circuit	District	Total
1789	6	—	13	19
1790	6	—	13	19
1791	6	—	14	20
1792	6	—	15	21
1793	6	—	15	21
1794	6	—	15	21
1795	6	—	15	21
1796	6	—	15	21
1797	6	—	16	22
1798	6	—	16	22
1799	6	—	16	22
1800	6	—	16	22
1801	5	—	16	21
1802	6	—	18	24
1803	6	—	19	25
1804	6	—	19	25
1805	6	—	19	25
1806	6	—	19	25
1807	7	—	19	26
1808	7	—	19	26
1809	7	—	19	26
1810	7	—	19	26
1811	7	—	19	26
1812	7	—	21	28
1813	7	—	21	28
1814	7	—	21	28
1815	7	—	22	29
1816	7	—	22	29
1817	7	—	24	31
1818	7	—	25	32
1819	7	—	27	34
1820	7	—	27	34
1821	7	—	27	34
1822	7	—	28	35
1823	7	—	28	35
1824	7	—	28	35
1825	7	—	28	35
1826	7	—	28	35
1827	7	—	28	35
1828	7	—	28	35
1829	7	—	28	35
1830	7	—	28	35

Year	Supreme Court	Circuit	District	Total
1831	7	—	28	35
1832	7	—	28	35
1833	7	—	28	35
1834	7	—	28	35
1835	7	—	28	35
1836	7	—	29	36
1837	9	—	30	39
1838	9	—	31	40
1839	9	—	31	40
1840	9	—	31	40
1841	9	—	31	40
1842	9	—	31	40
1843	9	—	31	40
1844	9	—	31	40
1845	9	—	33	42
1846	9	—	34	43
1847	9	—	35	44
1848	9	—	36	45
1849	9	—	37	46
1850	9	—	39	48
1851	9	—	39	48
1852	9	—	39	48
1853	9	—	39	48
1854	9	—	39	48
1855	9	1	39	49
1856	9	1	41	51
1857	9	1	41	51
1858	9	1	43	53
1859	9	1	44	54
1860	9	1	45	55
1861	9	1	47	57
1862	10	1	47	58
1863	10	1	48	59
1864	10	1	47	58
1865	9	1	49	59
1866	9	1	48	58
1867	8	1	48	57
1868	8	1	49	57
1869	9	9	49	67
1870	9	9	50	68
1871	9	9	52	70
1872	9	9	53	71
1873	9	9	53	71

Year	Supreme Court	Circuit	District	Total
1874	9	9	53	71
1875	9	9	53	71
1876	9	9	53	71
1877	9	9	54	72
1878	9	9	54	72
1879	9	9	54	72
1880	9	9	54	72
1881	9	9	55	73
1882	9	9	54	72
1883	9	9	57	75
1884	9	9	55	73
1885	9	9	56	74
1886	9	9	57	75
1887	9	9	59	77
1888	9	10	58	77
1889	9	11	58	78
1890	9	11	58	78
1891	9	11	64	84
1892	9	10	64	83
1893	9	19	65	93
1894	9	16	66	91
1895	9	20	65	94
1896	9	22	65	96
1897	9	22	66	97
1898	9	22	67	98
1899	9	22	66	97
1900	9	25	65	99
1901	9	25	71	105
1902	9	24	74	107
1903	9	26	70	105
1904	9	27	74	110
1905	9	28	74	111
1906	9	29	78	116
1907	9	30	81	120
1908	9	29	84	122
1909	9	29	85	123
1910	9	30	88	127
1911	9	33	91	133
1912	9	29	88	126
1913	9	28	92	129
1914	9	28	93	130
1915	9	32	93	134
1916	9	32	94	135

Year	Supreme Court	Circuit	District	Total
1917	9	33	93	135
1918	9	32	95	136
1919	9	33	98	140
1920	9	34	99	142
1921	9	36	96	141
1922	9	37	100	146
1923	9	41	110	160
1924	9	40	119	168
1925	9	42	128	179
1926	9	45	125	179
1927	9	45	125	179
1928	9	45	130	184
1929	9	47	140	196
1930	9	45	146	200
1931	9	48	147	204
1932	9	47	149	205
1933	9	48	148	205
1934	9	50	148	207
1935	9	47	134	190
1936	9	52	151	212
1937	9	51	168	228
1938	9	50	164	225
1939	9	52	165	226
1940	9	55	164	228
1941	9	55	181	245
1942	9	57	181	247
1943	9	57	185	251
1944	9	56	186	251
1945	9	55	183	247
1946	9	58	187	254
1947	9	59	198	266
1948	9	58	194	261
1949	9	58	197	264
1950	9	64	214	287
1951	9	65	218	292
1952	9	64	219	292
1953	9	63	215	287
1954	9	62	216	287
1955	9	65	236	310
1956	9	61	244	314
1957	9	63	240	312
1958	9	64	237	310
1959	9	62	232	303

Year	Supreme Court	Circuit	District	Total
1960	9	66	237	312
1961	9	61	232	302
1962	9	75	281	365
1963	9	74	293	376
1964	9	74	294	377
1965	9	73	291	373
1966	9	70	291	370
1967	9	83	312	404
1968	9	83	324	416
1969	9	85	330	424
1970	9	90	331	430
1971	9	92	370	471
1972	9	91	387	487
1973	9	94	387	490
1974	9	95	382	486
1975	9	97	388	494
1976	9	95	383	487
1977	9	88	372	469
1978	9	95	377	481
1979	9	94	392	495
1980	9	120	456	585
1981	9	124	474	607
1982	9	126	486	621
1983	9	127	484	620

Notes: From 1789 to 1881, the figures are from the successive judiciary acts and are for judgeships rather than actual judges. From 1882 to 1983, the figures are for actual judges and are based on counting the judges listed in volumes of federal judicial reports. Senior judges are excluded from the count, thus understating for recent years the effective number of federal judges below the Supreme Court level.

Table B.4. Filings per judge, district courts and courts of appeals

Year	District courts	Courts of appeals
1892	—	84
1893	—	37
1894	—	56
1895	—	51
1896	—	42
1897	—	42
1898	—	43
1899	—	47
1900	—	44
1901	—	41
1902	—	48
1903	—	42
1904	451	43
1905	472	46
1906	428	49
1907	454	46
1908	336	51
1909	325	51
1910	326	56
1911	319	44
1912	352	50
1913	344	52
1914	373	57
1915	378	51
1916	400	54
1917	400	44
1918	546	47
1919	676	46
1920	785	45
1921	903	51
1922	925	49
1923	925	48
1924	877	62
1925	892	60
1926	858	58
1927	844	56
1928	983	58
1929	940	62
1930	929	64
1931	905	60
1932	1,025	70

Year	District courts	Courts of appeals
1933	913	65
1934	474	68
1935	533	75
1936	499	68
1937	407	63
1938	417	65
1939	416	64
1940	415	63
1941	388	58
1942	380	57
1943	397	54
1944	379	55
1945	506	50
1946	490	45
1947	425	43
1948	365	45
1949	405	49
1950	387	42
1951	375	43
1952	399	46
1953	428	50
1954	427	54
1955	365	55
1956	339	56
1957	351	56
1958	380	56
1959	346	58
1960	341	57
1961	351	69
1962	305	64
1963	303	73
1964	316	81
1965	330	90
1966	336	100
1967	315	93
1968	307	107
1969	327	118
1970	370	127
1971	358	136
1972	365	157
1973	358	164
1974	369	172

Year	District courts	Courts of appeals
1975	408	171
1976	442	193
1977	458	217
1978	461	199
1979	475	215
1980	432	193
1981	445	212
1982	487	221
1983	572	233

Sources: Filings from Table B.2; number of judges from Table B.3.

Index